Renewing American Compassion

Other Books by Marvin Olasky

Fighting for Liberty and Virtue:
Political and Cultural Wars in Eighteenth-Century America (1995)

Loving Your Neighbor, co-author (1995)

Philanthropically Correct:
The Story of the Council on Foundations (1993)

Abortion Rites:
A Social History of Abortion in America (1992, 1995)

The Tragedy of American Compassion (1992, 1995)

Patterns of Corporate Philanthropy:
The Progressive Deception, co-author (1992)

Central Ideas in the Development of American Journalism (1991)

Patterns of Corporate Philanthropy:
Funding False Compassion, co-author (1991)

More Than Kindness, co-author (1990)

The Press and Abortion, 1838–1988 (1988)

Freedom, Justice, and Hope, co-author (1988)

Prodigal Press (1988)

Patterns of Corporate Philanthropy (1987)

Turning Point, co-author (1987)

Corporate Public Relations:
A New Historical Perspective (1987)

Renewing American Compassion

by MARVIN OLASKY

FOREWORD BY NEWT GINGRICH

THE FREE PRESS

New York   London   Toronto   Sydney   Singapore

THE FREE PRESS
A Division of Simon & Schuster Inc.
1230 Avenue of the Americas
New York, NY 10020

THE FREE PRESS and colophon are trademarks
of Simon & Schuster Inc.

Manufactured in the United States of America

10   9   8   7   6   5   4   3   2   1

Library of Congress Cataloging-in-Publication Data

Olasky, Marvin N.
    Renewing American compassion: a citizen's guide/ Marvin Olasky.
      p. cm.
    Includes index.
    ISBN 0-684-83000-0
    1. Public welfare administration—United States—Case studies.
  2. Public welfare—United States. 3. United States—Social
policy—1993– I. Title.
HV95.042 1996
361.8'0973—dc20   95-53992
                                            CIP

For Susan

Contents

Foreword: A Citizen's Guide for Helping the Poor

by Newt Gingrich

As Americans we can no longer escape this reality: three decades of social welfare policies have failed, condemning too many of our fellow citizens to lives of despair. Nevertheless, Americans want a compassionate society that will help the truly needy. In the mid-1960s the prevailing view was that this goal could be accomplished through high-rise bureaucracies in Washington. Unfortunately, that Great Society view set us on a track that has been an unmitigated disaster, a disaster more harmful to more Americans than the Vietnam war itself.

When we look at the murder rate among young black men, at the cocaine and heroin and crack addiction among young Americans of all races, at the illiteracy rate, at the number of children who have never known their father or had any father figure, at the devastation of our inner cities, we can see clearly that America's approach to helping the poor is doing great damage and that it is in urgent need of replacement. This means replacing a culture of poverty and violence with a wholly different culture of productivity and safety—not just helping the poor or focusing on the inner cities, but actually replacing one culture with another.

Efforts to repair or improve the current welfare system are

doomed to fail because they sidestep the holistic nature of the problem. In a holistic model, *everything* has to be taken into account—unlike a reductionist model, which breaks a problem down into a series of building blocks and decides which piece to deal with first. There's a very big difference between the two. In the holistic model, every piece depends on every other piece—deal with the totality or it does not work.

Piecemeal efforts to repair our system and its culture of poverty and violence are doomed to fail. We ask the poor, "Why don't you go to work?" And they say, "Fine." But if they do go to work, they lose Medicaid. If one of their children gets sick, they promptly lose all the money they just worked for. If they receive food stamps or Aid to Families with Dependent Children, the government will actually punish them if they try to save any money. They may not join Amway or Mary Kay or indeed do anything that would allow them to improve their lives. We have an interlocking system, in which change to any one piece without thinking through the change of the whole is pointless.

We must find a way to address the problems of the whole person. This is what Marvin Olasky explains so well: that to be effective, charity must be personal, challenging, and spiritual—requirements government cannot meet. To replace the whole culture of violence and poverty in this manner, we must address four key realities.

The first reality is that when individuals are caught within a dysfunctional culture they must transfer their loyalties, beliefs, and practices to another culture if they are truly to change their behavior. For instance, if you were a member of Alcoholics Anonymous, you would have to undergo a conversion experience. You would say, yesterday I was an active alcoholic; today, I am a recovering alcoholic. Yesterday, when I felt anxiety-ridden, I took a drink; today, when I feel anxiety-ridden, I go to my AA meeting and talk to my friends, or I pray. In AA there is a conscious effort to rebuild the entire person and to make the transition to this system from another system a decisive moment. In addition, there is constant support; if you don't have a support structure, something that helps you when you start to slide back, you are going to break down.

Part of the reason it is hard for us to really change things is that we underestimate the second reality, which is that cultural change is very hard. It requires tremendous persistence over a long period of time, and it can often only be achieved one person at a time. We tend to be impatient—we say, "Okay, I'm willing to do this for up to a year and a half." That is a little bit like the farmer who says, "I'll grow corn provided it's ready to eat in three weeks. If this seedling doesn't make it in three weeks, I'm throwing the sucker out and replanting." But important things do not happen overnight. To achieve breakthrough in a culture that needs a dramatic change of behavior means starting with one person, then going on to two and three, and then gradually beginning to peel away the whole culture, revealing a better one.

The third reality is that this kind of cultural change is best done outside government. I would argue that (with the exception of military boot camps) there is virtually no government program capable of producing such change—for the very reason that governments are not set up as agencies of acculturation. Moreover, as Americans we would be justifiably furious if bureaucrats tried to acculturate us. Who are they to tell us whether we ought to be in the circle or the square? They work for us—we don't work for them. We would strongly resist any call for cultural change delivered by government.

Such changes call for a kind of action that cannot be legislated. To truly help people requires discernment among their different needs. For some people poverty is a definable problem, such as occurs when they lose their job. But for many others poverty is only a symptom; if poverty is caused by alcohol or drug addiction, lack of education or mental illness, giving money will not help but will only facilitate escape from the real problem. True charity must understand each person's unique needs and target those needs—something government cannot do.

The kind of cultural change we are talking about requires missionaries. It requires the kind of person who will sit steadfastly at three o'clock in the morning holding the hand of someone who is about to commit suicide. Bureaucracy cannot do that. Yes, there are some wonderful government employees; you do find people who are individually fabulous. But you cannot recruit people to a bureaucracy on the premise that they will stay there as long as needed. To the contrary, you *can* recruit to a volunteer organization on that premise. The two are very different models. Yet we sometimes get mad at bureaucracy, asking it to do things it cannot do, instead of distinguishing between those things government can do well and those things some other part of society can do better.

To truly make a difference, we must move people out of this culture of violence and poverty and into a better culture. This is the fourth reality: we must actively involve ourselves. We cannot allow individual changes within the old culture to be overwhelmed by other aspects of that culture. We must make clear that a culture of poverty and violence, in which millions of Americans live right now, is not acceptable. What we must say to them is that it is better to work than to be dependent. It is better to be safe than to be in danger.

We are not talking about a small change. If we truly want healthy inner cities, if we truly want healthy Indian reservations, and if we truly want healthy West Virginia Appalachian poor neighborhoods, we are talking about one of the largest changes ever to be contemplated in American history. And we have to take it seriously—not pay mere lip service to it, not walk off saying, when a kid gets killed, "Gee, that's sad."

What I am suggesting is this. If we take that child seriously as an American, then we must decide in our generation that we are fed up with a system that encourages us to regret death or impoverishment but will not change to prevent it. We must do something to replace this failed system. All of us, including the poor, are taking on a big challenge, maybe in some ways one as big as the Cold War. It is not going to be a small challenge, and it is not going to happen overnight, but our goal should be to wake up one morning with the certainty that not one single child died during the night in a government housing project.

The questions each of us must ask are: where do I, as an individual citizen, begin? How can I make a difference in the face of such enormous problems? The answers lie, I think, in the book you are holding. *Renewing American Compassion* is filled with examples of what ordinary Americans are doing to make a difference. Marvin Olasky offers a guide on how we can make our charitable activity effective by focusing on the needs of one person—not the entire world, but just one person. If every American did that, our country would be a greatly different place.

Marvin Olasky unlocked for me the key of how to replace the welfare state. His earlier *Tragedy of American Compassion* was one of the most extraordinary books written in our generation. In it, he went back and looked at 350 years in which Americans dealt with poverty, tragedy, and addiction with much greater success than the current welfare state has done. It was primarily a history book that showed you, chapter by chapter, the consistent way Americans thought about poverty and helped the poor. It concluded that what the traditional reporters warned against is precisely what the welfare state ultimately did.

Now, in *Renewing American Compassion*, Olasky takes a quick look at his earlier arguments and evidence, but he focuses strongly on the future. He shows what mistakes of the welfare state we should give up, what we should pick up from our past that is best, and then how we can create a vision for 21st-century compassion that will truly make a difference in the lives of the poor.

Olasky teaches us simply but powerfully to move from entitlement to challenge, from bureaucracy to personal help, and from the naked public square to faith in God. He challenges Congress and state governments to develop ways for individuals and community institutions to take over poverty-fighting responsibility from the bureaucrats. He even discusses the provocative notion of completely doing away with the federal safety net. Olasky has traveled across America and seen firsthand what works and what does not work in helping the poor, and he shows us clearly what they are.

Renewing American Compassion should be read by all thoughtful and busy citizens. It is a book about America's future, one in which we need not dread turning on the local news every night for fear of hearing about ever more horrific tragedies that have befallen our children. Marvin Olasky points to victory in the 21st century rather than continued despair. If we believe in our Declaration of Independence, that all of our children hold certain unalienable rights, "among these Life, Liberty, and the pursuit of Happiness," then we must decide in our generation that we are fed up with a failed federal War on Poverty and that we as citizens are going to take up and shoulder our responsibility to one another.

Acknowledgments

This book arises from my education on the streets concerning the potential of community-based organizations. My first teacher in this regard was Bob Woodson, president of the National Center for Neighborhood Enterprise. Since then, I've learned much from leaders of community-based organizations in many cities, including Bob Cote, Virgil Gulker, John Woods, Hannah Hawkins, Marsh Ward, Robin MacDonald, German Cruz, Kathy Dudley, Freddie Garcia, David Perez, Jim Heurich, Deborah Darden, Lessie Handy, Noemi Motessi, George McKinney, Connie Driscoll, Wayne Gordon, Lee Earl, Eddie Edwards, Toni McIlwain, and Shelby Smith.

This book would not exist without the encouragement and support of a group of leaders who understand the need to renew American compassion; my special thanks go to Newt Gingrich, Bill Bennett, and Arianna Huffington. Progress & Freedom Foundation colleagues including Jeff Eisenach, Bill Myers, Rick O'Donnell, and Rachel Kracj; writers including John Fund, Karl Zinsmeister, Dan McMurry, Larry Arnn, and Michael Cromartie; foundation leaders Heather Higgins, Michael Joyce, Bill Schambra, and Patty Brown; and a number of governors, senators, and congressmen who have been not only helpful but kind. Michael Schwartz read the entire manuscript and made helpful suggestions, as did Bruce Nichols at The Free Press.

This book could never have been written apart from the satisfaction and solidity that my family affords. Susan, my wife of two decades, has a wise head and a loveliness that goes beyond narrative; her mettle was on display again in 1995 when she was in charge of four children while I had to be on the road a third of the time, promoting welfare reform and researching welfare alternatives. I thank also the four—Pete, David, Daniel, and Benjamin—who are all providing joy and deep satisfaction as they grow up to be godly men. Travel reminds me that family life is good, and particularly good for a man who is in love with his wife and children.

In closing, I am grateful to the Progress & Freedom Foundation for its financial support during 1995 and 1996.

The Need for Renewal

My youngest son is five. A year ago he and two friends slithered below the supposedly childproof iron fence surrounding a swimming pool. One of the three fell in and, unable to swim, sank to the bottom and stayed there. The pool owner looked out, saw two boys who didn't belong there by the pool, and yelled at them to get out. They knew they had done something wrong by going where they did not belong and, like Adam and Eve in the garden, went and hid.

Providentially, the owner came after them and Benjamin blurted out to her the grave situation: a boy was still in the pool. She screamed. One neighbor—a hospital worker who teaches others how to perform CPR on children—came running, dove into the pool, retrieved the boy, who at that point had been underwater for at least three minutes, and started breathing into his mouth. I got there some seconds later and helped out a slight bit by doing finger compressions on the four-year-old's chest. For at least the first minute, there was no reaction at all: the boy's eyes seemed dilated in death, his soul hovered between this world and the next, and the neighbor and I prayed between CPR puffing and compressing.

Only after what seemed an eternity did there come the

faintest of fluttering breaths, followed two minutes later by the slightest of coughs, and two minutes after that by the arrival of an EMS team, which took over and applied oxygen. This was on a Friday afternoon, and we worried about brain damage; amazingly, on Sunday the boy who seemed dead was running around in church, completely healed physically, and happy to be alive.

I thought about that boy's narrow escape as I read shortly afterwards a headline in the June 4, 1995, *New York Times:* "Gingrich's Vision of Welfare Ignores Reality, Charities Say." The story mirrored what became in 1995 the conventional way of dealing with the unconventional goal of replacing the welfare system over the next generation with one based in private, church, and community involvement. *Impossible . . . inconceivable . . . preposterous . . . ignores reality.* With words of that sort, ideas that could renew a nearly dead system of compassion were shunted aside, as many pretended that the situation was not so grave after all.

The goal of this brief book is not to prove that American compassion is now at the bottom of the pool, soon to be wrapped in a body bag unless someone intervenes. Many others have shown that, and I myself have written a history of the tragedy.* What I hope to suggest, to begin our discussion, is that dismissive words are not new in this century's welfare debate. More than seventy years ago, some leading social thinkers concluded that government should take from churches and community groups the prime responsibility for poverty fighting. Frank Dekker Watson, director of the Pennsylvania School for Social Service and professor of sociology and social work at Haverford College, argued in 1922 that local groups helped

---

*See *The Tragedy of American Compassion* (Washington, D.C.: Regnery Gateway, 1992).

individuals, but the central government could raise up the masses. "No person who is interested in social progress can long be content to raise here and there an individual," he wrote.

The idea of massive federal action, at a time when Washington's spending (except in wartime) was small, seemed ludicrous. But Watson and others argued that if private agencies continued to care for families, "it would be easy for the state to evade the responsibility." Watson praised one Philadelphia group for announcing that it would no longer help widows—for, only when private groups went on strike, would "public funds ever be wholly adequate for the legitimate demands made upon them."

Watson and other liberal visionaries, in short, were ready to force the issue, even if it meant eliminating immediate support not only for those who could fend for themselves, but for widows. How cruel! How mean-spirited! And in what a cause: to have the federal government, which then had only a small percentage of the resources necessary to meet needs, take away the leading role from big and powerful philanthropies. *Impossible . . . inconceivable . . . preposterous . . . ignores reality.* But conceive the new plan they did, and fight for it over a generation they did, and the result was, first (in the 1930s, helped along by the Great Depression), an enormous expansion of Washington's grasp and, second, in the 1960s, the reach for a Great Society.

We know now that the vision, even if noble to start with, was founded on tragic miscomprehension. Private charities had succeeded in helping many individuals because they offered compassion that was challenging, personal, and spiritually based. Government over time proved itself incapable of doing the same; instead, governmental charity emphasized entitlement rather than challenge, bureaucracy rather than personal help, and a reduction of man to material being only. Is it any wonder that we witness welfare failure?

In the same June 4, 1995, *New York Times* article, one official,

John Thomas of the American Red Cross, was quoted as saying, "This has been a 50-year history of government taking on added responsibilities. To try to undo that in a year or two is unrealistic." Mr. Thomas was exactly right about the lack of realism inherent in a year or two of undoing, but that was not the plan of those who want compassion to be effective once again: four-year-olds can recover quickly, but replacing a failed system will take longer. Frank Dekker Watson in 1922 did not say the government could immediately take over; welfare reformers now do not say that charities can immediately take over. The question in both cases was and is direction of movement, and ways to speed up the process of change.

Our situation in some ways is more troubled than that of 1922. Watson was confronted with a much smaller number of unmarried teenaged girls having babies or abortions, and their male counterparts shooting up or shooting each other, than we have today. Even so, he was willing to see widows lose every cent of their private pensions to force a crisis in order to build up the government's role in poverty fighting. Republicans in Congress have shown considerably more concern for individuals as they attempt to begin replacing the welfare state. They have in many instances increased spending, but to a lower level than Democrats wanted, and for their pains have been called pain inflictors. Never have so many accusations of meanness been thrown around with so little cause.

This book began as a response to requests for a quick display of the major themes of *The Tragedy of American Compassion,* and then grew into an attempt to present, in a nontechnical way, some still germinating ideas about replacing the welfare system. Chapter 1 opens the discussion by describing what has been widely regarded as the best welfare reform program in the most innovative welfare reform state, and then examines some of the other state-level reforms of 1995. Chapter 2 contrasts those government projects with community-based, nonprofit, and private alternatives. Chapters 3, 4, and 5 highlight themes and evidence from *The Tragedy of American Compassion,* setting the stage for chapter 6, which shows how ordinary people are becoming heroes once again in the 1990s, as their predecessors did in the 1890s.

Historically proven principles will achieve full effectiveness today, however, only if greater numbers of compassionate individuals and groups are able and willing to put them to work. Chapter 7 shows how government officials can play a useful support role by removing barriers to compassionate action; furthermore, legislators can develop practical plans to ensure that organizations with good reputations receive the material support they need. Chapter 8 then examines the opportunities to do what it takes to aid those in need, and looks particularly at the role of religion as motivator among both helpers and helped. The concluding chapter summarizes the essential principles; finally, four appendixes offer a pledge to action, an overview of biblical mandates concerning poverty fighting, additional information on a tax credit approach to replacing welfare, and an examination of how problems in education, crime prevention, and other areas relate to the poverty debate.

Overall, this book is closer to a first word than to a last. Some thoughts have been presented in a deliberately sketchy way, rather than with a specificity that would be arrogant at this point. What was missed in 1922 was a major debate on the vision of how best to make war on poverty, and as a result some legislation that emerged years later was not well thought out. My goal in this book is not to close discussion but to push open a debate on how all of us can help to renew American compassion, before all we are left with is a corpse on the swimming pool floor.

Chapter 1

Conventional Welfare Reform

The Kenosha County Job Center, located in the southeast corner of Wisconsin, with Lake Michigan to the east and the Illinois state line to the south, is the shiny face of state-level welfare reform, and its presence has launched a thousand trips. Twelve state delegations, dozens of reporting teams from networks and national magazines, and welfare managers from all over have come and marveled at 54,000 square feet of calibrated administration in color-coordinated offices.

Operations Manager Larry Jankowski notes that the *Washington Post* has come once, the *Los Angeles Times* twice, and Dayton, Ohio, officials four times. Even bureaucrats from Tanzania have taken the tour. Kenosha is important because it is said to be The Future: a successful attempt to provide social services with a human face. It is now widely understood that the primary problem of the modern welfare state is not its cost, but its tendency to treat people as cows whose feeding troughs need periodic refilling. Wisconsin, seeing human beings on the welfare rolls, has instituted a twenty-hour-per-week work requirement for many AFDC recipients, a two-year time limit on many welfare benefits, and a plan to eliminate cash benefits before the third millennium begins.

Those steps sound promising to conservatives—but Wisconsin has coupled them with a package of social worker-intensive programs that will continue to keep the welfare world safe for bureaucracy. Other states are doing the same: Michigan and New Jersey have Wisconsin-style programs and Massachusetts even hired Wisconsin's social services director to head its Department of Health and Human Services. Since Wisconsin's welfare reform generally, and the Kenosha County Job Center in particular, have become such popular poster children, Kenosha deserves a closer look; we'll then check on the progress and prospects of welfare reform plans in several other states.

Kenosha County itself is an hour's freeway drive from notorious Chicago slum high-rises like Cabrini Green, and a semibucolic world away. The county's population of 130,000 is 90 percent white and the unemployment rate is at about 3 percent. On the way from the interstate to the job center, drive-by shootings are not a concern, and drive-through fast-fooders are easy to find. Past Ponderosa Steakhouse, past the Big Buck Building Center, past the Stars-N-Stripes Restaurant and a home with a Jesus is Lord yard sign, the job center emerges, dominating a neighborhood of modest but tidy homes with well-kept yards and trimmed hedges. The center itself anchors a small shopping mall that includes a software store, a hobby shop, and a cinema fourplex. The parking area next to the center's main entrance has a few old cars on a Monday morning, but lots of clean Plymouth Voyagers and Ford Aerostars. This is the land of minivans, not clunkers leaking oil.

Next to the center is Aladdin's Castle Family Entertainment Center, and the facility itself has a Disneyland feel. On the way from the parking lot to the reception area, a sign on one wall promotes a workshop on self-esteem: "You are scheduled to begin an exciting adventure next week." For those used to welfare offices with bulletproof glass, scarred linoleum, and cramped cubicles, the reception area is a revelation: light wood, bright walls with prints of water lilies, purplish heather carpeting, circular wooden tables with padded blue seats, and an 18-foot ceiling with an overhead fan to complement the air conditioning. Next to the reception area is a bright and spacious children's playroom that has lots of toys and good books such as *Where the Wild Things Are.*

Further in, the adventure continues. Light blue-gray panels distinguish modular office areas in wide open spaces. Few welfare clients—no, they are called "participants"—need to wait for meetings with caseworkers; asked about the absence of lines, Program Director George Leutermann observes, "We're not into crowds." Posted newspaper headlines inform participants that they are visiting a site that will be historic: "Country looks to Kenosha for welfare reform ideas." Caseworkers convey to participants the sense that they are beneficiaries of an experiment that could change the nation, and the state employees themselves are encouraged to think of themselves as heroes.

Leutermann, receiving recognition at age forty-eight after a career in social services, recalls, "I told our people that their kids will be reading about them in the newspaper. They said, 'Sure. That's crap.' But they are getting what we promised." Jankowski, at fifty-one also a veteran manager of employment programs and welfare systems, tells employees, "If we can be successful here, that is your ticket to a job anywhere." Staffers know that the good press their program receives can translate into advancement in other states, should they choose to become evangelists for the Wisconsin welfare gospel.

That gospel is a crowd pleaser so far because it has three sides: liberal, conservative, and feminist. The liberal side of the equilateral triangle proposes big government programs, but with an awareness that bureaucratic hauteur is out, provision of services is in: "We treat our participants like kings and queens," Leutermann says, and he makes sure that the monarchs have a panoply of valets. "If they have a remediation problem, they can go to that instructor. If they have a training problem, they go to that person. We have a brokering process whereby the case manager helps participants access services." The Kenosha goal is not to bond the needy with caseworkers, who average 150 participants under their care and see each participant an average of once every three months; the goal is to place participants under the care of government-paid specialists, who at the job center are conveniently housed under one roof.

The conservative-sounding side of the triangle is the work emphasis. Participants quickly go through vocational assessment and receive information about careers, labor markets, job retention, and financial planning. They are required to develop a job-finding plan, and after an initial four-week module designed to build motivation and "self-esteem," to get on with the task of finding a job. Instructors stress, Jankowski says, that "there's a place in the job market for everyone. The unemployment rate is not the issue. The issue is motivating people to take the jobs that are available." Participants are required either to find a job or to put in a "simulated thirty-two-hour work week" of job readiness courses, practice interviews, etc.; the mushiness is evident, but at least participants are supposed to report on time. Those who do not cooperate lose $90 per month in benefits; that sanction pushes three-fourths of AFDC recipients to come to class regularly, and 90 percent of that final quarter to show up following sanction, according to Leutermann.

The base of the equilateral triangle is feminism, with chunks of New Age subjectivism thrown into the broth. Computer-printed signs dominate the walls of two large Kenosha training rooms: "A family doesn't need a man to be whole." "Stop waiting for Prince Charming, his horse broke down." Asked about the usefulness of dumping the Prince Charming goal—yes, AFDC moms should not be passively waiting, but marriage *is* the most-used exit from the welfare rolls—Jankowski says, "We tell them straight out that marriage is not the answer." Other signs suggest the answer: "I have the power within me. What I focus on expands." "You're a one-of-a-kind design."

Since that last exhortation seems to suggest the existence of a designer, a question logically follows: is something like the Alcoholics Anonymous concept of a "higher power" acceptable? "There's absolutely no reference to a higher power at this center," Jankowski insists. "This is a self-actualization technique." But one problem with a poster that says "If you think you're someone special, then you are" is that it implies a second message: if you don't think you are, then you're not.

Does the Kenosha triangle work? Or is its assumption that a huge investment in state-funded education and job training programs will reduce the welfare load fallacious? Fans and critics throw around statistics: yes, the Kenosha center has placed more clients in jobs than the typical welfare office, but it still has placed fewer than half of its participants, some of whom would have found jobs anyway. Yes, those leaving welfare in Kenosha are taking jobs at wages considerably above the minimum, but the county's booming local economy (with one of the nation's highest rates of job creation) and minority-rare ethnic composition makes its experience atypical.

Beneath those issues lie deeper questions. Governmental programs or incentives have not succeeded in reducing the number of children conceived out of wedlock, and extramarital pregnancy is now the leading cause of poverty. Over half of AFDC mothers have never been married, and raising children without a father, even with governmental economic support, is very hard: how will Kenosha help them? And how does Kenosha get at key questions of values among those who have grown up in a culture that already confuses liberty and license, and suggests that all "lifestyle choices" are created equal?

What if some participants are in not just economic trouble but spiritual bondage? The Kenosha goal is to change some habits; if effective, it may change a person on the outside, but it does not try to touch the inside—nor, perhaps, would we want a governmental program to so do. But is wiping the outside of the glass sufficient?

Whether or not the Kenosha model meets the needs of those on welfare, it certainly meets the needs of welfare careerists, while satisfying (for the moment) the public push for reform. The Kenosha model has now spread to Milwaukee, which has 36,000 AFDC cases to Kenosha's 2,000. The North Milwaukee Job Center opened in January with 56,000 well-organized square feet: Program Manager William Martin points out that there are "two chairs and two data lines at every work station."

Other bureaucrats are also turned on by the new center. Employment Training Manager Ruth Schmidt is "analyzing how units interface with other units so we can better integrate funding sources into service delivery output." Units can readily be moved around and recombined because, as Martin emphasizes, "everyone has the same kind of work station, and each work station is exactly the same." There has been lots of money spent in the pursuit of fraternity and equality; asked how much the desk and chairs and related furnishings cost, one staffer responded offhandedly, "Oh, a few hundred thousand dollars."

The only drawback evident at the North Milwaukee center is that it was built in the expectation that people would come, but several times on a May 1995 Monday afternoon only one of the two chairs at each of several dozen work stations was occupied, and that by a staffer. At 3 p.m., there were two child care workers but no children in the bright child care facility that is a clone of Kenosha's. At 3:15, one manager was talking excitedly about how the new computers at the center "are used constantly," but Classroom 27 had thirty-one new Omni-Tech computers with CD-Rom drives and "Intel inside" labels, and not a single person using them.

Different explanations were offered for the lack of warm, job-seeking bodies at the job center. Manager Schmidt said that clients were "out interfacing with job opportunities." One Milwaukee AFDC mom, Michelle Dudley, when asked about the job center's reputation in the community, said, "They want me to care about getting a job, but they're just trying to keep their own jobs." One director of a small inner-city business in Milwaukee, Jo Henderson, said, "They built a building. I haven't heard of their building relationships." Kenosha manager Leutermann said, "In Milwaukee they absolutely refuse to employ sanctions if people don't show up. They don't want to do it. Anything you can mention, they have an excuse."

Even with the apparent absence of clients, staffers on that Monday afternoon seemed busy. One was reading a manual, a second was checking computer files, and a third settled for low-tech paper shuffling. For the welfare system veterans, the line from an Old Milwaukee beer commercial is a good summation of life on the job in Kenosha or North Milwaukee: "It doesn't get any better than this."

For clients also, the decor and the decorum at such centers are far above the typical. It's no wonder that tourists from state bureaucracies are coming, because the Wisconsin experiment can satisfy their desires while placating conservatives who have forgotten what Robert Rector of the Heritage Foundation points out: "The bulk of the nation's welfare bureaucracy resides not in Washington but in the nation's [state] capitals. From Tallahassee to Juneau, these welfare bureaucracies are voluminous, left wing, and autonomous." A new "Welfare Works" program, announced in August 1995, may help the Wisconsin welfare system earn the praise it already has received, but so far it is less than meets the eye.

After Wisconsin, the three states often cited as welfare reform leaders are Michigan, Massachusetts, and New Jersey. Michigan took good first steps in 1991 by eliminating its state "general assistance" program, thus forcing some able-bodied males who did not qualify for any other program to look for work, and in 1992 by pushing the idea of a "social contract" within which AFDCers had to expend "productive effort" (besides that involved with their own children) in return for funding.

One concern, though, is that although one-fourth of AFDCers in Michigan now are listed as effort producers, compared to fewer than one in ten nationwide, most are taking courses or undergoing job preparation assessment by government caseworkers, not actually working. It is still early for a full assessment, but Michigan reforms have failed to shrink significantly the number of families on AFDC, and Governor John Engler is looking for ways to promote deeper change. *The New Republic,* in February 1995, noted in its catty way that most Michigan projects so far "have been pushed by state welfare directors for years. . . . Like most states, Michigan has adopted the 'human capital development' approach of the left."

Massachusetts' changes, often hailed in the press as the nation's most sweeping, went into effect on July 1, 1995, with the Welfare Department changing its name to the Department of Transitional Assistance. The goal is to make that change more than cosmetic by moving nearly a third of the welfare population from dole to job. About 20,000 able-bodied AFDCers with school-age children will be required to find work or take twenty-hour-a-week "community service" positions with agencies that will have them; the AFDC moms will not be paid, but they will continue to receive welfare checks for up to two years if they show up at their stations often enough to avoid complaints.

The change may provide justification for managers who house welfarists to hire additional staff, and it will certainly lead to an increase in government-funded day care slots. The new law also allows able-bodied recipients to receive welfare for only two years in a five-year cycle; officials may grant extensions to the two-year limit if the local job market is poor or if the recipient has hustled to no avail.

New Jersey has made many of the usual changes and is now best known for its "family cap," by which a two-child AFDC mom who has another child does not get a $67 monthly increase. Several other states also had caps in 1995, but it is too early to evaluate their effect. Quick declarations of victory should be suspect in welfare reform unless there are clear changes in values among recipients, because the main challenge is not placing a client in a job, but keeping him or her there. AFDC moms in particular tend to leave welfare temporarily for work, then cycle right back onto the lists. The critical question is whether internal values have changed sufficiently that the inevitable setbacks will be overcome with not just sporadic effort, but persistence.

Many state legislatures watched the Washington, D.C., welfare debates in 1995 and have not yet made significant welfare changes: much more is expected in 1996. The news is mixed from those states that were active. Ohio, for example, ended its "general assistance" plan, and many of the twenty or so similar programs in other states may not have long to live; those elastic clause plans are often the least defensible, since many of the checks go to able-bodied men. In Texas during 1995, the early talk was of "welfare crackdown," but the legislative walk ended up a stagger, with creation of another work force training agency probably the leading product.

Among the state reform efforts that did not garner much publicity, Virginia's was probably the most comprehensive. On July 1, 1995, it rolled many of the Wisconsin, Michigan, and Massachusetts innovations into one package, the "Virginia Independence Program," and added a few twists. For example, a new program of "diversionary assistance" offers emergency cash grants of up to about $1,000 to those who would otherwise go onto AFDC, on condition that they relinquish rights to AFDC eligibility for the next six months. Kay James, Virginia's Secretary of Health and Human Resources during 1995, insisted that the state will not be a softy should the $1,000 recipient come back for more a couple of months later: "We spell it out. People make choices and have to stand by them."

In Virginia and several other states, including Arizona (where Governor Fife Symington is eager for significant change) and California, a push to go deeper is developing. Michigan's Engler, searching for the next step, is among those inviting church involvement in welfare reform. Mississippi has been most explicit along these lines: its Faith and Families Project is designed to enlist churches in antipoverty work by using computers, in Governor Kirk Fordice's words, "to match each Mississippi family receiving public assistance with a participating church in their area. . . . If every church, synagogue, or religious organization in the State of Mississippi would adopt at least one welfare family and bring them to self-sufficiency in one year, we could remove all of Mississippi's families from the welfare rolls in twelve years."

Pushing the desire to go deeper is a growing realization that long-term poverty fighting depends on affecting not just the outside of a person, but the inside as well. Even the government programs that claim the greatest success in scrubbing the outside of the glass have yet to clean the inside, and what we might call "the rule of halves" thereby pertains: half of all AFDCers leave the rolls within a year, but about half of those are back within another year. Half of AFDC recipients have never been married and often continue to act irresponsibly in their personal lives, and half of all recipients thus are on the welfare rolls for a total of at least ten years.

Most people on welfare are white, but the percentage of recipients among blacks is higher, and the causes of problems in both racial groups go well beyond the tensions inherent in governmental programs. Shelby Smith, vice president of Mendenhall Ministries, a black-led, church-based organization south of Jackson, Mississippi, notes that "for a long time social programs were not incentive-based. That killed the desire to be productive. In the 1920s and 1930s we were productive, but now we're consumer-oriented. People don't want to produce, don't want to get a job. It used to be that a person's not working had a direct impact on his ability to eat. Now, folks that don't work are idolized—they're cruising around in a nice car, not having to work. We should be saying, 'We will help you if you help yourself.'"

Smith's organization itself, he noted, "has gone from giving away things to deciding how to charge for things. . . . Just giving to people is no good. At our thrift store it used to be people would come in, give a sob story, and get something. But we realized that it builds pride in individuals when they are able to go in and actually buy something. It takes a while to shift away from the entitlement mentality, and some people are critical: you get labeled Republican when you emphasize accountability. But that's the mentality you need if you're going to do better than the how-do-you-beat-the-system mentality. We need to remember that our problems on this side of the track are not due to the people on the other side of the track."

That type of thinking is becoming more common in poor areas across the country, and it's a different type of thinking than what pervades government offices. It's not necessary to travel from Wisconsin to Mississippi, however, to see what small community groups, often with a religious base, can do. In the shadows of the big government programs in Milwaukee, some innovative private groups are beginning to change lives.

Chapter 2

An Alternative Model

While the Kenosha model and its North Milwaukee clone garner press attention, several small, community-based Milwaukee groups, off the beaten path of welfare reform tours, change lives. They teach the beliefs and values that animated past generations of Americans to overcome poverty. They teach one-to-one the behaviors needed to keep a job: getting to work on time, dressing appropriately, staying until quitting time, and treating the boss and customers with respect.

In one corner of Milwaukee's Parklawn housing project, for example, an organization called the Right Alternative Family Service Center promotes cultural conservatism under the leadership of Deborah Darden. She is a black former welfare mom who still espouses political liberalism but sees what rot the left has wrought. Ms. Darden's essential message is contained in the lyrics she wrote to a catchy song called *Count Me In*:

> I want to go back, count me in, to a future that we left in the past.
> Do you remember when everybody in the neighborhood looked out for the children running wild?
> Take me back to yesterday when we followed my god's way.

17

> Leave behind these cold hard times and move on to brighter
> days.
> Do you remember when a father could provide and mother
> did not have those weeping eyes?
> I want to go back, count me in, to a future that we left in
> the past.

Ms. Darden, forty-one, dressed in a suit and big heart earrings, talks of her ideas while sitting in her program's headquarters, an old community hall/gym that still has basketball
backboards on the walls. The program plans to move to better
quarters within the housing project, but for now there is no
need to take a tour of thoroughly scarred linoleum and furniture that cost several hundred dollars rather than several hundred thousand. "We've seen the effects of the free, 1960s
lifestyles on our communities," she says. "When I began talking
about the need to have some discipline, there was opposition.
People said that to make a child say Yes, ma'am is returning us
to the times of slavery. But [respect is] one of the habits of the
past that really worked, so we need to revisit it."

Early in the 1990s, Ms. Darden worked with welfare moms
who live in the 518 units of the housing project to develop a list
of thirteen behaviors that mothers should follow as they begin
to embrace a culture of responsibility. The behaviors include:
"Reteaching our children to use Mr., Mrs., Ms. titles to all
adults. . . . Become more conscientious about the social behavior we allow our children to see. . . . Demanding that all guests
who visit our homes abide by the same value structure."

Current and recent welfare moms who attend Right Alternative meetings—almost all are black—embrace those behaviors. Donna Harris, wearing a flimsy jacket and a hat folded
back, says, "After I been here awhile, there was a big cloud coming over me, telling me I shouldn't be living with a man if I'm

not married." She now is married, and wants law and order in the neighborhood: "When I saw a drug sale to young boys, I called the police." Michelle Dudley rubs her braided hair and says, "I used to drink, smoke weed, do the pipe. I thought it was OK to sit home and watch TV all day. My four kids [ages five, six, seven, and twelve] used to be wild kids, it was because of me. Now I'm getting my GED, and nobody's allowed to do nothing in my house."

Deborah Lee, in T-shirt and sweatpants, says, "I thought it was OK to have a man in my house laying on me. You look at the TV, you think it's OK. But then I think, what will the child think about this? And now I say, Yes, ma'am, no ma'am." Cynthia Wilson, who is now engaged to be married, notes the "no profanity" rule within the thirteen behaviors and explains, "When you change, you'll see a change in your children. Now they say, 'Momma, you cussed,' when I slip." Lorene Lee, thin and quiet, says she now monitors the attention of neighborhood children: "Before, if I saw kids throwing stuff, doing bad, I'd just cuss them. Now, I'll go talk to their parents."

A change in values is the way for many moms to leave welfare, Ms. Darden and her disciples say: an honest woman can attract a diligent man, can impress employees through her own diligence and honesty, and can provide a model of good behavior for children to emulate. Ms. Dudley, explaining that traditional values attract men who want to marry, says, "Once I stopped being easy, then I started seeing gentlemen." Deborah Lee adds, "If you expect marriage, then you change the way you act. Now I make it clear: Johnny can't come to the house, get himself a little piece, and leave."

Cynthia Wilson, now engaged, specifies that she does not "want a boyfriend, I want a marriage. I was hard on men, I had to fight them, now I can want to help them be real men. Before, I didn't care about someone respecting me. I didn't mind someone laying over me. But I learned that I can't be half a woman and get a whole man." Ms. Wilson adds, "I have five children. The man I'll marry is not the father of any of them, but he loves me. The government says, You ain't gonna get no husband. We don't have to listen to the government. There is someone out there." Lorene Lee says simply but emphatically, "I'm going to get a husband, I'm putting myself into the relationship."

Many women planning to leave welfare do not know as much about the soap operas as they used to, but they almost invariably are thinking more about God. (They may have been in church as children, but they usually had no sense of how to apply biblical principles of work and family.) Donna Harris says, "Used to be, every time I heard the word God, I got mad. I didn't want to hear it, but before you know it, here I am, and I know God is the center of everything." Cynthia Wilson comments, "I didn't want to hear nothing about no God. And now, my friends and I are God-fearing people, and we try to do what is right."

None of these changes surprise Ms. Darden, who notes that a culture of immorality "is something you just buy into, without giving it a lot of thought." She blames societal leaders who "don't want to appear to have made a mistake. We tell the young girls that single parenting is a positive. It's not. We need to learn from our mistakes. We used to think that getting high, free sex, whatever feels good was fine. We said, don't be mean enough to your kids to raise them, just let them run free." That type of thinking is everywhere, including in the welfare system, and it needs to be fought." She concludes, "We're conditioned by something we can't see. People back off when you talk about values, but that's what we need."

In a sense, the Right Alternative could be called a first-stage assault on AFDC: women walk away from the beliefs and attitudes they have imbibed over the years and begin to appraise soberly the way the world works. (Even the *New York Times* occasionally stumbles across the core of the problem, noting— on October 22, 1984—that three-fourths of welfare recipients who leave the rolls later return, often lamenting "what they called their bad attitudes or insufficient drive.") The second stage, successful in the long term only if it is based on internally changed values, is an external attitude adjustment. The third stage is specific job training.

The Professional Receptionist Institute is one Milwaukee example of a second- and third-stage program. Begun by Lessie Handy, a black woman who is a former receptionist herself, the institute teaches women who want to leave welfare not only the skills to become receptionists, but the workplace culture as well. Ms. Handy, who wears dress-for-success clothes and has permed hair, is decidedly not multicultural in relation to her charges: "If they have a ring in their nose, they got to get it out. If they come in with their hair in braids, I tell them to get it permed. When they answer the phone, they can't say, Hold on; they have to be pleasant and use correct diction so they can gain and retain customers. They can't wear shorts."

Ms. Handy's students are receptive to her demands for change in habits and habit partly because they know she cares, and partly because they realize the financial payoff of being a good receptionist. The institute has 202 graduates and 186 of them are working, according to Ms. Handy, who comes from the same economic and racial background as most of her students and is available twenty-four hours a day for counseling: "People are still crawling when they leave here. They need someone who understands where they're coming from and will hold their hand as long as it takes; most government people can't or won't do that, and the ones that do are just there during office hours." Economically, those who have started to think long-term instead of getting by month-to-month, hand-to-mouth, are finally ready to turn their backs on the cheap grace of AFDC: student Angela Stearns says, "I'm tired of telling my kids, 'I can't afford that.'"

The differences between Ms. Handy's privately funded institute and the North Milwaukee Job Center are immense. The former uses every available bit of limited floor space; the latter is a vast prairie. The former is crowded with clients, the latter unpacked by participants. Paulette Christian, the institute's business relations manager, speaks readily of how she was called by Jesus Christ to offer a fresh spiritual start as well as training to those who come in; at the job center, God is still officially in exile.

At the institute, students talk of the men in their lives; at the job center, the theme song could well be Helen Reddy's sermon from the seventies: "I am strong, I am invincible, I am woman." The job center has the usual exhortatory signs about how "success comes in cans, not in cannots." At the institute, Ms. Christian says, "We don't sugar-coat anything. We don't tell them it will be easy, because it won't. We do a lot of shaking up around here. We shut the door, we put the mitts on, we let them know we're not from New Berlin [a Milwaukee suburb]. Everything we talk about we've experienced. What we want them to do, we've done."

The governmental job center programs, in comparison, largely operate at stage three, and have a feminist-flawed approach to stage two. They skip the changes in basic beliefs and values that often are needed, because such an emphasis would be politically incorrect. They stress the employment of numerous specialists rather than the one-to-one bonding that has been effective throughout American history. Jankowski of Kenosha, defending the caseworker method of brief appointments followed by referrals, says, "You don't have to sit down for an hour to have a meaningful dialogue with a person." Lessie Handy of the institute says, "No, you need ten hours"—and that governmental systems cannot afford.

The Right Alternative and the Professional Receptionist Institute are not the only shoestring, community-based operations in Milwaukee that are changing lives rather than bowling for bureaucratic dollars. Bill Lock, a black Korean War veteran, is operations manager of Community Enterprises of Greater Milwaukee, an inner-city organization housed across from a graveyard and designed to give birth to small, low-skill businesses. CEGM now provides space to half a dozen businesses, including a transformer assembly firm and an elderly home care service, and Lock speaks of how there is no reason to give up on low-skilled men: they can feel manly repairing everything from windows to small engines, and can then move on to training in trades like masonry and carpentry, where the demand for help exceeds the supply of competent individuals.

"The problem is not the availability of jobs," Lock notes. "The problem is minds that have been distorted." When those minds have been reconfigured, job training is easy, and for that reason, along with their own personal belief, many of the entrepreneurs with whom Lock works emphasize spiritual change as an underpinning to economic advance. Jo Henderson, director of a nursing concern, says, "When you have Christ, you become a new creation, and if you understand what that means, your work ethic changes."

Lock is a deacon at the Community Baptist Church, pastored by the Reverend Roy Nabors. Nabors dresses dapperly in a double-breasted suit with a pocket handkerchief, but he spits out sentences intensely over lunch at the Q F & H Diner, a black community fixture for thirty years. "It is God's plan that man and woman should live in a state of holy matrimony and then have children, with man as the primary breadwinner and woman as the primary nurturer," Nabors states. "When we move away from that, we have problems. . . . A lot of men, once they get married, see the need to support their family and start working hard, but the problem now is that many people are in shacking relationships, and the men don't take responsibility.

"We must face it: 75 percent of the children in this area are living in dysfunctional families," Nabors continues, wiping his face with a handkerchief and smiling wryly. "Here I'm making a moral judgment, but we need to say it straight: parents are raising children alone because of immoral behavior. Some do an excellent job, but it's an extremely difficult thing to do, and not a common occurrence to do it well. . . . I blame most of the churches for this cultural deprivation. What we are preaching is nothing but a watered-down, feel-good, mutual admiration society. African-American churches have been reluctant to confront the immorality, because most preachers depend on the shacking people to get paid. . . . At my church many couples have walked away because I confronted them on living out of wedlock with children, but you can't pussyfoot around that if you're serious about helping people lead godly lives. And no government program will help unless shacking people stop doing it."

The essential defect of the Kenoshalands is that they have as much relevance to the fundamental cultural problems that Nabors sees as Disneyland has to life outside of magic kingdoms. No bureaucracy, and no amount of money, can buy the reformation of morals that is desperately needed. Programs such as the Right Alternative are vital in that effort, yet in many government offices the most-asked question is the plaintive one offered nearly two decades ago at a dramatic moment in the first *Star Wars* movie: "But what will happen to the bureaucracy?" The apostles of Kenosha, going out ostensibly to preach good news to the poor, may make the new welfare world a safe place for themselves, but will the poor be helped?

Down the road, the challenge to Kenosha-style reform is likely to come from those animated by biblical ideas of personal involvement and spiritual challenge. A third element will also play a role: we might call the third factor "Kasich," after Representative John Kasich, energetic chairman of the House Budget Committee. Even if Kenosha were to work, would John Kasich and the new budget hawks in Washington and in state legislatures wish to pay for it, if there is a cheaper way of accomplishing the same objective?

"Even if the welfare system does more good than harm, which is questionable," Kasich asks, "is that good done at a reasonable cost? Can all those dollars be spent more effectively?" What if prospective Kenoshalands in other states have to justify their existence in comparison with church- and community-based programs around the country, such as those in Milwaukee and many other cities that are limited in budget but large of heart?

John Kenneth Galbraith a generation ago gave sound bites comparing private-sector affluence with the government sector's forced cheapness, but a look around today's welfare world shows the opposite. In Washington, the District of Columbia has been spending itself into bankruptcy, but privately funded programs like Children of Mine in southeast Washington or the Darrell Green Learning Center in the northeast are lean. If they had thirty-one new Intel-inside computers, they would not be sitting unused at 3:15 p.m., because children just out of school would be running to them. If far-thinking but frugal programs like the Gospel Mission, the Northwest Center, Clean and Sober Streets, and the Capitol Hill Crisis Pregnancy Center had half the square footage and furniture allowance that the Kenosha model requires, their managers would be shouting, Hallelujah.

Could we have a country animated by compassion and

Kasich? That is a question rarely asked during recent years, because for decades the welfare debate has been the same old-same old. Liberals have emphasized distribution of bread and assumed the poor could live on that alone. Conservatives have complained about the mold on the bread and pointed out the waylaying of funds by "welfare queens" and the empire building of "poverty pimps."

It is time now, however, to talk not about reforming the welfare system—which often means scraping off a bit of mold—but about replacing it with a truly compassionate approach based in private and religious charity. Such a system was effective in the nineteenth century and will be even more effective in the twenty-first, with the decentralization that new technology makes possible, if we make the right changes in personal goals and public policy.

Why is welfare replacement necessary? Because in America we now face not just concern about poor individuals falling between the cracks, but about the crunch of sidewalks disintegrating. An explosive growth in the number of children born out of wedlock—in 1995, one of every three of our fellow citizens was beginning life hindered by the absence of a father—is one indication of rapid decline.

Why is welfare replacement morally right? Because when we look at the present system we are dealing with not just the dispersal of dollars but the destruction of lives. When William Tecumseh Sherman's army marched through Georgia in 1864, about 25,000 blacks followed his infantry columns, until Sherman and his soldiers decided to rid themselves of the followers by hurrying across an unfordable stream and then taking up the pontoon bridge, leaving the ex-slaves stranded on the opposite bank. Many tried to swim across but died in the icy water. Similarly today, many of the stranded poor will soon be abandoned by a country that has seen welfare failure and is lapsing into a skeptical and even cynical "compassion syndrome"—unless we find a way to renew the American dream of compassion.

Why is welfare replacement politically possible? Because there is broad understanding that the system hurts the very people it was designed to help, and that the trillions of dollars spent in the name of compassion over the past three decades have largely been wasted. Conservatives who want an opportunity to recover past wisdom and apply it to future practice should thank liberals for providing a wrecked ship. And liberals should support welfare replacement because, given the mood of the country, the alternative to replacement is not an expanded welfare state, but an extinct one.

Why is welfare replacement practical? Because many specific strategies, projects, and tactics that emerge from an alternative welfare vision are now pushing their way onto the table. For example, not long ago, a tax credit for citizens who hope not to hurl more dollars down the federal Health and Human Services drain was a gleam in the mind's eyes of a few; now such a proposal is gathering steam. Other ways to get more funds to charitable institutions, both religious and secular, that can fight poverty far more effectively are now being developed.

The destruction of life through the current welfare system is not often so dramatic as that which occurred in 1864, but the death of dreams is evident every day. During the past three decades, we have seen lives destroyed and dreams die among poor individuals who have gradually become used to dependency. Those who stressed independence used to be called the "worthy poor"; now, anyone who will not work is worthy, and mass pauperism is accepted. Now, those who are willing to put off immediate gratification and to sacrifice leisure time in order to remain independent are called chumps rather than champs.

We have also seen dreams die among some social workers who had been in the forefront of change. Their common lament is, All we have time to do is move paper. Those who really care do not last long, and one who resigned cried out, "I had a calling; it was that simple. I wanted to help." Some social workers take satisfaction in meeting demands, but others, who wanted to change lives, become despondent in their role of enabling destructive behavior.

We have seen dreams die as "compassion fatigue" deepens. Personal involvement is down, cynicism is up. Many Americans would like to be generous at the subway entrance or the street corner, but they know that most homeless recipients will use any available funds for drugs or alcohol. We end up walking by, avoiding eye contact—and a subtle hardening occurs once more. Many Americans who would like to contribute more of their money and time are weighed down by tax burdens. We end up just saying no to involvement, and a sapping of citizenship occurs once more.

We have seen dreams die among children who never knew their fathers. In a very enjoyable movie from the 1980s, *The Princess Bride,* a character named Inigo Montoya has been chasing for over twenty years a six-fingered man who killed his father. Finally he has the six-fingered man at swordpoint, and says in words he has long rehearsed, "My name is Inigo Montoya. You killed my father. Prepare to die." The vile murderer begins to plead for mercy. Inigo Montoya, says, "Offer me money." The six-fingered man says, "Yes." Montoya says, "Power, too, promise me that." "All I have and more." "Offer me everything I ask for." "Anything you want," the six-fingered man says. Inigo Montoya then runs him through with the sword, saying, "I want my father back, you son of a bitch." A six-fingered government's programs have contributed to the removal of fathers, and nothing else can replace them.

Some would say that the death of dreams is inevitable. Big business . . . big government . . . big charity. Wake up and smell the cyanide. Mass civilization requires impersonal welfare. Yes, we lose the personal touch, but there is no alternative if resources are to be efficiently and equitably dispersed. That's the pessimistic position—but is it inevitable for the American dream of compassion to die?

Past performance—under circumstances as materially difficult as those of today—suggests that the answer is no. Today we have lots of theories about fighting poverty, but it is not necessary to be moving in the theoretical plane. Americans know how to fight poverty. We had successful antipoverty programs a century ago, successful because they embodied personal involvement and challenge, both material and spiritual.

This vital story has generally been ignored by liberal historians, but the documented history goes like this: during the nineteenth century a successful war on poverty was waged by tens of thousands of local, private charitable agencies and religious groups around the country. The platoons of the greatest charity army in American history often were small. They were made up of volunteers led by poorly paid but deeply dedicated professional managers. And they were effective.

Thousands of eyewitness accounts and journalistic assessments show that poverty fighters of the nineteenth century did not abolish poverty, but they saw movement out of poverty by millions of people. They saw springs of fresh water flowing among the poor, not just blocks of ice sitting in a perpetual winter of multigenerational welfare dependency. And the optimism prevalent then contrasts sharply with the demoralization among the poor and the cynicism among the better-off that is so common now.

What was their secret? It was not neglect, either benign or malign. It was their understanding of the literal and biblical meaning of compassion, which comes from two Latin words: *com,* with, and *pati,* to suffer. The word points to personal involvement with the needy, suffering with them, not just giving to them. "Suffering with" means adopting hard-to-place babies, providing shelter to women undergoing crisis pregnancies, becoming a big brother to a fatherless child, working one-on-one with a young single mother. It's not easy—but it is effective.

Our predecessors who helped others to move out of poverty and then turned their attention to the next group of immigrants and impoverished did not have it easy—but they persevered. Theirs were not the good old days. Work days were long and affluence was rare, and homes on the average were much smaller than ours are today. There were severe drug and alcohol problems and many more early deaths from disease. We are more spread out now, but our travel time is not any greater. Overall, most of the problems paralleled our own; the big differences are the increases in illegitimacy and divorce. Most of the opportunities and reasons to help also were similar; a big difference in this regard is that our tax burden is much larger, and many Americans justifiably feel that they are paying for others to take care of problems.

The differences are great, but the parallels make past accomplishments particularly instructive. Volunteers opened their own homes to deserted women and orphaned children. They offered employment to nomadic men who had abandoned hope and most human contact. Most significantly, our predecessors made moral demands on recipients of aid. They saw family, work, freedom, and faith as central to our being, not as lifestyle options. The volunteers gave of their own lives not just so that others might survive, but that they might thrive.

Clearly, Americans a hundred years ago did not have many of the advantages we have today—and yet, we have to be careful not to write off the past by simply claiming that "you can't turn back the clock." It is far better to ask a question similar to the one Ronald Reagan asked in 1980: *Are you better off now than you were four years ago?* It's instructive to compare the situation of a poor person now and a hundred years ago. The present holds many advantages, including antibiotics, refrigerators, and Power Rangers. But a century ago, poor people had to take responsibility for their actions, and were treated as citizens with souls, not just clients to be tranquilized. They received personal help, and their helpers were able to proceed confidently.

Today, of course, we have improved our poverty fighting. The bottom rungs of the ladder are no longer so low: we've removed the bottom rungs, leaving many people stuck on the ground. Over the past three decades, we have fought a war on poverty that has also struck down three of the best allies against poverty: shame, family, and God. When we take away shame, we take away deterrence. When we take away family, we take away the soil in which compassion best grows. When we kick out religion, we also remove the greatest incentive to help and be helped. *Newsweek* recently had a cover story about the need to bring back shame; maybe we are learning.

Some on the left say that, without welfare, poor folks are forced into "demeaning" jobs. But in the weekly newsmagazine I edit, *World,* we recently put on the cover a photo of a sixty-five-year-old man who has had a shoeshine shop in South-Central Los Angeles for many years, and is revered in the community. Teenagers come to him for counsel, and some use his wisdom to help them gain positions of trust and authority. (One person we quoted, who was full of praise for the "demeaned" shoeshiner, is now a police chief nearby.) We need to reemphasize the fact that it is not demeaning, but noble, to work hard to support a family.

There's a lot we can learn in this regard from a wonderful Western produced in 1961, *The Magnificent Seven.* It tells of how seven Texas gunfighters come to the defense of a village that previously had succumbed to a bandit gang; its best scene comes toward the end, when a gunfighter played by Charles Bronson is surrounded by a circle of admiring children. "We are ashamed to live here," one boy says. "Our fathers are cowards."

The gunfighter replies, "You think I am brave because I carry a gun, but your fathers are much braver because they carry responsibility for you, your brothers, your sisters, and your mothers, and this responsibility is like a big rock that weighs a ton. It bends and twists them until finally it buries them under the ground. And there's nobody that says they have to do this. They do it because they love you and because they want to. . . . I have never had this kind of courage, running a farm, working like a mule every day with no guarantee what will ever come of it. This is bravery. It's why I never even started anything like that. It's why I never will."

Some supporters of big government snarl about "turning back the clock" to smaller-scale approaches, but it is not bad to turn back the clock to that type of bravery. Besides, we truly turn back the clock when we stay stuck in the centralizing impulses of the 1930s and the 1960s. We need to turn to the future by giving up our twentieth-century mistakes, picking up what was best in nineteenth-century understanding, and making that vision work for tomorrow.

Furthermore, if we fall into the pessimistic view that people are problems, we are also turning back the clock, this time to the 1970s when zero population growth was hot. Population paranoia should have been laid to rest not only by the utter failure of Malthusian predictions, but also by the experience during the 1980s and 1990s of city-states like Hong Kong and Singapore: crowded and without natural resources, they have rapidly ascended in economic potency. Recent Asian experience shows once again that every mouth comes with a brain and a pair of hands, and that each brain and pair of hands, when trained, can perform wonders. Poor people are assets to be liberated rather than problems to be subsidized. They are resources, not victims.

The vision at its core is simple: people need to be treated as human beings made in God's image, not as animals to be fed, caged, and occasionally petted. The need to replace the welfare system is clear, but we will be able to choose the right means only if we learn from a period when that truth was more widely understood.

Chapter 3

From Wilderness to Neighborhood

When the Pilgrims came to the New World in 1620, they saw before them "a hideous and desolate wilderness," in the words of William Bradford, governor of the Plymouth colony. The colonial era of American history was a time of journeying into the wilderness and turning that wilderness into neighborhood. Good neighbors not only worked hard and cared for their families but also exercised compassion. Individuals and churches cared for widows, orphans, and others who had suffered destitution by disaster or were unable to help themselves.

The early understanding of compassion is different from what has prevailed in recent American history, however. Most settlers read their King James Bibles, where the word "compassion" appears forty-two times, usually as the translation of words coming from the Hebrew root *rachum* (womb) or the Greek root *splanchnon* (bowels of yearning). The linguistic connection underscores the close personal relationship that the person who offers compassion has with the recipient. Our predecessors knew that *suffering with* means not just sympathy but sympathy that is active and often painful, like giving birth.

American churchgoers through the mid-nineteenth century also were taught that Biblical compassion was more the culmination of a process than an isolated noun. Repeatedly, in Judges and other books, the Bible says that only when the Israelites had repented their sins did God, as a rule, show compassion. Second Chronicles 30:9: "The Lord your God is gracious and compassionate. He will not turn his face from you if you return to him." Nehemiah 9:27: "When they were oppressed they cried out to you. From heaven you heard them, and in your great compassion you gave them deliverers."

God's refusal to be compassionate at certain times made the pattern even more evident. Isaiah 27:11 describes Israel as "a people without understanding; so their Maker has no compassion on them." In Jeremiah 15:6, God says, "You have rejected me . . . I can no longer show compassion." The New Testament also teaches that those who have strayed from God must have the grace to cry out for help. Our predecessors did not worship a sugardaddy god.

This understanding of compassion as covenantal—requiring action by both parties—was critical in keeping the principle of *suffering with* from becoming esteem for suffering. The goal of all suffering was personal change. Those who refused to change did not deserve to be the beneficiaries of others' suffering. They might have to be left to themselves until their own suffering became so great that they gave up their false pride.

The colonial understanding that compassion should be challenging, personal, and spiritual provides insight into what early American philanthropies such as the Scots' Charitable Society (established in 1684) meant when they "open[ed] the bowells of our compassion" to widows but ruled that "no prophane or diselut person, or openly scandalous shall have any part or portione herein."* Sermons for several hundred years equated compas-

---

*For further reseach into the historical evidence cited in Chapters 3 through 5 of this book, consult *The Tragedy of American Compassion*, which is fully footnoted and deals at considerably greater length with issues summarized here.

sion with personal involvement that demanded firm standards of conduct among recipients of aid.

The belief that God did not merely establish principles but was active in the world contributed to a sense that man, created after God's image, also was to go beyond clockwork charity: "God values our *Hearts* and *Spirits* above all our Silver or Gold, our Herds and Flocks. If a *Man would give all the Substance of his House instead of Love,* the Loves of his Soul and the Souls of his House, *it would be contemned.*" Personal involvement always was key. Great care had to be taken with any material distribution: Cotton Mather warned in 1698, "Instead of exhorting you to augment your charity, I will rather utter an exhortation . . . that you may not abuse your charity by misapplying it."

The difference between Mather's restraint and our mechanistic redistributionism shows how much dominant ideas of human nature have changed. For the next two centuries, it was believed that many persons, given the option of working, would choose to sit. Based on that belief, Mather told his congregation, "Don't nourish [the idle] and harden 'em in that, but find employment for them. Find 'em work; set 'em to work; keep 'em to work."

Likewise, minister Charles Chauncey told members of the Society for Encouraging Industry and Employing the Poor to restrain "the Distribution of [their] Charity; not being allowed to dispense it promiscuously, but obliged to take due Care to find out suitable Objects; distinguishing properly between those needy People who are *able,* and those who are *unable,* to employ themselves in Labour."

Referring to the apostle Paul's maxim in Second Thessalonians 3:10—"If a man will not work, he shall not eat"— Chauncey said, "The Command in my Text is plainly a *Statute of Heaven,* tying up your Hands from Charitable Distributions to the slothful poor." It was both economically foolish and morally wrong to subsidize bad habits by "bestow[ing] upon those the Bread of Charity, who might earn and eat their own Bread, if they did not shamefully idle away their Time."

True compassion meant challenge rather than acceptance. The poor were seen not as standing on the bottom rung of the social ladder—with the only possible choices stagnation or upward movement—but as resting in the middle, capable of moving either up to economic independence or down toward "pauperism," characterized by a defeated spirit and dependent state of mind—as well as by a lack of income.

Some people, of course, became poor through circumstances beyond their control. They received personal care, often in neighbors' homes. The emphasis on *suffering with* meant that orphans during colonial times normally were adopted into families. As towns and cities grew, however, some institutionalization emerged: orphanages were established in New York, Philadelphia, Baltimore, Boston, and other cities.

At the end of the eighteenth century, some groups began providing small monthly allowances to working widowed mothers. "Widows who have the charge of two, three, four or five children," a Boston association declared, "are unequivocally proper subjects of alms." Even so, the Society for the Relief of Poor Widows with Small Children (established in 1797 in New York City) was cautious in distributing aid. Volunteers checked the means, character, and circumstances of each applicant, making sure that relatives were unable to help and that alcoholism was not contributing to misery.

Further, aid almost always was given in kind—food, coal, cloth—rather than in cash. During the winter of 1797–98, the society helped ninety-eight widows with 223 children; by 1800, 152 widows with 420 children under the age of twelve were listed on its books. Because the society accepted only those clients who "would rather eat their own bread, hardly earned, than that of others with idleness," it emphasized finding work. In one year, widows received nearly 3,000 yards of linen to make shirts and other articles of clothing in their homes.

Since compassion for widowed or abandoned women meant self-help whenever possible, the obligation of able-bodied men was even more exacting. Some twenty-three Boston charitable societies declared in 1835 that recipients should believe it "disgraceful to depend upon alms-giving, as long as a capacity of self-support is retained . . . [To] give to one who begs . . . or in any way to supersede the necessity of industry, of forethought, and of proper self-restraint and self-denial, is at once to do wrong, and to encourage the receivers of our alms to wrong doing."

Echoing Mather's warning of 150 years earlier, the societies stated that "a faithful avoidance of the evils [of] an injudicious bestowment of alms" was essential to "Christian alms-giving." For that reason, they all agreed that relief should be given only after a "personal examination of each case," and "not in money, but in the necessaries required in the case."

Alexis de Tocqueville, in the 1830s, observed that Americans "display general compassion" through personal interaction, unlike the European pattern by which the "state almost exclusively undertakes to supply bread to the hungry, assistance and shelter to the sick, work to the idle, and to act as the sole reliever of all kinds of misery." This difference, Tocqueville surmised, was due in part to the presence of small communities and strong religious ideas.

Americans understood that large-scale aid programs could not be discerning in that way and therefore intrinsically lacked compassion. An 1844 *McGuffey's Reader* ridiculed a "Mr. Fantom" who had "noble zeal for the *millions*" but "little compassion for the units." An English visitor observed that Ohioans did not favor building large institutions, but were compassionate on an individual and family basis: a "disabled Scotchman" received free "board amongst the farmers, sometimes at one house, and sometimes at another," while in another town a Dutch family impoverished by sickness were "provided with doctor and nurse, and in fact with everything needful for them, until they recovered."

As towns grew into cities, more organizations to help the "worthy poor" emerged. The goal throughout was to make city relations as much as possible like those of the countryside. The Boston Provident Association (established in 1851) gave food, clothes, and coal to those willing to work but in temporary need. The association refused requests from drunkards and asked supporters to give beggars not money but cards proposing that they visit the association's offices, where volunteers would examine needs, make job referrals, and provide food and temporary shelter. It developed a list of "the worthy" and also a "black record," which in 1853 contained the names of 201 "impostors"—able-bodied persons who refused to work.

Those who were ill generally received help (given nineteenth-century medicine, questionable help) regardless of background. The New York Association for Improving the Condition of the Poor frequently emphasized the importance of taking personal action. It reported "an increasing number of families and individuals who are willing to take charge of one or more, often of several, poor families." Similar associations emerged in New York, Baltimore, Boston, Philadelphia, Chicago, St. Louis, and other cities.

The South had fewer cities but similar patterns of compassion, as shown in historian Suzanne Lebsock's detailed examination of Petersburg, Virginia. Ms. Lebsock is typical of conventional historians in her bewilderment about the data she found. Describing Petersburg's economic difficulties during the 1830s and 1840s, and noting the lack of governmental response, she repeatedly indicates puzzlement and concludes, "How people got by, to repeat, is a mystery."

The mystery can be largely solved by recalling how compassion was then practiced: people got by when their neighbors showed true compassion. For example, women in Petersburg, Virginia, set up an orphan asylum in 1812, for they were "deeply impressed with the forlorn and helpless Situation of poor Orphan female Children . . . and wish to snatch [them] from ignorance and ruin." In Charleston, South Carolina, the Ladies' Benevolent Society in 1825 gave special support to a Mrs. Cowie, who suffered from blindness and leprosy; to Clarissa and Mary, two crippled black women; and to Mary McNeile, a free black with leprosy.

The first half of the nineteenth century, in short, witnessed a vast war on wilderness. The increase of neighborhood came not everywhere, not at all times, and, woefully, not for all races—but overall, the forward movement was remarkable. De Tocqueville was amazed by how strongly Americans felt "compassion for the sufferings of one another" and how—beginning with the establishment of the Female Humane Association for the aid of indigent Baltimore widows in 1798—women particularly were in the forefront of benevolent activity. Women founded and managed the Female Charitable Societies and Ladies' Benevolent Societies that started up in the early 1800s, first in large cities like New York and Philadelphia and then in towns both north and south.

Nineteenth-century sermons continued to define compassion as personal involvement: "To cast a contribution into the box . . . or to attend committees and anniversaries [are] very trifling exercises of Christian self-denial and devotion, compared with what is demanded in the weary perambulations through the street, the contact with filth, and often with rude and repulsive people, the facing of disease, and distress, and all manner of heart-rending and heart-frightening scenes, and all the trials of faith, patience, and hope, which are incident to the duty we urge."

Churches and charity organizations believed that professionals should be facilitators of aid, not major or sole suppliers: "there must, of course, be officers, teachers, missionaries employed to live in the very midst of the wretchedness, and to supervise and direct all the efforts of the people . . . [but] mark you! these officers are not to stand between the giver and receiver, but to bring giver and receiver together."

The compassion consensus was based on the development of personal relationships, often cross-class. A few proto-Marxists challenged that definition by declaring that compassion meant not *suffering with* but forcible redistribution of income. That idea, however, did not receive a widespread hearing until some editors of the "penny press"—newspapers that because of printing and circulation innovations in the 1830s could sell for one cent—became, for both ideological and mercenary reasons, self-appointed tribunes of "the poor" generally.

The first popular challenge to the compassion consensus came from mid-nineteenth-century American journalist Horace Greeley, who founded and became editor of the *New York Tribune* in 1841. A theological Universalist, Greeley believed that people were naturally good and that every person had a right to both eternal salvation and temporal prosperity. He probably never said the words most often attributed to him—"Go west, young man"—but he did advise many young men and women to fight poverty by joining communes in which the natural goodness of humans, freed from competitive pressure, inevitably would emerge.

Not accepting orthodox Christian anthropology—that man's sinful nature leads toward indolence, and that an impoverished person given a dole without obligation is likely to descend into pauperism—Greeley saw no problem with payment to the able-bodied poor who did not work. Rather than discuss the obligations of neighbors, Greeley argued that each member of "the whole Human Family" had "a perfect right . . . to his equal share of the soil, the woods, the waters, and all the natural products." There was no need for *suffering with* when everyone, by government fiat if necessary, was due an equal sustenance.

Greeley and his followers were only partially successful in undoing the definition of compassion that had been built over the previous two centuries. Henry Raymond, founder of the *New York Times,* was Greeley's principal opponent and emphasized individual and church action: "Members of any one of our City Churches do more every year for the practical relief of poverty and suffering, than any [commune] that ever existed. There are in our midst hundreds of female 'sewing societies,' each of which clothes more nakedness, and feeds more hunger, than any 'Association' that was ever formed." Raymond praised "individuals in each ward, poor, pious, humble men and women, who never dreamed of setting themselves up as professional philanthropists," but daily visited the sick and helped the poor.

Debates between Greeley and Raymond show clearly the conflict of views. Greeley contended that supporting a system of equal, society-wide redistribution was "the duty of every Christian, every Philanthropist, every one who admits the essential Brotherhood of the Human Family," and argued that evil resulted from "social distinctions of master and servant, rich and poor, landlord and landless." The way to end evil was to redistribute wealth by having the government tax the better-off and distribute food and funds to those who had less.

Raymond, however, argued that "before a cure can be applied or devised, the cause of the evil must be ascertained," and that cause was "the sinfulness of the heart of Man." The only solution lay in God's compassion toward man and man's subsequent compassion toward his brethren: "The heart must be changed."

The groups Raymond particularly applauded emphasized personal contact with the poor, even when some of their members were stunned by the firsthand experience. They refused to settle for the feed-and-forget principle or its equally depersonalizing but harsher opposite, the forget-and-don't-feed standard. They saw individuals made in the image of God, and when they saw someone acting disgracefully they responded with a challenge: *You do not have to be that way. You are better than this. We expect more from you than an arm thrust out for food.*

Personal involvement became the hallmark of nineteenth-century compassion. A consistent line of understanding and action runs from John McDowall in the 1830s, Robert Hartley in the 1840s, and Charles Loring Brace (who set up "orphan trains") through the late-nineteenth-century efforts of Humphreys Gurteen, Josephine Lowell, and other leaders of the Charity Organization Society movement. They wanted the rich to see without sentimentality. They wanted those with a pauper mentality to see the need to change and to know that they had neighbors willing to help. They helped poor Americans as well as the better-off to live in neighborhoods, not wilderness.

Following the Civil War, urban problems increased as industrialization accelerated—and the number of poverty-fighting societies grew commensurately. For example, in 1890 and 1891, in Baltimore, Chicago, and New York alone, about 2,000 organizations of various kinds were active:

• In Baltimore, the Association for the Improvement of the Condition of the Poor had 2,000 volunteers who made 8,227 visits in 1891 to 4,025 families. Nearly half the families were headed by widows who generally received material aid; most others were headed by able-bodied men who received help in finding jobs and in fighting alcoholism and opium addiction. An emphasis on personal involvement of rich and poor—not just material transfer—was evident in many ways.

• Other Baltimore groups emphasized self-help for the poor and material transfer only to those unable to work. In 1890, the Thomas Wilson Fuel-Saving Society helped 1,500 families save on the purchase of 3,000 tons of coal. The Memorial Union for the Rescue of Homeless and Friendless Girls offered free rooms in private homes for teenagers and young women until long-term housing and jobs could be found. The Presbyterian Eye, Ear and Throat Charity Hospital offered free beds and Bible readings to the poor and illiterate. While many groups had Protestant bases, Catholic groups also flourished: volunteers of the Society of St.Vincent de Paul of the City of Baltimore made 4,800 visits and relieved 345 families.

• New York's charity organizations also emphasized personal help and the exchange of time, not just money. The American Female Guardian Society and Home for the Friendless sheltered over 1,000 children "not consigned to institution life but . . . transferred by adoption to Christian homes." The Nursery and Child's Hospital provided free medical care and supported hundreds of unmarried pregnant women in return for an agreement "to remain three months after confinement to take care of two infants."

New York's 1,288 charitable organizations often employed professional managers, but their task was to coordinate activities of tens of thousands of volunteers who provided food, clothing, fuel, shelter, and employment; supported free schools and kindergartens; organized sea excursions and summer camps; staffed free hospitals and dispensaries; and constructed missions, reformatories, libraries, and reading rooms.

How effective was the late-nineteenth-century war on

poverty? That question is difficult to answer with certitude. Most overall statistics from the period are not thorough enough to be particularly useful. One page of the 1890 census report makes up in candor what it misses in accuracy by noting three times that "the results of this inquiry are comparatively value-less" and "the returns are so scanty that general conclusions can not be based on them."

Often we have to fall back on eyewitness reports and journalistic assessments, and here useful material is abundant. Author Edward Everett Hale analyzed the success of the Boston Industrial Aid Society in reforming alcoholics: "These women were most of them poor creatures broken down with drink, or with worse devils, if there are worse. But . . . five hundred people in a year take five hundred of these broken-down women into their homes, sometimes with their babies, and give them a new chance."

A middle-class volunteer in the slums was astounded when "with my own eyes I saw men who had come into the mission sodden with drink turn into quiet, steady workers. . . . I saw foul homes, where dirty bundles of straw had been the only bed, gradually become clean and respectable; hard faces grow patient and gentle, oaths and foul words give place to quiet speech." Writer Josiah Strong concluded in 1893, "Probably during no hundred years in the history of the world have there been saved so many thieves, gamblers, drunkards and prostitutes as during the past quarter of a century."

Strong and others were favorably inclined toward theistic values—but some who were deeply skeptical of the theology were nevertheless impressed by the practice. Muckraker Ray Stannard Baker was struck by testimonies such as that of a former "drunken wretch" whose life was transformed when he stumbled into the McAuley mission and came to believe "that Jesus Christ had the power to save me when I could not save myself."

Baker did not know quite what to make of the account and many others like it, but he was a good enough journalist, and a curious enough soul, to conclude that the saved person "knows what he has got, and those wretches who hear him—do they not understand intimately what he has suffered? And do they not also long blindly for the power . . . ?"

Baker also was struck by the realization that "it apparently makes not the slightest difference whether the man is an unlettered Christ or a university graduate; the power of reconstruction is the same." He called the McAuley mission "one of the most extraordinary institutions in the country" and noted that once the individuals "surrendered" to Christ, they were able to escape alcoholism, find jobs, and be reconciled with their families.

For those who scoff at both believers and skeptics, the most credible observer of the entire era may be liberal reformer Jacob Riis, author in 1890 of *How The Other Half Lives*. Riis lived his concern for the New York poor by hauling heavy cameras up dozens of flights of tenement stairs day after day to provide striking photographs of dull-eyed families in crowded flats. Riis documented great misery, but he also saw movement out of poverty and concluded that "New York is, I firmly believe, the most charitable city in the world. Nowhere is there so eager a readiness to help, when it is known that help is worthily wanted; nowhere are such armies of devoted workers."

Riis also wrote of how one charity group over eight years raised "4,500 families out of the rut of pauperism into proud, if modest, independence, without alms." He noted that another "handful of noble women . . . accomplished what no machinery of government availed to do. Sixty thousand children have been rescued by them from the streets."

Chapter 4

The Good Old Days?

J acob Riis and his contemporaries were not arguing a century ago that the war on poverty was won, or was even winnable in any final sense: Riis wrote that "the metropolis is to lots of people like a lighted candle to the moth." Those who climbed out of urban destitution were replaced quickly by others awaiting trial by fire. But dreams then were alive: the poverty-fighting optimism among Americans then contrasts sharply with the demoralization among the poor and cynicism among the better-off that are so common now.

What was their secret? They did not shower money on the poor, nor did they simply relax in an antistatist spirit: they knew that private agencies could be just as bad as government ones. No, charity workers a century ago were fired up by seven ideas that recent welfare practice has put on the back burner. For convenience of memory these seven seals of good philanthropic practice can even be put in alphabetical order, A through G: *Affiliation, Bonding, Categorization, Discernment, Employment, Freedom, God.* If we understand how these seven were applied, we'll at least be able to ask the right questions about our recent wrong turn.

Let's begin where poverty-fighting a century ago began, by emphasizing *affiliation: connecting with families and communities.*

Many men a century ago, as now, were abandoning their families. Church groups as well as the United Hebrew Charities fought the trend. Many young people were running away from home, and some of the elderly were out of contact with their children. Charity organizations responded by instructing all volunteers to work hard at "restoring family ties that have been sundered" and "strengthening a church or social bond that is weakened." The prime goal of relief, all agreed, was not material distribution but "affiliation . . . the reabsorption in ordinary industrial and social life of those who for some reason have snapped the threads that bound them to the other members of the community."

In practice, when individuals or families with real needs applied for material assistance, charity workers began by interviewing applicants and checking backgrounds with the goal of answering one question: who is bound to help in this case? Charity workers then tried to call in relatives, neighbors, or former co-workers or co-worshippers. "Relief given without reference to friends and neighbors is accompanied by moral loss," Mary Richmond of the Baltimore Charity Organizing Society noted. "Poor neighborhoods are doomed to grow poorer and more sordid, whenever the natural ties of neighborliness are weakened by our well-meant but unintelligent interference."

When material support was needed, charities tried to raise it from relatives and others with personal ties instead of appropriating funds from general income. "Raising the money required specially on each case, though very troublesome, has immense advantages," one minister wrote. "It enforces family ties, and neighborly or other duties, instead of relaxing them." Affiliation was important for both old and young. A typical case from the files of the Associated Charities of Boston notes that when an elderly widower applied for help, "the agent's investigation showed that there were relatives upon whom he might have a claim."

In another case, a niece "was unable to contribute anything," but a brother-in-law who had not seen the old man for twenty-five years "promised to send a regular pension," and he did. The brother-in-law's contribution paid the old man's living expenses and reunited him with his late wife's family. "If there had been no careful investigation," the caseworker noted, the man would have received some bread, but would have remained "wretched in his filthy abode." Similarly, abandoned young people were to be placed in alternative families, not institutionalized. Orphans were to be placed with families as quickly as possible—a century ago, that meant days or weeks, not months or years, in foster care.

Affiliation could also mean reinvolvement with religious or ethnic groups. The New York Charity Organization Society asked applicants what they professed or how they had been raised, and then referred them to local churches and synagogues. Some groups emphasized ethnic ties. The Belgium Society of Benevolence, the Chinese Hospital Association, the French Benevolent Society, the German Ladies' Society, the Hungarian Association, the Irish Immigrant Society, and many similar organizations did not want to see their people act in shameful ways. On an individual level, members of the same immigrant groups helped each other out.

When applicants for help were truly alone, then it was time for *bonding: helping one by one.* Volunteers in such situations became, in essence, new family members. Charity volunteers a century ago usually were not assigned to paper-pushing or mass food-dispensing tasks, but were given the opportunity to make large differences in several lives over several years. Each volunteer had a narrow but deep responsibility: the Philadelphia Society for Organizing Charitable Relief noted that "a small number of families, from three to five, are enough to exhaust all the time, attention, and friendly care which one visitor has." The thousands of volunteers were not babied by promises of easy satisfaction and warm feelings. Instead, the Philadelphia Society warned that volunteers would have "discouraging experiences, and, perhaps for a time little else," but would nevertheless be expected to maintain "the greatest patience, the most decided firmness, and an inexhaustible kindness."

There were failures, but success stories also emerged. The magazine *American Hebrew,* in 1898, told of how one man was used to dependency, but volunteers "with great patience convinced him that he must earn his living"—soon he was, and had regained the respect of his family and community. A man who had worked vigorously could no longer do so because of sickness, but was helped to develop a new trade mending broken china. Speakers at the Indiana State Conference on Social Work regularly told of those "transformed from dependent to respectable citizen."

The key was personal willingness to be deeply involved. Nathaniel Rosenau of the United Hebrew Charities noted that good charity could not be based on the "overworked and somewhat mechanical offices of a relieving society." The charity magazine *Lend a Hand* regularly reminded readers that they could not "discharge duties to the poor by gifts of money alone . . . Let us beware of mere charity with the tongs." Philanthropic groups such as the Associated Charities of Boston saw their role not as raising more money, but as helping citizens to go beyond "tax-bills [or] vicarious giving" by serving "as a bureau of introduction between the worthy poor and the charitable." *Charities Review* paid close attention to language abuse and emphasized the importance of understanding "charity in its original meaning of 'love,' not charity in its debased meaning of 'alms.'"

Involvement was not uninformed. Volunteers—typically, middle-class church members—were helped in their tasks by careful *categorization:* the goal was to *personalize* charity so that individuals with different needs could receive different treatment. Charities did not treat everyone equally—and, since they were private, they did not have to. Instead, charitable societies considered "worthy of relief" only those who were poor through no fault of their own and unable to change their situation quickly. In this category were orphans, the aged, the incurably ill, children with "one parent unable to support them," and adults suffering from "temporary illness or accident." Volunteers who were tenderhearted but not particularly forceful served as helpers to those who were helpless.

Other applicants for aid were placed in different categories and received different treatment. Jobless adults who showed themselves "able and willing" to work or part-time workers "able and willing to do more" were sent to employment bureaus and classified as "Needing Work Rather Than Relief." Help in finding work also was offered to "the improvident or intemperate who are not yet hopelessly so." However, the "shiftless and intemperate" who were unwilling to work were categorized as "Unworthy, Not Entitled to Relief." In this group were "those who prefer to live on alms," those with "confirmed intemperance," and the "vicious who seem permanently so." Volunteers who agreed to visit such individuals had to be of hardier stock and often of rougher experience; often the best were ex-alcoholics or ex-convicts.

How would agencies know the categories into which applicants fell? Background checks helped, but "work tests" were a key self-sorting device, and one that also allowed the dispensing of aid with dignity retained. When an able-bodied man in almost any city asked an agency for relief, he often was asked to chop wood for two hours or to whitewash a building. A needy woman generally was given a seat in the "sewing room" (a child care room often was nearby) and asked to work on garments that would be donated to the helpless poor or sent through the Red Cross to families suffering from the effects of hurricanes or tornadoes.

In 1890, wood yards next to homeless shelters were as common as liquor stores are in 1995, and the impact was sobering: work tests allowed charity managers to see whether applicants who held out signs asking for work were serious. Work tests also allowed applicants to earn their keep. The work test, along with teaching good habits and keeping away those who did not truly need help, also enabled charities to teach the lesson that those who were being helped could also help others. The wood was often given to widows or others among the helpless poor. At the Friendly Inn in Baltimore, for example, the count was exact: 24,901 meals worked for in 1890 and 6,084 given without work. The New Orleans Charity Organization Society described its wood yard as a place "where heads of families can earn household supplies, and the homeless food and lodging," with assistance given "in a way that does not pauperize."

Categorization, Jacob Riis wrote repeatedly, was crucial: the way to fight "real suffering in the homes of the poor" was to hang tough—"no work, nothing to eat." Many organizations during the 1890s kept careful records. At Boston's Associated Charities in one typical year, 895 volunteers visited 2,094 families requesting relief (the goal was one volunteer for two families). The visitors found that 18 percent of all applicants were "worthy of continuous relief" because of old age, incurable illness, or orphan status. Some 23 percent were "worthy of temporary relief" because of accident, illness, or short-term trouble. The 33 percent categorized as "able to work" (a few were unemployed not by their own choice and others were the "shiftless or intemperate where reform may be hoped for") were sent to employment bureaus that had jobs aplenty. The remaining 26 percent were "unworthy" of support because they had property or relatives to fall back on, or because work tests and investigation had indicated that they were without "desire to change."

With Associated Charities' help and pressure, 817 clients found and accepted jobs that year and 278 refused them ("98 refusals with good reason, 170 without"). In addition, Associated Charities gave loans to eighty-one persons (the repayment rate was 75 percent), legal aid to sixty-two persons, and medical help to 304. Volunteers helped 185 families to save money, influenced fifty-three relatives to offer aid, and pushed 144 alcoholic breadwinners to make progress in temperance. Nearly 600 children were helped directly by volunteers. They found adoptive families or guardians for orphans, influenced truants to attend school more often, and placed other children in private day nurseries or industrial schools.

The New Orleans Charity Organization Society also emphasized "personal investigation of every case, not alone to prevent imposture, but to learn the necessities of every case and how to meet them." Some 1,328 investigations in a typical year there led to 926 individuals being classified as worthy of help, 276 as "unworthy," and 126 as doubtful. In the "worthy" category were 271 individuals found unemployed but willing to work, 252 who had jobs but wanted additional work, 205 who were ill, and sixty-four who were aged; forty-eight women had been abandoned by their husbands. Among the "unworthy" were forty-one drunkards and professional beggars uninterested in changing their conduct, 143 who were "shiftless" and unwilling to work, and seventy-two who were found not to be in need.

Categorization and self-categorization went along with discernment—or as we say today, *responsible giving.* The tendency toward caution grew out of the benign suspicion that came naturally to charity workers who had grown up reading the Bible. Aware from their theology of the deviousness of the human heart, nineteenth-century charity workers were not surprised when some among the poor "preferred their condition and even tried to take advantage of it." The St. Louis Provident Association noted that "duplication of alms is pursued with cunning and attended most invariably with deceit and falsehood."

One magazine reported that a "woman who obtained relief several times on the ground that she had been deserted by her husband, was one day surprised at her home with the husband in the bedroom. She had pretended that the man was her boarder." The husband turned out to have a regular income. Jacob Riis noted that some claims of illness were real, but other times a background check revealed "the 'sickness' to stand for laziness, and the destitution to be the family's stock in trade."

Only discernment on the part of charity workers who knew their aid seekers intimately could prevent fraud. Baltimore charity manager Mary Richmond wrote that her hardest task was the teaching of volunteers "whose kindly but condescending attitude has quite blinded them to the everyday facts of the neighborhood life." To be effective, volunteers had to leave behind "a conventional attitude toward the poor, seeing them through the comfortable haze of our own excellent intentions, and content to know that we wish them well, without being at any great pains to know them as they really are." Volunteers had to learn that "well-meant interference, unaccompanied by personal knowledge of all the circumstances, often does more harm than good and becomes a temptation rather than a help."

Discernment by volunteers, and organizational barriers against fraud, were important not only to prevent waste but to preserve morale among those who *were* working hard to remain independent. One charity worker noted that "nothing is more demoralizing to the struggling poor than successes of the indolent or vicious." The St. Louis solution was to require volunteers "to give relief only after personal investigation of each case. . . . To give what is least susceptible of abuse. . . . To give only in small quantities in proportion to immediate need; and less than might be procured by labor, except in cases of sickness. . . . To give assistance at the right moment; not to prolong it beyond duration of the necessity which calls for it. . . . To require of each beneficiary abstinence from intoxicating liquors. . . . To discontinue relieving all who manifest a purpose to depend on alms rather than their own exertions for support."

Doles without discernment not only subsidized the "unscrupulous and undeserving" but became a "chief hindrance to spontaneous, free generosity": they contributed to "the grave uncertainty in many minds whether with all their kind intentions they are likely to do more good than harm . . . Only when "personal sympathy" could "work with safety, confidence, and liberty," would compassion be unleashed. The New Orleans COS tried to impress on its volunteers maxims of discernment by printing on the back cover of its annual reports statements such as "Intelligent giving and intelligent withholding are alike true charity" and "If drink has made a man poor, money will feed not him, but his drunkenness."

It was also important for every individual approached by a beggar to be discerning—and teaching that proved to be a very difficult task! *Charities Review* once asked the designer of an innovative program whether its success satisfied "the 'gusher' who desires to give every evening beggar 25 cents." S. O. Preston responded, "No, nothing satisfies the 'gusher'; he will persist in giving his (or someone else's) money to the plausible beggar as often as he appears." The magazine was filled with criticism of "that miscalled charity which soothes its conscience with indiscriminate giving."

Our predecessors did not pussyfoot around. Charity leader Humphreys Gurteen called giving money to alcoholics "positively immoral" and argued that if givers could "foresee all the misery which their so called charity is entailing in the future," they would "forgo the flutter of satisfaction which always follows a well intentioned deed." New Haven minister H. L. Wayland criticized the "well-meaning, tender-hearted, sweet-voiced criminals who insist upon indulging in indiscriminate charity."

The drive to stop foolish "compassion" continued throughout the 1880s and 1890s. *Charities Review* quoted Ralph Waldo Emerson's famous self-criticism: "I sometimes succumb and give the dollar, but it is a wicked dollar, which by and by I shall have the manhood to withhold." Sociological analyses of the "floating population of all large modern cities" showed the homeless including some "strangers seeking work" and needing temporary help, but a larger number of "victims of intemperance and vice"—not all that different from today, with studies showing a majority of the homeless in major cities suffering from alcohol or drug abuse.

Charities Review criticized "that miscalled charity which soothes its conscience with indiscriminate giving" and proposed that individuals and groups restrict "material relief to those cases in which such relief would be given by the true friend." True friendship was not encouraging "lazy imposture," for "such mercy is not mercy: it is pure selfishness." Instead, true friendship meant helping to deliver a person from slavery to a bottle, a needle, or his own laziness.

Affiliation and bonding, categorization and discernment— when the process was working well, the next key element was long-term *employment* of all able-bodied household heads. *Demand work,* magazines such as Charities Review stressed, proclaiming that "labor is the life of society, and the beggar who will not work is a social cannibal feeding on that life." Indiana officials declared that "nothing creates pauperism so rapidly as the giving of relief to [able-bodied] persons without requiring them to earn what they receive by some kind of honest labor."

An emphasis on work would have been savage had jobs not been available—but, except during short-lived times of "business panic," they were. (In 1892, charity experts from several major

cities were asked whether honest and sober men would spend more than a short time out of work: they all said such a situation was "rare" or "very exceptional.") A single-minded work emphasis also would have been unfair if alternatives to begging did not exist during short-lived periods of unemployment—but private charities in every major city provided the opportunity to work for food and lodging, as we have already discussed.

Most of the able-bodied poor accepted the work obligation, partly because of biblical teaching and partly because they had little choice. A New Haven mission manager reported that fewer than one out of a hundred refused to work in the wood yard or sewing room, perhaps because "there is no other institution in this city where lodging can be secured except by cash payments for same." Had there been alternatives, bad charity might have driven out good, for charity leaders argued that it took only a short time for slothful habits to develop. After several years of easygoing charity in Oregon, N. R. Walpole of Portland "found among the unemployed a reluctance to work, and regarded compulsory work as the only solution of the problem."

Take a hard line, charity leaders demanded, or else problems would worsen: New York charity leader Josephine Lowell wrote, "The problem before those who would be charitable, is not how to deal with a given number of poor; it is how to help those who are poor, without adding to their numbers and constantly increasing the evils they seek to cure." Jacob Riis agreed; when some New York groups appeared to be weakening, Riis foresaw a tribe of "frauds, professional beggars . . . tightening its grip on society as the years pass, until society shall summon up pluck to say with Paul, 'if a man will not work neither shall he eat,' and stick to it." Riis, like other Christians a century ago, kept coming back to the apostolic teaching. Jewish leaders, meanwhile, were stressing that poverty was not a desirable status within Judaism, and that a person unwilling to work could not justify his conduct even by citing a desire to study the Bible: they quoted a Talmudic saying, "All study of the Torah that is not accompanied by work must in the end be futile and become the cause of sin."

Within the Talmudic tradition, avoiding dependency was so important that even work on the Sabbath was preferable to accepting alms: Rabbi Jochanan said, "Make thy Sabbath a weekday and do not be reduced to need the help of human beings." All charity leaders argued that even poorly paying jobs provided a start on the road from poverty; since travel down that road required solid work habits, true friendship meant challenging bad habits and pushing a person to build new, productive ones.

Along with an emphasis on employment came a focus on promoting *freedom*—which was defined by immigrants not as the opportunity to do anything with anyone at any time, but as the opportunity to work and worship without governmental restriction. To *promote freedom* meant to provide opportunity to drive a wagon without paying bribes, to cut hair without having to go to barbers' college, and to get a foot on the lowest rung of the ladder, even if wages for that job were low. Freedom was the opportunity for a family to escape dire poverty by having a father work long hours and a mother sew garments at home.

This freedom did not make for an instantly successful war against poverty at a time when 200,000 persons were packed into one Manhattan square mile. Snapshots of abject poverty could show horrible living conditions, but those who persevered had roles in a motion picture of upward mobility. My grandparents, for example, all came from the Russian empire shortly before World War I and found the streets paved not with gold but with liberty—which, in the hands of people who wanted to work hard and were encouraged to do so, amounted to virtually the same thing.

It was clear to leaders a century ago that government subsidy could not provide the kind of freedom that was important. In 1894, Amos G. Warner's mammoth study, *American Charities,* compiled what had been learned about governmental charity in the course of the nineteenth century: "It is necessarily more impersonal and mechanical than private charity or individual action. . . . There is some tendency to claim public relief as a right, and for the indolent and incapable to throw themselves flat upon it. This feeling will always assert itself whenever it is given an opportunity to do so. . . . In public charities, officialism is even more pronounced than under private management."

Warner prophetically continued, "The degradation of character of the man on a salary set to the work of relieving the poor is one of the most discouraging things in connection with relief-work. . . . It is possible to do so much relief-work that, while one set of persons is relieved, another will be taxed across the pauper line. . . . the burden of supporting the State tends to diffuse itself along the lines of the least resistance; consequently, money which is raised for the relief of the poor may come out of pockets that can ill spare it. . . . The blight of partisan politics and gratuitously awkward administration often falls upon the work. . . . Charitable institutions are spoils of an insignificant character, thrown frequently to the less deserving among the henchmen of the successful political bosses."

The goal of charity workers, therefore, was not to press for governmental programs, but to show poor people how to move up while avoiding dependency, depicted as slavery with a smiling mask. Minister Joseph Crooker noted that "it is very easy to make our well-meant charity a curse to our fellow-men." Social worker Frederic Almy argued that "alms are like drugs, and are as dangerous," for often "they create an appetite which is more harmful than the pain which they relieve."

Governmental welfare was "the least desirable form of relief," according to Mary Richmond, because it "comes from what is regarded as a practically inexhaustible source, and people who once receive it are likely to regard it as a right, as a permanent pension, implying no obligation on their part." But if charity organizations were to do better, they had to make sure the poor understood that "dirt and slovenliness are no claim to help; that energy and resource are qualities which the helper or helpers will gladly meet half-way." Freedom could be grasped only when individuals took responsibility.

Affiliation and bonding, categorization and discernment, employment and freedom . . . and the seventh seal on the social covenant of the late nineteenth century was concern about the relation of God to all these things. *Rely on faith in God* was a constant refrain; "true philanthropy must take into account spiritual as well as physical needs," a frequent theme of charity magazines. Poverty will be dramatically reduced if "the victims of appetite and lust and idleness . . . revere the precepts of the Bible and form habits of industry, frugality, and self-restraint," Pennsylvania charity commissioners declared. The frequent conclusion was that demoralized men and women needed much greater help than "the dole of organized charities."

There were some differences between Christians and Jews as to what that help was. The biblically orthodox Christians of the late nineteenth century worshipped a God who came to earth, suffered with us, and died for us. Christians believed that they—creatures made after God's image—were called to *suffer with* also, in gratitude for the suffering done for them, and in obedience to biblical principles. (The goal of such suffering, of course, was to promote those principles, and not to grease a slide into sin.) Jewish teaching, however, emphasized the pursuit of righteousness through the doing of good deeds, particularly those showing loving kindness (*gemilut chasadim*). The difference was significant—but both approaches led to abundant volunteering.

Similarities in theistic understanding led both Christians and

Jews to emphasize the importance of personal charity, rather than a clockwork deistic approach. The Good Samaritan in Christ's story bandages the victim's wounds, puts him on a donkey, takes him to an inn—the Samaritan walks alongside—and nurses him there. The Talmud also portrayed personal service as "much greater than charity," defined as money giving.

Christians and Jews had many similarities in understanding because they both read an Old Testament that did not portray God as a sugar daddy who merely felt sorry for people in distress. They saw God as showing compassion while demanding change, and they tried to do the same. Groups such as the Industrial Christian Alliance noted that they used "religious methods"—reminding the poor that God made them and had high expectations for them—to "restore the fallen and helpless to self-respect and self-support."

In addition, Christians had the expectation that the Holy Spirit could and would rapidly transform the consciences of all those whom God had called. Those who believed in poverty fighting through salvation were delighted but not surprised to read in the *New York Herald* of how "the woman known as Bluebird up to a year ago was one of the worst drunkards in the Lower East Side. . . . Scores of times she had been in the police courts." Then she was met with by an evangelist, agreed to go to the Door of Hope rescue home, was converted, and decided to help others. The *Herald* reporter told how he visited "the Five Points Mission Hall. A big crowd of ragged, bloated and generally disreputable looking men and women were seeking admission. . . . a very pleasant looking young woman dressed neatly in black and having a bunch of flowers at her waist . . . spoke to them of love and hope. The crowds kept coming until the break of day. No one would ever think that the neatly attired young lady speaking so appealingly had once been the terror of the slums, always alert to get in the first blow."

Some one hundred of Bluebird's former gang associates changed their lives over the next several years as, in the words of the *New York Times*, she was "transformed into one of the most earnest and eloquent female evangelists who ever worked among the human derelicts in dark alleys and dives" and "threw her whole soul in the work of evangelism among her former associates." Most of those hundred changes were permanent, a follow-up years later concluded.

Affiliation, bonding, categorization, discernment, employment, freedom—and in the end, God's grace. Those were the principles developed by poverty fighters who did much more than the standard textbooks report, and who accurately warned us of the long-term consequences of the government programs that the standard textbooks praise. But hard questions still nag at us: did the late-nineteenth-century war on poverty work? What was the direction of movement—for how many was dire poverty only a short-term curse? To what extent did charity and challenge help individuals escape poverty? Was it fair that most would advance—some very slowly—but some would not?

To answer those questions accurately, we need to avoid both sentimentality about the past and snideness toward it. Clearly, the good old days were hard, and living conditions for many of the urban poor, particularly in crowded Manhattan (the 1880 census showed six wards in lower Manhattan with over 200,000 persons per square mile), were terrible. Without antibiotics, illness could ravage families overnight; without modern machinery, work was often long and physically exhausting; without modern heating and cooling systems, cold fronts and heat waves took a toll. Societies at different times have differing degrees of difficulty in their poverty fighting; materially, our predecessors' task was harder than ours.

Given conditions a century ago, how did poverty fighters acquit themselves? Various writers answered those questions in different ways, but the person I trust the most is Jacob Riis, who before he became an acclaimed writer was himself a penniless, homeless immigrant. Riis's most famous work, *How the Other Half Lives,* is a particularly noteworthy combination of sad realism and thoughtful optimism. New York's "poverty, its slums, and its suffering are the result of unprecedented growth with the consequent disorder and crowding," he wrote, and argued that what government welfare there was made life worse by creating an "incentive to parents to place their children upon the public for support."

Riis, knowing through his own reporting the dire situation of many, still insisted that material distribution to the able-bodied, by the state or private charities, led to "degrading and pauperizing" rather than "self-respect and self-dependence." Instead of calling for governmental programs, Riis praised New York's Charity Organization Society and "kindred organizations" for showing "what can be done by well-directed effort." With the understanding that antipoverty progress was incremental and tied to economic growth, he pointed to problems but declared that "the thousand and one charities that in one way or another reach the homes and the lives of the poor with sweetening touch, are proof that if much is yet to be done . . . hearts and hands will be found to do it in ever-increasing measure."

The good news, according to Riis, was that through many charitable efforts, "the poor and the well-do-to have been brought closer together, in an every-day companionship that cannot but be productive of the best results, to the one who gives no less than to the one who receives." He concluded that "black as the cloud is it has a silver lining, bright with promise. New York is to-day a hundredfold cleaner, better, purer, city than it was even ten years ago. . . . if we labor on with courage and patience, [these efforts] will bear fruit sixty and a hundred fold."

Chapter 5

Twentieth-Century Debacle

Some Americans did not labor on. Books and articles at the beginning of this century were filled with an unwillingness to go on patiently helping people, one by one. The process of turning wilderness into neighborhoods seemed too slow. A changed view of the nature of God and the nature of man led to impatience.

The older view saw God as both holy and loving; the new view tended to mention love only. The older anthropology saw man as sinful and likely to want something for nothing, if given the opportunity. The new view saw folks as naturally good and productive, unless they were in a competitive environment that warped finer sensibilities. In the new thinking, change came not through challenge, but through placement in a pleasant environment that would bring out a person's true, benevolent nature.

Such thinking packed a political pistol, for it soon became customary to argue that only the federal government had the potential to create a socioeconomic environment that would save all, and that those who were truly compassionate should rally behind the creation of new programs. Others, however, argued that compassion required "coercive philanthropy"—

forced redistribution through taxation—that would "establish among us true cities of God."

Hopes were high. "Social misery and wrong" could be ended by officials with "a genuine and earnest and passionate desire for the betterment of mankind." Welfare programs could "become the outer form of the altruistic spirit—the unselfish, loving, just nature of the new man." Since people were naturally inclined to goodness, why go slow?

Part of this revisionist definition was based on the revived belief that man is naturally good and productive unless a competitive environment warps finer sensibilities. Reporter Ray Stannard Baker saw that *suffering with* compassion was having an impact—"Whenever I went downtown to see [the] work [of one mission] I always came away hopeful"—but worried about those who did not undergo change. One-by-one compassion was based on hand-picking of fruit ready to be harvested, but an apple-grabbing machine presumably could motor through the orchard. Baker distinguished the mission's method from what he hoped could be a new one by titling one of his articles, "Lift Men from the Gutter? or, Remove the Gutter? Which?"

For those working within the biblical understanding of compassion, the question was not either/or. The goal was to remove as much of the gutter as possible so that no one would have to live in it. Yet, they had the grim expectation that some would seek out parts of the gutter that remained, or build new sections, and sometimes drag their children and others into it: "The poor you always have with you" (although not any particular poor). Those who believed the story of the prodigal son argued that times of torment were not wasted; some people needed to hit bottom before they were ready to move up.

One Charity Organization Society official conveyed this understanding: "The question which we try through investigation to answer [is,] Are these applicants of ours ready to work out with us . . . some plan which will result in their rescue from dependency . . . ? If such elements are entirely lacking—no basis of good character, no probability of final success—then we do not assume the responsibility of asking societies or churches or private persons to help, and may even, if our advice is asked, urge them to refrain from blind interference with natural educational agencies."

The goal, our predecessors insisted, was not "that poor families should suffer, but that charity should accomplish its purpose." Mission workers steeled themselves to bid farewell to those who would not accept the challenge to change. Some who left never came back, but as one volunteer wrote, "The prodigals commonly returned confessing their weakness and laboring earnestly to prove their penitence."

Such thinking was unacceptable to those who saw no need for hearts to change. Those who saw mistakes but not sin, foolish acts but not evil, also believed that problems originated in social conditions, not moral corruption. They argued that "the social evils of the day arise in large part from social wrongs." They argued that environment determined action, so a good environment would save all. They reinterpreted compassion to mean acceptance of self-destructive behavior and postponement of pressure to change until all were in a good environment.

Since such theological liberals believed that persons freed from material pressures also would be freed from the sinful tendencies arising from those pressures, a focus on material need emerged. Popular novelist Hall Caine described the extent to which material comfort was believed to drive moral progress: "The world is constantly growing better and happier. . . . there can hardly be any doubt about this [when one sees] the changes which the century has brought about in the people's health, education, and comfort. . . . People are better housed, and for that reason, among others, their morality has improved."

If utopia could be attained through mass redistribution, personal compassion was unnecessary. Compassion could become synonymous with sending a check or passing redistributionist legislation. A new stress on professionalized social work accompanied increased government action. The New York Charity Organization Society's Summer School of Philanthropy, established in 1898, soon became the Columbia University Graduate School of Social Work.

Such moves brought misgivings. One Charity Organization Society official worried that professionals were being "exalted . . . at the expense of the volunteer," and noted a "certain opinionated and self-righteous attitude in some of the trained social workers [who saw the world as a stage] upon which we professional workers are to exercise our talents, while the volunteers do nothing but furnish the gate receipts and an open-mouthed admiration of our performances."

But the band played on. National Conference of Social Work president Owen Lovejoy announced in 1920 that social workers would have a new kind of task. While volunteers had endeavored "to ameliorate evil social conditions, to lighten the burdens of poverty, to reduce the volume of ignorance, combat the ravages of disease and otherwise labor diligently to assuage the flood of human sorrow and wretchedness," social workers and their allies would be "social engineers" capable of creating "a divine order on earth as it is in heaven. . . . [S]imply making the earth a place that will be humanely endurable and stopping there [is] an intolerable belittling of the innate qualities in man."

In short, the idea that all (even the voluntarily idle) were entitled to a piece of the pie gained vast intellectual and theological support in the early twentieth century. Materialism triumphed among the academic and journalistic elite groups in American society. Lecturers and writers stopped teaching the truth that it may be good to send money to a charity, but that such action is not compassionate activity. Political scientists stopped teaching that legislation may be wise or foolish, but that it cannot be compassionate. (It can erect barriers to compassion.) Those who were supposed to be the intellectual shepherds of society forgot that compassion means adopting a child, suffering with an adult trying to reform, or (like the Good Samaritan) binding up the wounds of a mugging victim.

As some leaders forgot that compassion means *suffering with,* they looked more and more to government. They combined power seeking (for the good of others, of course) with social universalistic faith. Social gospel leader Washington Gladden was among those who believed that God is unfair if all are not saved from hell (if there is a hell), and government is unfair if all are not saved from poverty (which Gladden knew did exist). Universalist soteriology, proposing that all must be saved regardless of belief, was matched by universalist sociology demanding that all receive provision.

Other changes followed. If provision of material aid was primary, programs could be measured by the amount of material transferred. Nonquantifiable considerations could be overlooked. The nineteenth-century concern that state charity would supplant private efforts—the "crowding out" effect— was turned upside down. Some began to call for less private charity, arguing that such efforts let government off the hook: no one should make it "easy for the state to evade the responsibility." Grants from private groups to widows got in the way of governmental expansion.

Increasingly, some saw charitable organizations as a sign of government weakness rather than as a sign of social strength. As professionals increasingly dominated the realm of compassion, opportunities for charitable work decreased and volunteers departed. At United Charities of Chicago, by 1915, "interested laymen were as likely to be consigned to a desk job as they were to be assigned to a family." When board members at one organization wanted more involvement, its president announced, "Our staff is so well organized that there is very little for our Board Members to do. . . . "

Boards did, however, retain one major function: fund raising. Historian Kathleen McCarthy has noted that, "under the exacting gaze of a freshly certified professional elite, boards were remodeled into fund-raising bodies. . . . " Increased economic segregation and mediated compassion allowed the better-off to "measure community needs through abstractions: publicity, lectures, the photographs in annual reports. Communications innovations, like professionalization, separated the twentieth-century donor from the object of his largesse. [Donors] could exercise the obligations of stewardship at a safe remove from the problems they were helping to solve."

By the 1920s, University of Chicago sociologist Clarence Glick was finding that suburban residents were unlikely to venture into poor areas. One woman explained, "[The slums are] too dirty and besides it's too dangerous. I can't see how anyone could get a kick out of doing that. Merely the idea of it is nauseating to me." A willingness merely to spend money grew as the desire to expend time decreased: "Like some of Shakespeare's characters [rich people] have developed a habit of flinging purses at the least provocation and crying: 'Spend this for me!'" One wealthy Chicagoan, when asked why her peers were not involved in person-to-person activity, said, "Organizations look after everything, and they give to them, so why think about it?"

By the 1930s, the long-term trend toward redefinition was already on its way to making cash king. Decreased personal action was easy to justify when problems seemed overwhelming, and when an emphasis on community chest cash transfers provided "the ultimate in bureaucracy—an anonymous public supporting anonymous machinery supporting anonymous clients." Philanthropy had become "as cold as the payment of taxes." One journalist noted, "Indeed the objectives of the two are often the same." The New Deal emphasis on compassion as income transfer was generally accepted because the ground had long been prepared.

When a major economic crisis emerged in the early 1930s, many believed it not only natural but inevitable to rely on governmental programs run by professionals and emphasizing material transfer rather than individual challenge and spiritual concern. During the Depression, when millions of individuals were not responsible for their own plight and jobs were not readily available, Mormons set up an effective church welfare system and other groups could have been helped to revive their own programs, but few thought in those terms. Instead of supporting the replication and expansion of church- and community-based programs, the federal government set up a new charity order.

Some governmental programs made moral sense (although the required expenditures may have prolonged overall economic misery) as temporary expedients. But later, when programs were institutionalized at a time when jobs were available, the potential problem grew. Throughout the 1940s and 1950s, governmental systems were like a guillotine poised to sever compassion from thought. As long as most families were intact and most people saw benefits not as rights but as backups only for use during dire emergencies, the blade did not fall.

There was a deeper problem, though. In 1938, one editor wrote that "personal conscience in the United States has fallen to a new low in our history as a nation. It has been largely lost to our sight in all the din and dither that have been raised about that other moral concept, the social conscience, which, we are constantly reminded, has a nobler and more widely embracing function. And, the more we hear of the one, the less we hear of the other. The personal conscience has been steadily submerged; the very foundation upon which any broader conception of individual responsibility towards society must rest is being washed away."

Influenced by ideas of the left, many social work leaders argued that an emphasis on personal change was a "trivial and reactionary" practice that "imposes on the individual the cruel burden of adapting himself to a psychotic society, and, insofar as it succeeds, constitutes a brake on social action." A typical writer on the subject, Grace Marcus, reported that "trained social workers in the relief field are helping fundamentally to bring about a new social order [through] the reorientation of clients from the still prevalent viewpoints of 'rugged individualism' to the newer social philosophy dictated by the interdependent, complex society of today."

For a time, even after the federal government jumped into the social welfare puddle with two enormous feet, the social universalistic impulse was held in check. Two gatekeepers—the welfare office and an applicant's own conscience—scrutinized each applicant. As late as the mid-1960s, only about half of those eligible for welfare payments were receiving them, and many of the enrolled were taking only part of the maximum allowance. Attitudes changed during that decade, however, as a postmodern welfare system emerged alongside a postmodern cultural system.

Postmodernism in welfare meant, in theory, that there was no right way to act. In practice, it meant a war on the biblical understandings that still underlay even New Deal governmental welfare—for example, the idea that able-bodied people should work. Biblical writers never argued that it is better to receive alms than to glean, but in the 1960s, Michael Harrington, author of the influential book *The Other America,* complained that some who were out of work for a long time "would take low-paying jobs" and in that way "accept humiliation rather than go on the public dole." Until the 1960s, the public dole for those who did not need it *was* humiliation.

By the 1960s, a New York City lecture series by theological liberals was emphasizing the new conventional wisdom: "the age-old plague" of poverty will end as soon as "proper direction" and "imaginative planning" bear down on it. "We have reached the stage where old concepts of charity and almsgiving no longer apply. . . . There will always be the need for the spirit of generosity and neighborly benevolence, but it will act on a higher and happier level." That happier level was massive wealth redistribution, based on "a five-year or a ten-year or a fifty-year plan . . . to end this abject poverty."

While liberal theologians planned tours of the celestial city, Lyndon Johnson declared his intention to create "a Great Society: a society of success without squalor, beauty without barrenness, works of genius without the wretchedness of poverty." Johnson's legislative triumphs during 1964 and 1965—the Economic Opportunity Act, food stamp legislation, Medicare, Medicaid, public works programs, and so on—were immense. The speed of passage, unrivaled since the New Deal, showed a disregard for real-life effects, and was more remarkable in not being prompted by the mood of crisis so evident in 1933. Great Society legislation was truly a triumph of faith, the social gospel walking on earth.

Yet, as nineteenth-century charity leaders had warned, government programs lacked true compassion and tended to produce social folly at the margin. The War on Poverty meant that some Detroit autoworkers could earn more by quitting their jobs and joining job-training programs; in Johnson, Rhode Island, seventy-three parents of children in a poverty program owned more property—fifty-eight homes and 113 cars—than typical nonpoor residents.

Reports of such inequities were embarrassing, but underlying materialist assumptions predominated. One administration official said, "The way to eliminate poverty is to give the poor people enough money so that they won't be poor anymore." One columnist wrote that for $12 to $15 billion a year (2 percent of the gross national product at that time), "poverty could be abolished in the United States"—as if a change in material circumstances would inevitably alter attitudes that, left unchanged, would create new poverty.

Crucially, the War on Poverty became a war on God. The successful antipoverty pushes in American history have been religiously based. They have worked on the inside by changing hearts and not just temporarily changing habits. Yet, government funding of groups that emphasize spiritual challenge was excluded by regulations concerning welfare. The 1960s-style welfare system was rooted not only in the separation of church and state but, with governmental programs dominating social service provision, in the separation of church and needy. That, in turn, meant a separation of program and effectiveness.

Books of the period generally equated compassion with redistribution and argued for compassion not just to widows, orphans, and other victims, but to those who had victimized themselves and wished to continue in self-destructive pursuits. Some of these books claimed to be based on the Bible, and others were explicitly Buddhist. The common theme was compassion as "a vision that dissolves division" and that teaches "seeing the unity in things." With that understanding, attempts to distinguish the deserving from the undeserving were seen merely as legitimizing inequality.

The political agenda in this use of compassion was evident. Government expanders such as Sar Levitan wrote, "Only through greater reliance upon programs that offer the promise of opportunity as envisioned in the Great Society is the nation likely to reject policies of negativism and retrenchment." The theologically liberal National Council of Churches called for "the extrication of stewardship from its almost indelible association with economic capitalism." A typical "Christian left" writer, Douglas Hall, demanded "a new look at the socialist alternative" and a "search for new forms of community— including a 'New Economic Order' that can more adequately reflect our faith's concern for justice, equality, and mercy."

By the 1980s, observers such as Clifford Orwin noted abundant misuse of the concept of "compassion": "Our century has hardly seen a demagogue, however bloody and monstrous his designs, who has not known how to rally compassion and mine its potential for sympathetic moral indignation." Writer Mickey Kaus noted that Americans were supposed to have "compassion for the unmotivated delinquent who would rather smoke PCP than work. Compassion makes few distinctions . . . which is why a politics based on mass-produced compassion leads naturally to the indiscriminate dispensing of cash in a sort of all-purpose socialized United Way campaign."

Despite such warnings, a bull market in compassion raged throughout the 1980s, particularly on the issue of "homelessness." The *Washington Post* typically used "compassion" as a euphemism for "more heavily funded": when Speaker of the House Tip O'Neill favored more spending on the homeless, his "compassion was the size of his frame." O'Neill's successor, Jim Wright, was likewise praised, as was Washington, D.C., Mayor Marion Barry. Professor Dwight Lee concluded, "The notion that compassion toward the poor requires favoring expansion of government transfer programs has achieved the status of revealed truth."

As the 1980s came to an end, leading newspapers also equated compassion with leniency. Chicago lawyers asked a judge for compassion when sentencing a sheriff's deputy for selling cocaine. California lawyers asked a jury to have compassion for an accused murderer by letting him off. Baseball star Steve Garvey asked for compassion for having exercised passion through bigamy or trigamy. At times the word was even less defined: a music reviewer complained that an LP record was filled with "make-out ballads" for "the wine-and-cheese crowd," but was saved by "the mix of spiky aggression and compassion." A California music group was praised for trying to "communicate" the idea of compassion in a "noncognitive way."

Such ludicrous examples abound, but the misconception became more tragic than comic. Prior to the 1960s entitlement revolution, marriage was both a social and economic contract. Economically, it was a compassionate antipoverty device that offered adults affiliation and challenge while providing children with two parents. So strong was support for marriage in the 1950s that 85 percent of single pregnant women got married before their babies were born. Those who did not had a second option: placing a child for adoption. Fewer than one in ten pregnant women chose single parenthood for fear of social ostracism and lack of financial support.

While marriage under pressure certainly was not optimal, it did not leave a woman alone. Placing a child for adoption also was difficult, but one result of the marriage/adoption emphasis was that children had fathers during their early years.

In the 1960s, as part of the new definition of "compassion," government obligations to single mothers increased while marital obligations decreased. As no-fault divorce laws spread, women knew that husbands were allowed to be unfaithful with little penalty. Sociologist Jack Douglas noted, "Almost all women have enough economic common sense to realize that the marriage contract has been tremendously devalued by the legal changes. Since any potential husband can fly free of his family at the first impulse, women have far fewer incentives to get married, even when they are pregnant."

The reduction of social and financial barriers to single parenting made it seem logical to raise children alone, even though they often grew up not only materially poor—three out of five were in poverty—but emotionally impoverished as well. Their mother's husband, in essence, was the federal government. These children never knew what it was like to have a father who could love and discipline them.

In a sense, the blade on this social guillotine had been ready to fall ever since the 1930s, when children born out of wedlock first became eligible for AFDC help and harm. The blade did not fall until the 1960s, when—under conditions of prosperity rather than duress—a cultural revolution led to attacks on any kind of categorization and investigation of welfare applicants.

The War on Poverty of the 1960s was a disaster not so much because of its new programs but because of their administered emphasis on entitlement rather than need. Opportunities to give aid with discretion disappeared as welfare hearings became legal circuses and depersonalization triumphed. Talk of affiliation and bonding was seen merely as an attempt to fight wars on poverty cheaply.

Small efforts at categorization and discernment similarly were seen as plots to blame the poor rather than the socioeconomic system that trapped them. "Freedom" came to mean governmental support rather than the opportunity to work and move up the employment ladder. A *Time* magazine cover asked whether God was dead: he certainly seemed that way in much of what went by the name of philanthropy.

Many programs described as "compassionate" were actually the opposite, since they made neighborly or familial help less likely. To gain a full share of government-funded services, pregnant teens had to be on their own, without support from families or children's fathers.

There was no clear evidence that government entitlements

led women to become pregnant, but they did influence decisions to choose single parenting over adoption, welfare dependency over marriage, and living in an apartment rather than a family home or group home. Adolescents were aware of opportunities for government support and increasingly often "did not consider the expense of raising a child as a barrier" to setting out on their own. To a poor teenager, monthly AFDC stipends could look like a good deal—and they were available only if bonds were broken. As single mothers moved into their own apartments, government spending was actually reducing the level of true compassion by providing incentives for social isolation.

The destruction was obvious, but many who had bet their careers on Great Society success refused to acknowledge it. At a reunion of Johnson administration officials in Austin, Texas, twenty-five years after the War on Poverty fired its first cannonade, the mood of reminiscence was akin to Wordsworth's memory of enthusiasm following the French Revolution: "Bliss was it in that dawn to be alive. . . . " Sargent Shriver exulted that the Reagan years had not essentially damaged Great Society programs, most of which were "still in existence, all helping millions of Americans today." *New York Times* columnist Tom Wicker proposed that it was time to stop moaning and instead drink a toast to "vision and aspiration, confidence and compassion."

Vision, aspiration, and confidence were all there. But was compassion? Not if the word is given its historical and literal definition of *suffering with*—and we need to bring back that original emphasis on personal involvement and challenge. Not only is the current misuse notorious, but current confusion among those who say they want to help shows no signs of abating. The conclusions of political scientist James Fishkin typified the early 1990s tendency to punt on third down: "Some great revision in our assumptions or in our actions is required. But because I feel genuinely caught in this dilemma myself, I am not now advocating any particular resolution."

Throughout the early 1990s, as politicians, journalists, and scholars continued to sit and debate, or increasingly gave up, a generation continued to roll down the slippery slope to destruction. Crack babies in inner-city hospitals trembled and twitched uncontrollably. Teenage mothers, alone with squalling children, fought the impulse to strike out. Men in their twenties called job holders "chumps" and went on a rampage in Los Angeles. Women in their thirties, abandoned by husbands, waited in welfare offices for their numbers to be called. Homeless men, aged beyond their years, lined up impatiently at food wagons. They then shuffled off to eat and drink in alleys smelling of urine.

Meanwhile, in middle-class areas, those who complained about income transfer through taxation were seen as lacking compassion. Private charity also changed as telethons and jogathons became typical activities. Stars on television for twenty-four hours, or those who ran long distances at so much per mile, suffered to raise money to pay professionals who in turn would help the needy.

These were good-hearted activities, even if the horseshoes pitched were at best leaners rather than ringers. Government groups and many charities, in turn, tended to offer not challenge but what might be called "Velcro compassion," with the poor treated as perpetual children unable to tie their own shoes and needing a supply of sneakers with Velcro closers.

Upset by ineffectiveness, Americans joined a backlash against welfare expansion that has grown consistently over the past three decades and accelerated during the past three years. If it had not been for media teachers instructing us that anyone who opposed welfare lacked "compassion," reform action could have been taken a decade or two ago, before the problems became as severe as they now are.

Now that we have waited, the welfare system has gotten incredibly out of whack. A person who knows how to take in not only the relatively miserly AFDC payments but also housing allowances, food stamps, medical help, and other tax-free benefits loses money by taking an entry-level job that would lead to something better over time, but in the short run reduces disposable income and especially disposable time.

A recent Cato Institute examination of the benefit levels of just the six (out of seventy-seven) most common types of federal welfare payment—AFDC, food stamps, Medicaid, housing, nutrition assistance, and energy assistance—showed that in thirty-nine states the welfare package is economically superior to an $8-an-hour job. In sixteen states, welfare payments provide more income than would be gained by working at a $10-an-hour job, and in eight states, including New York and Massachusetts, welfare pays more than a $12-an-hour job; that's two and a half times greater than the minimum wage.

Payments are out of whack, but the worst aspect of welfare, again, is the effect on aspirations. If a person's expectations are low, if a person knows that no matter what he does or how often he fails, or how obvious it is that he has stopped even trying, he is still guaranteed by law a place to sleep, food to eat, and some money to spend; if all he has to do to keep these benefits is to stay poor; and if working hard probably will not improve his standard of living in the short run, then why go to the trouble of working?

The typical response to such a statement is that the benefits are not all that great, that few people would settle for them if they had real choice or access to good jobs with transportation and day care provided, and that it is societal rather than individual failings that are to blame. Again, however, individuals vary enormously, and for those who have grown up in the dog house and know its walls intimately, it seems like home.

Chapter 6

That Was Then—This Is Now?

The full version of the history summarized in chapters three through five has been attacked in three ways.

First comes the accusation of romanticizing the past. That is easy to refute. The outpouring of charitable activities in the nineteenth century is well-documented, as are the great difficulties through which our predecessors persevered. They did not live in good old days; the times were bad in many ways, and Americans faced problems of drugs, crime, and assimilating immigrants.

A century ago, Americans were far poorer on average than we are today, and epidemics sometimes devastated communities. They had less divorce and illegitimacy but far more orphans than we have. Overall, they had problems. We have problems. The only glow from the past is this: they dealt with their problems; we whine about ours.

Next comes a criticism from members of the religious left. They say the Bible requires us to transfer whatever resources we can to the poor, for Christ said, "Whatever you did to the least of these my brethren, you did it to me." That verse should be taken very seriously, but before it is blindly used to justify the welfare state a question needs to be posed: who are the least of these in America and what kind of help is real help? Is giving to panhandlers money that goes for drugs akin to sticking heroin into Jesus's veins?

Christ does not include in his list of commended charitable acts, When I was strung out you gave me dope. Since various biblical passages were cited repeatedly during the 1995 welfare debates, Appendix B provides an overview of a consistently biblical antipoverty position.

The third criticism is the most frequent: old times are best forgotten because, although an outpouring of compassion in the past did occur, that history is irrelevant to "our more complex society today." People today, it is said, will not go above and beyond the call of economic logic. They will not remember dreams and volunteer to bring them to life. They are so cynical about the large leaps promised by past political leaders that they will not start with small steps. Since affluent individuals are removed more from the everyday experience of poverty than our predecessors were, they will not feel the urgency of action—and in the absence of that sense of urgency, the motivation to act sacrificially will not be present.

There is some logic behind this argument, but it points to the need to go faster in changing the welfare system, not slower. As long as governmental welfare remains, it leads potential helpers to sit back, since they are paying for someone else to do it. Bad charity drives out good. Groups capable of replacing the welfare state will not emerge in full strength before they are desperately needed, but the governmental safety net masks the emergency. Urgency is the mother of motivation, and in the American welfare debate right now we have frustration but still not urgency.

Furthermore, as long as tax revenue needed to pay for government welfare comes from working individuals who sometimes need two jobs to pay the freight, those individuals can rightly say that they have little time for volunteering. Many young mothers are pressed into the work force when they would prefer to stay home with children and then volunteer part-time. If the tax rate now was similar to that of the 1950s, they would be able to do just that. For every government social worker paid to help preserve families, there are families falling apart under government-created financial pressures.

The suggestion that ordinary people will not give of themselves compassionately, however, is partly belied by the experience of recent years. Tens of millions of Americans regularly do volunteer work, but all such gross statistics can be misleading because they lump together those who merely serve on charity ball committees with those who walk down mean streets daily. The deeper story is that despite all the bureaucratic obstacles that those who wish to be compassionate often face—more on this in the next chapter—it is heartening to see how many truly commit their lives to the task.

Here I have to get personal, because I am having the opportunity now to meet many heroes. Actually, they are ordinary people who become heroic as they show, through hard suffering, that the American dream of compassion is not dead.

Look, for example, at Bob Cote of Denver. He is a six-foot-four white exboxer who spent a year on the streets as an alcoholic in the early 1980s and then pulled together a few of his fellow winos and junkies to start a program that has become known as Step 13. In his organization's four-story building, mostly dead people from off the streets can, step by step, come back to life. They can get jobs of increasing responsibility and build up their own savings accounts. They can progress within that building from dormitory space to alcoves to separate rooms of their own; at the end of the process, they own their own furniture, have their own telephone accounts, and are ready to go out and rent apartments of their own. They go through a tough, time-intensive process of counseling and spiritual rebuilding as well, but Cote has gone through it himself and is there to help others.

Cote is angry about the existing welfare system. He has seen the destructiveness of false compassion and knows that "you don't just give a street drunk a bed and a meal and some money. He knows how to work the system too well. You've got to get him out of his addiction." He has seen enormous amounts of money wasted in government programs and has learned how to resurrect dreams at a cost much less than governmental programs charge for killing them. Step 13, for example, costs about $3,000 per man annually, one-fifth of what it costs to keep a person for only twenty-eight days in some fancy detox center. Residents pay about half the cost out of the wages they earn and donations take care of the other half.

Look, for example, at Hannah Hawkins, who lives in Anacostia, the poorest part of Washington, D.C. She is a retired school administrative aide and the widowed mother of five grown children. At the rundown, formerly abandoned community center that houses her program, Children of Mine, fifty children from five to fifteen look for attention in the late afternoon. Volunteers do everything, and Hannah Hawkins walks around her building and gets children in the study area to settle down and start on their homework: she knows each of her sheep by name, and they know her. One sixth-grader reports getting good grades and Mrs. Hawkins says, "Go ahead, girl." Two little children come in the front door by themselves, in time for dinner, walking past the druggies and hookers outside on Mount View Street (but there's no mountain in view), and Mrs. Hawkins gives them instructions in table manners and prayer.

Hannah Hawkins is gentle with her children but shows barely controlled anger when asked what the welfare system has done for her neighborhood. "Oh, there's lots of government money floating around Anacostia," she says. "I look at the budgets and I see la di da administrative cost, eighty-five thou a year. Assistant to the assistant, sixty thou a year. Services, null and void." She skewers the jostling line of government grantees who "say they help the needy but are really the greedy." She tells of money-flush but program-poor organizations asking her to bring several dozen children on particular days when federal funders were around, so that fat-cat facilities would not look like ghost towns: "When I first started, I used to go because I didn't know nothing. Now I'm well seasoned. I see the pimping of these children, and I will not have any part in it."

That Hannah Hawkins is no pimp is evident as she stops one child who is running by and asks, "Do you have homework?" "Yes, ma'am." "Then sit down. We can't have you running back and forth, can we?" "No, ma'am." One junior-high boy makes a threatening remark to another, and the steely-eyed woman who has lived in Anacostia for over four decades reminds him quietly, "People who pick fights end up either dead or in jail." Hannah Hawkins calls her program Children of Mine because she insists that social progress comes not when professionals take on needy children as clients, but when ordinary people treat the semiabandoned children of others as their own. A strong Christian belief underlies Mrs. Hawkins's willingness to serve and keep serving: "Without Jesus you're empty. You're just out to sea, floating, and don't know where to go."

Hannah Hawkins says she would rather be where she is than hanging out at the White House across town: "The impression you make there means nothing. But your impression here is everlasting." To keep going she gleans food, books, and shoes from local businesses and churches, and she is unabashed when phone calls come in: "Excuse me. Children of Mine. Yes, I need me some dough, re, mi." Glancing at some financial records she adds, "We are flying on a wing and a prayer. Tell your neighbors to wake up little Susie."

Defenders of the welfare state should also spend time with Freddie Garcia, a softhearted but hardheaded Hispanic exaddict. Garcia, head of Victory Fellowship in San Antonio, became a Christian and a drug fighter three decades ago. Before his conversion, he had been not only an addict but a hater of white non-Hispanics. Immediately after his conversion, he "saw a Mexican-American girl holding hands with her Anglo boyfriend. It was a sight that had never failed to infuriate me, but now the anger was gone." At present, during lunches at his home and all through the day, he patiently counsels and teaches those of all skin colors whom everyone else has abandoned. Over the years, he has led hundreds of people out of substance abuse and trained many in the techniques of helping others.

Among those he discipled is David Perez, a veteran who came back from Vietnam "strung out on drugs, and . . . kept doing it." After years in the pits, however, Perez's uncle pressed him to go to church, and Perez saw there "all kinds of drug addicts. Men and women I knew on the street, they were praising the Lord, their lives were changed. I said, 'Man, what's going on here?' And then Pastor Freddie was preaching, and I gave my life to Christ." Garcia taught and mentored Perez for several years, and Perez then became head of a Victory Fellowship chapter in Austin, seventy miles north of San Antonio. He has been working there at bare subsistence pay for fifteen years and has influenced hundreds of addicts and alcoholics during that time.

Perez, like Garcia, scorns the federal welfare system's fostering of dependency and its insistence that the way out is through job training. He points out that many homeless and apparently hopeless men are not without skills and solid job experience, and the Austin chapter's intake forms show that. Some of the addicts and alcoholics cannot read or write and have never held responsible jobs, but most have large amounts of productive experience as teachers, machinists, computer repairmen, certified welders, carpenters, licensed plumbers, auto mechanics, electronic technicians, tailors, and so forth. Cocaine, heroin, and alcohol, not tough job markets, have brought them down; as Perez puts it, "They're not untrained, they're in bondage."

The way out, he says, is through God, personal help, and discipling. One of Perez's disciples, Gene Lucio, recalls that "the first few days here were really rough. I still had the temper that had gotten me into fights at stoplights and in supermarkets. Gradually, though, I got some structure and discipline in my life. Delivery from drugs took a few days, but it was the delivery from rage and violence that took a long time. I told Pastor David, 'Help me to change, please, don't be easy on me, if anything be double-hard on me.' He worked with me day after day, helping me to see myself as self-centered. He rebuked me but also gave me love."

Lucio has now been placed as leader of a chapter of Victory Fellowship in San Marcos, thirty miles south of Austin—far enough away to require some on-the-spot decisions, close enough to be under supervision. For the eight men who live there, he is Pastor Gene. From Garcia to Perez (and many more) to Lucio (and many more), Garcia's disciples have spread his life-changing teaching throughout the southwestern United States and as far south as Peru.

Bob Cote, Hannah Hawkins, Freddie Garcia and two generations of disciples . . . all have created challenging, personal, and spiritual programs that work, without a dime of government money, and there are hundreds more like them. None of them knew the best ways to help others when they began the practice of effective compassion; none was an accomplished speaker or program manager. Each developed under pressure, and others can too.

It is particularly impressive to see the way that soft-hearted people lose their soft-headedness as they accumulate experience

in helping others. Seven years ago, for example, Marsh Ward
came to Washington, D.C., to build a haven for homeless alcoholics and addicts. His ideal was a detox program with no rules
("They're all adults, aren't they?") and no pressure to prepare for
a job ("Nothing good available under capitalism, anyway"). In
1988, Ward recalls, "we believed that if you brought people in off
the streets and gave them food, they'd pull themselves together
and get on with their life."

That did not work with alcoholics and addicts, though: "If
you treat them that way, you're killing them. You're enabling
them to stay with their disease." When Ward and a partner, Julia
Lightfoot, set up Clean and Sober Streets in line with their liberal philosophy, "drug dealers set up here. They could deal all
day, then come back here for a room and hot meal, get their
food stamps and welfare, then go back out and deal the next
day." Soon, to protect residents who did want to beat their
addictions, Ward established rules: "Real simple: no violence, no
sex. If you sit down, get too comfortable, make no progress,
you're out. Any stealing, you're out. No alcohol, no drugs—not
even legal ones, unless I've approved them. If you miss the cur-
few by one minute, you're out."

At first, Ward's tendency was to accept excuses for violations:
"We did it sometimes just out of mercy, or sympathy, because
we like the guy—but it never worked out. Every time we let
someone get by, he screwed up again. It's hard to kick people
out, but you also have to think of the effect on the honest people." Walks through Clean and Sober Streets show that law and
order has taken over what once was a zone of anarchy. Interviews with many of the eighty residents show that they welcome the hardball approach and are ready to report on rule
breakers. (One resident said, "This program is saving my life. If
someone messes it up, I have no hesitancy going to the office
and telling them about it.")

Graduates of the program have responsible jobs and are building families. "I've found that this society has a place for everyone who is sober and responsible, who has a skill and is willing to work," Ward now says. One definition of a neoconservative in politics is "A liberal mugged by reality." Ward's experience is similar: "Yes, there's racism and injustice. But, on the other hand, if I take a guy from outside, sober him up, teach him how to read, and teach him the computer, there's a hole in the wall for that man. He goes right through."

He goes right through. That could also be the motto at Boys Town, still based in Omaha but now expanded across the country. House parents are generally not charismatic individuals— one effective leader, when asked how and why he hooked up with Boys Town, said truthfully, "Failed as a farmer"—but they show children with unstable pasts the hole in the wall. Boys Town has worked out a sensible procedure of handing out points to reward good behavior, and it can be applied by people of normal parenting skills. Boys Town has found that children from troubled backgrounds will respond when the adults around them finally do the big people's job of creating an environment that is safe and nurtures growth, so that the weight is off shoulders too small to bear it.

He goes right through. That is what leaders of the Oak Cliff Bible Fellowship just south of Dallas have learned. As the Reverend LaFayette Holland explains, Oak Cliff is in the "transforming business," and the methods of transformation are prayer and teaching that concerns not only belief in God, but what God expects of man. Ordinary people see from the Bible that God values work, marriage, respect for employers, peaceful conflict resolution, careful stewardship of time and money, and excellence in craftsmanship (Holland says, "God gave us his best, we should give him our best"). When students absorb those lessons, they get jobs and begin working their way up; after years of thinking of themselves as stuck within walls, they see the holes and they go right through.

What's most important, again and again, is time rather than money—and time well spent leads to the discerning use of money. The experience of Patty Brown is a case in point. Patty majored in urban anthropology at the University of California at Los Angeles, then received an M.B.A. in finance from the University of Southern California. In 1985, after work in marketing, she joined the Bettingen Corporation, a foundation begun by Burtie Bettingen to help runaway children, child prostitutes, and other truly needy homeless persons.

If Patty had followed normal foundation staff procedure for assessing an organization, she would have made an appointment to swing by a facility to inspect its pipes and hear of its goodness from some carefully chosen clients. She would have eaten lunch with several members of the board. She would have exercised due diligence by examining the group's financial statements and then written a recommendation. But Patty colored outside the lines. "I wanted to find out what nonprofits actually provided," she recalls. "I wanted to find out why kids used some services and didn't use others, and where there was a void. I listened to presentations by organizational development directors, but in market research you need to find out what the buyers think. I was thirty-two in 1985 and able to pass as a street person not much older than the kids, so I started living in the shelters."

A foundation official living in homeless shelters? Yes, and not just for a short time either: three days here, a week there, in San Francisco and Los Angeles, many months in all. When Patty wanted to find out about Children of the Night, a privately funded Los Angeles outreach to young prostitutes, she invested several Saturdays in the program's hotline training, then worked as a three-hour-per-week volunteer for several months. To learn more, she frequently went out in the van that goes around to hookers' hangouts from 11 p.m. to 2 a.m., went on foot patrols as well, and hung out during those times at the joints the kids frequent. She traveled with police and juvenile officers as they encountered teens living in abandoned buildings.

Patty Brown's practice is strange in the philanthropic world, where most staffers have no business background, evaluate programs by good intentions rather than results, and spend more time in air-conditioned organization offices than on the mean streets. Those board members who have business experience often do not apply it in their foundation work. Some compartmentalize their brains and do not think that bookkeeping has any relation to doing good; others do not care if someone else's money is misused, because they will not be personally embarrassed or taken to task.

But Patty has learned through her personal research that "much of what is presented by fund-seeking organizations has no relation to reality." And she also has had a direct influence on others. Patty recalls how she was accepted into street culture: teen hookers who were pregnant asked her what she thought about abortion. She thought about it and realized that, by some standards, teenage prostitutes were exactly the people who should have abortions—but she said she was against it because abortion "destroys a life that is unique, that has a purpose."

What happened next was remarkable. As Patty recalls, "That conversation had a result I would not have expected. When I said there was hope and purpose for the unborn even under such tough circumstances, they started to believe that there was hope and purpose for themselves. They saw themselves as throwaways, but I had come to believe that they were important in God's eyes and in mine. It was hard for them to believe that they had some purpose besides just surviving day by day, but once some of them started thinking in those terms, that made all the difference." They saw that there was a hole in the wall, and some of them went right through.

How effective are such groups? In addiction, it is common for Bible-based groups to have success rates of well over 50 percent and for government organizations to be down in the single digits. In fighting teenage pregnancy, groups that teach abstinence have been far more effective than their condom-pushing counterparts. In education generally, children from poor socioeconomic groups who go to church-affiliated schools have done demonstrably better than their public school counterparts. Statistics keeping in many areas is suspect, but those figures that are available consistently suggest that spiritually based programs are much more successful than secular approaches.

More telling than the statistics themselves, however, are the stories that exaddicts and alcoholics tell; one anecdote by itself, of course, means little, but I have now heard hundreds of autobiographical tales, and a pattern is evident. A typical several hours of listening came on a cold night in February 1995 at the Gospel Mission, a mile from the Capitol in Washington, D.C. With me that evening were Arianna Huffington (a friend and colleague at the Center for Effective Compassion) and a *Washington Post* reporter. We sat around a table in a small, bare room and heard resident after resident tell his story.

One resident, forty-five-year-old Rudy Jones, told us how he grew up in a middle-class household and as a teenager reacted, sixties-style, to school "regimentation." He became a voracious reader of political thrillers and worked for Hubert Humphrey's campaign in 1968. Then he went to a college where drugs were more important than studies and learned about LSD, speed, and surrealistic painting. After college, Jones moved to Los Angeles and "tried to get into the film business. That's where I really got into some fast circles. I was doing a lot of powdered cocaine out there." The infantilized gratification seeking that characterized late-sixties politics and culture stayed with him as he worked at a television station as a production technician and then as film and tape editor.

A stripper in a striptease joint introduced Jones in 1984 to crack cocaine, which he had heard of before as a drug that led middle-class people to "sell their houses and break up their lives." He had scoffed at such reports, but when he took his first hit "the bells were going off in the center of my brain." The mid-1980s were filled with more cocaine and more disintegration in life: "It was like a slow-motion train wreck. A big long pileup." Unable to work consistently because of his drug use, Jones left his job in 1988 and began a series of freelance assignments that would give him the money for crack without the obligation of regular labor.

The culmination came in September 1994, when he received a check for $1,500 from a public television station: "I just went nuts. Didn't sleep or eat for four days in a row, doing crack all the time. That's when I realized I needed to do something drastic." Drastic for Jones was entering a live-in, religion-based anti-addiction program. Ironically, it was sixties reasoning—Don't think about right and wrong, just show me where I can get a buzz—that led him into a program built on right and wrong. Jones based his decision to enter the Gospel Mission not on faith in God, but on research showing that religious antiaddiction programs are more successful than others: "I wanted to get results, I didn't care how."

Pragmatism changed to awe as Jones participated in Bible studies and counseling programs, however. The transformation, he says, began when he stopped thinking of God as "a bunch of physics laws" and started to see Him as "a personal entity that man could relate to." Suddenly he could pray, for he knew someone was listening. Suddenly there was purpose that went outside self-pleasing, for someone was watching. Suddenly there was power to change, because someone was helping.

After five months Jones felt "completely changed." In February 1995, he spoke of no longer living for each day's pleasures as he had done since the 1960s, but of dying to self—seeing God rather than man as the center of things. Complete changes sometimes short-circuit; time heals all wounds and also tests all spiritual swoons. But at the end of 1995, Rudy Jones was still clean; he lived with and cared for his mother, who is now in her eighties and in need of help; he was working in telecommunications and volunteering twice a week to teach English and writing to newcomers to the Gospel Mission.

Arianna, the reporter, and I sat and listened to another forty-five-year-old man, Ferdinand Banks, talk about the skin disease he has had from infancy that left him hating to look in the mirror, and hating the alcoholic father who treated his unattractive son with contempt that became physical abuse. Banks smoked marijuana when he was twelve and then regularly "started getting high, or drunk. That was the only thing that made me feel like a regular person." A tour in Vietnam was followed by service in Washington as a street cop beginning in 1974. For a decade, Banks scared bad guys and, souring further in the process, did more drugs. In 1985, he was convicted of drug selling, dismissed from the force, and put in jail for a year.

The day of his release, Banks did crack. Over the following five years, he had many different jobs but lived in shelters and in the street, because every time he received a paycheck he would immediately use it for drugs. Despite his conviction, he also received a retirement check for $16,000 from the police department and went on a drug binge. The money was gone in a week. Banks remembers that finding jobs and making money was not a problem: "The last job I had was driving a trash truck, making very good money, almost $1,000 a week. It all went to support my habit." He flamed out in four different state-approved antidrug programs and always ended up in city shelters that were full of drugs and sported occasional murders.

His laconic answers to questions about life there illustrate the nature of government "compassion": Did anyone ever help you in any way in the shelters? "No." Not at all? "No." What did they do for you? "They gave me a cot, and a blanket, and a shower. That's it." Did they ever try to help you change? "They had counselors. They knew I was getting high. I looked terrible every day. They never came to me." One day, Banks, trudging along, saw the cross at the front of the Gospel Mission. "That day I had done a drug run and still had $300 in my pocket," Banks said, "but I was tired and I wanted to be healed. I stumbled through the glass doors."

Banks had a very hard first two weeks but was "scared to go outside the building, because if I went out I would not come back. . . . I prayed and cried and prayed some more and made it." Banks stayed then and for two years. He now works for the Metro system and has a girlfriend who is capable of looking beyond appearance to a newly scrubbed spirit. The skin disease has not gone away but Banks says, "I don't have the pain anymore. Now that I know I'm made in God's image, I feel like a regular person."

We sat and listened as a third man, forty-one-year-old Jerry Minor, opened the furnace door of his past and looked into hell. "I couldn't—I couldn't hold a job," he recalled. "Drugs and alcohol." Minor, who started using heroin and cocaine when he was nineteen, was married at twenty-two and over the next few years turned from "recreational user" into a drug-focused wreck of a man. Mrs. Minor accepted the occasional use, but as it mastered her husband and he became unable to hold a job or act decently in the home, she "just couldn't put up with it anymore" and left in 1984. Minor hit the streets, selling crack cocaine and heroin but not netting much cash in the process, "because I was using as much as I was making. Most of the money went right back into my body."

Minor was also "off and on" in jail for selling drugs. When not behind bars, he would see his wife and children every few weeks; she would plead with him to stop doing drugs, but "it was just beyond my control to stop." He sometimes stayed at big, government-funded homeless shelters, but he found there "a lot of the same things that I was always doing. A lot of drugs, a lot of fights." He walked into the Gospel Mission in 1992 not because he had any Christian belief, but because he was desperate. "I was tired of doing the things that I was doing. I was tired of going in and out of jail. And that was it. The shelters fed me and clothed me but they gave me no rest. I was just tired, you know?" He was also functionally illiterate and deciding it was time to do something about that.

In the new program, constructive envy started to set in. "I started seeing other people accepting the Lord, and realized they were getting better. I wanted some of that, because I had tried everything else. And there were people here showing me that they cared about me. People helped me learn to read, they helped me to understand the Bible. And it was the grace of God that finally did it." Minor developed a strong faith in God and decided to stay at the mission and help others; he is able to work as a drug counselor because the Gospel Mission doesn't care about his lack of classroom hours in counseling or his poor reading skills. He is particularly valuable because he knows the tricks of the drug trade and isn't easily taken in by scams; he's stood up to bullies before and isn't easily possessed by fear; he's learned to live with little and isn't readily subject to greed.

Arianna was enthralled by such stories. I had heard similar ones before, but in an age of hopelessness about drug abuse found them moving. I looked over at the reporter and thought of Ray Stannard Baker, the skeptical reporter a century ago who was impressed despite himself at the "earnestness and simplicity" he found in similar accounts of sin and redemption at the McAuley Mission in New York, which he ended up calling "one of the most extraordinary institutions in the country." I thought that perhaps the reporter would note some of the testimonies, but in a Style section story that he wrote about Arianna, there was deep coverage of dinner parties but not a word about what she and he had heard that night.

It is not only reporters who have their eyes elsewhere. Ask members of a typical middle-class audience to raise their hands if they have ever talked with a homeless person, and the atmosphere is almost entirely undisturbed. And yet, those who live in or near a fair-sized city and are tired of learning about homelessness only from media reports could do an easy experiment. Many urban shelters for the homeless have cards that volunteers can hand out. The cards typically have the address of the organization and a pointed offer: "Good for a night's lodging and two free meals." Anyone who wants to find out whether those with signs such as "Hungry, need a meal" or "Will work for food" are truly starving or actually desiring to work can hand out cards to the first ten panhandlers encountered and point them in the right direction if they express any interest.

Such an experiment has been tried in at least four cities, and probably many more. In 1995 Rita Kramer of *City Journal,* a New York City magazine, gave twenty homeless Manhattanites tickets from the McAuley Mission that promised them three nights lodging, food and clothing, counseling, and further assistance. Only one person seemed interested. In 1991, in Washington, D.C., I passed out ten numbered cards from the Gospel Mission there; the numbers allowed me to call a few days later and see if the several men who said they were hungry actually had shown up for grub and a bunk. None had.

On a larger scale, Bob Cote tried to bring more homeless men into his Step 13 program from 1989 through 1994 by passing out 90,000 coupons reading "Good for One Free Meal." At the bottom of the coupon in smaller type came the words "Need a job? A place to live? Step 13 offers you a chance to take charge of your life!" Over those five years, twenty-four persons came for a free meal; of the twenty-four, not one entered Step 13 and accepted work. Randy Willis, an Austin, Texas, businessman and rancher who was ready to employ homeless men, stopped at Austin freeway entrances forty times to ask men with signs if they indeed wanted to work; not one accepted. This does not say that the homeless generally do not want work; some do, and in cities like Austin they assemble early in the morning at "work corners" where they are picked up by those who hire day laborers. But many prefer to rely on the false kindness of strangers and use their preferred substances throughout the day.

Compare the panhandler by the subway stop or the freeway with the man or woman who enters a good program. The former is likely to be similarly down and out next year and the year after, while the latter will probably be heading up and away. How can there be more good programs, and how can people receive the productive pressure that leads them to change their lives? How can good programs be replicated and bad ones exposed? How can we help good programs to receive the right amount of resources—not too much, lest they be overwhelmed, or too little, lest they be frustrated?

In short, happy is the land that needs no heroes, but that is utopia. Happy also is the land that breeds heroes, but when a country is in greatest need the quantity of born leaders is likely to be insufficient. In what ways can we encourage the development of more?

Chapter 7

Pushing the Back of the Envelope

The once ordinary people spotlighted in chapter 6 all became heroes of antipoverty work because at one point in their lives they felt a sense of urgency. Governmental programs over the past several decades have been designed to lift the burden from ordinary people by allowing them to write a check to pay the professionals who would solve problems. This chapter proposes exactly the opposite: it is time for Congress to increase the pressure by phasing out federal programs and pushing states to develop ways for individuals and community-based institutions to take over poverty-fighting responsibility. In that way, Washington can promote compassion and not just fail again by attempting to provide it.

The use of the words "promote" and "provide" is deliberate and crucial. Our predecessors understood the Constitution's charge to provide for the common defense but promote the general welfare as ensuring an environment within which individual and community action could flourish.* Occasionally,

---

*The term "general welfare" in the preamble to the Constitution did not have welfare state connotations in 1789, but it did mean that government should promote a social framework in which justice is the norm of public life and opportunity is open to all. These are not characteristics of the day-to-day experience of many poor Americans now.

when Congress would go over the line into providing, presidents used veto pens. For example, when Congress in 1854 responded to impassioned pleading by Dorothea Dix and passed legislation for federal construction and maintenance of mental hospitals, President Franklin Pierce vetoed the bill.

Pierce explained that he wished to help the mentally ill, who were not responsible for their plight, but argued that even worthwhile appropriations would push the federal government down a slippery slope: "If Congress has the power to make provision for the indigent insane, it has the same power for the indigent who are not insane." He also contended that the law actually would be "prejudicial rather than beneficial to the noble offices of charity," since federal funds would end up substituting for local assistance: "Should this bill become a law, that Congress is to make provision for such objects, the foundations of charity will be dried up at home. . . ."

Pierce's veto was sustained. His concern about "dried up" charity was typical of the era: municipal aid to the poor could dry up private charity; state relief could dry up city aid; federal programs could dry up state efforts. Any time appropriations were made at a higher level than they had to be, "the powerful workings of generous and compassionate feeling" at the next lowest level were dampened.

The concept of the modern welfare state, however, placed responsibility for fighting poverty not at the lowest level but the highest: national entitlement programs came to dominate the social services scene. The reversal of Pierce's doctrine was so complete that, in the 1980s, even conservatives who favored reducing the growth of welfare programs still talked of the importance of maintaining a federal safety net. They did not understand that the federal safety net was not only inefficient, with most of the money designed to help the poor being snatched away by managers and employees of the poverty industry before it reached those in need, but conceptually mistaken.

What? Criticize the safety net itself? Yes. When I took my children to the circus recently, I realized how infrequently the Ringling Brothers safety net is used. For an acrobat, a fall to the safety net is failure; if he does it stunt after stunt, he will be fired. Most people during the Depression had the psychology of the acrobat: the newly installed federal safety net was to be used only when the choice was between it and a hole in the ground. But over time, as attitudes softened and welfare programs expanded, that desire to avoid use of the safety net was often lost. The destigmatizing of welfare in the 1960s meant that the acrobats no longer needed to strain for those extra inches, because the audience would still applaud even if they fell into the safety net every time.

Do away with the safety net? Yes. "Lead me not into temptation," the Lord's Prayer says, but the welfare system has tempted millions. Although some recipients have retained the esprit de corps of trapeze artists, others have been tempted into not getting up early on a cold morning, not working that extra hour, not shaping up. Circuses need safety nets because without them performers are injured and the show does not go on, but in American society the federal safety net has become not a rare lifesaver but a frequent place to flop. Seeing that, the hardheaded and hardhearted say, No safety net. Let people fall, and those who are softhearted and softheaded say, Hammocks for all. The compromise reached over the years is a dilapidated safety net with gaps, so that some individuals do fall through and others weave bunches of frayed strings into hammocks that resemble webs.

Do away with the safety net? Visits to families supposedly protected by the safety net show how some do not receive the help they desperately need and how others flop around in the net for years, resenting its presence even as they stay stuck to it.

Life within the safety web is miserable enough that many relatively wealthy Americans look at it and wonder how someone can be tempted not to do what is needed to climb out—but here is where we have to step outside the warm glow of our own good intentions, as nineteenth-century reformers suggested. It is tempting to approve of a slightly reformed safety net, one not dyed in such vibrant colors that it is the first thing an acrobat sees after arriving in the big tent. But that is not fair to people who need challenge, not entitlement.

Yes, do away with the safety-net concept that proposes that one net is adequate for all, on the supposition that people will fall only occasionally, and that when they do they will want to climb right back up. The vastly differing attitudes toward work and challenge in current American society, and the inescapably personal nature of true compassion, point us toward making not one safety net but a vast variety of small trampolines suited to individual needs, movable so as to be present for individual crises, and providing a level of bounce fitted to the skill level and psychology of the individuals they are designed to save.

The government role under such a plan is clear: eliminate the negative by getting rid of constraints on the construction and movement of trampolines, and—if it does not appear that enough trampolines will be produced—accentuate the positive by providing incentives to get more. In that way, government can promote the general welfare.

Eliminating the Negative

Washington and state-level task forces should detail the ways in which government bureaucracies have frequently obstructed the effective operation of small trampolines by trying to turn them into large safety nets. For example, in 1992, the Los Angeles charity, Children of the Night, opened a shelter for eleven-to seventeen-year-old exprostitutes who wanted to rebuild their lives. (How extraordinary it is that a twelve-year-old could be an ex!) But, as Children of the Night president Lois Lee recalls, "Regulations were a problem. They wanted us to have handicapped-access rooms. I told them that all the kids here were prostitutes, they don't need handicapped rooms. Kids in wheelchairs carry dope."

Mrs. Lee's logic was impeccable but the government was unmovable. She finally agreed to put in a ramp that would connect one door to a yard area. (To this day, it never has been used.) And until the ramp actually was in place, she had to agree that no one would ever open that particular door to go into the yard. She promised that if a handicapped teenage prostitute were to show up, the young woman and her wheelchair would be carried down the three steps. No, officials insisted, no one could go out that door—and they had their way.

Such problems are common throughout the country. In western Pennsylvania, when the Light of Life Mission bought a farm to serve as a facility for recovering drug addicts, officials ordered the group to retrofit the buildings to make them wheelchair-accessible. No one in a wheelchair would be coming to the farm, protested the director. That did not matter. All right, the organization would erect an entirely new building that met the wheelchair specifications. Not good enough. The farmhouse had to undergo major reconstruction, at huge expense, in order to be prepared for a circumstance that was almost certain not to occur.

That antidrug facility at least opened; in one well-reported situation, nuns of the Missionaries of Charity—Mother Teresa's organization—gave up their plans to spend $500,000 to convert an abandoned New York City building into a four-story homeless shelter when they were told that an additional $100,000 or more would be required to include an elevator in the reconstruction. The nuns explained that their vows of poverty obliged them to avoid the use of modern conveniences, so they would never use the elevator; if a homeless man could not ascend the stairs, they would carry him up. When the nuns were told that the law could not be waived, they decided not to waste money on something that would not help the poor.

Just as the nuns were frustrated, so are some doctors. Those who wish to serve the poor enlarge their exposure to malpractice claims and find their insurance premiums dramatically increased; now, it is financially easier for doctors to go on medical missions abroad than to volunteer in their own cities. There are relatively simple ways to reduce these barriers to Good Samaritan conduct. For example, two hundred Los Angeles-area doctors and nurses provide medical care for the poor by volunteering at the Azusa Evening Clinic. They are able to do so because Los Angeles County covers the cost of malpractice insurance for the volunteers. As clinic founder Dr. George Ferenczi recalls, "Initially, the county was shocked. They couldn't believe that doctors and nurses would want to work for free." Many more people across the country could be similarly shocked if governments made it their business to promote the general welfare.

Senator Dan Coats has proposed a Medical Volunteer Act that would aid the process of medical volunteering. As David Stevens, executive director of the Christian Medical and Dental Society, said concerning the need for such a bill, some members of his society "have decided to devote their careers to serving the needy. In recent years, however, the constraints of medical practice liability have made it increasingly difficult for our members to provide charitable care." The Medical Volunteer Act would help by extending federal tort claim coverage to any health care professional who provides free medical services to a medically underserved person. (Such coverage is already provided for medical services in Indian health facilities and in community migrant, homeless, and public housing centers.) Stevens says that the Coats legislation, by freeing medical volunteers from the fear of devastating lawsuits, could "knock down the barriers that have hindered health care for the poor."

Legislation in other areas could eliminate many obstacles charities generally face. That would be helpful, but regulations designed to ensure that no one is left out also constrict the opportunities that small businesses provide to entry-level workers. A Sherman, Texas, restaurant—Raviolli's—employed eighty-five persons until one of them, a dishwasher, began to display sores on his neck and arms. The owner, Carlo Morelli, saw the sores, heard Jeremy the dishwasher's bad cough, and asked him what was wrong. "He said he had AIDS," Morelli recalled. "An AIDS patient has no immunities. That means Jeremy caught everything that was going around—when he caught a cold, it darn near would turn into pneumonia. TB is a problem, and I just couldn't have someone who came into contact with every utensil in the restaurant passing along communicable diseases. That's common sense."

Morelli continued, "I didn't want to fire him, so I asked him to move out of the kitchen, maybe run errands for me, do some gardening and groundskeeping. I even gave him a raise for that." But Jeremy returned with lawyers and bureaucrats who told Morelli that moving Jeremy to another job restricted equal opportunity. As word about the AIDS patient in the kitchen spread through the community, many people stopped coming and Raviolli's receipts declined by 75 percent. Morelli's lawyer told him that if he moved Jeremy it could cost as much as $1 million to defend the restaurant in court, so Morelli closed the restaurant and eighty-five jobs—personal trampolines—disappeared.

Government officials, like doctors, should be committed to the principle "Do no harm"—yet many regulations end up eliminating the bottom rung of the ladder for those who could otherwise climb out of poverty. For example, if small business owners are to give job applicants with poor work records a new chance, the businessmen should be free during the first few months of employment to fire at will those who do not work out. If employers are subject to wrongful termination lawsuits or huge charges to their unemployment insurance accounts, they will not take a chance.

Furthermore, if an employer cannot single out a new hire for a surprise drug test and be able to fire him if the test comes out positive, that employer also is unlikely to take a chance. If the new hire comes in late and leaves high, and after being fired turns up with a Legal Services lawyer, sues, and gains a settlement, he is being taught how to shake down the system. In all such cases, employers are being taught to just say no the next time they are approached with a plan to increase job opportunities. Government is doing harm to both those who need help and those who could offer it.

State task forces should examine these types of barriers and recommend their removal. State legislatures should eliminate the negative, and Congress should do the same when federal statutes contribute to the harassment of compassion. At the same time, the positive question should be posed: how can the state promote the production of additional trampolines?

Accentuating the Positive

Congress in 1995 tried to push the back of the envelope by breaking with decades of more-funds-available-on-request entitlement thinking. The plan was to block grant amounts to states; for the five years from 1996 to 2001, Washington would collect hundreds of billions of dollars in taxes and then return them to the states, minus postage and handling, of course.

President Clinton's veto kept states from having more flexibility to design their own programs than in the past—but block grants were only a transitional device anyway. A new Congress in 1997 should take the next logical step, either by passing a charity reform act that would establish tax credits for contributions to poverty-fighting organizations or by voting to place in the hands of state officials all decisions about welfare and the financing of it.

Under the first alternative—national tax credits—taxpayers would be able to receive a dollar-for-dollar credit for contributing a certain sum of money to organizations that have as their primary purpose the prevention or alleviation of poverty. In legislation introduced by Senator Coats, the amount is $500, or $1000 for married couples. Senators Ashcroft and Santorum, Representatives Knollenberg and Kolbe, and other legislators have also proposed such measures, sometimes with different dollar amounts. The common objective is to break the federal welfare monopoly and provide a pool of capital for community organizations like those in Milwaukee and around the country that are doing a far better job than their governmental counterparts.

Passage of Coats's 'Comprehensive Charity Reform Act' would also allow the 71 percent of taxpayers who do not itemize to deduct charitable contributions from their tax liability, thus broadening the base of giving in America. In addition, the bill would extend the deadline for charitable giving from the end of the year to the tax filing deadline of April 15, thus increasing the incentive and opportunity to reduce tax liability by giving to charity. Finally, the bill would require full public disclosure by government welfare programs of the amount of money they spend that actually benefits the poor. This would bring greater public accountability to public spending programs and expose them when they are inefficient or ineffective.

Furthermore, to avoid placing the emphasis solely on money—because, as we have seen, the expenditure of time is often more crucial—a companion Coats bill, the Compassion Credit Act, provides a small but good incentive to people who open their homes and their lives to some of the most vulnerable members of society: the homeless, those requiring hospice care, women in crisis pregnancies, and battered women and children. To receive a $500 credit, taxpayers would have to house individuals referred to them through a qualified 501(c)(3) organization that has as its primary activity provision of care for the needy.

Historical precedents for governmental help that encourages families of average means to take in poor neighbors are clear. Early American leaders opposed direct welfare spending by the federal government, but town councils provided subsidies to those who housed the poor. A $500 credit will not cover the cost of care, and people who are willing to open their homes to needy individuals will not do it for the money. Some who want to, however, are stopped by finances. The credit would encourage a greater opening of homes and hearts and make the option available to more than just the affluent.*

These are all excellent ideas, and well worth passage. Appendix C discusses the national tax credit idea further, provides additional rationale, and proposes a fast pace of movement along that route, if that is the route chosen. Nevertheless, the rest of

---

*The current tax code is deficient in this regard. Now, a taxpayer who turns a spare room in his home into an office can deduct the costs of that room as a business expense. Yet, if he is a volunteer at a local homeless shelter, sees the progress toward responsibility that one of the shelter residents is making, and decides to turn that extra room into a bedroom so he can mentor that individual, there is no deduction. People should be encouraged to offer shelter to homeless individuals (discernment is needed here), to abandoned young women going through crisis pregnancies, and to others in need. A taxpayer willing to make that commitment should have it treated in the tax code as equal in importance to a business expense.

this chapter will put on the table a more revolutionary proposal: placing in the hands of state officials all decisions about welfare and the financing of it, and then pressing them to put welfare entirely in the hands of church- and community-based organizations.

In this second, radically decentralist scenario, Congress would acknowledge that block grants violate common sense: far better to leave the money in the states in the first place. Congress would acknowledge that block grants reduce accountability: the goal of block grants is to free state governments from centralized control, but they also tend to free state governments from taxpayer control because the funds are viewed as "free money" blown in from Washington. Congress would acknowledge that block grants tend to breed scandal: without real accountability to either the national capital or the state citizenry, funds are wasted and pressure mounts for Congress to attach not just strings but ropes to hold in the sides of the box.

But in this scenario a bold Congress, pushed hard by the newcomers of 1994 and 1996, would not fall into the "same-old same-old" and recentralize. Instead, Congress would pass, effective at the end of a transitional period, a massive tax cut, with federal taxes decreasing by the amount no longer block granted.

States would then use their own taxing authority to implement new programs or duplicate the old ones if they chose to do so. If a new Congress were to make that decision in 1997, states would then begin entering the post-federal welfare era. They could tax residents adequate amounts to care for the poor, but provide incentives for citizens to contribute sizable amounts of time or money to local poverty-fighting charities by providing exemptions to the new tax.

It is not as if a dollar-for-dollar replacement for the $350 billion annual cost (in 1994) of federal and state welfare spending

(70 percent of it coming from Washington) is necessary: we know that much money is wasted and worse than wasted, actually causing harm. Yet, if more trampolines are needed, we should not be opposed theoretically to governments, once they have worked to reduce barriers, also working to promote the general welfare.

The major way for state legislatures to do this would be to offer the average taxpayer a deal of the following kind: Come the year 2001, under the Welfare Replacement Act of 1997, your federal tax burden will be reduced by an average of $3,000. We certainly do not want to be accused of being cruel or mean-spirited, so we will raise state taxes by an average of $2,500 for social welfare purposes. However, we also want to promote personal involvement with community-based organizations that offer effective compassion to the poor, and if you provide to such an organization a combination of money and time totaling at least $3,000—thus leaving the quantity of societal commitment to the poor unchanged—you will be exempt from the new tax.

This would obviously represent a sweeping change from the current system. Now, taxpayers who itemize can deduct from their taxable income the contributions they make to a wide range of religious, charitable, and educational organizations, at their marginal tax rate (low is 15 percent, high is 39.6 percent). This is helpful but not good enough, and movement toward a flat tax might eliminate that deduction anyway. States, under the new system proposed here, would be pushing taxpayers in a massive way to become involved with groups that provide direct social services to the poor, and offering exemption from taxation for such purposes to those who were helping others in their own way.

A dozen critical questions about such a revolutionary departure from current practice immediately arise:

1. What percentage of taxpayers would choose to support local charities and thereby gain exemption? That is very difficult to predict, but with four years of preparation it is likely that many would, with a tremendous boost to nonprofit finances and a large increase of citizen involvement resulting. Those who did not become involved would pay the new tax, and states could use that fund to pay for any missing trampolines.

2. Would church- and community-based organizations be ready to expand or replicate themselves in order to make use of the new resources they would have in a new century? They would have time to prepare, and the encouragement of a new system would blow away the compassion fatigue that has built up over the years. (The related question of whether religion-based groups should be allowed to participate will be covered in the next chapter.)

3. Would acceptance of exemption-creating contributions force poverty-fighting charities to accept governmental control? Now, charitable organizations that seek government grants come under government oversight; some church-related programs have gained financially but lost their souls in the process. Even nonreligious charities accepting public funds have been forced to treat all of their clients bureaucratically, within the parameters set by law and regulation, rather than dealing with each human being on an individual basis.

The advent of "new tax" exemptions would not automatically free up religious groups and other community-based institutions to participate as equals in the social services sector. Despite precedents set by the GI Bill and other programs that allowed consumer choice, the ACLU would not be amused by the removal of secular liberalism from its established, privileged place.

Still, the offer of an exemption (signifying a right not to pay because of other services rendered) is as clear a hands-off statement as a legislature can make. Exemptions offer a greater degree of protection than deductions, credits, or especially vouchers, since the latter require government not only to overlook revenue but to send out checks. A political coalition strong enough to obtain tax exemptions should be strong enough to keep them from being abused by antireligious zealots.

4. Wouldn't some exemptions from taxation go for funds sent to phony, needless, or simply ineffective projects? Wouldn't these cases be cited by partisans of the welfare state as reasons for opposing the exemption system? Certainly, and those cases would make an impact on people who are startled to find that some among their fellow human beings are foolish, incompetent, or gullible.

Markets work not because everyone exercises perfect judgment, but because, on balance, most people make good judgments most of the time. Even with all the anticipated human error, a charitable sector in which the funds are allocated by individual private decision is likely to be less wasteful than the current system. Besides, with more resources at stake, more careful analysis of charitable effectiveness is likely to become common. Publications that examine charities the way *Consumer Reports* examines products would emerge.

5. Wouldn't acceptance of volunteer time as part of the exemption-creating contribution open the door to fraud? It is true that proof of the giving of money tends to be clearer than that of the giving of time, the valuation of which can be complicated. Still, emphasis on the crucial meaning of compassion—suffering with—is vital, and a plan that provides incentives for contribution of money but not time is incomplete.

Many goups already keep records of volunteer hours, so bookkeeping would not be an insurmountable problem. Corruption could be kept to a minimum by keeping the general credit for exemption purposes at the level of the minimum wage—enough to provide a bit of compensation for work time lost and to signify societal commitment to compassionate action, but not enough to promote widespread cheating.

6. What would happen to health care for the poor? Medicaid is the single biggest element of current federal and state welfare expenses: of the $324 billion that federal and state agencies spent on welfare in 1993, $132 billion went for that one program. And yet, many cities have free or sharply reduced-price clinics where some dedicated doctors and nurses volunteer their time. What can governments do to help such organizations?

In Jackson, Mississippi, for example, the Voice of Calvary Family Health Center sees about 8,000 patients each year and would like to expand its operations or grow other clinics like it. Center director Lee Harper contrasts her clinic with higher-budgeted state operations and concludes, "When you have more money, you tend to waste more"—but still, she needs more funds. Job one, however, is getting more hours from volunteer doctors, dentists, and nurses: "If we get the health professionals, we'll get the money."

Such an urgent need translates into a specific proposal that could be implemented at the federal level in lieu of all the macroreform proposals of the 1990s: give medical professionals tax credits for hours regularly worked at clinics. If a typical doctor, dentist, or nurse worked one day every two weeks at a clinic or in a similar way spent time to provide health care to poor individuals, billions of dollars in medical expenses could be saved. Participating health personnel, in return, could receive a tax credit equivalent to 10 percent of their salaries. Such a credit could be the cornerstone of the personal alternative to bureaucratic health care plans that are rightly regarded with skepticism.

7. Why substitute a state tax (with exemptions) for a federal one? Why not simply reduce taxes and allow individuals to spend the money as they see fit? Advocates of individual rather than governmental responsibility have the personal emphasis right, but will a reliance merely on individual goodwill and effort lead to the production of enough trampolines? For those who emphasize original sin rather than natural goodness, there is a middle ground between government and individual: call it societal responsibility, within which government requires payment but leaves to the individual taxpayer how the money is to be spent.

8. Would it be possible to restrict tax-exempting contributions to those organizations that are actually engaged in fighting poverty and its associated pathologies? In some cases, the correct category will be obvious, but in others careful judgment will be required. For example, it would seem that general donations to a college or a private school should not be used for exemption purposes, but donations to college or school scholarship funds for poor students should be. General donations to a church should not produce an exemption, but those to a church's specific poverty-fighting endeavors (an antiaddiction program, for example) should be. General donations to a hospital should not; donations to a free or reduced-rate clinic for the poor should.

Such categorization would be necessary, even though it could cut into the individual flexibility that straightforward tax reduction would allow. No matter how carefully state legislatures define the new tax category for poverty-fighting organizations, officials would have to write and apply regulations implementing the new tax; that potentially could give a state agency the opportunity to exclude organizations that it did not favor for ideological, theological, or political reasons, and it also means that some organizations might change what they do and the way they do it in order to conform to the regulatory standards.

Such a threat does not mean that the new system could not work; it does mean that eternal vigilance will continue to be the price of liberty.

9. Why not rely on pure voluntarism to do what is necessary? The seeds of welfare replacement are already planted, as chapter six suggested; if we wish to move quickly enough to save a generation of children during the first decade of the twenty-first century, those seeds will need lots of water. If men were angels, no incentives for goodness would be necessary, but devolution to the states and further devolution through an exemption system is a good way for human beings to shift resources from the public sector to the private sector. Such a shift would provide a pool of capital for worthy charities to use in replicating themselves and thus replacing the welfare state.

The stimulation of voluntarism through tax exemption is an impure tactic but our predecessors in this country, with their realistic view of human nature, were not above using impure motives to promote virtue. Colonial settlers who took in a poor person received compensation from the township, and some of them may occasionally have profited a bit (although that would have been more than made up for by the time they spent mentoring the needy person). A farm family that adopted an orphan gained a farmhand (again, the economic advantage was more than paid for by the hard task of being new parents to someone who had grown up under tough conditions).

10. Why require $3,000 to receive the exemption from payment of $2,500? If some people hesitate to give (in money or minimum-wage time) the greater amount necessary to receive an exemption, that is fine: the quality of their giving would probably be low. Some personal contribution by the taxpayer is important to build a sense of involvement with and responsibility for the work of the charitable organization. The goal is

to have as many taxpayers as possible think through their giving, and not merely respond to direct-mail appeals.

11. Why would taxpayers be expected to make better decisions about which groups to support than government officials have? Competition has made the American economy the strongest in the history of humanity and the American political system the envy of the world. The American people have proven themselves capable, on average and over the long haul, of making good economic and political judgments. Taxpayers who invested $500 of their own money and time in order to direct $2,500 to satisying projects would be likely to make equally good judgments in the charitable sphere.

Decisions about where funds shall go would no longer be a function of political struggles over the budgets of government agencies, but would result from the decisions of millions of individual donors. Independent charitable organizations would for the first time in generations be on a level playing field with those groups favored by government. Some errors would occur, but there is every reason to expect this system of delivering assistance to the needy to be far more effective than the current model of top-down government monopoly.

Yes, some innovators would fail, but isn't it better to win a football game fifty to fourteen than to play so defensively as to fall into a three-three tie? Given the growing body count of damaged children and ruined adults under our current regime, isn't it better to take the rational risks that could liberate millions, rather than for it to be always winter and never Christmas?

12. Could the Coats national tax credit provisions be combined with this state-emphasizing approach? Possibly: Washington could retain some social services taxing authority and implement limited national tax credits, but most of the funding expectations could be returned to the states along the lines dis-

cusssed. Following both paths does seem complicated, however; one approach probably would become dominant.

National Versus Decentralized Approaches

Which is better, the national or state-by-state approach? Either would represent a substantial improvement. I would be delighted to see national plans pass, but—in general—decentralization offers the best shot for each state to innovate in the way that is right for its unique population and specific problems. Since we do not know precisely which legislative plan would best promote the offering of individual compassion, an emphasis on state-level action maximizes the opportunities to find out for sure which tactics work best. Furthermore, there may be more opportunity to move quickly in some states than in Washington.

While each state would have to sort out its particular problems, all would have to deal with rising rates of illegitimacy. Abstinence programs are a start. When pregnancy nevertheless results and marriage does not, states should foster group living arrangements for women during pregnancy and during the next year or two, so that those who would otherwise be alone would have a support network. Biases against adoption should be challenged and the advantages to the child of adoption at birth (or up to age two, at the latest) stressed. Having a baby out of wedlock should not bring with it the reward of any governmental cash payments. Appendix D examines a variety of poverty-related subjects that legislators should visit.*

---

*Following completion of this manuscript I received from the Beacon Hill Institute at Suffolk University (Boston, MA) an excellent, book-length examination of poverty-fighting tax credits. Interested readers should consult that work: the authors are James P. Angelini, William F. O'Brien, Jr., and David G. Tuerck; the title is *Giving Credit Where Credit Is Due: A New Approach to Welfare Funding.*

Some programs already put into limited practice could be expanded. The Wisconsin Policy Research Institute recently reported on 70 "Time Dollar" programs now up and running in 30 states, where individuals commit time to helping others but receive credit for their hours so that the givers can receive help when they need it. Concerning state tax credits for poverty-fighting, it is worth noting that several states already provide tax credits to businesses that contribute cash, materials, or services to nonprofits.

Such developments are significant—yet we should remember that no public policy measure can take the place of the personal changes that are necessary to raise high the standard of American compassion. With supportive laws and rules, compassionate individuals can make real progress toward reducing some of our most serious social pathologies, but the crucial change is still the one that goes on in each individual soul, not in the federal or state capitals.

Chapter 8

Down the Drain?

As chapter 6 suggests, compassionate individuals and groups are still at work in the 1990s, much as they were in the 1890s. And as chapter 7 proposes, legislators can play a useful support role by removing barriers to compassionate action and developing practical plans to ensure that organizations with good reputations receive the material support they need. But a harder question remains: do we, as this troubled century closes, have the optimistic willingness to do what it takes to renew American compassion?

During my early teenage years, from 1963 through 1966, I spent many Saturdays at Fenway Park in Boston, cheering on the Red Sox as they lost game after game. They were terrible then, and there always seemed to be a loud-mouthed fan behind me shouting, as the Sox fell behind, "Down the drain." That cry still resounds in my mind when talk at public policy conferences turns to our nation's present plight.

There is no doubt that America is in trouble. Bill Bennett's "index of leading cultural indicators" shows us the depth of the problems in many areas: underachieving schools, overachieving criminals, and illegitimacy swamping us all. Even greater than the problems that can be measured are those that cannot. The last two Democratic presidents were ridiculed for talking about a national "malaise" or "funk," but the evidence of "compassion fatigue"—a cynicism about the possibility of helping others—is evident.

If history were a slippery slope, we would already be so far down that it would seem impossible to scramble back up. But the historical flow is not so straight. There are historical precedents for cultures rubbed as raw as ours making astounding comebacks. For example, the British upper classes at the time of the American Revolution were morally sick, but the efforts of Member of Parliament William Wilberforce and others who fought for Bible-based renewal from the 1790s through the 1830s helped to give England a much improved nineteenth century.

Another example of national revival comes from the United States itself. Although conventional history books generally leave this out, the 1840s and 1850s were decades of spiritism and free lust—New Age theology and sexuality—throughout the North and to some extent in the South. Then came the Civil War, with its loss of 600,000 lives and much of the southern economy, and the troubled Reconstruction era. And yet, the reunited states recovered and witnessed economic and moral growth through the remainder of the nineteenth century. Huge problems such as racism remained, but American citizens were able to assimilate millions of immigrants and extend compassion to them and to millions of the native-born without enabling destructive behavior.

Today, the United States needs to recover from the social civil war that has raged since the 1960s. On the one side are those who scorn words like responsibility, discipline, and maturity; some are affluent enough to act foolishly and not be out on the streets, but the poor who imbibe the propaganda of a radical elite have no such margin for error. On the other side are leaders like Sister Connie Driscoll, who founded and heads St. Martin de Porres House of Hope in Chicago, a hundred-bed shelter that is operated without any government funds.

The women who come to her, Sister Connie notes, "almost always have the money to pay their rent, but they often spend it on something else, and they don't pay the rent on time, month after month, until the landlord evicts them." The main cause of homelessness, Sister Connie says, is "an often total lack of understanding of personal responsibility and discipline." When women are willing to accept discipline and strive toward responsibility, she has had great success in turning around lives.

We often hear today that the problems of poverty are incredibly complex, but if that is true the success of some fairly simple programs is even more remarkable. There is nothing fancy about the Gospel Mission programs that helped to turn around the lives of Rudy Jones, Ferdinand Banks, Jerry Minor, and hundreds of others. Nor is there much more than meets the eye— love, Bible, discipline, fun—behind the success of Kathy Dudley, a young woman who began Voice of Hope in Dallas and has helped to turn around the lives of numerous inner-city children and teenagers. She walked down an inner-city street there a dozen years ago with a soccer ball under her arm and an invitation to children: play, learn about God through Bible studies, and work at rehabbing deteriorated homes in the neighborhood. During the past decade, crime rates among the boys she works with and pregnancy rates among the girls have been much lower than those in the surrounding community.

There is nothing all that complicated about the work of pregnancy help centers such as the Capitol Hill Crisis Pregnancy Center in Washington, D.C., where unmarried, pregnant teenagers learn responsibility. Toni McIlwain of the Ravendale area of Detroit would be the first to say that advanced degrees are not needed to help neighbors work with each other to fight drugs and make their city blocks safer. It does take hard work, though, and she worked to set up Neighborhood Watch clubs on thirty-five high-crime blocks. (Battling alongside a Joy of Jesus group that pushes for spiritual revival, she has seen a significant drop in her area's crime rate.) In many areas—promoting abstinence, facilitating adoption, helping the handicapped, pushing young men to accept their responsibility as fathers—we already have working models.

Furthermore, it does not take elaborate flowcharts to motivate people in suburban churches and other religious institutions to become involved with their inner-city neighbors. In this regard, the experience of Virgil Gulker, head of KidsHope USA (which connects children with adults willing to help), is instructive. Gulker has learned to stress specificity. Inviting people to a general war on poverty overwhelms them, and it even "did little good to ask churches if they could 'supply tutors for learning-disabled children.' The request was too broad. Once, however, we asked if there was anyone who could help a little boy named Johnnie. We told church members that he was a fourth grader who was unable to read and, because he could not read, the other children made fun of him and would not play with him. I was amazed at the response. It seemed as though everyone wanted to tutor Johnnie. We had to tell volunteers that we were sorry, but Johnnie was already being helped. Perhaps they would like to help Becky or Kimberly learn to read? They did."

The best place to learn more about what works is not in a graduate program of social work oriented toward government models. State welfare headquarters also tend to be great dismal swamps, although there is much to learn from shake-up-the-system innovators such as Kay James of Virginia or Eloise Anderson of California. Just as Wisconsin state welfare is an improvement on the typical but not good enough, so welfare administrators and social workers whose livelihoods depend on the current system generally push programs that taste great but are far less filling than what private groups offer. No, the best way to learn more about effective compassion is to hear from those who practice it on mean streets.

In California, for example, we should listen to the experienced poverty fighters of a gospel-proclaiming inner-city church such as St. Stephen's Church of God in Christ. There, in southeast San Diego, the fellow playing the bongos on stage may have been a drug addict a year ago, and the man in a suit in the next pew a recently released convict—but a spiritual transformation has swept both of them, and hundreds of others, into a new life. As church leader Richard Smith points out, the church's goal is to deal with not just poverty, which is a relatively easy material problem, but "impoverishment—long-term hopelessness, humiliation, and degradation, a culture unto itself. It takes more than money to redeem the lives of those who have become spiritually destitute."

In Georgia, rather than listening to those who believe in magic—flick the wand, provide new housing, and the problem of poverty goes poof!—we need to hear explanations such as the one coming from Summerhill Neighborhood head Douglas Dean: "We're not just talking about changing people's physical environment. We're talking about spiritual change, changing people's hearts." In Oregon, we will want to learn from Don Michel, a mission director who has watched people trading food stamps for drugs and now tells reporters how his attitude has changed: "I thought just handing out food and clothes without question was a very compassionate thing to do. But I think now that when you give things out without accountability, you're participating in that person's harm. . . . It's never been true that there is an absence of service. . . . there is an absence of motivation."

What Michel calls the "absence of motivation" is the missing link to reality in much naive talk about homeless people restoring some order to their lives or people on welfare going to work. Necessity is the mother of change, and our removal of urgent necessity from the lives of many poor people has also taken away the impetus for productive behavior. Steve Gilkenson, program administrator at the McAuley Mission and a man who has been through tough times himself, suggests that "the problem today is nobody's able to hit bottom, they just bounce around the bottom, and every couple of months someone picks them up." That is the safety net problem again; if welfare payments decrease, Gilkenson says, "our chapel would be fuller and our audience would be soberer."

Gilkenson points to a key issue: do we want audiences to be sober, if the condition is that chapels are also full? Government officials for the past thirty years have in essence decided that it was more important to shut out religion than to back the most effective means of fighting addiction and alcoholism. Yet, drug and alcohol abuse are frequently related to lack of a religious commitment in a person's life: nine of ten alcoholics in one study said they lost interest in religion during their teenage years, and researchers found a strong religious commitment to be a consistent predictor of not using illicit drugs. Religious belief has been shown to be the most powerful force for recovery from alcoholism.

Such evidence points to one of the inescapable correlations of late-twentieth-century life: intellectual elites may continue to proclaim the death of God, but programs that fight substance abuse, as well as the hopelessness that underlies all forms of long-term American poverty, need a living God if they are to be successful. Theoretically, philosophers can contend that this need not be so, but in practice the evidence is overwhelming. Religious commitment, particularly church attendance, correlates negatively with delinquency. Frequent church attendees have lower crime rates than infrequent attendees. Belief in an afterlife (with the threat of divine punishment) is also associated with lower crime rates. Former prison inmates who are religious have a significantly lower recidivism rate than their nonreligious peers.

Religious beliefs also have an effect on the supply side of charity. In 1993, individual donors gave $102 billion to nonprofits, and a Russ Reid Company study showed that the best predictor of giving behavior continues to be the intensity and nature of spiritual commitment. In terms of money, individuals who give to religious groups contribute a total of 66 percent more than nonreligious givers. In terms of time, the difference is probably even greater. Only when helping the poor is a calling rather than a career do those capable of service stick with the hard cases.

Some government social workers in Wisconsin call the hard cases FUBBs. The only cost-effective treatment for a FUBB (and his more genteel cousin, the MUBB, for "messed up beyond belief") is to give up on him. Take the case of twenty-eight-year-old Willie Wilson, a cokehead who started freebasing six years ago while working in a restaurant and deejaying at a nightclub: "I started using more drugs. The more drugs I took, the better I felt I was on the turntable, making people dance. I was snorting in the DJ booth."

Love had a chance to change Wilson. A woman he moved in with—whose sister was on crack—demanded that he stop using the drug. He stopped for a week but then started lying to her, and soon disappeared for days at a time. Strike one. The woman gave him another chance, and he stopped using cocaine for two months. She was happy, until she found out Wilson had switched to alcohol and slept with another woman. Strike two.

That woman became pregnant and had their child, and Wilson "promised to give her and the baby all the money I could. . . . But when I had money in my hand, I bought a small portion of crack cocaine, maybe a $50 rock, planning to leave . . . but then I wanted to test its quality right away . . . and once I tested the crack, I couldn't go nowhere, because I got paranoid, so I ending up spending all the money at the crack house." Strike three.

Wilson kept promising to do better and was able to hold a job, but each week he received a check for $280 "and everything would just go. No money the next day." Strike four. Wanting more money one day after sleeping at the crack house and being turned out on the street, Wilson "went to my mom's house. She knew something was wrong. But she left me in the house alone for a few minutes. I went into the bedroom and took her $200 camera, ran out, and sold it for a $50 rock of cocaine." Strike five. Managers at a Burlington coat factory gave Wilson another chance, but after only a few days he "got high and couldn't go to work. So, they fired me." Strike six.

Then Wilson stayed with his aunt and stole $300 in cash, along with her television, VCR, and microwave: "I took them to the crack man. He gave me money." Strike seven. Wilson entered a twenty-eight-day, government-funded detox program in Laurel, Maryland. It was the same old thing: the program treated a symptom of his problem, not the problem itself, so when he came out he fell into the old pattern of giving up cocaine only to embrace alcoholism once again. Strike eight. Wilson found a job, the paychecks started coming—and crack was back: "It seems like every time I got money in my hands, I started using crack. And I saw myself blowing everything I have in the paycheck. I spent $598 in one day." Strike nine.

Did spiritual deliverance finally come in 1993 when he started going to church? That would make a happy ending, but Wilson dropped cocaine only to start drinking again. Strike ten. A church in suburban Washington gave him a paying job and he started using cocaine again; then he stole equipment from the church and sold it for drugs. Strike eleven. He had an enormous high, then came down and "wanted to jump in front of the Metro, because I was so disgusted with myself. How can I take from the house of God? How can I take from people who care about me?"

There's more to the Wilson story, including not just one but three children fathered at various times, and other problems as well. His self-recrimination aside, at this point Wilson is clearly a MUBB, right? Anyone who tries to help him is a fool, right? Maybe—but at the Gospel Mission, where Wilson has lived over the past year, residents, staffers, and volunteers see themselves as fools for Christ. Wilson is in the Mission's antiaddiction program, has gone back to school, is working on a commercial driver's license, and subjects himself to random drug tests. So far the tests show that he has stayed clean.

Conversation with Wilson certainly reveals a willingness to confess past actions and a desire to go and sin no more. "Only the power of Jesus will let me do that," he says. Life at the mission also puts him in constant contact with "the guys who have been in the program longer. I get strength from them, because I can see where they came from, and where they're going." Will that be enough? Stay tuned. And why do Gospel Mission staffers and volunteers stick with Wilson at a time when government would have given up? As long as Wilson confesses and strives, the answer is simple: they believe that Christ changes lives.

Take a rocklike faith of that sort, rub it against a rocklike state bureaucracy, and sparks fly. During the 1990s, highly effective groups that emphasize biblical rather than secular ways of fighting addiction and alcohol have had run-ins with state licensing authorities in Oregon, Pennsylvania, and many other states. In the most highly publicized case of 1995, Teen Challenge of San Antonio stood firm against state pressure by maintaining its effective policy of treating alcoholics and addicts. It continued to teach about Christ and in that way fill holes in souls. Teen Challenge was not receiving any government grants, but the Texas Commission on Alcohol and Drug Abuse nevertheless subjected the organization to arbitrary licensing and credentialing procedures. Counseling that emphasizes religious belief is not real treatment, the state insisted: turn in your license!

Teen Challenge eventually survived, but only after putting on a rally at the Alamo and having its case brought to wide public attention by several journalists and activists. Texas Governor George W. Bush, facing an uprising from Christian and conservative voters who had helped to elect him, said, "I support faith-based programs. I believe that a conversion to religion, in this case, Christianity . . . by its very nature promotes sobriety. There is logic to what Teen Challenge is doing, and I support it strongly." He agreed to push for new laws and regulations that, at least as far as the state government is concerned, would create an alternative licensing agency run by religious organizations themselves. Florida already has such a system; other states need one.

The Teen Challenge episode and others like it point to a problem growing out of the curious interpretation of the First Amendment's religion clauses that has become dominant. Now, government funds bankroll many programs that promote atheism or at least marginalize God, but they cannot be used in religious programs that show materially and spiritually poor people what will meet their needs. Even licensing, the government's seal of approval, may be withheld from religion-based organizations that believe strongly enough in what they profess to want to share that faith with those who walk through their doors.

Government funds may be used by religious groups that have set up religionless programs, government look-alikes that are rarely effective—but any program that communicates to clients the need for religious conversion, no matter how effective, faces a ban. With many first-rate programs out of bounds, government often buys into the second-rate.

No rational business leader trying to develop an effective product would eliminate from consideration many of the most impressive prototypes. But the ACLU and similar organizations have made it their business to foster an eccentric interpretation of the religion clauses, even though it was certainly not the intent of the framers of the First Amendment to ban religion from the public square, or to press a lawsuit on any recipient of government funds who says the G-word.

Even Thomas Jefferson, who was not involved in the Constitution-framing discussions but spoke his piece later, would be surprised to find out that, in his name, conversations about spiritual matters, or reflections on the most important topics, must either be expunged altogether or conducted in such an antiseptically censored way that they cannot seriously address the questions that lie in our hearts. How has it come about that any activity funded by the government must be conducted as if atheism were the established religion? Why should we tolerate such bias against a vital dimension of our existence that has demonstrably made a difference in the lives of millions?

Halfway covenants will not suffice here. Jean Rogers, a key division administrator within the Wisconsin Department of Health and Social Services, notes that a plan adopted late in 1995 will allow explicitly religious groups in her state "to bid on segments of the [social services] operation . . . as long as groups can stay away from direct proselytization, we can be legally safe." That is a well-intentioned attempt, but the groups that are most effective often view Bible studies and "proselytizing" actions to be the engine of their ship.

A more comprehensive attempt to provide religious liberty came in Washington late in 1995, when the Congress approved a proposal by Senator John Ashcroft "to allow religious organizations to contract, or to accept certificates, vouchers, or other forms of disbursement" for federally paid social service programs "on the same basis as any other provider without impairing the religious character of such organizations. . . ." Antireligion groups went predictably ballistic. The provision "could lead to the creation of an unprecedented church-government relationship," American Civil Liberties Union lobbyist Liz Symonds screamed.

The reaction came even though the Ashcroft proposal had a catch—federal grants could not be "expended for sectarian worship, instruction, or proselytization." That gag rule evidently was needed to pass the proposal, but it overlooked something essential: Christian efforts take a bite out of poverty because of Christ, and other serious religious groups also attribute their effectiveness not to niceness but to spiritual transformation brought about by worship, teaching, and theological advocacy. Yet, those are the very functions that the proposal explicitly disallowed.

Furthermore, the proposal did not affect all religious groups equally. Churches that had become political or social clubs could readily accept government money because they had already lost their salt and become government lookalikes. But Christian, Jewish, and Islamic groups that had remained theologically tough would either turn down the money and its restrictions, or go soft also—unless they cheated by sliding money from one category to another.

Senator Ashcroft did well to spotlight discrimination in funding, but his proposal—part of the welfare bill vetoed by President

Clinton—might have led more religious groups to place their funding hopes in bureaucratic hands, instead of looking to contributors or to help from a tax credit system within which Washington never gets its hands on the money.

Grant-seeking temptations have ensnared many groups. For example, an organization elegantly named HOBO—Helping Our Brothers Out—started up in Austin, Texas, in 1987. Homeless men could get some clothes and food while also being exposed to some Bible study and prayer. The program was small and often crude, but it did some good. In 1989 and 1990, however, the HOBO board of directors faced a choice: remain a financially challenged, Bible-based organization or hit a governmental jackpot. As Director John Porterfield put it, "We became aware of grants that we could just pick up. We knew there were strings attached, but . . . the money was there in our hands, the only question was whether we should put it in our pockets."

The answer was not an obvious one for those who had become involved in poverty fighting because they cared about both body and soul. Board members faced a terrifying choice: supply material help to many using government funds, or supply material and spiritual help to a few and suffer nightmares about those who slipped away. HOBO leaders chose to take the government money and drop their ministry orientation. Soon, HOBO sported legal services, a health clinic, afternoon Sharon Stone movies for homeless men, and hot and cold showers— everything that could enable an addict or alcoholic to remain homeless. All that was gone was the pressure to change. At HOBO, God was dead and so was real hope.

The Ashcroft provision could have provided a greater degree of protection in some states, but the effect of any law depends on the interpretation of courts and the degree of enthusiasm of local and state government officials. Only when there is a welling up of citizen compassion so great that it will not take the ACLU's frowns for an answer, and only when that bottom-up movement is supported by civic leaders' top-down enthusiasm, will change occur.

One city with a promising combination of top-down and bottom-up impetus is Indianapolis, led by Mayor Steve Goldsmith. Although his own faith is Jewish, in 1992 he had the city contract with a strongly evangelical Christian group, the Institute in Basic Life Principles, to deal with juvenile offenders. The program has expanded each year since then as tough teens "have seen and adopted values that they never would have gotten in the court system," Goldsmith says.

Leaders of the Christian organization were amazed at the speed with which their operation got off the ground: no lengthy licensure process, permits zipping through the bureaucratic maze, health and fire inspections carried out without axes to grind. Goldsmith has also called together directors of religious charities throughout Indianapolis and asked them how his office could help them to do their work more effectively. Get the government off our backs, he was told, and we'll help the city provide the services it wants to provide.

Goldsmith has worked to eliminate the negative while accentuating the positive. He "uses the mayor's office as a bully pulpit," says Russ Pulliam, editor of the *Indianapolis News*. "He tried to keep the vultures off Christian nonprofits." In public appearances, the mayor praises the work undertaken by religious charities. He issues special commendations and mentions specific ministries by name all around the state. "The person who dismisses that as ceremonial doesn't understand that this is an essential function of government," Pulliam notes. "The government will pick on such Christian nonprofits unless they see that kind of support from the top.

Indianapolis so far is an unusual situation: a well-established organization, a secure mayor, and a sympathetic newspaper editor combining to support effective compassion. Recognition of the effectiveness of the religious groups might encourage other cities to follow the Indianapolis model. Still, the goal overall should be to move from a grants economy to a charity marketplace where individual taxpayers will be able to increase support to what they approve of without being forced to underwrite what they abhor. The more Goldsmith rationality the better, but overall, the development of a national tax credit or state tax exemption system will best promote the expansion of religion-based programs in a way that raises fewest hackles. Only decentralization can drive a tunnel through the mountain of litigation that opponents of religion are prepared to bring forth whenever they feel threatened.

This is not to say that the churches, synagogues, mosques, and other houses of worship are instantly ready to replace the welfare office whenever the ACLU gives up its rearguard action. Many religious organizations inhabit the valley of the biblical prophet Ezekiel's vision in the Old Testament, where he saw "a great many bones on the floor of the valley, bones that were very dry." As David Caprara, director of Virginia's Department of Housing and Community Development, puts it, "By allowing government to take over the functions that are rightly the responsibility of families, religious organizations, and local communities, we have become less inclined to parent, mentor, lend a helping hand, instruct our young, and perform other important duties."

In Ezekiel's vision, God connects knee bones to thigh bones, and provides tendons, flesh, and breath so that the revitalized creatures "came to life and stood up on their feet—a vast army." A key question for Americans in the next decade will be whether the modern knee bones, thigh bones, and—most important—backbones of community groups can be reconnected in their own parched valleys.

The state with the best likelihood of sorting through church-state issues may be the one where Patrick Henry and James Madison debated the question in 1784.* Virginia Governor George Allen's Commission on Citizen Empowerment has proposed that the state emphasize its role not as provider of welfare but as promoter of community clearinghouses that could "match people in need with services available in the community." State officials are to "review all current regulations to ease restrictions on citizens" and to "engage religious and nonprofit organizations in creative community-based programs."

A church/nonprofit/government conference in September 1995 brought together 350 religious leaders, community activists, and officials from around the state to discuss ways of accomplishing that. Kay James, then Virginia's Secretary of Health and Human Resources, noted that "we haven't achieved what we really wanted to achieve with welfare: helping poor people." She emphasized that no one is content with the current system and that the recipients themselves are among the most critical. She made it clear that the welfare battle is not an us versus them class warfare frontal assault, but a struggle to reassert values of work and family that hold for all racial and ethnic groups.

The conference also went beyond either welfare reform or welfare elimination by showcasing programs that are the seeds of welfare replacement. Church- and community-based groups that teach sexual abstinence outside of marriage, offer mentors for young mothers and for children, provide child care and housing, promote literacy and fatherhood, connect suburbanites with the urban poor, and do a hundred other things all told their stories in well-attended workshops. Conference participants noted that if volunteers do more and current welfare recipients

---

*My book *Fighting for Liberty and Virtue: Political and Cultural Wars in Eighteenth Century America* (Wheaton, IL: Crossway, 1995) examines this debate.

escape dependency, government will save substantial sums. Such savings, however, were always presented as a by-product of freeing poor people sunk in dependency and welfare workers mired in drudgery.

Other states need similar meetings that will attempt to end the battle of hard hearts and hard heads versus soft hearts and soft heads, and instead attempt to develop tough-minded, warmhearted leaders; as noted in chapter one, Mississippi and several others are embarked on this journey. Significantly, a new understanding of biblical ideas about fighting poverty is developing among a new generation of church leaders. Many ministers and lay leaders had fallen for the line of the religious left: God has a "preferential option" for the poor, which means that forced redistribution of income is next to godliness and a poor person is entitled to material help with nothing asked in return. Now, however, the Biblical emphasis on challenge for both rich and poor is starting to be heard once again. (Appendix B provides a theological base for the rediscovered approach.)

The practical application of the deeper understanding comes out in conversation with new leaders such as Shelby Smith, a thirty-eight-year-old father of three and vice president of Mendenhall Ministries, a black-led Mississippi organization. "For a long time social programs, government and private, church and nonchurch, were not incentive-based," Smith says. "That killed the desire to be productive. In the 1920s and 1930s we were productive, but now we're consumer-oriented. People don't want to produce, don't want to get a job. It used to be that a person's not working had a direct impact on his ability to eat. Now, folks that don't work are idolized—they're cruising around in a nice car, not having to work. We should be saying, We will help you if you help yourself."

Smith notes that Mendenhall Ministries "has gone from giving away things to deciding how to charge for things. In the school, for example, it's imperative that parents pay their third—they can pay some through work, but they have to pay some cash. Just giving to them is no good. . . . At the thrift store, used to be people would come in, give a sob story, they'd get something. But we realized that it builds pride in individuals when they are able to go in and buy something at an affordable price. When you emphasize accountability, people say, That's a Republican mentality, that's a probusiness mentality. But that's the mentality you need if you're going to do better than the how-do-you-beat-the-system, how-do-you-get-things mentality."

Those who can best teach about accountability, Smith notes, are those who model it in their own lives and then disciple others. Understanding the true meaning of commission remains essential: "Compassion comes when you're involved in an intimate basis in a person's life," Kay James says. "I've never seen a government body that can do that." The experience of those who have rolled up their sleeves points to an essential truth that bears repeating: when any of us complain about a spendthrift modern welfare state, we are right about the costs but are stating the problem backwards. The major flaw of the modern welfare state is not that it is extravagant, but that it is too stingy. It gives the needy bread and tells them to be content with that alone. It gives the rest of us the opportunity to be stingy also: we can soothe our consciences as we scrimp on what many of the destitute need most—love, time, and challenge.

What does that mean, realistically, for Americans as we prepare to enter the twenty-first century? Here are ten summarizing propositions:

1. We should have confidence in the American people, unless it is proven that past successes are no longer possible. When we look at past poverty-fighting successes, we need to ask: why

can't we do the same? Were Americans then a different people than we are today? Have we become so corrupted that we don't care about others? Have we become so lazy that we are unwilling to suffer with those in need? Perhaps, but it is more likely that we simply have become used to having someone else do it for us—even though we know that a professional social worker, with a caseload of 150 in "good" programs and sometimes double that number elsewhere, can't do much more than shuffle paper. Bad charity drives out good: government welfare leads potential helpers to sit back, since they are paying someone else to do the job.

2. Our problems would be fewer if private groups could be trusted to act on proven poverty-fighting principles. Alas, independence from the state is a necessary condition for effective philanthropy but not a sufficient one, for some private charities are as bureaucratic, unchallenging, and downright foolish as their governmental counterparts. Bad charity has undermined the good throughout America: few people sign up for a program emphasizing discipline as long as they can choose another program that simply passes out checks. Most homeless men in Washington, D.C., given a choice between staying at the Gospel Mission, where they have to leave their bottles outside, and the Center for Creative Non-Violence, where drug-induced creativity has been welcome, choose the latter.

3. It is especially important that societal leaders, in their callings and in their volunteering, model the type of behavior that needs to be general. A minister should preach about the biblical model of effective compassion and then show throughout the week that the teaching goes beyond rhetoric. A business leader should work to create new jobs and train employees to move up; he should also establish policies to support employee volun-

teering and then go out himself to tutor a child. A political leader should work for public policy measures that do no harm to community institutions and promote citizen involvement. She might then provide a room in her home for a young woman going through a crisis pregnancy.

4. Americans a century ago understood that true welfare—the state or condition of being well—is most likely to occur when people are in families. The War on Poverty of recent years, however, has been in many ways also a war on family. Here's one telling statistic: 50 percent of unmarried women of all ages go on AFDC soon after having their first children, but only 10 percent of married teen moms and only 5 percent of married moms twenty or older. Marriage makes the difference; family makes the difference. But our current welfare system discourages marriage and encourages teenaged moms to leave their parents and set up "independent" households. That's a great victory, until a baby cries and cries, and a lonely young mother at wit's end responds in anger.

5. The greatest cause of poverty in America today is abandonment of children by men. Some deliberately slink from responsibility, but others see their children cared for regardless of what they do and lose the incentive to set aside immediate gratification. The current system does not even require the establishment of paternity for children receiving AFDC. That should be basic. Any system that gives men a green light to wander leads their children directly into not only material poverty but psychological, educational, and spiritual deprivation as well. Children without a father who loves and disciplines them have a hard time comprehending the nature of a God who does the same (but without making mistakes). Children deserve the wealth of having a mother and a father when-

ever possible, not the poverty of one parent or the insecurity that develops when a variety of conflicting voices attempt to replace everyday stabilizing forces. (It takes a whole village to confuse a child.)

6. Turning around the welfare ravages of seventy years will take a generation. We need to recognize that the real question about welfare—the one that opens up opportunity—is not the one most often voiced: how do we get people off the welfare rolls? A different question needs to be at the forefront: how do we keep new people from getting on? Abstinence and adoption are the keys to avoiding the single parenting that makes welfare rolls grow. Instead of compartmentalizing problems—welfare here, educational choice there, sex miseducation here, overregulation there—we need to connect the dots.

7. People change from the inside out: the crucial factor is not social or physical environment but belief, which is the basis of attitude, which is the basis of behavior. The successful antipoverty programs in American history have been based on provision of not only jobs but spiritual challenge as well. Income transfer by itself would not last unless a transfusion of values also occurred—and values are most frequently tied to religion. In the 1960s, however, liberals declared a war on poverty that was actually a war on God, since the Bible was excluded by judicial fiat from governmental antipoverty work. Now we need what could be called the New Pragmatism: religious programs receive no special preference but no special antagonism either. If a program gets people off governmental welfare it should not receive adverse discriminatory treatment, whatever its philosophical basis. A system of state-based taxpayer exemptions or national tax credits is the best way to proceed, although other devices to rise above antireligious bias are also worthy of support.

8. Decisions on welfare should be made at local levels, with the guiding principle of facilitating *suffering with*. Those who wish to lead and not just complain should give of their own lives by adopting hard-to-place children, making available rooms in homes for poor women going through crisis pregnancies and hoping to avoid entry into the welfare world, mentoring boys without dads through Big Brother programs or Little League coaching, and contributing time in other ways. Some problems—for example, mental illness and hard-core homelessness—will continue to require specialized care, but states should experiment with ways to provide ordinary citizens with small incentives to give time as well as money, and those who contribute of themselves should be honored.

9. What these propositions point to is a sense that realism today means taking into account more than material conditions. The War on Poverty defined realism as emphasizing dollars and cents rather than children's need for a two-parent family. Realism today means putting children first by finding ways to reverse the trend toward fatherlessness and family malformation. The extent of our cultural loss is conveyed in an anecdote offered by Anne Gordon, who lives with her intact family in the very poor North Lawndale area of Chicago. She recalls the visit of a woman who "came to our house one night at dinner time. She knocked on the door and we were all sitting around the dinner table eating and she said, 'Do you all do this every night?' . . . It seemed to her like a big event, whereas to us it was just part of family life and very normal." All of the improvements in North Lawndale will avail little unless attitudes change so that the tender mercies of a family dinner become normal activities.

10. Overall, keeping massive numbers of new people from entrapment in welfare rolls is not a mystery. The formula is simple: we make a societal commitment, as our forebears did, to

godly patterns of sexual practice and family development. We emphasize abstinence and personal responsibility among both males and females. We work toward an adoption-friendly society by stressing the needs of children, regardless of race, for two parents and a stable home life, and by making it financially possible for families at all economic levels to adopt. We know that good programs designed to meet these goals can work because they worked under somewhat different but equally difficult circumstances a century ago. We do need to find ways to apply these old lessons in new contexts.

Chapter 9

Proclaiming Liberty Throughout the Land

This book suggests that each reader go beyond the failed governmental war on poverty by starting his or her own. We need to show love for our own families and then resolve to help at least one other person or family out of poverty. How can we love others? Let me count a few of the ways: tutor a child. Mentor students or young adults. Be a Little League baseball coach. Counsel an unmarried mother. Be a volunteer librarian at a church school in a poor neighborhood. Teach rich and poor what the Bible has to say about wealth and poverty. Help a poor person negotiate the legal system. Employ a jobless person. Lead a neighborhood association in a poor part of town. Start a crisis pregnancy center. Give a pregnant teenager a room in your home. House a homeless person. Adopt a child.

Friends at the Progress & Freedom Foundation have kindly suggested that it might seem unfair of me to press others to action without acknowledging that I have pressed myself. Revealing such personal stories leaves me uncomfortable but the friendly comments make sense, so here goes: my wife and I have helped out a bit by doing at various times the things listed in the above paragraph, and others. Most of these experiences have turned out to be useful to poor individuals and satisfying to ourselves, but not all. Since the introduction to this book began on a personal note, this closing chapter can begin in the same way, with a mention of two of the personal efforts—one successful foray that began a decade ago, one current attempt that at this writing is a decided failure.

The first effort involved an unmarried, Hispanic nineteen-year-old college student—call her Isabella—who became pregnant. When her twenty-five-year-old boyfriend—call him Chuck—learned she was pregnant, he dumped her. Her traditionalist father made it clear that she had shamed the whole family and was not welcome at home. Summer vacation came but Isabella could not go home or afford an apartment, so she sought help at our local crisis pregnancy center, which offered her shelter in a home—ours. She lived with us for six months until the baby was born.

Isabella became in one sense part of our family, joining us around the dinner table, praying with us, and playing with our children. At the same time, however, she was a stranger in strange terrain, often feeling the need to retreat to her bedroom and mourn there alone. She worked during most of that period at a local convenience store so as to save money for an apartment, and that was sometimes hard. A month after giving birth, Isabella moved into an apartment with two other women her own age.

The story does not end there. Chuck, after seeing the tiny being he had fathered, began to grow as fast as the baby did. He fell in love with his daughter, then fell in love with Isabella all over again. They married, and over the next several years had two more children; their marriage, while suffering some ups and downs as do others, is now well established. Isabella graduated from college. So did her husband, pushed to gain maturity.

Ten years later, my wife and I stay in contact with Chuck and Isabella. Their first daughter, who might have been aborted had

Isabella not been so determined to keep her and hope alive, and whose first home was our home, is a beautiful young lady. Isabella's husband works at rehabbing homes, a task that requires some heavy lifting at times, and he has given my two teenage sons their first outside-the-home jobs. (They have better muscles than me and have earned their pay.) All in all, a tale that is certainly satisfying to tell.

This second one is not. One day my pastor met in a restaurant a thirty-eight-year-old ex-convict—call him, creatively, John Doe—and invited him to church. John had expressed belief in Christ while serving eight years in prison and was showing discipline in reporting to a restaurant job every day, but he still had difficulty in controlling impulses and planning ahead. Church members offered him biblical teaching, financial counseling, suggestions for improving job skills, transportation, listening, and encouragement; I was one of the helpers. We always made it clear that we could not carry John to a better life: we could help, but the responsibility was his.

As it turned out, he could not handle that responsibility at that time. After quarreling with a roommate he hit the streets, working day jobs at times, drinking at times, and perhaps gaining other immediate gratifications at times, but doing nothing to set up a long-term ascent. His emotional instability did not make it appropriate for him to live in a home where women and children were present. We urged him and helped him to enter two local programs that could have given order to his life, but he did not stick with either for more than three days. On his own, John got into a brawl, went to jail, and eventually was shipped off to prison for violating parole.

John's attitude showed improvement the last time he and I talked; maybe he will be released soon and can start over again. But, to help John and others like him, the essence of his problem must be understood. There is much talk in Washington of the need to create more low-skilled jobs, and it is true that many city manufacturing jobs have disappeared in recent decades, but finding work is not a problem for John and those like him in most cities. Many entry-level jobs that would lead to stability and a solid income, if John stuck with them, are available. Beginning workers have to put aside immediate gratification, and that is especially hard when a person is thirty-eight and eager to make up for time lost in prison, but the success of many recent immigrants shows that opportunity is still present and that patience breeds success.

We also hear about the unavailability of low-cost housing, and it is true that ill-conceived governmental urban renewal plans eliminated many single-room occupancy buildings and inexpensive apartments; it is also true that unnecessary governmental building codes and specifications keep other low-income apartments from being built, or drive up their cost. But even so, and even in Austin with its high rates of apartment occupancy, John's problem was not housing (unless it is assumed that every homeless man has a right to his own house or apartment). John's problem was finding a congenial roommate and getting along with people generally. John is intelligent and physically capable; his problem, like the problem of many Milwaukee AFDC moms who do not enter the Right Alternative program, like the problem of Washington addicts who do not stick with the Clean and Sober Streets program, has been attitude.

After all, think about what Marsh Ward of Clean and Sober Streets learned after years of thinking that the poor were imprisoned within societal walls: Ward saw that when attitude changes, a formerly homeless alcoholic or addict finds a hole in the wall and *goes right through*. Ward saw that attitude and behavior, most of the time, make all the difference. Is it true that, if all attitudes changed, the economy would be unable to provide or grow jobs for all? It probably would, but macro questions of that sort are irrelevant to the decision of any particular poor individual: if attitude changes there is a hole in the wall, and *he goes right through.*

More Republicans in Washington and around the country need to stress the historical and current evidence that shows there is a hole in the wall for those whose behavior changes. More Democrats need to understand that governmental programs work poorly because their tendency over time, even when they start out solidly, is to substitute entitlement for challenge, bureaucracy for personal help, and the naked public square for faith. Our predecessors made use of the seven principles of effective compassion summarized in chapter four; we can even simplify them into an emphasis on help that is challenging, personal, and spiritual.

We can teach fellow citizens to remember the basics in the same way that millions of Americans now know the meaning of the letters CPR. They know that when death is near, as with the four-year-old submerged in the swimming pool, cardiopulmonary resuscitation may restore normal breathing. Similarly, now that American society is in dire straits, we need to teach CPS: compassion that is challenging, personal, and spiritual. (Those three letters also begin the three syllables of the word "com-pas-sion.")

Lifesaving CPR has three defined elements, and the first is heart massage by the exertion of pressure. A person using CPR does not press down faintly on the chest of a person close to death. He challenges the heart to respond, and it is important that the push in CPS also be hard. A century ago, homeless shelters were not enablers that maintained alcoholics and addicts in their lifestyles and asked little or nothing of them. Instead, they followed the challenging advice that the apostle Paul gave in his epistle to the Thessalonians: if an able-bodied man does not work, he shall not eat.

An emphasis on challenge at the present time suggests that we need to stop talking about "the poor" in the abstract and start distinguishing once again between those willing to struggle and those just looking for an enabler. Just as our national and state public policy measures should promote economic growth, so should our individual and community efforts emphasize work, not make-work or excuses. Industrious women on AFDC and men desperate to support their families deserve concentrated help, not the pittance they receive when they are lumped in with those who merely want to work the system. Alcoholics, addicts, drifters, and irresponsible parents must be challenged to change their destructive behavior; if parents abuse their children, adoptive parents are ready to take them in.

When we think of the second element of CPR—clearance of air passages to the lungs—an intense image may come to mind: the volunteer performing mouth-to-mouth resuscitation, occasionally stopping for a second to half-mutter, half-pray, "Breathe . . . Breathe." Effective compassion needs a level of *personal* involvement almost as great, and that's what the second letter of CPS stands for. In many poverty-fighting situations, lives and values also have to be resuscitated, and people learn more from an individual they respect (and perhaps love) than from a textbook.

Here again there are lessons from the past: a century ago, charity volunteers usually were not assigned to massive food-dispensing tasks, but were given the narrow but deep responsibility of making a difference in one life over several years. A typical magazine story reveals how one "demoralized" woman was helped: "For months she was worked with, now through kindness, again through discipline, until finally she began to show a desire to help herself." For months: "Breathe! Breathe!" Today, it is hard to buy the level of personal involvement that is needed to be next to an addict as he is going through withdrawal pains—but at Victory Fellowship chapters and similar organizations, a person who recently escaped addiction himself and wants to help one other person do the same sits by a kicking addict's bedside.

Similarly, the cost of providing the professional support needed to stand by all the unmarried, pregnant teenagers who are going through the pain of abandonment by boyfriends and parents would bankrupt governments. But true, personal help arrives when a married couple with compassion for a tough-talking but frightened teen gives her a room in their home and a place at their dinner table. We should participate in and support programs that emphasize one-to-one approaches. We should not overlook bonds that, even if torn, already exist. We should support attempts to reunite aid seekers with families and friends, for as history shows and Psalm 66 states, "God sets the lonely in families."

The third element of CPR is use of appropriate medications. The idea is to take what is of proven effectiveness and apply it immediately. No one doing CPR goes to a medicine cabinet and tries whatever the snake-oil salesman of the week has peddled. In the same way, there is a medication of proven effectiveness for the poor who see themselves as worthless: successful antipoverty work, past and present, has given the poor self-esteem not by offering easy, feel-good praise, but by reminding them that a wonderful God made them in His image and has a purpose for their lives. "True philanthropy must take into account spiritual as well as physical needs," poverty fighters a century ago noted, and that is why the third letter in CPS stands for "spiritual."

Sadly, the federal War on Poverty of the 1960s presented a rummaging around in the medicine cabinet. Religious teaching, instead of being embraced by bureaucrats at least as a way of helping roaming individuals to think about their purpose in life, was excluded by judicial decree and administrative design. Instead of letting Christians, Jews, Moslems, Buddhists, and others all compete in doing good—over time we would see who is the most successful—they were all excluded unless they were willing to embrace in daily practice a philosophy alien to their beliefs. We've discussed in several chapters ways to overcome that error; there is nothing more essential than to seek God's help once again, and to fight a war on poverty that is personal and spiritual.

CPS: it's easy to say, but let's not pretend that the type of change proposed here will be easy. We need to reject the notion of material redistributionists that change is as easy as passing a bill or writing a check. Every successful person in society can look back at the human and spiritual capital that has been invested in him. Grandparents, parents, teachers, mentors, and others have successfully communicated values of discipline, planning, and long-term commitment; sometimes, God has touched and altered lives. Without the intervention of God and man, all of us fixate merely on short-term gratification, and that is the path to poverty, regardless of how much money we have at the start.

The good news is that radical transformations of individual lives do occur, and in abundance. Furthermore, we should realize that the amount of compassion in a society is not fixed. In 1995, newspapers emphasized the demand side, speculating on enormous needs versus the limited ability of current charities to fill them. We now need to focus on the supply side, realizing that giving increases as contributor confidence concerning the wise use of funds and the need for commitment grows.

Overall, the evidence indicates that when charity is challenging, personal, and spiritual, antipoverty work can be effective. The crisis of the modern welfare state is a crisis of government, but it is also a crisis of individual giving and nongiving. All of us need to learn how to apply CPS: some will have more time to give; some will have more dollars; but everyone can do something that will help and not hurt. Everyone can do something.

He goes right through. That statement could characterize the way that the American welfare system, which for thirty years defied serious reform, suddenly changed in 1995. Serious change brings with it not only opponents but skeptical participants; as the Israelites walked through the Red Sea, some probably muttered, It's all an optical illusion. But welfare reform, if pushed even harder over the next several years so that it moves from reform to replacement, is no illusion. Nor is it an illusion for people concerned about poverty whom I met during 1995 in New York and Virginia, Michigan and Wisconsin, Mississippi and Texas and Oklahoma, Colorado and Arizona and California, and other states. They are hopeful about welfare for the first time in many years because they can see the opportunity to go right through.

More people are capturing the understanding that the major flaw of the modern welfare state is not that it is extravagant but that it is too stingy, giving the needy bread and telling them to be content with that alone. More people are saying, in the words of the Bible that are inscribed on a bell in Philadelphia, "Proclaim liberty throughout the land, and to all the inhabitants thereof." If more Americans during the next five years give of themselves to accomplish just that, many of the poor will be free men and women as they enter a new millennium. And what about "John Doe"? He too can have true liberty, if he lives by the principles that the Bible and American history teach, and is not satisfied to be either a lone wolf or a paternalized pet.

This book has been written for the sake of my friend in prison, and others like him.

Appendix A

A Pledge to Action

Sometimes, when we finish reading a book that proposes action, we know exactly what we can do; sometimes, we do not know where to begin. If you want to help and are already involved in a truly compassionate activity, go to it. If you are not sure where to begin, though, read the following pledge that summarizes the principles of effective compassion, take the brief self-diagnosis quiz following the principles, and check out the organizations in your community that operate in your areas of interest. Then let the Center for Effective Compassion know what you find out; there is a form at the end of this appendix, and an address to which it may be sent.

Preamble

The tragedy of America's underclass is chronicled daily in our newspapers and on the nightly news. Today we watch, seemingly helpless, as generation after generation of children are condemned to lives of squalor, violence, and, all too often, premature death. We know it is wrong—deeply, fundamentally, morally wrong. But we seem powerless to do anything about it.

Why are we failing? Some argue that the government has not

spent enough on antipoverty programs. And yet, the trillions of dollars we've spent on welfare programs over the past thirty years have failed to alleviate poverty. Indeed, the big government approach appears to have made many of our most pressing problems, from joblessness to family disintegration, even worse. The destruction of bonds among givers, receivers, and mediating organizations has laid waste to once productive communities of helpers and helped.

Some reformers call for private charities to step in and shoulder more of the burden. That's the right idea, but much of our private assistance network—like a muscle that's too long been unused—has begun to atrophy. Fund-raisers for charities complain of "compassion fatigue"—dwindling donations from people who are either overwhelmed by the size of our problems or assume that they're the government's responsibility. (What else are they doing with my taxes? they figure.) The understanding that people should make charitable contributions to organizations in which they volunteer or about which they are knowledgeable has often been lost.

It's time to transform the way we help those in need. On one point the country has reached consensus: we need a major overhaul of the welfare system. And yet, we must be clear about the reasons for reform. Governmental welfare programs must be confronted not because they are too expensive—although, clearly, billions are being wasted—but because they are inevitably too stingy in what only individuals can give: time, love, and compassion.

The welfare state should be abolished not out of fiscal responsibility, but out of moral responsibility. The casualties of America's war on poverty have been the poor themselves. The evidence of history can no longer be ignored: the welfare state is cruel, not merely misguided. As Americans, we can and must do better.

Private charities can do a better job than government. The history of American philanthropy is one of our country's greatest legacies. And yet, some private programs or partnerships do a pale impersonation of the government initiatives that have so dismally failed. Some private charities also suffer from bureaucratization, centralization, the mass production of benefits, and an exclusive focus on the material nature of poverty. We need to focus once again on moral questions, on the processes that build character. Charity that treats the capable as incapable robs people of capacities.

Seven Principles

To renew American compassion, we commit ourselves to the seven principles of effective compassion contained in this pledge—principles that can help revitalize the volunteer community, resolve our most pressing social problems, and restore the moral authority of our country as a beacon of freedom for the world.

Principle #1: Affiliation (Connect With Families and Community)

A century ago, when individuals applied for material assistance, charity volunteers tried first to "restore family ties that have been sundered" and "reabsorb in social life those who for some reason have snapped the threads that bound them to other members of the community." The first question asked by charity was, Who is bound to help in this case?

Today, before creating new antipoverty programs or contributing to a private charity, we too must ask, Does it work through families, neighbors, and religious or community organizations? For instance, many homeless alcoholics have families, but they do not want to be with them. When homeless shelters simply hand out food, clothing, housing without asking hard questions, they run the risk of enabling an addiction while furthering the alienation at its root.

To renew compassion, we must help reconnect those in need with their brothers, sisters, spouses, parents, children, and community. We also need to help the helpers: it is hard for a family to take in a relative with a drug addiction problem, and our compassion needs to be directed to courageous families as well.

A radically new approach to our problems must recognize that effective compassion is a far more complex and richly woven responsibility than simply tossing a few coins at a street person or pulling the ballot lever for the political candidate with all the answers. Effective compassion asks whether our efforts help reinforce family bonds and strengthen community ties or whether they perversely serve to increase an individual's isolation.

Effective compassion also asks whether a program of aid to an unmarried teenage mother increases the likelihood that she will be reunited with those whom she actually depends on, whether she admits it or not (e.g., parents, the child's father), or offers a mirage of independence. It is good to give Christmas presents to poor children, but effective compassion asks whether the gifts are given to parents to wrap and place under a tree—or whether parents watch on the sidelines while Santa doles out the goods.

Concerning this principle and those that follow, various organizations may have different means to the same end. A homeless shelter and a tutoring/sports program for teens both need to connect recipients of help with families and communities, but their means are very different. The Pacific Garden Mission in Chicago probes the family backgrounds of homeless men and tries to make connections, while Voice of Hope in Dallas requires parents of children in the program to show up periodically and help out. But both are devoted to seeing those they help as members of families and communities, not as lone wolves.

Principle #2: Bonding (Help One-By-One)

When applicants for help are truly alone, effective compassion means working one-to-one to become, in essence, new family members. Charity volunteers a century ago usually were not assigned to massive food-dispensing tasks but were given the narrow but deep responsibility of making a difference in one life over several years.

Today, when a boy is growing up without that combination of love and discipline that only a father can provide, a volunteer at a Big Brother program can show him a different model of manhood than the fighting-and-impregnating version that dominates some barren cityscapes. When an unmarried pregnant teenager is dumped by her boyfriend and abandoned by angry parents who refuse to be reconciled, a volunteer family working through a local crisis pregnancy center can provide her a room in their home and a place at the dinner table.

Sure, it may be easier to give someone the phone number of the right agency; that might ease our conscience with the illusory gratification of having "helped." But effective compassion recognizes that one size does not fit all—only a personalized, face-to-face approach tailored to the individual (or sometimes the family) offers any hope for turning lives around. Institutions should be bond makers, not bond breakers; Alcoholics Anonymous is a prime example of creating a community that is not geographic or economic and promoting bonds within that community.

For Father Clements, a Roman Catholic priest, this approach began with his adoption of one homeless child and blossomed into the aptly named One Church-One Child—a program that spread to thirty-nine states and resulted in the adoption of 40,000 children. The program was such a success that he has now applied its community-intensive, individualized strategy to tackling the problem of substance abuse by launching One Church-One Addict.

Father Clements demonstrates the spirit of the Talmudic expression, recently recalled in the movie *Schindler's List,* "He who saves one life, saves the world." To renew American compassion, we must apply this wisdom to each person we approach.

Principle #3: Categorization (Treat Different Problems Differently)

The individualized approach of effective compassion recognizes that two persons in exactly the same material circumstance but with different histories, abilities, and values may need different treatment—ranging from material help to new skills to a spiritual challenge and a push. Historically, this approach is one that produced results. Those who were orphaned, elderly, or disabled received aid. Jobless adults who were "able and willing to work" received help in job finding. And "those who prefer to live on alms" and those of "confirmed intemperance" were not entitled to material assistance.

Volunteers used "work tests" to both sort applicants and provide relief with dignity. For instance, when an able-bodied man came to a homeless shelter, he often was asked to chop wood for an hour or two or to whitewash a building. In that way, he could provide part of his own support and also help those unable to chop. A needy woman generally was given a seat in the "sewing room" (often near a child-care room) and asked to work on garments that would be donated to the poor or sent through the Red Cross to families suffering from the effects of natural disasters. The work test, along with teaching good habits and keeping away those who did not really need help, also enabled charities to teach the lesson that those who were being helped could help others.

To renew American compassion today, we must stop talking about "the poor" as an abstract phenomenon haunting society and start talking in practical, ground-level, concrete, individual terms about how to help. What do you need? What can you do? Where have you been? By asking such questions, we can begin again to distinguish between those who truly want help and a second chance and those who want an enabler.

Work tests can provide some early indication of a willingness to accept responsibility. Why shouldn't able-bodied homeless persons remove graffiti, clean up streets, and pluck weeds at parks? Why shouldn't a new church that worships in a ballroom and needs to put up and take down chairs each Sunday ask a homeless person to help in that effort, and stay for the service and dinner afterwards, instead of sending him on his way with a few dollars?

The question to ask is twofold: what do you need, and what can you do? By putting people to work, effective compassion helps create workers. By giving applicants something to care for, it helps create people who care. By treating people as unique individuals rather than stray pets, it helps restore humanity and dignity.

Principle #4: Discernment (Give Responsibly)

Block grants may work on a governmental level, but they do not work on the streets. Effective compassion does not simply hand out blank checks—it discriminates between those who are truly hungry and those who are looking for a free lunch. If individuals have habits or are engaged in practices that are contributing to their own downfall, material assistance may only speed their progress toward oblivion—just as a broken engine is not fixed by simply fueling it with more gas.

A century ago, poverty fighters trained volunteers to leave

behind "a conventional attitude toward the poor, seeing them through the comfortable haze of our own intentions." Aid given with "no strings attached" and "no questions asked" may feed the ego of the giver as he contemplates his largesse, but it can often hurt more than it helps. Indeed, one of the most deep-seated misunderstandings about effective compassion has been the ironic equation of indiscriminate, anonymous giving with the values of equality and dignity. Even today, we see bumper stickers and tee shirts urging us to "commit random acts of kindness." That is a vast improvement on random acts of violence. But kindness is not random. Kindness is specific.

Providers of effective compassion always recognized that barriers against fraud were important not only to prevent waste, but to preserve morale among those working hard to remain independent. The same applies today to the need for tough standards within compassionate institutions. For example, Clean and Sober Streets is a haven within the District of Columbia for drug and alcohol addicts who are trying to pull their lives together. Addicts receive the close attention and caring that are unlikely in a government institution. At the heart of the project's success are recovering addicts who have successfully completed six weeks of treatment and act as mentors to new arrivals. But the program also has a big stick: residents who drink or use drugs on the premises are immediately kicked out. Rule-bound government shelters have difficulty ejecting addicts who backslide or assault fellow residents—and as a result, they make it harder for those who want to turn their lives around.

Today, lack of discernment in helping the poor is rapidly producing an anticompassion backlash, as the better-off, unable to distinguish between the truly needy and freeloaders, have an excuse to give to neither. To renew American compassion, we must help wisely—giving with our heads as well as our hearts.

Principle #5: Employment (Demand Work)

If a grown son needed a place to stay after, for instance, losing a job or house, we would undoubtedly want to welcome him back to his old room—perhaps even kept intact with his old football trophies or high school yearbook. We probably would ask him to help out around the house, maybe to do the grocery shopping or mow the lawn—and we would expect him to look for work. It would be inconceivable, no matter how much we loved him, for us to advocate his staying on indefinitely, to discourage him from lifting a finger around the house, to forgo any mention of a job search, and to subsidize his idleness with free food, unlimited television, and a rules-free environment. Families do not operate that way.

Many charities and welfare programs do. Historically, practitioners of effective compassion have recognized simple rules of supply and demand: if individuals are paid not to work, unemployment multiplies, chronic poverty sets in, and generations of young people grow up without seeing work as a natural and essential part of life. Government aid programs are most vulnerable to falling into this trap: because they operate outside the market, government assistance is often seen as flowing from a practically inexhaustible source. Like air or water or sunshine, assistance comes to be regarded as a right, as a permanent pension implying no obligation.

Today, programs that stress employment, sometimes in creative new ways, need greater emphasis and deserve our support. For example, more of the able-bodied should receive not housing but the opportunity to work for a home through "sweat equity" arrangements in which labor constitutes most of the down payment. Some who start in rigorous programs of this sort drop out with complaints that too much sweat is required. But one applicant who completed a tough program summarized what his new home meant to him: "We are poor, but we have something that is ours. When you use your own blood, sweat, and tears, it's part of your soul. You stand and say, 'I did it.'"

Special efforts need to be made in helping the physically disabled or the mentally below par, but even for these harder cases, work is useful. For example, one program has trained those with IQs below the Forrest Gump level to work well as supermarket baggers; occasionally they start putting gallons of milk on top of bread and need some retraining. And the movie itself, fictional though it is, displayed in its portrayal of the double-amputee Lieutenant Dan the important fact that even those without legs can find appropriate tasks, and in doing so regain their dignity.

Principle #6: Freedom (Reduce Barriers to Compassion and Enterprise)

Thomas Jefferson coined the axiom that "government can do something for the people only in proportion to what it can do to the people." Our founders firmly grasped the inverse relationship between state power and individual freedom—they knew that government-provided services, no matter how well intentioned, inevitably carried a coercive virus of rules, regulation, and numbing bureaucracy. Perhaps this was the wisdom behind charity workers' past reluctance to ask government to come in and take charge of the poor; they chose instead to show the needy how to move up the ladder while steering clear of perpetual dependency.

Freedom was the opportunity to drive a wagon without paying bribes, to cut hair without having to go to barbers' college, and to get a foot on the lowest rung of the ladder even if wages there were low. Freedom was the opportunity for a family to escape dire poverty by having a father work long hours and a mother sew garments at home. Life was hard, but static, multi-generational poverty of the kind we now have was rare.

The twentieth century has witnessed the march toward greater and greater politicization of life. Big government, once viewed with suspicion, came increasingly to be seen as omniscient, omnipotent, and infallibly beneficent. We are more inclined to redistribute wealth than to give people the tools to create it. We are more inclined to march on Washington than to walk into inner cities ourselves, offering our services.

By viewing the free market as the creator of poverty, we have regulated and restricted it, impeding one of the most reliable vehicles to independence. Today, in our eagerness to hoist those at the bottom of the ladder out of poverty, we have raised its lowest rungs out of the reach of many of those left on the ground.

Regulations designed to protect workers on the job, for example, increasingly make employers reluctant to hire those with drug backgrounds or other indications of potential instability. Small businessmen who desire to be compassionate in their hiring need to be free to take on workers without clean records; they need to be able to do drug testing and to fire workers (without legal or financial repercussions) during an initial trial period if they misbehave. Liberating small businessmen will create more opportunity for the poor to begin climbing the ladder.

Principle #7: God (Reliance on the Creator and His Providence)

Some people think of poverty fighting like they think of dinner table discussions: it is a violation of etiquette to emphasize the importance of religious beliefs. But the facts leave us no choice: successful antipoverty work, past and present, has allowed the poor to earn authentic self-esteem not by offering easy, feel-good praise, but by pointing them to God. Most successful programs in America have stressed biblical religion. Some have spoken of a less-defined "higher power," but all have reconnected poor individuals—who may only have been thinking about the next meal or the next fix—to life's spiritual dimension and higher purpose.

Antipoverty workers of the past understood that self-respect is based on having a purpose in life, on understanding that we are created in God's image and thus have value. They knew that those who were not committed to running a consistent race over a long period of time would most likely worship the gods of immediate satisfaction, including drugs, alcohol, and adultery. Given that understanding, they knew that the antidote to poverty was an infusion of new values, not cash, for an irresponsible person and his money soon would be parted.

The federal government's gradual entrenchment in America's public service sector created an increasingly inhospitable environment for charity's religious elements. Too often today, the spiritual inspiration fueling much of our country's grassroots volunteer work is branded as sectarian and (if it applies for taxpayer dollars) banned as unconstitutional. When religion was banished, a variety of experimental social programs were ushered in, but none touched the pessimistic core values of the welfare mentality. Antidrug programs without a spiritual base, for example, have success rates in the single digits. Such programs contrast starkly with those that provide God-centered medication rather than simple bandaging of wounds.

Lots of programs ask people to have faith in themselves or the latest social work doctrines, but in general nothing changes until faith in God transforms values. Moms getting off AFDC through the help of organizations like the Right Alternative Family Service Center in Milwaukee are witnesses to the way value changes lead to behavior changes that allow individuals to hold a job and build a cohesive family. Government programs often emphasize job training, but unless the basics are first dealt with, long-term success is rare.

The same pattern pertains to children at risk, as Hannah Hawkins shows daily in Anacostia. She gives an eternal gift that government cannot provide—Bible lessons showing the difference between right and wrong—and in so doing begins to construct a foundation strong enough to resist the temptations of street culture. Given all the evidence of the importance of spiritual approaches in fighting poverty and drugs, even those who do not believe in God should appreciate the social utility of allowing religious groups of every kind the same opportunity to develop and fund programs that secular groups now have.

A Call to Dedicated Action

Americans can be proud of our nation's long history of compassion for those in need. But the condition of our cities, the epidemic of drug addiction and violent crime, the crisis of teen pregnancy, the crushing poverty and endemic homelessness—these are all causes for shame.

In recent decades, we have allowed true caring to be replaced by the myth of institutional compassion—the idea that we can fulfill our sincere desire to help those in need by writing a check to some institutional charity (government or private) that will do the rest for us. The cost of that myth is measured daily in the lives of three generations of children who have grown up in a culture of poverty.

It is time to dispense with the myth and substitute for it the principles of effective compassion that Americans long have known. For more than two centuries, those principles guided our efforts to provide opportunity for those in need. It is time to reclaim wisdom only recently forgotten. The renewal of American compassion will not occur immediately, and I know that revitalization will not be easy. But each year of delay is a year of increased suffering.

The good news is that the revolution has begun. Individuals, church groups, and volunteer associations are rediscovering the principles of effective compassion that have historically made American generosity a shining example for all the world. People have caught on to the folly of relying on arbitrary benchmarks of spending or numbers served and have begun to count compassion the only way that really matters: one person, one family at a time.

What's needed now is personal dedication. Therefore, I pledge to practice the principles of effective compassion in my own life by identifying, volunteering at or contributing to, and informing others about at least one nonprofit organization that practices effective compassion; an evaluation sheet is shown on page 166. My specific goal is to help one person or one family over the next year; that means taking personal, hands-on responsibility (perhaps shared with friends, relatives, or colleagues) for one person, one problem, one littered edge of America's community square.

SELF-DIAGNOSIS QUIZ

Helping people who are poor may require you to move outside your comfort zone. At the same time, with the host of problems that demand action, it's important to pick an area of endeavor that emotionally resonates with you. These questions may help you to pin down areas to pursue.

1. The most moving, or most troubling, personal encounter I've had with someone in poverty was

   _____

   _____

   _____

2. The last news story I read or saw about some aspect of poverty that made me want to do something was

   _____

   _____

   _____

3. Concerning the problems that have moved me, I feel capable of volunteering in this way:

   _____

   _____

   _____

4. Organizations in my area that work on those problems include

   _____

   _____

   _____

5. Organizations in my area worth visiting, in light of the four questions above:

   _____

   _____

   _____

EVALUATION SHEET

Please mail to Director, Center for Effective Compassion, 1301 K St NW, Suite 650 West, Washington, D.C., 20005.

Name of organization:

_____

Address:

_____

_____

_____

Contact person, telephone number:

_____

_____

Brief description of organization's purpose:

_____

_____

How does the organization emphasize affiliation?

_____

_____

_____

How does the organization promote bonding?

_____

_____

How does the organization practice categorization?

_____

_____

How does the organization show discernment?

_____

_____

_____

How does the organization demand employment?

_____

_____

_____

How does the organization promote freedom?

_____

_____

How does the organization rely on faith in God?

_____

_____

_____

Overall: Ask yourself if the organization offers compassion that is challenging, personal, and spiritual. If it falls short in any of those areas, please note that below and explain why it might still be considered a model worthy of replication.

_____

_____

_____

And, before you sign up, two more questions are vital:
Judging from management reputation, budget, apparent level of efficiency, etc., does the organization seem to be well run?

_____

_____

_____

Is there an established and satisfactory procedure for training volunteers?

_____

_____

_____

Your name, address, and telephone number:

_____

_____

_____

Appendix B

A Biblical Base

The Bible was cited often during Congress's 1995 welfare reform debates—and often inaccurately.* The religious left has often twisted Scripture to make it conform to modern liberal ideology, but the Bible is a much deeper document. What follows is a quick survey, first of the Old Testament, then of the New.

Old Testament

Let's begin with something on which religious left and right can agree: throughout the Old Testament we are commanded not to sit back when there are poor people among us. God's redemptive work in bringing Israel out of Egypt provides a motivation for mercy ministry. Deuteronomy 15 notes, "If there is a poor man among your brothers in any of the towns of the land that the Lord your God is giving you, do not be hardhearted or tightfisted toward your poor brother. Rather be openhanded and freely lend him whatever he needs."

---

*See, for example, March 23, 1995, *Congressional Record,* 104th Cong., 1st sess., p. H3713.

Similarly, Psalm 82:3 prompts us to "defend the cause of the weak and fatherless," and Isaiah 1:17 similarly commands, "Defend the cause of the fatherless, plead the case of the widow." As God is merciful to us, we are to be merciful to others, and in the process learn the truth of Proverbs 22:9: "A generous man will himself be blessed, for he shares his food with the poor."

God promises blessings for obedience, but never an all-expenses-paid vacation. Here it is important to understand the biblical concept of labor, both before and after the traumatic events in the Garden of Eden. If work were something that had to be done only because of man's sin and fall from grace, we would be right to treat it as something to be endured only until "Miller time" arrives—but Genesis 2:15 (pre-fall) tells how "the Lord God took the man and put him in the Garden of Eden to work it and take care of it." Adam had a good combination of intellectual and physical labor: it was his job to name the animals (a name was supposed to reveal the essence of the creature, so finding the right name required hard thinking) and also to work the garden. Adam's work was not endlessly frustrating, as work sometimes is today, for then it was without thorns. He enjoyed perfect dominion over the earth.

That all changed with man's independent and rebellious grasping for the knowledge of good and evil and consequent expulsion from the garden. Genesis 3:17–19 summarizes the outcome: "Cursed is the ground because of you; through painful toil you will eat of it all the days of your life. It will produce thorns and thistles for you, and you will eat the plants of the field. By the sweat of your brow you will eat your food. . . . " Man must now do tiring work to live, but the pre-fall nature of work shows us that man does not work for bread alone: we miss one of God's gifts to us when we do not seek productive work.

Work now is painful but useful both for survival and for

character development: work is a tuition-free education in diligence. Throughout the Bible, and in Proverbs specifically, character and economic success go together: "Lazy hands make a man poor, but diligent hands bring wealth. . . . He who works his land will have abundant food, but he who chases fantasies lacks judgment. . . . Diligent hands will rule, but laziness ends in slave labor. . . . Do not love sleep or you will grow poor; stay awake and you will have food to spare" (Prov. 10:4, 12:11, 12:24, 20:13). That there are annual exceptions to these general rules is clear—farmers may work hard throughout the summer and lose their crops to a sudden storm—but over a lifetime their applicability is equally clear.

The moral value of labor is emphasized in the way Proverbs lampoons the lazy: "The sluggard buries his hand in the dish; he will not even bring it back to his mouth. . . . The sluggard says, 'There is a lion outside' or 'I will be murdered in the streets.'" (Prov. 19:24, 22:13). For the most part, though, God's writers contrast the present-mindedness of paupers with the willingness to delay gratification that is the engine of economic progress: "A sluggard does not plow in season; so at harvest time he looks and finds nothing. . . . The plans of the diligent lead to profit as surely as haste leads to poverty. . . . He who loves pleasure will become poor. . . . In the house of the wise are stores of choice food and oil, but a foolish man devours all he has. . . . The sluggard's craving will be the death of him, because his hands refuse to work" (Prov. 20:4, 21:5, 21:17, 21:20, 21:25).

The folly of some among the poor, however, does not mean that they can be treated as subhuman, for poor as well as rich are created in God's image. The Old Testament anticipates the New in noting that wrong action toward the least of God's people shows a lack of faith in their creator: "He who oppresses the poor shows contempt for their Maker, but whoever is kind to the needy honors God" (Prov. 14:31). This passage and others nowhere suggest mandatory redistribution of wealth, but they do emphasize God's abhorrence of dishonesty, legal shenanigans, and other tendencies to twist the market to gain unfair advantage. Proverbs condemns those who "share plunder with the proud" and states flatly that "the Lord detests differing weights; dishonest scales do not please him" (Prov. 16:19, 23:23).

Amos 5:11–12 provides the clearest statements of this sort: "You trample on the poor and force him to give you grain. . . . You oppress the righteous and take bribes, and you deprive the poor of justice in the courts." Amos's withering criticism is aimed at those who use governmental power to force the poor to do what they would otewise not do, often by building public-private partnerships that enable those with wealth to get more by wielding tax and courtroom power. Honest business pursuits are no vice, but "skimping the measure, boosting the price and cheating with dishonest scales" tramples the needy (Amos 8:4–6).

Those with wealth are to provide opportunities for the poor to rise out of poverty; the typical starting point in the Old Testament was gleaning. As the book of Ruth most clearly shows, landowners were to leave the corners of their fields unharvested and the upper branches of fruit trees unpicked, so that those willing to work hard would not starve. Character counted: Boaz married Ruth for several reasons, but he began to pay attention to her when he saw that she worked hard all day long. (She may also have been pretty, but we are not told that; we are told that Boaz and Ruth, a Moabite woman who came to believe in God, became the great-grandparents of King David and thus ancestors of Christ.)

The institution of gleaning offered opportunity to aliens such as Ruth who had no land, and also to those within Israel who had lost their inheritances. The Old Testament also mentions several other devices, including the sabbath year and the jubilee year, that God gave as a way of offering new opportunity. Israelites could buy and sell freely everything except land, which could be offered only for long-term lease, with rental payment varying according to the length of contract; once in fifty years (the jubilee year) all contracts were to conclude so that land would revert to the families of the original owners, and thus allow a new generation new opportunity.

In situations where there was no opportunity for people to earn bread by the sweat of their brow, God did provide—but in a manner that always provided a spiritual lesson along with material help. In Exodus 16:31, God gives the Israelites manna that is not only life-sustaining but tasty, "like wafers made with honey." The next phase of God's providence was not so pleasant, however. When people were not content with their daily bread but demanded daily meat, the Lord provided another feeding connected with teaching—but this time, with people not crying out from necessity, God answered their petitions and kept answering: "The Lord will give you meat, and you will eat it. You will not eat it for just one day, or two days, or five, ten or twenty days, but for a whole month—until it comes out of your nostrils and you loathe it—because you have rejected the Lord . . ." (Numbers 11:18–20). Disease followed.

In this passage and others, God shows us that he will ordinarily supply our needs but not our wants. Significantly, God's people are not immune to the results of spiritual disobedience. In this passage and others, disobedience always has consequences, and when an entire society embraces ungodliness, even those who have had tough lives are not excused. We have to work hard to earn more than the basics, and we have to behave decently to retain even the minimum: when Israel goes foul, God declares that He will not "pity the fatherless and widows, for everyone is ungodly and wicked, every mouth speaks vileness" (Isa. 9:17). Part of the tithes that God's people are commanded to give may go to help the poor, but the poor always have responsibilities as well.

Above all, there is no "preferential option" for either poor or rich. God is a theological determinist, and belief is more important than status. Representative Glenn Poshard of Illinois stated, "If there is one thing evident in the Scriptures, it is that God gives priority to the poor"—and yet, what is evident is that God says that we should not give class-based preferences. "Do not follow the crowd in doing wrong," Exodus 23:2 states. "When you give testimony in a lawsuit, do not pervert justice by siding with the crowd, and do not show favoritism to a poor man in his lawsuit."

Passage after passage shows that biblical justice means the offer of a fair hearing: "Do not deny justice to your poor people in their lawsuits" and "do not show partiality to the poor or favoritism to the great, but judge your neighbor fairly" (Exod. 23:6, Lev. 19:15). Justice means the upholding of contracts; God is on the side of the poor when the rich use political power to place themselves above the law: "Woe to him who builds his palace by unrighteousness, his upper rooms by injustice, making his countrymen work for nothing, not paying them for their labor" (Jer. 22:13–17).

This theme receives particularly pointed examination in chapter five of Nehemiah, where the emphasis is on not using courts to oppress working people and on lowering taxes: "Neither I nor my brothers ate the food allotted to the governor. But the earlier governors—those preceding me—placed a heavy burden on the people and took forty shekels of silver [about one pound] from them in addition to food and wine. Their assistants also lorded it over the people. But out of reverence for God I did not act like that. Instead, I devoted myself to the work on this wall" (Neh. 5:14,15).

Where do these passages and many others, correlated with

each other, leave us? Quick summary: we're told to defend the rights of the poor, particularly widows, orphans, and aliens. We're told that work is good, although now impeded by thorns. We're told that the provision of food should be coupled with the provision of spiritual lessons. We're told that justice means giving the poor full legal rights, but not treating them as more worthy than the rich just by virtue of their class position. We're told that the poor should be given opportunity to glean and that provision through tithing should be made for some, but that God condemns laziness. We're given examples of the affluent and powerful, like Nehemiah, who voluntarily give up some of their perks to help rebuild the walls of a once godly culture that was almost down the drain.

Now, to the emphasis that the New Testament provides, and the example set by Christ himself.

New Testament

An old rhyme explaining the relationship of Old and New Testaments goes "The New is in the Old contained, the Old is by the New explained." That is certainly true regarding poverty fighting, as the New Testament carries through on the themes of the Old.

Concerning work, for example, Ephesians 4:28 states that "he who has been stealing must steal no longer, but must work, doing something useful with his own hands, that he may have something to share with those in need." The apostle Paul's injunction to church members is particularly strong: "In the name of the Lord Jesus Christ, we command you, brothers, to keep away from every brother who is idle. . . . we gave you this rule: 'If man will not work, he shall not eat.' We hear that some among you are idle. They are not busy; they are busybodies.

Such people we command and urge in the Lord Jesus Christ to settle down and earn the bread they eat" (2 Thess. 3:6, 10–15).

Some New Testament books directly parallel in their message some of the Old. For example, James matches Amos's condemnation of those among the rich who use governmental power to exploit the poor: "Are they not the ones who are dragging you into court?" (James 2:6). Employers and employees can negotiate whatever wages they wish, but an agreement must be honored: "Listen you rich people, weep and wail because of the misery that is coming upon you. . . . Look! The wages you failed to pay the workmen who mowed your fields are crying out against you" (James 5:1,4).

God also does not provide entitlements in regard to provision of food generally: as in the Old Testament, material sustenance has a spiritual purpose. The famous feedings (reported in Matthew, Mark, and Luke) of four and five thousand men, plus women and children, came after many hours of Jesus's teaching, with people in a place (like the desert in Exodus) far from food supplies; the multiplication of loaves and fishes fed many and also showed Jesus's divine power.

Since the Bible repeatedly emphasizes the importance of helping widows and orphans, both of whom are in a difficult position through the mysterious workings of God's providence, it is striking to see that great care should be taken even in aid to widows. "Give proper recognition to those widows who are really in need," Paul writes to Timothy; "really in need" means lacking family, for "if a widow has children or grandchildren, these should learn first of all to put their religion into practice by caring for their own family and so repaying their parents and grandparents, for this is pleasing to God" (1 Tim. 5:3,4).

When widows have no children or grandchildren, Paul continues, they are eligible for aid, but he emphasizes that "no widow may be put on the list of widows unless she is over sixty, has been faithful to her husband, and is well known for her good deeds, such as bringing up children, showing hospitality, washing the feet of the saints, helping those in trouble and devoting herself to all kinds of good deeds." Paul then notes, "As for younger widows, do not put them on such a list," and explains why: "They get into the habit of being idle and going about from house to house. And not only do they become idlers, but also gossips and busybodies, saying things they ought not to. So I counsel younger widows to marry, to have children, to manage their homes and to give the enemy no opportunity for slander" (1 Tim. 5:9–11, 13–14).

This passage is especially striking because Paul is talking about the class of suffering people who are nearest and dearest to God. And look at the precautions he takes when recommending even aid to widows within the church: first, family responsibility; second, help only to those over sixty; third, help only to those well-known for good deeds. From all this we learn much about the particular problem of helping widows in the church, but we should also draw a logical conclusion: how much more careful should we be before putting others on the list? And how careful should we be in making up a list of those to be aided by government?

Other parts of the New Testament similarly show that God is not obligated to help even widows when ungodly belief and behavior has come to dominate a culture that arrogantly assumes God's favor: Jesus, warning the residents of his native area of Galilee, explains that "there were many widows in Israel in Elijah's time, when the sky was shut for three and a half years and there was severe famine throughout the land. Yet Elijah was not sent to any of them, but to a widow in Zarephath in the region of Sidon" (Luke 4:25–26).

The New Testament also parallels the Old in prodding the better-off to help those in need. Need is defined as it was in the desert—be thankful for manna rather than yearning for meat—in passages such as I Timothy 6:8: "If we have food and clothing, we will be content with that." Redistribution for the sake of material equality, therefore, is not called for; charity to people who are truly destitute is. (This is particularly true when spiritual debts are involved, as Paul noted [2 Cor. 8] when requesting the Christians of Greece to come to the aid of those in Jerusalem.) Just as Nehemiah voluntarily gave of his economic abundance so that the walls could be rebuilt, so Christians who owned substantial real estate sold some of their holdings so that the truly needy could also be part of building a new community in a hostile place (Acts 4:32–37).

The New Testament intensifies the Old, however, in several crucial ways. First, and most obvious, is the clarification of the meaning of compassion. *Suffering with* (the word's literal meaning) is central in the life of Christ: God came to earth to suffer with us and die for us. Matthew 8:17 suggests the fulfillment of Isaiah's prophecy: "He took up our infirmities, and carried our diseases." Matthew 16:24 shows what those of us who profess to follow Him are charged to do: "If anyone would come after me, he must deny himself and take up his cross and follow me."

Taking up the cross involves crucifying the flesh—killing sin in our lives—and learning to suffer with others. Christ's life and parables taught true compassion: probably the most famous parable, that of the Good Samaritan (Luke 10), tells of how a priest and a Levite crossed to the other side of the street when they saw a mugging victim, but a despised Samaritan "took pity on him. He went to him and bandaged his wounds, pouring on oil and wine. Then he put the man on his own donkey, took him to an inn and took care of him. The next day he took out two silver coins and gave them to the innkeeper. 'Look after him,' he said, 'and when I return, I will reimburse you for any extra expenses you may have.'"

The Samaritan did not go to the other side of the street; nor do we have any record of his lobbying to set up a governmental department of Travelers' Health and Human Services. Instead, he suffered with a person in need. Christ's followers are to do the same. Paul wrote to his supporters, "If we are distressed, it is for your comfort and salvation; if we are comforted, it is for your comfort, which produces in you patient endurance of the same sufferings we suffer" (2 Cor. 1:3–6)

The New Testament also reemphasizes the Old Testament's connection of God's compassion to personal change, a process God sovereignly sets in motion. In the Old Testament, crying out to God is essential: "When they were oppressed they cried out to you. From heaven you heard them, and in your great compassion you gave them deliverers" (Neh. 9:27). Turning back to God is essential: "The Lord your God is gracious and compassionate. He will not turn his face from you if you return to him" (2 Chron. 30:9). Many prophets explain that God is not a sugar daddy who hands out sweets regardless of behavior; Isaiah calls Israel "a people without understanding; so their maker has no compassion on them" and Jeremiah quotes God as saying, "You have rejected me. . . . I can no longer show compassion" (Isa. 27:11, Jer. 15:6).

The New Testament makes the process more vivid in Christ's healings and stories. In chapter twenty of Matthew's gospel, those with sight overlook the evidence that Jesus is God but blind men do not, and when they cry out for mercy they receive it: "Jesus had compassion on them and touched their eyes. Immediately they received their sight and followed him" (Matt. 20:30–34). The prodigal son who squanders his wealth and hits bottom also changes his thinking and decides to cry out: "I will set out and go back to my father and say to him: 'Father, I have sinned against heaven and against you. I am no longer worthy to be called your son; make me like one of your hired men.' So he got up and went to his father." The father was "filled with compassion for him; he ran to his son, threw his arms around him and kissed him" (Luke 15:17–21).

Another great emphasis of the New Testament is that God's grace is for all who believe, not just members of one ethnic group. Again, some ingathering was present in the Old Testament: many non-Hebrews joined the exodus from Egypt, and for a millennium thereafter aliens such as Ruth or the Hittite soldier Uriah were welcomed into Israel. King Solomon also spoke of God's extending the covenant to other nations, and the book of Jonah shows how Assyrians devoted to evil could change: "When God saw what they did and how they turned from their evil ways, he had compassion and did not bring upon them the destruction he had threatened" (Jon. 3:10). But in the New Testament that understanding is made explicit: the apostle Peter says, "I now realize how true it is that God does not show favoritism but accepts men from every nation who fear him and do what is right" (Acts 10:34).

Grace, compassion, and fair treatment from God; faith, labor, and spiritual challenge among men: these are all New Testament emphases that clarify those of the Old. God does not show favoritism and neither should we: individuals from every nation are acceptable to Him and should be to us. The crucial question for economic help is whether aid will be used rightly and effectively. Again, as Paul states in First Timothy 5:16, the goal is not to throw more water into the soup, but to make sure that "the church can help those widows who are really in need." That is the challenge for today: to help those who are really in need, and to give them the type of help that can set them on the path to escaping future need.

Along this line of thought, one quotation frequently taken out of context may point us in the right direction. In Matthew 5:42, as Jesus is telling his disciples how to respond to adversaries, he says, "Do not resist an evil person," and goes on to state (in reference to a Roman rule that soldiers could force innocent bystanders to do short-distance carrying for them), "If someone forces you to go one mile, go with him two miles. Give to the one who asks you. . . . " To wrench that last line into a call for undiscerning handouts is extreme textual manipulation, but some good can come of the attempt if it leads us to a broader question: when a person does ask us for spare change, what are we to give?

The answer may be suggested by the response of Peter in Acts 3 to a crippled beggar's request for a handout: he did not give money (the liberal solution), nor did he proffer a job as if that alone would solve deeper problems (the secular conservative solution). Instead, he told the man to arise and walk in the name of the Lord Jesus Christ; the man does so and is transformed from a helpless person who looks at passersby hoping to get something from them, to a tiger who walks and leaps through the temple courts and stands before the Sanhedrin, praising God.

A similar change, although not always one as physically dramatic, comes among poor persons (and rich) who gain faith in Christ. The gospel does have material effects: among many poor persons who become Christians, it leads to a change in values, which produces a change in behavior, which normally leads to a job, which leads to material improvement. There is no guarantee that spiritual change will lead to material change, and the process should not be regarded mechanistically—but there is a general principle at work here.

Applying the principle requires discernment. Representative Poshard quoted early in 1995 one of Jesus's most famous teachings: "He said in the day of judgment: . . . 'When I was thirsty you gave me drink, when I was hungry you fed me, when I was naked you clothed me, when I was in prison you visited me.' And we will say in that moment, 'Lord, when did I do those things?' And he will say, 'When you did it to the least of these my brethren, you did it to me.'"

That is a terrific passage, but if we are to deal with it fairly we need to understand that today's poor in the United States are the victims and perpetrators of illegitimacy and abandonment, family nonformation and malformation, alienation and loneliness and much else—but they are not suffering thirst, hunger, or nakedness, except by choice, insanity, or parental abuse. When we lack discernment, we give money to panhandlers that most often goes for drugs or alcohol. Christ does not include in his list of commended charitable acts, "When I was strung out you gave me dope."

What are we truly doing to homeless men when we enable them (through governmental programs, undiscerning nonprofits, or tenderhearted but weak-minded personal charity) to stay in addiction? Here's the reality: when I was an addict you gave me money for drugs; when I abandoned the woman and children who depended on me you gave me a place to stay and helped me to justify my action; when I was in prison you helped me get out quickly so I could commit more crimes.

If we take seriously Christ's words, "When you did it to the least of these my brethren, you did it to me," giving money that goes for drugs is akin to sticking heroin into Jesus's veins. The Bible, however, points us to a life that is disciplined in work and worship, living and giving. It teaches us to glorify God and to enjoy his providential workings, both in this life and forever.

Alternative Welfare Replacement Methods

There are at least four ways to use government to promote the delivery of resources to programs that can provide effective compassion. One, shifting tax power along with pro-grammatic authority to the states, is discussed in chapter seven. A second, giving religious groups equal access to funding under the Ashcroft provision, is discussed in chapter eight. This appendix touches on two more: massive federal tax credits and social service vouchers.

Tax Credits

My philosophical preference is for states rather than Washington to call the shots—but if it turns out that Washington is ready to move ahead and states are not, then a change in the federal tax code could provide the resource base for a rich harvest of new programs that would help the poor and allow for the free exercise of religion. That would be worth fighting for.

Currently, individual income taxpayers can deduct from their taxable income the contributions they make to a wide range of religious, charitable, and educational organizations. This is good, but not good enough. If leaders in Washington are serious about replacing government welfare programs with private charity and do not choose to wait for state action, they can accept the Coats proposal discussed in chapter seven and then go one step further by establishing a massive system of tax credits for funds sent by individuals to groups within a new tax-exempt category. That category would include organizations that provide direct social services to the poor (as distinct from the many educational and religious organizations that can receive tax-deductible contributions).

Here's my proposal in its simplest form (and we'll deal shortly with the complications and drawbacks): individual taxpayers could take a tax credit of 90 percent of the value of their donations to nonprofit poverty-fighting organizations, up to a maximum of 50 percent of their tax liability. For every dollar sent to such trampoline-building organizations by credit-receiving taxpayers, expenditures for the federal safety net would decrease by a dollar. In 1993, federal welfare spending totaled $234 billion and total individual income tax receipts amounted to $510 billion; if this system had been in effect in 1993 and all taxpayers had used the maximum amount of their credit, $230 billion that came to federal coffers would have gone to the poverty-fighting nonprofits.

In economic terms, this reform would amount to a massive redistribution of poverty-fighting expenses. Now, nearly all of that money is going to the U.S. Treasury and then trickling down to the needy, in the form of cash or in-kind services, after passing through a complicated maze of bureaucracy. When it finally arrives at its destination, it is spent according to a complex set of regulations in ways that are widely recognized to be extremely ineffective. Under the tax reform proposed here, most of that money would be distributed to poverty-fighting organizations according to the individual preferences of millions of taxpayers.

On the other hand, if taxpayers did not use their credit—and some would not because of resistance to paying out of their own pockets 10 percent of the total amount going to an organization, or because of a belief that government will do a better job than a private organization—funds would be left for government-run programs, which would then have more popular legitimacy than they do now. Since the poorest states would (in dollar terms) be adversely affected by the end of federal redistributionism, a "compensation fund" could be created; some $26 billion would compensate those states.

The system would work for an individual taxpayer in this way: over the course of the year he contributes a certain amount to qualifying charitable organizations. In preparing his tax return, he follows the same procedure as now (unless, of course, a flat tax comes in). If he itemizes deductions, he may still deduct the amount he contributes to his church, to a medical research organization or environmental group, to a college or museum, or to other nonprofit organizations that do not have a poverty-fighting mission. Then, when he calculates the amount of tax he owes, he subtracts from the amount of tax due 90 percent of the amount he has given to qualifying charities.

Here's an example: if a taxpayer owes $4,800 in taxes and has made $2,000 in creditable contributions, he subtracts $1,800 (90 percent of $2,000) from his tax due, so that he owes only $3,000 in income tax. The amount credited may not exceed 50 percent of the tax due (or $500, whichever is greater), so if the hypothetical taxpayer above had made $3,000 in contributions, his credit would only be $2,400 (50 percent of $4,800) instead of $2,700 (90 percent of $3,000). It is probable, as the public became accustomed to using the charitable tax credit, that most taxpayers would send enough to charities to take the maximum tax credit.

The tax credit approach diminishes the government's role as

a service provider or even fund allocator, but allows the government to promote the general welfare. The actual provision of services would shift toward privately run charitable organizations, which would be able to place more emphasis on helping the needy in ways that are personal, challenging, and spiritual. Decisions about where funds shall go would no longer be a function of political struggles over the budgets of government agencies, but would result from the decisions of millions of individual donors. And the already large contributions Americans make to charitable organizations will grow over time to several times their current level.

Vouchers

If the "new tax" exemption plan proposed in chapter seven does not gain steam, there is a way that a welfare choice campaign based on vouchers could still work at the state level. Vouchers are often proposed in relation to schooling, but there is a great difference between parents who are generally responsible and deeply concerned about the education of sons and daughters and welfare recipients who vary greatly in degree of responsibility. Some recipients would do fine with vouchers that they could use for any social services, but it would be irresponsible to place unconstrained vouchers in the hands of addicts, alcoholics, and others who are not committed to changing their lives.

However, there are ways to bring into action the fundamental principles of paying for performance and rewarding success. What if a voucher could be redeemed by a participating organization only as the social service client showed progress toward self-sufficiency? For example, a homeless person could present a voucher that would pay service providers nothing for warehousing individuals, a small amount for getting individuals established in transitional housing, and the full amount only when a client had a permanent home in which he had resided for a year.

Other needs could be dealt with similarly. A welfare mother's voucher could be redeemable in stages as she achieved certain thresholds in becoming independent: obtaining a high school diploma, marrying or getting a job (and holding it for a year), and so on. An organization that helped an addict would receive payment only if he were tested a year after completing the program and still was clean. We should emphasize achievement rather than programs that continue to get funding regardless of what happens to the people they are supposed to be helping. That goes against the current standard procedures, but those procedures have produced built-in incentives to keep clients dependent: a big caseload is a good argument to use for a budget increase. Those incentives need to be reversed so that rewards come not for maintaining people in dependency but for liberating them.

Appendix D

Connecting the Dots

Problems of poverty, crime, education, and family formation are interrelated. Instead of circling one dot and moving on to the next, legislators should go dot to dot and draw a picture. They should assess statutes and regulations for their effect on the opportunity and incentives for individuals to help others. Environmental impact statements have become bureaucratic nightmares and charity impact statements probably would fare no better, but thinking about interrelatedness is a practice that should be fostered.

Government's ability to promote compassion rather than provide services is directly connected to improving its performance in areas that are at the center of its mission. Again, look at the preamble to the Constitution:"ensure domestic tranquillity" means preventing a civil war within the nation, but it is also a reminder of the need to prevent civil war in the streets. When an angry pimp is trying to break down the door of the Children of the Night shelter in Los Angeles to snatch back a teenager who has been his meal ticket, and the police get a squad car to the shelter and a helicopter over it within five minutes, government is doing things right.

Government is rarely doing right by poor neighborhoods,

though, on questions of crime. Criminal activity is the norm in many poor neighborhoods; victimization rates are many times higher among the poor than among those who are more afflu-ent. Criminal behavior poisons every aspect of life in those communities where it is dominant. Voluntary action of the kind promoted by numerous neighborhood watch groups or organi-zations such as Mad Dads in Omaha can help make streets safer in poor neighborhoods. Antigang activities like those pioneered by some church and youth organizations can help. But such efforts need to be spearheaded by tough but fair police activi-ty—which is yearned for by most residents of poor neighbor-hoods—and backed up by a judicial system that actually convicts criminals and a penal system that actually punishes them.

A reasonably high proportion of criminal cases—especially those involving violent crime—are closed with arrests. But even among those criminals who are apprehended, there is a very good chance that they will evade conviction and an even better chance that they will receive no punishment, even if convicted. As a result, crime is perceived—often accurately—as a low-risk activity that pays off better than work. Anyone who complains about "welfare queens" should speak out more vociferously about crime kings.

Enforcement of drug laws is particularly vital. Proposals to decriminalize drug use are now frequently heard; drug use is so widespread that enforcement would inevitably be arbitrary and ineffective, some pundits say. Such statements are not only counsels of defeat in the face of large-scale criminal activity, but counsels of despair with respect to lifting the poor out of dependency. Alcoholism and addiction are proximate causes of much of the unemployment, family disintegration, and crimi-nal activity so epidemic among the poor. To permit the twin boa constrictors to continue to crush human lives is irresponsible, especially since their backs can be slashed by the many excellent treatment programs—such as Teen Challenge—now in existence.

In at least one instance it has been shown that the mere threat of criminal prosecution is sufficient to motivate drug users to seek and stay with treatment. During the mid-1980s, physicians in Charleston, South Carolina, were concerned about the number of crack cocaine-addicted babies they had to care for. They had warned the mothers during pregnancy that their children would suffer serious damage if they did not stop using drugs, but these warnings were to little avail: the teaching hospital in Charleston consistently had about thirty crack babies a month.

That miserable situation changed in 1988, when doctors asked the local prosecutor to back up their medical warnings with a legal warning: expectant mothers who were using drugs could choose between going into treatment or going to jail. The mere threat was sufficient. Without ever having to prosecute a single mother, enrollment in drug treatment programs became routine and the incidence of crack babies was cut by 80 percent. Sadly, after a few years of successful operation of this program, the federal government moved in and ordered the prosecutor to stop threatening to enforce the law: since more black moms than white moms were affected, the ACLU had sued on grounds of racial discrimination; a judge had thrown the case out of court, but in 1994 the Department of Health and Human Services in Washington threatened a cutoff of all federal health money to South Carolina if the program continued. The 800-pound gorilla won. Mothers no longer stayed in treatment programs. The number of crack babies went back up.

In other realms as well, government is doing little to ensure domestic tranquillity, even in areas where it has created problems. Sequestering the poor in public housing where residents are not required to be responsible is bad enough, but the situation becomes intolerable when—and this, amazingly, is now standard—residents cannot be expelled for being drug dealers. If there is to be any government-subsidized housing, the privilege of living in it should be contingent on maintaining the standards proper to a good neighbor: keeping the house or apartment reasonably clean and orderly and not using it as a headquarters for criminal activity. If drug dealers demand a right to public housing, they should be accommodated in penitentiaries.

The impact of crime in poor neighborhoods is exceeded only by the impact of miseducation. Public schools in many poor neighborhoods feed poverty and crime by giving up on discipline and learning and becoming holding cells. Some poor parents make extraordinary efforts to earn the money needed to pay private school tuition; most try to make the best of a terrible thing. Some poor children try to overcome an environment in which teacher expectations are low and any attempt to meet even those expectations produces scorn among classmates; most succumb.

The public education safety net has failed and the failure is particularly obvious when public and private schools in the same neighborhood, and drawing students from similar socioeconomic groups, are compared: the inner-city private schools are trampolines. Children in such schools, of course, have parents who care enough to make sacrifices, so the comparison may be unfair to those public school teachers and administrators who have not given up. And yet, how many more parents could be challenged to care more if they, like parents who are reasonably well off, did not have to scramble so hard to place their children in a better school?

Poor parents, unlike their affluent counterparts, generally can afford neither tuition nor residence in a better neighborhood. They have to take schools without discipline and without learning, where mere attendance may be physically dangerous and where graduation may not necessarily signify basic literacy. Schools like that are able to exist only because they have a captive clientele, students who are there only because they are not able to go anywhere else. There is one way to get rid of bad schools like that, and it's simple: give parents the power to decide freely where their children shall go to school. When it becomes a matter of survival for schools to attract students, there will be discipline, there will be learning, and there will even be innovation and perhaps excellence in every school.

School choice also has another advantage, which is generally not noticed, and that is its good effect on parents. Many poverty-level parents (often young unmarried mothers who did not complete their own education) feel intimidated by the responsibilities of parenthood, especially in comparison with the well-dressed, educated teachers their children encounter. But when those same parents have the power to make the final decision— not just to "have input"—about what school their children attend, they are given a renewed sense of their own dignity and worth as persons and their rights as parents. The exercise of responsibility builds the capacity for responsibility.

Vouchers have been the main tool seized upon by proponents of school choice, but the poverty-fighting tax exemptions discussed in chapter seven would work better. Here's the process: taxpayers could receive tax exemptions for making contributions to children's educational opportunity funds (or similar organizations) that provide poor students with partial or full scholarships. Poor parents could use those scholarships to place their children at a wide variety of private or church schools. Vouchers are a step up from our current system because they give parents choice, but many Christian school leaders worry about strings attached. The introduction of tax exemptions would not eliminate those concerns, but they are three steps further removed from state control because government officials never get their hands on the money, unlike with vouchers.

Furthermore, educational contributions/tax exemptions could build more of a sense of citizenship than vouchers and be less open to charges that advocates are interested only in activities that benefit their own families. The new pool of capital for scholarships would help the least among us, those who currently are deprived of a decent education. The exemption would not help middle-class parents, but most are not in the desperate situation in which poor parents zealous for their children's education find themselves. The best way to help middle-class parents would be a dramatic increase in the federal per-child tax exemption and the inclusion in any flat tax plans of a similarly child-friendly base.

For mothers with younger children, the cost of child care is often seen as an overwhelming impediment to work and additional child care funds are regularly demanded, but the answer to the problem lies within the cohort of the poor itself: if goals of reaffiliation and bonding are kept in mind, crises become opportunities. The average welfare mom has two children; three welfare moms could form a child care group within which one would take care of the children, either in homes or in play areas provided within housing projects, and the other two would go to work. The child care provider could be subsidized with "new tax" funds as long as she provided that useful service for two other mothers.

Of course, as noted before, the long-term goal would be a revival of the two-parent family; while public policy measures cannot accomplish this, they can promote the general welfare through establishment of a family-friendly environment. Numerous studies show now what those on the cultural left would not admit during the 1992 political campaign when Dan

Quayle raised the subject: a strong family structure is anti-poverty insurance. A solid family can compensate for many of the disadvantages of simple material deprivation. Family members encourage one another and share a mutual sense of responsibility. And, of course, intact married-couple families have more ways of earning and more ways of saving money, which is one reason why poverty is unusual among married couples but rampant in those mother-child family fragments we call single-parent families.

Families, of course, are not created by the government, and strong families can exist under any form of government. But governmental innovations have, for example, created no-fault divorce, a concept that renders every marriage unstable. In a civil sense, marriage is a contract between a husband, a wife, and society to establish and maintain a family. Under traditional divorce law, society held the husband and wife to that contract unless it could be proved that one party had seriously violated it; society was on the side of maintaining the stability of marriages. Only in recent years has either spouse been allowed to withdraw from the contract unilaterally, for any reason, without suffering disadvantage.

Now, the law tolerates stable marriages, as long as neither spouse objects, but is on the side of dissolving marriage whenever a conflict arises. The consequent lack of marital stability is a major cause of poverty. So is another consequence of the devaluing of marriage: the rise of governmentally approved sexual activity outside of it. Instead of passing out condoms (which are often successful in preventing conception on any given occasion but not over a period of several months or a year, because sooner or later the condom is not used, misused, or faulty), abstinence programs that have proven their success should be in place in every school.

Programs such as Elayne Bennett's Best Friends in Washington, or those offered by Carenet-affiliated crisis pregnancy centers, have demonstrated that the abstinence message can be communicated successfully even to children from extremely disadvantaged backgrounds. Early sexual activity and the accompanying high rates of teen pregnancy are not inevitable. Reducing teen pregnancy by changing teenage behavior patterns not only alleviates one of the major direct causes of dependency, but also builds the character strengths needed to succeed in school, at work, and in taking on family responsibilities.

And as we make connections between areas of public policy and society that often are compartmentalized, we should note that criminal activity also plays a part in the surging incidence of illegitimacy. A study of 46,500 births by California teens in 1993 showed that in 71 percent of the births to teens aged eleven to eighteen, the father was on average five years older. A Seattle survey of 535 moms aged twelve to seventeen found that the mean age of the father was twenty-four. The age difference raises the question of why statutory rape laws are not enforced. Just as we need to get tough with adults who corrupt kids with drugs, so we need to enforce laws against adults who corrupt kids with sex.

Overall, proper public policy measures can help to liberate children to be children, students to be students, and citizens to be citizens. If government helps to establish a sound environment for citizenship, productive change can come. During the next few years, state governments rather than the federal government may be able to take on the primary responsibility for providing social services and the means to compete in innovation. With more latitude to experiment, diminishing financial assistance from Washington, and incentives to strengthen the private charitable sector, most states will change the way they deliver social services, if the proposals of welfare decentralizers are enacted.

At the same time, we should resist the temptation to look to public policy for salvation. Those who truly help the poor will continue to be not public policy planners, no matter how smart they are, but compassionate individuals on the front lines. They perhaps will be given new resources under a new system. They should certainly be given the opportunity to suffer with others without looking over their shoulders at a government trying to push ahead so as to get in the way.

Index

About the Progress and Freedom Foundation

A private, non-profit, non-partisan idea center established in 1993, **The Progress & Freedom Foundation** aims to create a positive vision of the future founded in the historical principles of the American Idea. It brings together a diverse group of thinkers and policy experts and shares their work with the American people through seminars, conferences, publications, and electronic media of all forms. The Foundation is tax-exempt under Section 501(c)(3) of the Internal Revenue Code.

The Center for Effective Compassion, a project of the Progress & Freedom Foundation, works to educate the public on ways to help the needy through a people-focused approach that is personal, challenging, and spiritual. The Center's activities include research, publications, and a major public education campaign designed to fundamentally change the debate over how to assist those in need. Among its objectives is the development of a nationwide network to encourage financial and volunteer support for effective charities.

For more information, contact:

The Progress & Freedom Foundation
1301 K Street, NW
Suite 650 West
Washington, DC 20005
E-mail: mail@pff.org
http://www.pff.org

AUTHORIZED
PERSONNEL
ONLY

OTHER FORGE BOOKS
BY BARBARA D'AMATO

Killer.app
Good Cop, Bad Cop
Help Me Please

AUTHORIZED
PERSONNEL
ONLY

M
D'AMATO

Barbara
D'Amato

A Tom Doherty Associates Book
New York

AUTHORIZED PERSONNEL ONLY

A Forge Book
Published by Tom Doherty Associates, LLC
175 Fifth Avenue
New York, NY 10010

www.tor.com

Forge® is a registered trademark of Tom Doherty Associates, LLC.

Library of Congress-in-Publication Data

D'Amato, Barbara.
    Authorized personnel only / Barbara D'Amato.—1st ed.
        p. cm.
    "A Tom Doherty Associates book."
    ISBN 0-312-86564-3 (alk. paper)
    1. Police—Illinois—Chicago—Fiction. 2. Chicago (Ill.)—Fiction.
3. Policewomen—Fiction. I. Title.

PS3554.A4674 A96 2000
813'.54—dc21   00-057270

First Edition: December 2000

Printed in the United States of America

0 9 8 7 6 5 4 3 2 1

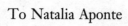

To Natalia Aponte

ACKNOWLEDGMENTS

Thanks to Mark Zubro for seagulls, and to Edward O. Uthman, M.D., for his discussion of autopsies

MONDAY

CHAPTER ONE

Monday, 1:30 P.M.

"WE LOST SIGHT of them in traffic, squad," the voice on the radio said.

"Get a plate?"

"Never got close enough." It was 3-32, a car from the Third District talking. The Third was well south of the Loop.

The dispatcher said, *"Where you at?"*

"Eighteen hundred south on Michigan. Breaking off."

"All units in the eighteen hundred south Michigan area, we're looking for a two-door green Ford containing two male whites, approximately twenty, twenty-five years old. Heading northbound. These two gentlemen held up a currency exchange on Jeffrey and are armed. Repeat, they are armed."

"In broad daylight," Suze Figueroa said.

Bennis said, "Yeah. What's the world coming to?"

Officers Norm Bennis and Suze Figueroa were rolling east in their squad car on Roosevelt Road heading toward Lake Michigan, minding their own business, which basically meant minding the business of the law-abiding or not-so law-abiding public out there. They had both front windows down for air. Chicago squad cars don't have air-conditioning. Figueroa was driving. Bennis wanted to drive all the time, but Figueroa loved squad cars, loved the lights and siren, and reminded him of department rules. In a two-man car, the manual said each man should drive four hours. Even if one of them is a female.

"Hang a right on Michigan," Bennis said.

"Aye-aye, Captain."

"Now mosey into the right lane and slow down."

"Jeez, why don't you just drive and be done with it?"

"Told you I would."

"Never mind."

Bennis was thirty-six years old, a black man who was medium height and built like a wedge, wide shoulders, narrow waist and hips, fairly skinny legs but a great runner. Figueroa was twenty-six years old, Irish and Hispanic. Bennis had been on the job ten years longer. That made him the boss. He thought.

"Comin' up in the rearview," Bennis said.

"What?"

"Your basic two-door green Ford with two extremely basic male whites."

"I hate it when you're right."

The Ford passed them, going slower than it had coming up behind. It moved sedately into the right lane ahead of them. Obviously the driver didn't want to be pulled over by a cop car for some minor violation. This was fine with Bennis and Figueroa, though. It put the Ford right where they wanted it. Figueroa hit the lights and siren. Bennis was on the radio.

"One-twenty-eight. We got them on view, squad," he said reading off the Ford's license plate.

And at that moment, the Ford took off like a bat.

"Shit! Move it!" he said.

"Like I couldn't guess." Figueroa floored the accelerator. They flew past Eleventh, Ninth, and Eighth Streets—there was no Tenth—all of which came in from the left and dead-ended at Michigan Avenue. The Ford screamed around three or four cars, then cut into the right lane again, just barely clipping the front bumper of a Toyota Celica. The Celica's driver jammed on his brakes—a poorly considered move that caused him to lose control and swerve onto the sidewalk, where, thank God, there were no nearby pedestrians—and Figueroa swore at him under her breath, fighting the wheel to pass him on the left, then swing back into the right lane.

Ahead the brake lights of the Ford went on, just for a split second, but giving Figueroa some advance warning. It swung sharply right, fishtailing as it turned onto Balbo.

The Ford's driver was heading straight toward the lights at Balbo and Lake Shore Drive. Ahead of him was Lake Michigan. His choices were only left or right, unless he planned to sleep with the fishes.

Bennis said, "Eastbound on Balbo," to the radio.

"Ten-four, twenty-eight."

"Not anymore," Figueroa said.

The Ford shot through the intersection with the light against it, screeching sharply left. A blue pickup got out of its way too fast, sideswiping a Jeep.

"Nobody knows how to drive anymore," Figueroa said.

At one-thirty in the afternoon, Lake Shore was busy but not as full of cars as it would be at three when the rush hour started to build. The Ford sped up, going forty, then fifty, then sixty, cutting back and forth around cars, one lane to another. Buckingham Fountain flew by on their left.

Most of the traffic saw the light bar on their squad car and some even pulled over to the right, giving the Ford a free lane and more space for more speed.

"Don't lose him!" Bennis yelled.

"Good thinking, boss."

"Northbound on LSD," he yelled at the radio.

At seventy miles an hour they passed everything on the road. The Ford was weaving, dodging traffic, sliding around the stopped cars at the Jackson intersection, then the Monroe crossing. Speeding up, with the yacht club on the right, it was running too fast into the curve at the north end of Grant Park.

"Oh, shit! There he goes!" Bennis said.

The Ford slewed sideways into the center guardrail, flattening a section, and then spun out across the southbound lanes, miraculously missing six southbound cars, and up the embankment onto the golf course Mayor Daley was so proud of. A golf course in the middle of the city.

Figueroa piloted the squad car bumpily over the flattened rail more carefully than the Ford, and then she cut across the southbound lanes in a gap in traffic.

Ahead of them, the Ford churned into the soft earth of the golf course, the driver still trying to get away from the cops. Golfers ran for the trees, scattering clubs and bags and hats.

Figueroa drove the squad car across the grass, following the Ford.

"Hey! You're messing up the green," Bennis said.

"It's a rough."

"It's a rough now, that's for sure. At least stay in his tracks. The mayor's gonna kill us."

"They're getting out!"

Figueroa shoved the gearshift into park. Bennis was already out of his side, running. The two men jumped from the Ford and ran. The one from the passenger seat turned. He was holding an automatic weapon.

"Bennis! Look out!"

Bennis was chasing the driver. The first guy took a one-handed Rambo stance, feet spread wide, automatic weapon held in his right hand only, and fired at Bennis. He missed, and Figueroa thought, *Thank God.* Figueroa didn't have time to pull her sidearm and she didn't need to. By the time he fired she was on him, just plain jumped him with all her weight, which wasn't much, but if a hundred and ten pounds hits you dead-flat-on, you notice it. She grabbed the gun. Her momentum carried the guy backward with her on top of him and then she rose up and let herself drop on him hard, one knee right in the middle of his abdomen. The air went out of him with a sound like a popped balloon and so did all the fight.

When she looked up, Bennis and the other guy were disappearing over the hill toward Randolph Street and half a dozen squad cars with their light bars flashing were coming up Lake Shore Drive.

Monday, 3:30 P.M.

"I'M SAYING THAT Gentleman Bandit guy had to have the IQ of a rutabaga," said Corky Corcoran, leaning heavily on the bar from his side.

"But handsome I heard," Sandi said from the customer side of the bar.

Suze Figueroa said, "Well, see, that's the thing. When they're handsome they think they can get away with all kinds of stuff."

"Who?" said Kim Duk O'Hara. There were nine of them, just off second watch, all unwinding in the Furlough Bar.

"This armed robber," Corky said. "Weren't you listening?"

"No," said Kim Duk.

Corky laughed. "See, this happened on my next-to-last day, just before I pulled the pin." A former cop, Corky had left the department two years earlier. "Got in all the papers, too. What a send-off! The robber—they called him the Gentleman Bandit—specialized in convenience stores," Corky said.

Mileski said, "Those places! Just banks by another name. Cash withdrawal by Smith & Wesson, twenty-four-seven. Have some cigarettes and Twinkies while you're at it."

"No, that's 7-Eleven," the Flying None said.

"Twenty-four-seven means twenty-four hours a day seven days a week," Corky said, waving his arms hugely and smiling. Mort groaned deeply. Corky and Mort co-owned and ran the bar, Corky having bought a half interest just two years back. Mort was also a former cop, but unlike Corky, didn't talk much.

He was irritable and crabby, which didn't seem to bother his customers. Figueroa believed that cops took a perverse delight in crabby bartenders. Still, most of the cops who hung out here thought Mort had driven his first partner away with his bitching and moaning. The partner had sold out to Corky. Corky was the perfect foil for Mort; he just laughed when Mort snarled.

He said, "So what I'm sayin' is in he goes. I mean, he's done maybe fifteen, eighteen stores we know of by that time, and he's gotta know we're looking for him, but he goes in anyway."

"Yeah, well, he also got away with it fifteen, eighteen times," Kim Duk said, making a not-bad point.

Corky merely beamed on Kim Duk. "It was the media called him the Gentleman Bandit because he's polite, see? Sheesh. Make him a hero, right? So anyway he goes into this convenience store on Kedzie. He's swaggering; he's cool; he's handsome. And he's got a thirty-eight. Goes behind the counter and tells the sweet young thing to please give him all the money out of the cash register and all the cigarette packages she can stuff in this big brown bag. And she does."

"I would too," said Kim Duk.

"Says stuff like 'if you don't mind,' and 'thank ya kindly, honey.' Then he's ready to go. But he wants an efficient getaway. Now, his other masterful jobs have been in Ravenswood, South Shore, Old Town, Back of the Yards, I mean all over the city, but not right here in the middle of the Loop where there's a hell of a lot of one-way streets, so he asks her, 'Say, honey, what's the best road to the Kennedy Expressway?' Being sweet, see? She says, 'Take Randolph Street.' "

"You're kidding me."

"Never. So he says thanks and good-bye, and I'm here to tell you he actually gives her a quick kiss on the cheek, and he quick-steps out of there. Soon as he's out the door, she dials 911 and informs Dispatch about the robbery and says, 'He's gonna be taking Lake Street to the Kennedy.' Naturally, the 911 operator asks how she's so sure, and she tells him. And we get the word. So my partner Jimmy-Jones Sharpe and I are out there on Madison, scream a couple of blocks over, and pick him up. It's easier than netting minnows in August."

"If they were all brain surgeons," Norm said, "we'd never catch 'em."

"I would," said Mileski.

"Jeez. Mort," Corky said, swabbing the bar surface with a rag, "do you have to leave beer goo all over the counter?"

"Keeps the yuppies away," Mort said.

"No yuppies is one thing," Corky said. "But how about basic sanitation?"

Mort snarled and leaned against the ice maker. They were the odd couple, Corky cleaning and Mort bitching.

"So, Susie," Corky said, changing subjects while he scrubbed the counter, "I hear you're a hero." The bar behind him was the only thing close to trendy in the place. Five tiers of wall-length glass shelves totally filled with bottles spread before a not-too-clean mirror. The mirror was a source of constant wrangling between Mort and Corky. Mort believed that washing it would destroy the ambience, though he would never have used the word "ambience." Even the word "character" wasn't one he admitted to knowing in this context. He said, "You ain't gonna hookerize my bar."

The Furlough was a typical cop hangout, dark, no ferns, small windows that hadn't been washed since Eisenhower was president, and every kind of booze known to humankind. God forbid the district commander should stop in and ask for something they didn't have.

"Don't call me Susie. It's Suze."

Norm said, "Rhymes with booze."

"Or coo—" Mileski began.

"Do *not* go there!" Figueroa said.

"So you're a hero," Corky repeated.

"Please! I'm not."

"Tackled a guy with an automatic weapon. Saved Bennis's ass. What I hear."

"Guy thought he was Rambo," Figueroa said. "Shooting one-handed. Those pieces rise when you fire them, which is why you gotta hold them two-handed, but the idiot didn't know that. He was firing way over Bennis's head."

"Still," Mileski said, "that wasn't bad action."

Figueroa said, "You know what I was thinking when I decided to tackle him?"

"You're going to tell me. I know that much."

"That it would take way less time and agony to tackle him 'by hand' so to speak than to spend the rest of the day and evening sitting in front of a round table inquiry explaining why I 'discharged a firearm.' "

"You got *that* right," Corky said fervently.

"Sad but true," said Mileski.

"And the hell of it is," Bennis said, "that the asshole I was chasing got away. Ran down the slope to Randolph. I mean, I was right on his tail, but when he got where there were pedestrians, he took a bunch of cash out of his pocket, paper money from the currency exchange, and threw it up in the air."

"No shit?"

"Yeah, and people just fell all over it. I couldn't get *through*. My guess is when he got to Michigan Avenue he grabbed a cab."

Figueroa said, "Some of the money from the currency exchange—a whole lot of money—was in the car, but I guess he'd stuffed his pockets with whatever he could grab."

"Say, you know what," Mileski said. "At least that guy wasn't *so* stupid."

"Yeah. I bet he was smart enough to keep some, too," Figueroa said.

"It's a funny old world," said Corky, setting up more glasses.

Speaking of the world, there was nothing on earth, Figueroa reflected, as satisfying as letting your guard down after work, coming in and having a beer to unwind. Especially among others of your kind, who understood your problems. You *need* it. Non-cops just don't understand. Other professions unwind after work too, but she believed cops were different.

She had always secretly kind of liked being the only woman in the Furlough after the tour. It gave her a sense of being one of the guys. But they had a new female officer these days.

Sandi Didrickson, the Flying None, was bellied up to the bar. The gang called her the Flying None for a couple of reasons, partly because she came in after the tour, drank three beers, the first two fast, and then after the third glided out, flying on wings of hops.

Figueroa was a-one-beer-and-I'm-outta-here kind of person. For one thing, she needed to get home to the kids and Sheryl. The nurse was supposed to leave at five o'clock.

"But *why* didn't they let you through?" the Flying None said. Of course this was the other reason for her nickname. Sandi wasn't the sharpest knife in the drawer.

"They wanted to pick up the money."

"But they could see you were a police officer."

Bennis said, "And I'm sure that was a *huge* deterrent, Sandi."

Figueroa stood up. "Bye, guys," she said.

Everybody mumbled something or other. But as she pulled on her jacket, Bennis caught her eye and mouthed, "Thanks."

CHAPTER TWO

FIGUEROA'S HOUSE WAS painted a dark plum red with cream trim, which looked better than it sounded, stick-built in 1890 or so of thousands of pieces of yellow pine that had cured in the following hundred years to the hardness of cement.

It was on a street full of other Victorians—at least, Figueroa believed they were Victorians, although one of the cops she worked with said they were really Queen Anne style. At any rate, they were large ornate wooden structures, all about the same age, with occasional squat ranch houses of late 1940s to early 1950s vintage cowering on lots between the grander, older places. Driving down the street, you could easily see that at some point not long after World War II the owners of some of the big old places had had to raise money and sold off their side yards.

Most of the old places had the contrasting color trim style, which had been rediscovered a few years ago and was considered accurate to the period. The one next door to Figueroa's was a deep dusty blue with pale green trim. The one next to that was pumpkin and gray.

But this wasn't a wealthy neighborhood, just middle class, just getting by. People kept saying someday the rehabbers would discover these houses, but so far that hadn't happened. The houses were kept freshly painted, mostly, but gutters sagged here and there. The roofs of some showed patches of unmatching shingles—people saving up money for a few years in anticipation of a full reroofing. The yards had not been professionally landscaped, and although they were maintained with a great deal of pride, the work often had been done with more pride than skill. Now, in the last week of May, some grass already looked scalped and feeble from too-aggressive mowing, and much of the shrubbery was overpruned.

The neighborhood was extremely convenient, being just three miles northwest of the Loop. The street itself had all the usual Chicago problems—clogged drainage, not enough parking, and too many potholes.

Suze Figueroa found a parking spot only two and a half blocks from the house. Her secret personal horoscope held that if the parking space was less than two blocks away, that was a good omen and the rest of the day would be especially fine. If it was more than three blocks, bad luck, watch out for trouble. In between? Well, that was like partly cloudy. Or scattered showers. Not very predictable.

Figueroa put her handcuffs in their case and the case into her back pocket. Then she used her cyber-clicker to lock up the car.

She drooped from the heat and a full day's hard work. It was four forty-five when she reached the house and let herself in the back door. Her son J J would be home soon, on the five o'clock bus from school. At seven years old, he stayed after the regular school day to play soccer. Her sister's two daughters, Maria and Kath Birch, would be home at five-fifteen; Kath, who was twelve, from band practice and Maria, the teenager not quite from hell, from a friend's house, where they would ostensibly have been doing homework. Doing homework at that age meant trying out new colors of eye shadow and talking about tenth-grade boys.

As Figueroa closed the back door behind her, she looked around to make sure the house hadn't been broken into by crazed maniacs. Alma Sturdley, the nurse—actually a certified caregiver, not an R.N.—was in the kitchen making tea.

"Hi, Miss Sturdley," Figueroa said.

She would have liked to call the nurse Alma, but Miss Sturdley was determined not to be so informal, and refused to call her Suze, so she was stuck. They had hired Alma Sturdley from a pool of three possibles, and had picked her because she looked so *clean*. By and large, they were happy with her.

Sturdley said, "Good afternoon, Ms. Figueroa."

Since there seemed to be no crazed maniacs, Figueroa pulled out her sidearm as she went through the hall to the coat closet, where she dumped her raincoat. She stopped there and locked the trigger guard on her .357 Magnum Colt Python revolver. In a house with three children, there was no place for a loose loaded gun. Even after Figueroa had made it safe, she put it back in its holster under her arm. Like most cops, she felt exposed to the whims of malign fate without it.

Crossing the hall, she leaned into Sheryl's room.

"Hi, babe!" she said. "How's it going?"

"Bastard," Sheryl said. For some reason, when Sheryl wanted to say "better" she said "bastard." It was one of the few predictable words she used.

Sheryl had been injured in an accident on the Kennedy Expressway six months earlier when her car flipped end over end off a ramp. For several hideous days, Sheryl's husband Robert, Suze, Kath, Maria, and J J thought she'd die. Once she was stabilized, the broken bones healed quickly. But although the body recovered, the effects of the closed-head injury, as the docs called it, were horrifying. Even now, four months after being released from the hospital, Sheryl couldn't walk without help because her entire left side got mixed messages from her brain. She also had a big problem with formulating words.

"Well, I'll be back down in a few minutes," Figueroa told her.

"Good," Sheryl said, perfectly clearly.

Figueroa went up the narrow rear service stairs, which all these old houses seemed to have. The front stairs were quite grand, rising in a graceful curve from the hallway near the front door. A curving railing with turned spindles framed the stairs and a huge oak newel post stood proudly at the base.

The back stairs were steep, cramped, and unadorned. In her imagination Suze passed the ghosts of a dozen Victorian maids carrying piles of towels and sheets from the basement laundries, damp hair straggling loose from their tightly pinned rolls, sweat running down their necks, in those days before air-conditioning.

J J and Suze lived on the third floor, where there were four bedrooms, two of them unused except for boxes of stuff nobody could bear to throw out, and a couple of racks and piles of winter clothes. Sheryl's husband Robert and their two girls had their bedrooms on the second floor, which had five bedrooms and two baths. When Sheryl recovered, they fully expected to move her to the big bedroom Robert occupied. Right now it was safer to have her on the first floor so they could get her out fast in case of fire.

Figueroa let the nurse go, started to stir up peanut butter cookies, and got out the ingredients for dinner. Pasta tonight. Rigatoni marinara. Extra garlic.

Peanut butter cookies, she reflected, are truly not brain surgery. A cup of peanut butter, a cup of sugar, brown and white mixed, a cup and a half of flour, butter, salt, an egg, and mix it all up while the oven heats. Cookies made a house smell happy, however simple they were. Roll the dough into balls, mash them down with a fork. The cookies baked while Figueroa sliced onions, garlic, zucchini, and fresh tomatoes for the marinara sauce. She set the veggies aside to wait for dinnertime.

Then she spent just a few minutes sitting on the end of

Sheryl's bed, telling her about the day. The funny parts, not the dangerous stuff.

The man in the backyard watched the inner wood door open inward, and then the screen door open outward. A twelve-year-old girl came out, dwarfed by two huge black plastic garbage bags, which she carried with arms thrust around their middles, as if she were waltzing with two fat grandmothers.

"Why do I alllllllways have to take out the garbage?" she said over her shoulder.

Someone inside answered, patiently, "You don't always do it. You do it Monday and Wednesday." A slender, dark-haired woman came to the back door, still talking as she opened the screen. "Maria does it Tuesday and Thursday. J J does it Friday and Saturday. And you know this." The girl grinned at her.

The woman leaned against the door frame, studying the girl. "Oh, wait a minute, here. Kath, you're pulling my chain, right?"

The girl started to giggle. "Got you, Aunt Suze."

"Yeah, yeah, yeah." She laughed, too. "Hop to it."

The man had watched the woman closely, his eyes slightly narrowed in recognition. The screen door closed. The inside door stayed open.

The girl walked down the cement path to the alley, not hurrying.

She had on such a short little gray flippy skirt, the man thought. And just a fuzzy pink sweater over that lithe little-girl chest. He stood unmoving, only half hidden behind two blue spruces that guarded one side of the path. He didn't expect to be seen. People rarely looked anywhere except straight ahead.

The sweet little girl moseyed closer, dancing little-girl dance steps despite the big bags. One of the bags hiked up her skirt on the left side. He could see the white underwear she wore.

Such a dangerous thing to let your nice little girl go out to the alley all by herself wearing almost nothing. Why, look. You could almost see downy hairs standing up on her smooth thighs. Such a short skirt. Such a short, short little skirt. Such soft skin on such smooth, slender legs.

She swished past him, one bag brushing the spruce nearest the path with a sound like a fingernail on a blackboard, the other just catching its bottom for a second on a terra-cotta pot filled with scarlet geraniums.

He could smell her smell, that wonderful, soapy, shampooey smell of little girls.

She turned right at the end of the path and started down the alley toward the place near the short driveway that led into her father's rickety wooden garage. Three big garbage cans stood at the junction of the alley and driveway. He heard her feet scraping gravel in the alley as she went.

He watched her come back, doing a little skipping dance. *Skitch-skitch, tap-tap!* She went in the back door, and the screen door slammed itself behind her, but he could hear no voices. That meant the dark-haired woman most likely had left the kitchen. And the inner door still stood wide open.

Quickly he walked up the path to the house. He held his hand up as if to knock, just in case anyone was inside. Pausing just a second or two to gaze through the screen and make sure no one was near, he let himself in the back door.

CHAPTER THREE

ALMA STURDLEY HAD left at five o'clock. The deal was for her to be in the house from eight A.M. to five P.M., while Robert and Suze were at work and the kids were in school. Since on Figueroa's present shift she left early in the morning, Sheryl's husband Robert Birch waited until Alma arrived. On days when Figueroa had to work late, she called Robert at work and he would get home early. Also Maria was supposed to let Suze know if she planned to go to a friend's house, so Figueroa could get hold of her if they needed the teenager to come home and take over. The whole thing was pretty complicated. Alma fed Sheryl and bathed her, got her to the bathroom, washed her clothes, and so on. Alma also put Sheryl through her prescribed daily exercises, a full series in the morning and a second series in the afternoon. Sheryl could walk a little, but only with support because of the weakness on her left side. Alma was at the house Monday through Friday, which meant the family took care of Sheryl on Saturday and Sunday, and of course nights. A special therapist came in for an hour and a half five mornings a week at nine—the maximum the insurance would pay for—Monday, Tuesday, Wednesday, Thursday and Saturday for specific muscle work that Alma couldn't supervise. This odd schedule meant Sheryl never had to go more than one full day without her muscle-stretching and leg exercises, and the electrical stimulation of a few muscles that wouldn't contract without it. A neurological consultant came every Thursday and administered tests. She arrived at four-thirty and stayed an hour, so that day nobody had to be home until maybe five-thirty, as long as they were sure she was here. Alma could let her in before she left. Figueroa called every Thursday at four forty-five to be absolutely certain.

"Hey!" Kath said as all six of them finally got collected around the dinner table. Sheryl was in her wheelchair, held upright in place with a woven chest belt, just to be on the safe side. It seemed an indignity, and usually she could sit pretty well by herself, but she had fallen out once and hurt her jaw badly. Her right side was extremely strong, overcompensating for the weakness on the left. The problem was that if she started to tip, she could grab something with her right hand, but she wasn't usually able to recover her balance.

Figueroa stood in the doorway, just about to go out to the kitchen.

"Hey what?" she said.

"The band is going to the inauguration! We're gonna march in the parade! Isn't that great, Dad?"

"How much is it going to cost us?" Robert asked.

Kath's enthusiasm faded slightly, but she was ready for this question. "Maybe nothing. We've got more than six months, so we're gonna do lots of bake sales and car washes and sell candy."

Sheryl's head bobbed up and down as it did when she was excited. She said, "Abate money."

For some reason Kath understood her best of all of the family and translated. "She said, 'That's great, honey,'" Kath told them. Proud of her mother.

Even Kath could not understand her all the time, not even as much as half the time. The muscles of Sheryl's mouth just did not do what the brain wanted them to. In addition, Sheryl was frequently confused. Figueroa believed that the months of limited mobility, the huge life change from being a competent, self-reliant human being, a highly paid computer engineer to a terribly ill, dependent, and physically weak person had disoriented her. Maybe it was the efforts the brain made to recon-struct itself, the irregular fits and starts of improvement and backsliding, but something gave her bouts of hallucinations.

Figueroa left Kath to explain all the excellent details of the planned Washington trip to her dad. She didn't want to hang over them, and she had more dishes to get from the kitchen, anyway. Being the odd person out in the household was often difficult. Figueroa was sure Robert appreciated the work she contributed, and he seemed to appreciate the care she gave Sheryl. After all, the nurse was here only nine hours a day, five days a week—forty-five hours that left a hundred and twenty-three hours a week when the rest of them had to cope. Partic-ularly when it came to bathing Sheryl and getting her to the bathroom, Suze was afraid that the basic, unpleasant care might damage Robert's relationship with her. There were men who can step into a caregiver role and feel closer to their wives, but Robert did not seem to be one of them.

The rigatoni marinara in a huge bowl was keeping warm in the turned-off oven. She brought it into the dining room, checked to see that the grated cheese, the salad, lemonade, and milk were already on the table, and finally sat down.

"And we're gonna reenact that really famous picture of the Revolutionary War band. You know the one. Mrs. Spears says it's called 'Yankee Doodle,' or 'The Spirit of '76,' and it was painted by Archibald McNeal Willard. There's two drum play-ers, and a fife player. I get to be the fife."

"Well, that makes sense," Maria said in the voice of the older, condescending sister. "After all, you play the flute."

"Yes, isn't it *excellent*?" Kath asked.

"Is the flute player the one with the bloody bandage around his head?" J J asked.

Kath said, "Yeah! I get to have it all gross and bloody."

J J said, "Way cool! Do you get to meet the President?"

"Sure, I guess. Maybe."

J J said to Suze, "Can I go, Mom?"

"I don't think so, honey. You're not in the band."

He made a disappointed face, so Suze said, "And besides, since it'll be January, you'll probably have a basketball game."

"Oh. Oh, yeah."

Robert said, "How come there's no meat in this?"

"It's got marinara sauce. The doctor said we should all eat less meat and more veggies."

"Well, I like it with sausage."

Figueroa sighed. "Next time I'll make a side of sausage."

She snuck a glance at Sheryl. Even though Sheryl couldn't talk properly, when she was clearheaded, Figueroa thought she was entirely aware of all the nuances of everything that went on in the house. She gave Suze a small lopsided smile of sympathy with the right side of her mouth.

Not for the first time, Suze thought that she and J J had to get a place of their own soon. But she couldn't leave Sheryl right now. She was still too fragile.

The kids giggled and teased each other and told Sheryl and each other extremely dumb jokes. J J said, "Why do seagulls fly out to sea instead of in to the bay?"

"I don't know," Kath said.

"Because then they would be bay-gulls. Bagels, get it?"

Maria groaned.

This was much better for Sheryl than being solemn. When their mother, Suze's and Sheryl's, came over to visit, she spoke in a whisper, as if Sheryl were dying, and shushed the kids. *Jeez!* Figueroa thought. *Talk about a totally wrong approach.*

"My turn to take out the dishes," J J said. He was such a good little guy, doing his part.

"And Maria's turn to load the dishwasher," Kath said, the younger sister just checking to be on the safe side.

"J J, bring in the cookies while you're out there. Okay?" Suze said.

"No prob, Mama-san."

"Where did that come from?" she asked Robert, but he only shrugged.

"School," JJ said, returning. "Second grade is China and Japan."

"Oh. Well, what's third grade?"

"Dunno."

"The Fertile Crescent," Kath said. "Mesopotamia and all."

"Oh." Suze stared at the platter of peanut butter cookies. "JJ, did you eat some of those?"

"No, but I *will*!"

"Seriously. I thought—" Mmm. She really thought there had been a bigger pile of cookies when she left them to cool. But then, it had been a long day. She was tired. Her brain might be on overload. Who knew?

At two A.M., when the house had been quiet for a couple of hours, the man started toward the stairs. He suspected that the old, shrunken boards that floored the attic might creak, so he had stayed quiet as long as he could. He had been lying on a lumpy pile of discarded winter clothing, and he was now very stiff and sore. Plus, during the day, the attic was unbearably hot, and it had cooled as slowly as grease congealing.

So fortunate, he thought, to have both back stairs and main stairs. But then, that was life. Sometimes you got good luck and sometimes you got bad.

Passing slowly across the splintery wood, he stepped onto the narrow back stairs. Probably the attic had housed servants once upon a time. There was some dumb floral wallpaper still clinging in faded shreds to the wall next to the landing.

When the stairs reached the third floor, the wallpaper got newer. White roses on a blue background. The third floor, he guessed, had either housed the more important servants or maybe a nursery. Or both.

Here he became very, very quiet. He peered into the dark third-floor hall.

It was fascinating, he thought, how you could close your eyes and still know what was what and who was where. The third floor smelled warm and woody and like fabrics, but not dusty, so you knew it wasn't used just as storerooms; people lived here. There was a faint smell of bubble bath. That meant there was either a woman, a girl, or a young child, which confirmed what he already had observed about the family. Also, there was an outdoors smell, like grass or earth, probably earth, the more he thought about it. So maybe the kid played outdoor sports.

He stepped the last two steps down into the third-floor hall.

The nearest door was open. Did he dare risk peering in? Stepping as softly, he thought, as snowflakes falling on feathers, he moved forward carefully until he had covered about a yard or so, and he could see diagonally into the bedroom. No perfume smell, some leathery smell. In the dim spill of light from a streetlamp, he could just make out a form in the bed. Very small. Hockey stick on the wall, baseball mitt on the wall, both as decorations, and a soccer ball on the floor as if it were in constant use. Shouldn't leave things on the floor. People could trip and fall. *Wall, small, ball, hall,* he giggled silently to himself. *And that's not all.*

Yes, the boy child was in this room. That certainly was obvious, wasn't it?

The child snuffled and the man backed slowly out.

On the stairs once more, he stalked very carefully down to the second floor. There was a light at the far end of the second-floor hall, maybe forty feet away. He could see an open door a little distance from him, but the two closest doors, one on the left and one on the right, were shut. He leaned next to the keyhole of one and inhaled. There was an aroma of flowers, roses or lilacs maybe, he didn't know much about flowers, but he decided it was perfume, not live flowers. So—maybe one of the girls was in there. Maybe the soft, smooth little one with the short little skirt.

He sniffed the air, savoring the scent as if it were the bouquet of a fine wine.

He gave up on this for now and went down to the first floor, where the landing presented him the choice of continuing down to the basement or entering the kitchen.

It was the kitchen for him. A yellowish alley light shone through the window over the sink, and although he didn't dare turn on any other lights, it was enough.

He stood for a minute or two, just absorbing the smells and glorying in the thrill of being in other people's intimate space, a ghost in the innermost room of their house. Wasn't the kitchen the heart of a house? And here he was in their heart. And nobody knew.

Then he unzipped and urinated in their sink.

It was a long, long stream and gave him immense satisfaction. There was no bathroom in the attic, and he didn't dare use any of the bathrooms anyway, at least not at night. He suspected that he could flush the third-floor toilet in the morning, after the woman and the boy who lived on that floor had gone down to breakfast. There would be so much moving around and water noise all over the house with the girls getting ready for school—everybody said girls spent hours in the bathroom—and the Suze-person probably cooking breakfast, that nobody would notice.

Now he opened the refrigerator. Light spilled out into the kitchen, blinding after the darkness. Maybe the woman in the downstairs bedroom would see it. Maybe not. It didn't matter. The spaz could hardly talk.

Plus, kids raided refrigerators all the time, didn't they?

What wonderful fun it had been to listen to the dinner conversation. All those sweet little-girl stories. And the spaz woman going *glub-glub-glub*. And him standing on the back stairs, four steps up, eating cookies.

Holding the refrigerator door open with his shoulder, he lifted a bowl from the shelf. Some kind of pasta.

He stood there with the door open. Slowly, he fed himself with his fingers, eating right out of the bowl. Not bad, but the stuff needed some meat. The hoity-toity male voice at dinner had been right about that.

He put the bowl back, confident that no one would notice any food was missing. In a house with three children, how could anybody ever remember exactly how much food they had? He would, of course, if it were his house. But other people were such slobs.

He rinsed his fingers in the sink, swishing the urine spots away, too. When the sink was clean, he went back to the refrigerator. In a drawer he found some sliced salami. It was in a square plastic deli package, about three-quarters full. He took two slices, careful to leave four, which was still most of it, then closed the plastic down methodically. No one would ever notice.

Delicious.

So now, he thought, it was time to explore the basement.

CHAPTER FOUR

AN OLD MAN stood in the middle of the street, in front of the Chicago Police Department at Eleventh and State, looking down at his toes on the white line, trying to figure out if it was very late at night or very early morning. His face was almost invisible under a growth of beard and long, uneven hair. What little skin showed, mostly nose and forehead, was gray with dirt. He wore the pants from a rusty brown suit and the jacket from a navy-blue striped suit over a tan knit shirt. All three items of clothing had been given to him at a Salvation Army someplace, but he couldn't exactly remember where it was, now. He wore sneakers he had found in a trash can in Lower Wacker Drive. A pair of socks, mottled brown from mud, hung loosely in folds around his ankles. Despite the heat, he wore a threadbare black raincoat he'd had for as long as he could remember—from the old days when he was still somebody—flapping over the whole outfit.

His hands were quite clean. He had just washed them in a rest room at Union Station, before the transit cops moved him along.

He was staring at the police department headquarters when a horn sounded behind him. He'd been thinking about other things. It was night but he hadn't noticed the headlights coming up. Quickly he shuffled out of the street, hobbling onto the curb on sore feet and arthritic knees. He limped over to stand near the police department doors.

Fifty-one years ago he had married his high school sweet-heart. Barbara Jean, sweet as cream, the fall prom queen, he thought. Twenty-four years ago he was still married, happily as far as he could tell. No children. That was not so good. Then he retired. Two years later, his wife had left him, tired of his gloom.

Once upon a time the man had been a police officer. He had retired after twenty-five years on the job, with a full pension, sixty percent of his final year's salary. He found he had no friends who weren't cops. Funny he'd never realized it before. That year he and his wife tried spending the winter in Sarasota—it sounded so wonderful, sunny days, no ice, no snow, no shoveling, no stuck cars—but they didn't know anybody down there and the people they met, though perfectly nice, weren't like their Chicago friends. And they couldn't get used to the climate. Boring. They came back to Chicago. The people he knew best hadn't yet retired. Most of them didn't have their time in. He had started young in the job, twenty-two years old. Most of his buddies came on the job later than he had, in their mid or late twenties, and still had a few years to go.

He tried hanging around the district, tried to pass the time of day with his old friends, go to lunch maybe, but the cops had work to do. They'd talk a little bit, making an effort to be nice, but then they'd go back to the job.

An amazing thing, really. One day you were one of the guys, exchanging rude comments about the top cops, complaining about stupid new department policies, dissing civilians, stopping together for a beer and war stories after a tour. And then the next day here's the crew throwing you a retirement party, all good fellows together, friends, fellow soldiers, brothers almost. They loved you. And then the day after that, you were nobody. Like pulling down a window shade. Out. It was over.

He'd heard about it from other retired cops. Who hadn't? But you never quite believed it would happen to you. Like death. Or getting old. You never quite believed it would happen.

In order to get out of the house, for a while he spent his days sitting on a bench near his old station, the Eighteenth District, over on Chicago Avenue, but it hurt him too much seeing the squad cars going in and out, rabbiting out of the lot, Mars lights flashing, doing stuff that looked so important and glamorous from outside, even though he knew it wasn't always important and almost never glamorous. But he wanted so bad, so bad, *so bad* to be back.

There were a couple of old guys he knew, retired cops his age, and he hung around with them some, but they drank too much and complained too much, and after a while so did he.

So his wife left. He didn't blame her. She was only going to have one life, and it might as well not be spent with a gloomy drunk. He assigned her fifty percent of his pension. He didn't begrudge it; she deserved it. She'd stuck with him many years. But after a few years, he lost the house. Finally, what little was left of the pension seemed just barely enough to buy drink and maybe an SRO hotel for two weeks out of every month. And little by little everything just basically fell apart.

He stared up at the CPD building. They were going to move, he'd heard. Move the central offices to a big new building someplace. They were gonna tear this building down. Hard to believe.

For two years, 1971 and 1972, he actually worked in this building. He was secretary to the Commander of Personnel. Everybody had to go through him to get to the commander. Glory years.

While he leaned on the wall, a couple of young cops came out of the department doors.

"Hey, Pops," the tall, skinny one said. "You gotta move along."

"Oh, sure, sure, officer," he mumbled. He felt in his pocket for the bottle he carried. Just to make certain it was there. He always felt for it when people made him nervous.

"Get going," the shorter cop said.

The tall one seemed uneasy about moving him along so abruptly. "Want to go to a shelter, Pop?"

"Oh, no. No, no, no." Shelters were dangerous. Full of crazies. And dirt. And disease. If it had been zero degrees and snowing, maybe. But tonight the weather was plenty warm.

He began to move away, to show he was complying. They lost interest in him as he moved north.

There was an alley running east off State Street. He'd go lie down there. Roll up his raincoat and use it for a pillow. Done it a hundred times. A thousand.

Half a block into the alley, with the glow from the peach-colored streetlights of State Street reaching faintly all the way back here, he stopped. Unobtrusively, he shook the bottle of cheap wine in his pocket and he could tell just from the weak slosh that it was nearly empty. He'd have to beg for some money before lying down. Couldn't get to sleep without a drink. He fished in the pocket of the raincoat and found the McDonald's coffee cup he carried and used for begging.

Then he realized how late it was. He didn't exactly know the time, had to be two or three A.M., and he'd forgotten again that it was so late because State Street was always bright, there were always cars going by, and the night was hot. But where would he find pedestrians to drop some coins in his cup at this hour? Cops coming out of the building? He should have asked the two young guys for money. Although—no—he could never force himself to do that—except—

When a shadow fell on him, he turned, surprised. You had to be careful on the street, but at this hour the worst attackers— the most unpredictable and most vicious attackers, swarms of teenagers—wouldn't be in a place like this. If they were out at this hour, they'd be at the El stops looking for late-shift workers.

"Can you spare some change?" he said immediately, hearing the desperation in his own voice.

"I think I can help you."

TUESDAY

CHAPTER FIVE

From the *Chicago Sun-Times*,
Tuesday, May 31:
[City News, section B, p. 2]

More than 220 homeless men and women will share a $300,000 settlement among them, an amount decided upon when District Judge Morton Eidesman ruled today that seizure of their personal property was a violation of their rights. Two years ago city workers cleaned Lower Wacker Drive, and in the cleanup the homeless lost their belongings.

The class action lawsuit charged sanitation workers' sweep of Lower Wacker violated the homeless rights in destroying their property.

"It was a denial of our humanity," said William Lyall, one of the plaintiffs. "The judge did the right thing, God bless him."

The city has admitted no wrongdoing.

Tuesday morning, 7:30 A.M.

SERGEANT PAT TOUHY was in her General Patton mode at morning roll call. Touhy had two modes. Clint Eastwood once said to a director that he had two facial expressions and he had given him both. Well, Touhy too. There was General Patton, which was unpleasant enough but you knew where you were with it, or Understanding Superior Officer. Which was a bitch.

You never knew with Ms. Understanding whether the understanding smile was real or a suck-in.

She finished the educational five-minute updating on what probable cause for search meant. Then she said, "Let's get to the day and read some crimes."

"They ever find the other currency exchange asshole?" Bennis asked. "I'd know him if they got him."

"No. And the one you guys got won't talk."

"Shit."

"Except to say Figueroa used excessive force capturing him. Says his liver's bruised."

"Jeez, Sarge," Figueroa said. "He hadda weigh two-fifty. I'm maybe a hundred twenty after two Quarter Pounders with cheese."

"Says you dropped on him when he was down."

"I surely did—"

"You shoulda shot him," Mileski said.

"Yeah. I'll know better next time."

Sandi the Flying None said, "Why didn't you shoot him, Suze? I can't remember why you said you didn't."

Several people groaned. "Humanitarian instincts," Figueroa said.

"Wait a minute!" Bennis said. "Figueroa saved my life. The suits'd better not get any idea of jamming her up!"

"Oh, give it a rest, Bennis," Touhy said. "I know that. The brass knows that. They're going through the motions. Cover their ass. And by the way, Figueroa, get yourself up to Branch 71 soon as we're done here. The ASA on the case wants to interview you before the arraignment. Now, moving right along, we got a problem. The Detective Division had a little medical situation, so some of you—Didrickson, Mileski, O'Hara, Figueroa, and Bennis—are going over to Area Four to do some canvassing for them today. You will also follow up on your own existing cases from yesterday. Bennis and Figueroa—

don't pretend to forget you're still on the pickpockets! We've got a whole lot of highly pricey stores seriously upset."

"Wait a minute, Sarge!" Bennis said. "This means we're doubling. We're working *two* jobs."

"And your point is?" Touhy asked.

"What medical situation?" Mileski asked.

"Last night was the dinner honoring Chief of Detectives Ramon Bartlett on his retirement. Most of the off-duty detectives were there. Maybe two-thirds of the dick roster. They all have food poisoning."

"Some detectives *they* are!" Bennis said.

"What did they eat?" Figueroa asked.

"Apparently they had onion soup gratiné, boeuf bourguignonne, baby peas—"

"I guess it was really barf bourguignonne," said Mileski.

"As a matter of fact, no," said Touhy, who had no sense of humor to speak of, and was certainly not going to put up with one in anybody else. "They think it was the crème anglaise sauce on the dessert. Some of the eggs weren't cooked enough. Or maybe the sauce was held at room temperature too long. Hot weather like this, see. Salmonella, they think. Forty percent of the detectives are off."

"Off for how long?"

"Couple, three days at least. Okay. Here's what we're gonna do. Mileski and Didrickson go as a team, O'Hara all by his lonesome, and Figueroa and Bennis soon as Figueroa gets done with the state's attorney."

Kim Duk O'Hara asked, "But what about speeders and double-parkers and like that, Sarge?"

"I guess Chicago will just have to take its chances today."

At which point they were sent out.

The ASA doing the Herzog case, Herzog being the guy Figueroa had flattened on the golf course, naturally wanted to talk

with Figueroa before the arraignment. Because he was important and Figueroa wasn't important, she was supposed to go to
him. Fortunately, Branch 71, one of a dozen Cook County
criminal courts, was in the same building as the CPD HQ and
the First District police station. In a matter of months, this
agglomeration of offices would all be history. The First District
was moving to new quarters at 1700 South State. The CPD
main offices were getting a whole new building of their very
own. The courts were going God knows where. And the present
building was going to be demolished. "All this history gone!"
some said.

Most said, "And high time too."

For now, not only was the ASA and the court and the First
District in the present building, but as a matter of fact, Herzog
also was in the building, in the men's lockup on the twelfth
floor, just below the women's lockup, on thirteen, called the
"penthouse" by the cops.

If Figueroa had been in some distant district, she would
still have had to go to the ASA. As it was, she gave Bennis a
Hershey bar—with almonds, who said she wasn't a saint?—told
him she hoped she'd be right back, and headed for the elevator.

The ASA, Francis Xavier Malley, was tapping his foot when
she tracked him down in the wide piece of hall that constituted
the back end of the Branch 71 courtroom. Court was not yet
in session. Besides tapping his foot, he had his arms crossed and
his briefcase wedged between his left leg and the adjacent wall.
Suze thought, *And we call the perps assholes.*

"Officer Figueroa?"

"State's Attorney Malley?"

"I asked you to come up forthwith. Herzog will be brought
in any minute now."

"Came as soon as I was told, sir," she said with just a slight
edge in her voice. Back in the academy, an instructor she admired had said, "Don't risk your job for the idiots. There's too

many of them, and a new batch is born every day," and he was absolutely right. She couldn't resist adding, "Course if you ever talk to anybody in charge of speeding up the elevators—"

"Let's get to work. Why'd you pick on Herzog in the first place?"

"Pick on him? Have you read the case report?"

"Yeah. Humor me. His PD wants to go to trial. Says Herzog doesn't want to plead. I need to know how you'd do on the stand."

"We were patrolling on Roosevelt Road, heading toward Michigan Avenue. We got a call from the dispatcher about the robbery, and they had the description of the car, a two-door green Ford, which was presumed to be heading our way. Two male whites. Saw them less than a minute later. Soon as we got behind them they rabbited. Isn't the fact that the cash was on them proof enough?"

"Cash can belong to anybody."

"Oh, please! Both of them running like hell? What about the currency exchange operator? He ID the guy? Description match?"

"It matches, what there is of it, but he didn't see his face. He wore a stocking mask."

"Oh, great. What about the other guy? The guy driving the car?"

"What about him? The currency exchange manager never saw his face at all. He stayed outside in the car with the motor running. Anyway, he hasn't turned up anyplace. You people are supposed to find him, not me."

"Okay. Well, what about dealing with the one we have, get him to give the other guy up? Can't you plead this one to a lesser charge? If maybe this one really wasn't the planner—"

"Malley!" said a voice.

A man in a dark suit with a fine white stripe appeared next to Figueroa. Though no expert on clothes, she could tell the suit was probably half the price of Malley's. Therefore, this had to be the public defender.

"Ben," Malley said without enthusiasm. He added, "Ben Jenks, this is Officer Figueroa."

Jenks held out his hand, but while they shook, he said, "Mr. Herzog is pleading innocent."

Figueroa said, "So why'd he run?"

"You know, officer, a lot of people are afraid of the police. He didn't know what you wanted him for."

"Didn't know but he was pretty sure it was something bad, huh?"

Malley said to Jenks, "We've got him dead-bang on possession of an unregistered firearm."

"I think you've also got him on attempting to kill a police officer," Figueroa said angrily.

As if none of this mattered, Jenks added, "Plus, you used unnecessary force in subduing him, Officer Figueroa. He has the bruises to prove it."

"Jeez, maybe he ought to try not shooting at the cops if he doesn't want bruises."

"We ought to get into the courtroom pretty soon," Malley said to Jenks, as if Figueroa were an idle bystander.

"And the guy is bigger than I am, besides," Figueroa said.

"Doesn't matter," Jenks said.

There was a call in the court, and people started to take their seats.

Malley said, "That's all, officer."

As she turned to walk out of the room, Figueroa saw Herzog. He was coming into the holding pen next to a jail guard, and Jenks, the public defender, went to meet him. Figueroa detoured a few feet and said, "Hiya, Herzog."

Then she moved to stand right next to the prisoner, turned and bumped shoulders with him and caught Jenks's and Malley's gaze. Herzog stood fifteen inches taller than Figueroa. One of his thighs was as big as her whole body. He had to weigh 250, minimum.

Jenks and Malley exchanged glances, as Figueroa knew they would. They were both visualizing a jury taking a look at this picture.

Without a further word, allowing herself just a tiny nod but no smile, she turned away and strode to the elevators.

"Oh, this is so cool!" Figueroa pounded the dashboard in a brisk *rat-tat-tat* as they took off in the car for Area Four.

Bennis said, "What's your problem?"

"I always wanted to be a detective. This is truly the very finest!"

"Well, your calm reserve and stolid, conservative person-ality is a great reassurance to me at all times, given the risky nature of our endeavor," Bennis said.

"Phooey!"

"Hey! Aren't you the young lady who told me that getting home for JJ every day was such a priority? Remember how happy you were that patrol cops put in a regular eight hours and then can go home?"

"Well, sure, but—"

"Most people think cops put in long hours. We know bet-ter. And thank you, union. But detectives sure as hell do."

That was true and it brought Figueroa up short. It was almost impossible to have an unpredictable twelve- or maybe fifteen-hour-a-day job and take good care of a child. Maybe she could get a part-time nanny, she thought. Oh, sure. With whose money? Plus, right now when he was young was when JJ needed her. And there was Sheryl, too, to think about—

Damn.

"Listen," Figueroa said, "JJ isn't going to be seven forever. And anyway long hours is gonna be good practice for when I get to be District Commander."

"Oh, right. I forgot that was the plan."

"And for when I get to be Superintendent of Police."

"Oh, of course!"

"I'll make you Chief of Patrol."

"I'm holding my breath."

She ignored the sarcasm. Bennis was her buddy and if now and then he wanted to pretend to be an asshole, that was his business. But with maybe a bit of retaliation in mind, she asked, "Hey, Bennis! How's Yolanda?"

"Yolanda! What'chu asking about Yolanda for?" he said, doing his street-talk imitation. "You know I haven't seen Yolanda in months. I'm going with Amanda now."

"Yolanda, Amanda, sounds incestuous somehow."

"You got a dirty mind, girl! Besides, Deirdre was between Yolanda and Amanda."

"Between? I'm not gonna touch that with a ten-foot pole."

"And since Mileski isn't here, we don't got ourselves a ten-foot Pole."

CHAPTER SIX

"WASN'T THE CRÈME anglaise," Detective Mossbacher said, pronouncing it to rhyme with cream and grace. Which is how Figueroa would have pronounced it, but she had a feeling Bennis would soon instruct her otherwise. "And not salmonella. Worse."

"Worse than salmonella?" Figueroa said, because she knew he expected her to.

"They think it's E. coli. The bad kind of E. coli." He flipped a memo and pointed a thick finger at a line. "E. coli 0157:H7. Probably in the salad."

Bennis said, "Salad is supposed to be good for you."

"No kidding. They think one of the kitchen employees was a carrier and, much as I hate to say this, guys, did not use proper bathroom cleanliness procedures."

Figueroa said, "Ukkk!"

Since the sick detectives had come from every police area center in the city and therefore every area was depleted, the brass had decided to call in a few patrol cops from each district within each area. This spread the drain on the districts. On the one hand, you couldn't strip the districts, but on the other hand, when you have a homicide, you had to collect the facts ASAP. Eyewitness memories fade, or get falsely augmented by gossip or by inaccurate newspaper and TV reports. Trace evidence gets stepped on or blown away.

So Bennis and Figueroa had been sent over to Area Four. In Chicago, patrol officers work out of districts, of which there are twenty-five, and detectives work out of areas, of which there are five. The First District was part of Area Four, which was located way the hell west at 3151 W. Harrison. It covered Districts One, Ten, Eleven, Twelve, and Thirteen. This made it sort of an elongated east-west slice of the very center of the city.

Bennis and Figueroa and the rest of the First District crew had waited in the main room for their assignment. The place seemed quieter than usual to Figueroa, although she had never spent much time here. She thought in the last two years she'd been here at most maybe four times, tops, for one reason or another. Maybe the detectives were all out rushing around at double speed, covering for their sick colleagues.

Mileski and Sandi the Flying None got called in first. Mileski and Sandi got the job of canvassing businesses and restaurants around the scene of an armed bank robbery that had happened last evening. Kim Duk O'Hara got to canvass a luxury Loop hotel all alone about the death by choking of a beautiful young lady—a plum assignment, indoors and in air-conditioned premises. But the ingrate grumbled about it. He really loved tooling around in a squad car with Mars lights and sirens. And who could blame him?

Bennis and Figueroa were called last. "See Detective Mossbacher. Left door at the end of the hall."

Mossbacher was the "Grizzled Veteran." Old-style cop. Red face. Shiny shoes. His hair was cut very short on the sides and long on top. Figueroa's mind produced a picture of him at age twenty-two, a new recruit, short sides and long on top, the "in" style at the time. Probably he had been in style once or twice through the years, and again now, and never in his life changed his haircut.

"Have I got a deal for you," he said, grinning.

CHAPTER SEVEN

THE HOUSE WAS dead quiet. Stifling heat soaked the attic, and it wasn't even ten A.M. yet. His watch still ran, another piece of good luck. Maybe one of those batteries that go on forever because the company forgot to put in the obsolescence factor. After the horrible luck on Monday, he deserved a whole lot of these little pieces of good luck.

The bad luck right now was the heat. The attic didn't even have an exhaust fan, and the dark-shingled roof hung hot right over his head. He could actually feel the direction of the radiating heat—it glowed in at him, coming from the east side of the roof, as if it were a space heater. Afternoon would be even worse.

Didn't these people know you should have an exhaust fan in your attic? Didn't they realize how much money you could save on your air-conditioning if you got rid of the heat up here? Fools!

Then he remembered how much money he had not saved in his life. Of course, that hadn't been his fault. He'd had a problem, that was all, and it ate money. Lawyers ate money.

He was dripping sweat. He hated to sweat. It was unsanitary.

Maybe he could go down to the third floor and spend the day there. It would be cooler, and as long as he didn't fall asleep, it would be okay. None of the family would get home before three-thirty at the earliest, would they? And he knew from yesterday that the cop got home about five, and the man had got home yesterday at six.

Maybe he could sleep on the kid's bed. Who'd notice? Little boys were sweaty, dirty monsters anyhow, weren't they?

He moved slowly and softly down the back stairs, stopping to listen. He reached the third-floor landing. It was so quiet he heard the refrigerator door close, two flights down, although that was partly because the kitchen was right next to the foot of these back stairs. He heard the nurse say, "There. Now let's see."

She was talking to the paralyzed woman. He heard her feet clump across the hall and into the spaz's room. God, what a clumsy, stupid person. He moved down another flight, to the second-floor landing.

"Now, Ms. Sheryl," the nurse said, "how about a nice bath?"

Bath! Oh, God, how he'd love a bath. He had to have a shower or a bath. Had to. Had to. *Had to!*

"Now you just wait. We'll make a nice lukewarm one. Too hot today for a hot bath, don't you think? We could get in a short bath before the therapist gets here."

"Margle. Uz."

Margle uz! he thought. What a retard.

"Or I suppose you might want it after you do all that exercising. No, I guess this is the best time. All right?"

Then he heard the bathwater running, and he got the brilliant idea. Rushing back up the stairs as fast as he could without making a sound, he hurried into the third-floor bathroom and turned on the water in the tub. He held his arm in the stream so that it wouldn't splash. A couple of inches of cool water was all he needed. Maybe a little more.

With the pipes running the bath for the spaz, there would be pipe noise. The old pipes in this old house were predictably clanky. Surely the stupid nurse wouldn't notice a little more gurgling and bumping.

What if she did?

He kept his eyes on the open door to the hall. If she did—? Well, now, if she did—if she did hear, if she did appear, if she did see him, well, these old houses had steep, old stairs. Why, they weren't even up to current building codes. She'd probably just have an unfortunate fall.

CHAPTER EIGHT

Tuesday, 10 A.M.

"POOR GUY!" FIGUEROA said. "The poor old guy!"

Bennis said, "Yeah," very subdued. "He looks just like my grandfather."

"Bennis, your grandfather is black."

"So? Also he probably looks just like *your* grandfather, Figueroa."

"Yeah, he surely does."

"He looks just like everybody's grandfather, you know?"

"Yes," she said, sadly, "I know."

"If you guys are gonna get sick, just leave," the pathologist said.

Figueroa said, "I'm *not*," with more force than was absolutely necessary. And she meant it.

Bennis said, "No ID at all?" He gestured at the clothes and "effects" on the rack eight feet back from the autopsy table. The only effects were a bottle with a label of some cheap wine and an inch or so left in it, and a McDonald's coffee cup. And eighty-eight cents—two quarters, three dimes, a nickel, and three pennies.

The diener, who had stripped the body for the autopsy, said, "Nope. Plus most of his pockets had holes in the bottom."

"Poor old guy," Bennis said, echoing her. That's one of the reasons Figueroa liked Norm Bennis, she thought to herself. Eleven years as a cop and he still hadn't lost his center. He was actually able to be tough on the job without being heartless.

"Well, now let's see." The pathologist, a chubby man in his early sixties, clapped his hands once. He had a Santa Claus beard and wore bright green-and-yellow checked pants finished off with oxblood tassel loafers peeking out under his lab coat. Most of the M.D.s here wore scrub suits and booties. Autopsies were a messy business. Dr. Percolin, however, wore the long lab coat and clear plastic covers over his stylish shoes, leaving his trouser bottoms open to possible splashing. He drew on two pair of gloves with that slapping noise people who wear surgical gloves love to make. *Puts the rest of us nonprofessionals in our place,* Figueroa thought. Although to be fair, Dr. Percolin here was accessible and friendly. "So you're the newbies!" he said. "Well, this is gonna be different. Ever seen an autopsy?"

"Of course," Bennis said.

"During training," Figueroa said. "The academy schedules autopsies for us. And twice when we filled in for one of the detectives."

"You're experts then, huh?" Before they could protest, he said, "Don't mind me teasing you. I've been doing this for twenty-two years and I still learn something new pretty much every day. Which is why I love it, mmm? And by the way, if you ever run into a pathologist who says he knows every-thing"—he fixed them with a very serious face—"run fast. Guys like that are a menace. Guys like that send innocent people to prison. Always check their results, mmm? But enough of this cheery chitchat."

Percolin studied the exterior of the naked body minutely, using a magnifying glass now and then to aid his eye. Then he directed the diener to make extra photos with a Polaroid CU-5 close-up camera of certain parts, including the nose.

He and the assistant turned the body over. After studying the back for hypostasis, which they found, they turned it again. With the body once again supine, he mumbled the usual intro into his foot-activated mike. "The body is that of a poorly nourished white male, seventy-one inches in length, one hundred and thirty-two pounds, hair gray, eyes brown. Rigor just passing off in the jaw and neck. We have what appears to be an appendectomy scar, normal size and location."

Suze couldn't see any fresh wounds on the body except a slight abrasion on the nose, which the doctor had included in his recorded notes. There seemed to be no obvious cause of death. "Hypostasis consistent with lying on back," Percolin said to the mike.

Mike off, Dr. Percolin pointed at the face and said, "Strangulation, I guess. Say, look at this."

"Dirty," Bennis said.

"I shouldn't have said look at this. I should have said smell this."

"We already do."

"Not that."

The body gave off a ripe, sweaty odor, in addition to the usual smells of feces and urine that cling to death. But Dr. Percolin had his nose right down near the corpse's unlovely neck.

Bennis leaned forward. The old man's chin rested above a filthy chest. And at that instant a bug, a real living insect, crawled out from the left armpit.

"Yo!" Bennis said.

The doc said, "Little critter must've just warmed up. They're real quiescent in the cooler."

The bug dropped onto the floor. The doc and the diener ignored it.

"Let's have you do this methodically. Look at the body as a whole," Percolin said.

Suze looked. The hair around the crotch of the old man was stained, and some of the gold granular stuff might be crystallized urine. The ankles were dark brownish gray with grime, darkest just above where the socks might have ended. But Fi-

gueroa said to Dr. Percolin, "The hands and face are clean."
The face was unshaven, with a three- or four-day beard, but
what skin could be seen was pink and washed.

"So he stopped someplace and washed up," Bennis said. "So
what?"

Percolin looked at Bennis and waggled his head. "Not
good, officer. You're a detective now."

"Okay. Tell me."

"Now. Like I said before, smell this."

"Yeah, yeah, okay."

Bennis leaned over the corpse and smelled where Percolin
pointed. First the face, then the hands. After Bennis, Figueroa
smelled, too. She said, "Hey! They're different!"

"Exactly." Figueroa received a big Santa Claus smile.
"What do you deduce?"

"He washed his hands with some kind of liquid soap. Cheap
stuff, like in public bathrooms and court buildings. I've used it
a thousand times myself."

"And the face?"

"Different. It could be one of those pre-moistened towelette things. Lemon-scented."

"Exactly."

"But why not use the same stuff for both your hands and
face?"

"Who knows? That's the question, isn't it?"

Figueroa realized that Percolin had gone through this sniff-
ing process before making a cut. He didn't want to confuse the
external smells with blood odors.

Dr. Percolin placed a block under the man's neck, angling
the head back. He revealed a yellow-brown, papery-dry groove
around the front and sides of the neck. With the wrinkled and
drooping skin covering it, Figueroa had not noticed the groove
before, even when the body had been turned facedown and then

onto its back again. "How'd you know that he'd been strangled?"

"Genius," Percolin said. "I wish. Actually, it's about as subtle as saying a guy was shot when he has a circular hole in his
chest with powder burns around it. See, his face is swollen. Not
so obvious as some cases, because he's old, but enough to notice.
And look at the eyes. See these little hemorrhages in the
whites?" He pulled the lids back to show the eyes to her. "Petechial hemorrhages, they're called. They're in the other mem-
branes around the eye, too, but you can see them better against
the whites. And there are more here on the skin of the face.
See?"

"I see. So if a victim is hanged or strangled, you see these
petechial—"

"No. Not hanged. Strangled. If the victim is truly hanged,
the body falls from a height. There's a sharp drop and all the
arteries in the neck are closed down instantly. But when you
strangle somebody, the interior arteries running up near the
vertebrae go on pumping. But at the same time the veins carrying the blood back are compressed, so the blood has nowhere
to go."

"And pressure builds up."

"Exactly. Now let's take a look at the groove around the
neck. See, it goes only three-quarters of the way around. The
back of the neck shows no groove."

"Strangled from behind," Figueroa said.

"Sure. But we'll put that together with the roughish abrasion on the nose—"

"Strangled after being pushed onto his face!" Figueroa said.

"Or simply held facedown. The cord around his neck was
pulled up from behind. And maybe then he struggled. You're a
studious type, are you? Hmmm?"

Bennis said with some vigor, "She certainly is."

Santa Percolin smiled broadly and asked, "Or an ambitious type?"

Figueroa shrugged. "A cop is what I always wanted to be. I'd like to make detective. I'd like to do everything there is on the job."

"Well, my dear, why not? You only go around once in life."

He opened the body with a Y incision, from each shoulder to the breastbone and then down to the pubis, filling the air with a meaty smell. He cracked the chest, humming as he did. He detached the organs in one large unit. Most of his work was done with just one knife, its blade about a foot long and very sharp. The diener swung the dissecting tray near the torso and then he and Percolin lifted the organ bloc onto the tray. Percolin cut into the pericardial sac around the heart and felt inside the pulmonary artery for clots. "Heart's not bad-looking, considering," he said to Bennis and Figueroa. "He could have gone on a fair number of years, poor old guy."

Percolin was sympathetic enough, Figueroa thought, without being maudlin. Unlike the doc in her first autopsy, who made hideous jokes at the expense of the deceased to tease the recruits, Percolin respected the dead man's dignity, covering his genitals when not actually cutting there. But he hummed like a bee as he worked: "Roamin' in the Gloamin' " and "You Take the High Road."

As he continued, stepping on the foot pedal frequently to trigger the audio recording device, Dr. Percolin lost some of his jolly Santa persona. Figueroa wondered why the change. Maybe he was finding evidence of another, mysterious cause of death in addition to the strangulation, or maybe an unexpected disease. However, his comments to the recorder didn't suggest it.

Having reached the digestive system in his dissection, he ladled out the contents of the stomach. "No food in here," he said. "Just booze. Smells like scotch. What do you think, Officer Bennis?"

"Scotch. Good scotch, in fact," said Bennis, who was a gourmet.

"I think you're right. Good scotch. Which is a little odd, when you've got eighty-eight cents in your pocket, isn't it?"

But Percolin's pensiveness had begun before the scotch, so that was not the cause.

The dead man had a small ulcer. "Which is no wonder. That's pretty much to be expected with a drinker who doesn't eat," Percolin remarked aside.

He found liver disease, moderately advanced, which was no surprise, either. "I still say he could have got a few more years of life out of this body." No appendix, consistent with the appendectomy scar. Nothing much else. Percolin took samples of blood for a tox screen and the vitreous humor of the eye for ethanol. And tissue samples. And stomach and intestinal contents samples.

"You can start reassembling the guy, Jimmy," he said. "You did the prints, right?"

"Always."

"I knew that."

"I'd like a copy of the ten-print too, if it's okay," Bennis said. "I want to run it through AFIS and the FBI records."

Figueroa said, "That's it? We're done?"

Percolin said, "We're done *here*. The tox'll take a week to ten days."

"That's too long," she said, worrying that they would be sent back to being patrol officers before then.

Percolin said, "Don't worry about it, Officer Figueroa. I'd be astonished if anything special showed up. I think you've got what you've got."

"All right, Doc. Then what's bothering you?"

His pink cheeks bunched up in a smile. "I like you, Figueroa," he said. "You've got all your marbles."

"Thanks. But what is it?"

"Tell you what I'm gonna do. Jimmy, get me some vials and sterile water."

The assistant brought sealed packages. Percolin changed gloves, then opened a plastic stoppered tube. He set it next to the dead man's shoulder. Then he ripped open a package of sterile gauze. The assistant poured water on the gauze in Percolin's hand, and Percolin wiped one side of the clean part of the victim's face with the wet gauze. Immediately, he put the piece of fabric in the tube and stoppered it. He repeated the whole process with the other side of the face. Then the clean forehead.

"I'll see if we can get an analysis of what was used to wash his face. There are several ways to detect very small traces of chemicals. Assuming most of them haven't evaporated. Who knows? The point is to get a profile of the wiping fluid."

Figueroa said, "Don't you mean what *he* used to wash his face?"

"I doubt it. I think we're going to find out what *somebody* used to wash his face."

"The *killer* washed his victim's face?"

"I hardly think it was an idle passerby, do you?"

Bennis said, "No, of course not. But why? Why would you even think so? It's not like he couldn't have washed his hands, say, at the bus depot and then got hold of a Wet Wipes wherever he bought his scotch."

Percolin was grim. "I'll tell you why. I had a peculiar case a week or ten days ago. A drifter—a homeless man, I suppose. Smothered with some extra clothing he carried around in his bag. Not strangled. His hands were quite dirty. But his face had been washed, and the skin smelled just like this."

Out in the squad car, Bennis said, "Does the doc think we've got a serial killer?"

"With just two possibles? I don't know."

"It's far-fetched."

"And a killer who washes faces?" Figueroa said. "It's nuts."

"So? Killers are sometimes nuts. Maybe usually."

"But somebody washed the faces of those two men."

"They washed their own faces."

"Wait a minute," Figueroa said. "There *is* a way we can tell whether it was the killer who washed the dead man's face. We can look at the site search."

"For what?"

"For the used lemon-scented Wet Wipes or Handi Wipes or Wet Ones or whatever. The evidence techs should have picked everything up. If the wipe was lying near the body, the dead man might have used it himself or the killer might have used it and dropped it. But if it's gone, then the killer took it away, which means the killer washed the guy's face."

"Hey, that's brilliant." Then Bennis's expression changed. "No, wait. It's not brilliant. Sorry—brilliant but not conclusive. The victim could have washed his face someplace else and left the Wet Wipes there."

"Oh! Damn! You're right."

They drove in gloom for several minutes. Then Figueroa said, "No, there *is* a way to tell."

"What?"

"Stop the car! I've got to call Dr. Percolin."

"Use my cell phone."

"The victim's nose was abraded while he was lying on the ground being strangled by the killer. Okay. If he washed his own face earlier, the nose abrasion should be dirty. If the abrasion is as clean as the rest of the face, *the killer washed him after he was dead!*"

CHAPTER NINE

"**HERE ARE THE** files on the earlier case," Detective Moss-bacher said. He shoved a large manila folder across his desk at Bennis and Figueroa. "Some homeless guy named James Manualo. Body found in the alley under the El the morning of May twenty-first, and he was probably killed just a few hours earlier. But I doubt you'll get anywhere with it."

"We want to go back over the interviews on the Manualo thing in light of this new killing."

"Yeah, well, two senior detectives worked it for a week."

"Full-time? For a week?"

"Of course not full-time."

"Anyway, we have more information now than they had," Figueroa said. "At least we have another case—" Before the end of her sentence, though, they heard a scream from the hallway outside.

All three of them bolted to their feet and went running out, Bennis and Mossbacher jamming together shoulder to shoulder in the door. Figueroa pushed Bennis hard from the back and he popped out the other side.

Even though the three of them had their hands on their sidearms, as soon as they got into the main lobby it was clear they didn't need weapons. A secretary—what the cops called "a mere lowly civilian"—was standing rigid in the central hall screaming. She was looking at a man who was obviously a detective. He wore civilian clothes, but he wore a sidearm and you could always tell a cop, anyway, Figueroa thought. Blue suit, white shirt, shiny black shoes. The man had fallen to his knees and was vomiting on the floor.

A second man was rushing to help him.

"Back!" Mossbacher barked. "Stop right there, Godfrey!"

"But he needs help."

The sick man staggered to his feet.

"Godfrey! Get away! Paul! Sit down! Don't even try to get up." Mossbacher yelled at the desk. "Anne, call the EMTs!" Godfrey turned and headed for the desk sergeant's telephone, but Anne, the desk sergeant, was already punching in the number.

"I don't need any help," the sick man said. "I'm okay."

Godfrey turned back again to help him.

"Freeze right there, Godfrey," Mossbacher said. "For all I know you and everybody else here can get contaminated with E. coli, and *you* sure as hell don't know it's impossible."

"I don't need the paramedics," the sick man said.

And just as Mossbacher said, "I say you do," the man's eyes rolled up in his head and he fell forward, limp as a dead squid, right in the mess.

Mossbacher said, "Bennis. Figueroa. What are you standing here for?"

"See if we can help," Bennis said.

"You can help by taking the fucking file and getting out of here. Shit, your whole case is just a couple of homeless bums anyhow!"

Figueroa had a message on her pager to call Dr. Percolin. Bennis still held the file of the Manualo case.

"Let's go read that in the Furlough," Figueroa said. "And call the doc."

"Are you nuts? You can't go in a bar while you're working."

"Why not? We really *are* working."

"Oh, stifle that. Everything's image," Bennis said. So they

went back to the First District and sat at a table in the break room with the coffee, candy, and chips machines.

"You know that cop who collapsed at Area Four? Can E. coli take that long to develop?" Figueroa asked.

"Indeed, Suze, my man. It usually comes on in twenty-four hours, but it can take longer. There could still be quite a few more cases."

"When it takes longer, does that mean it's more serious or less serious?"

"E. coli 0517:H7 is always serious, and it's often fatal. The detectives have a real problem." Bennis sounded gloomy.

"How come you always know everything?" Figueroa asked, to lighten him up.

"You should be grateful."

Figueroa used the phone. She came back grinning.

"Your guess was right," Bennis said.

"Yup. The old man's nose abrasion was clean."

"Shit. The killer got him drunk. Flipped him on his stomach. Strangled him while he was lying on his face. Then turned him over and washed his face! This is one cold bastard, Suze."

Her smile vanished. "Yeah. He's gotta be a real madman."

Sergeant Touhy marched in, heading toward the candy machine. "What are you two doing here?"

"Working." Figueroa pointed at the files spread out on the table.

"Oh, good," Touhy said, looking at the papers. *What is this?* Figueroa wondered. *Sergeant Touhy—not crabbing at us, not snarling, not folding her arms and waiting for a better answer? No huffy snorts?*

"What's wrong, Sarge?" Figueroa asked.

"One of the detectives died. The E. coli got to his kidneys."

"Young guy, black hair, skinny, first name Paul?" Figueroa asked, thinking of the man who had collapsed in front of them.

"No. He was fifty-eight."

"Oh."

"He was my partner for a year, back when we were both uniforms."

This was getting worse and worse, Figueroa thought. Touhy with a heart? What next? Quiche and a chilled Chablis in the break room at lunch?

CHAPTER TEN

"HEY, MORT" MILESKI said, leaning both elbows on the bar. "Why did *you* pull the pin?"

"Ah, you don't wanna know." Unlike his partner Corky, Mort had always been a man of few words, and most of them grumpy. The gang was hanging around the Furlough Bar, about ten people just off the second watch.

Mileski said, "Yeah, I do."

"Nothin' much. You don't wanna know."

"Yeah, we all do," Mileski said, sending his gaze around the room very slowly. Everybody did a radio-show chorus of "mm-mmm" and "oh, doubtless" and "yo!" and "we do, we do."

"Ah, hell, I just got tired of getting pissed on."

"By your sergeant? The ungrateful public?"

Mort said nothing. Just shrugged. Figueroa said, "You know you gotta tell us now. You really can't just stop the story there."

He frowned horribly at her, but finally said, "Nah. I got tired of getting pissed on. My last case. I wasn't a detective, see. I'm on patrol, minding my own business, Nineteenth District, I get this radio call, check the well-being."

Mileski said, "Sure."

Silence. Three people simultaneously said, "Go on!" and Mileski added, "Dammit!"

"Oh, all right. All right. Dispatcher says check out a woman at this apartment building. So I go. Well, check the well-being indeed!" Having once started, he seemed ready to keep talking. "Female maybe twenty years old, back bedroom, dead at least three days, hot weather too, mother snuffling and wringing her hands and pacing back and forth. Body's bloated, but you can see the blood on the shirt and bed, and I call it in."

"Yeah. So then what?"

"I figure they knew she was dead for a coupla days at least. I mean, this is all one apartment, and only three bedrooms for what looks like seven people—mother, father, girl, four brothers. So they called when the girl got so ripe they didn't know what else to do. And the brothers are all 'and shits.' "

Kim Duk said, "Huh? What's that?"

Mort stopped, Kim Duk having broken the grudging flow, but Mileski flapped his hands to the side like a conductor and nodded fiercely.

Mort said, "They're like they never heard of 'and so forth' or 'etcetera' or 'and so on.' Or even 'and like that.' "

"I don't get it," Kim Duk said.

"They say like 'I'm going to the store for bread and shit.' Or 'we met him in the alley and bashed him and kicked him and shit.' "

"Oh."

"What ethnicity?" Bennis asked.

"Middle European. The parents speak with an accent. But 'and shit' is the universal language."

Figueroa said, "Yeah. Surely is."

Mileski said, "Go on."

"So I call it in and I close the bedroom door, 'cause it reeks, and I go wait in the hall to tell the guys where the body is. And I'm goin' down the hall past the four brothers and they open their flies and piss on me."

Dead silence. Finally, Figueroa said, "What did you do? Arrest them?"

"By myself? By the time the two detectives come in the door, like twenty minutes later, the brothers are gone. Plus, what am I gonna arrest them for?"

Kim Duk said, "Assaulting an officer?"

"Oh, no doubt, Kim Duk. I'm gonna want to be known as the man who was assaulted by four penises. Make me feel like a big man, wouldn't it?"

"Well, they shouldn't be allowed—"

"Forget about it. I had twenty years in then. I basically quit."

The Flying None said, "Why didn't they like you? Had they killed their sister?"

Mort shrugged. Then he decided to utter a few more words. "Naw. The boyfriend killed her. Stabbed her."

"So then why?"

"Number one, they didn't like cops. Number two, if we picked up the boyfriend they couldn't get to him."

"Get to him?"

"They didn't think the criminal justice system was firm enough. As soon as they found him, they were going to take care of him their way."

Figueroa left the bar in plenty of time to pick up some groceries on her way home to start dinner.

Today's closest parking space was three and a half blocks away in front of a blue, white, and muted salmon house. By her reckoning three-plus blocks was a medium-bad omen. She'd have to watch her back for the rest of the day.

Really, I'm not that superstitious, she told herself as she walked, carrying the bags of groceries. Mainly it gave her something to do while she was walking home.

Robert, of course, got use of the garage, but it was so rickety that someday either a stiff wind or a thick, wet snow would collapse the old structure. *Better on his car than mine.*

It was nearly five o'clock, and this time of year it wouldn't be dark for a couple more hours, but the sun was hot orange in the western sky when Suze walked in the door. She dumped the groceries and then went through her usual firearm-safety routine.

She poked her head into Sheryl's room. Sheryl said, "Umph!" Suze didn't know what this meant, but didn't need to when Sheryl turned away from her. There were tears in Sheryl's eyes, and Suze knew she didn't want anybody to see them.

Suze backed out quickly, saying, "I'm hot and I better wash up. Back in five." And she hiked fast up the back stairs to her floor.

Shucking her jacket, she walked into the bathroom. The first thing she always did, even in cold weather, was to splash water on her face and give it a good rub. She knew that symbolically she was erasing the effects of eight hours in the squad car and cop-shop, and the residue of nasty people, pitiful people, drugged people, bruised people, and angry people.

Next she always washed her hands. She washed her hands as often as she could on the job, very conscious of the fact that a lot of the people she came in contact with could have drug-resistant TB. Partly she was protecting herself, of course, partly protecting Sheryl, who in her condition was terribly vulnerable to lung infections, even ordinary flu and colds. And partly she was protecting Maria, Kath, and J J.

She picked up the soap.

It was damp.

Damp on top, wet on the bottom.

How very odd, she thought. *Alma never comes up here.* Suze took care of the third floor herself, vacuuming and cleaning both her room and J J's. Anyway Alma didn't clean the house or sort clothes or anything like that. Her job was Sheryl. J J and both girls had left home at quarter to seven this morning. Suze had dropped them at school herself on her way to work. The school had an early social hour, which the school called "breakfast club," for children whose parents had to get to work. Robert hadn't left by then, having to wait with Sheryl until

Alma got there, but he had his own bathroom on the second
floor. Besides that, he was always out of the house by eight-
fifteen at the latest. It was now four-thirty in the afternoon.

Suze went downstairs intending to ask Alma why she'd been
up on the third floor, trying to figure out a way of phrasing the
question so that it didn't imply any sort of criticism. But when
she got downstairs she remembered Sheryl's sadness and then,
looking into the room, Suze realized from the twitching of
Sheryl's right leg that she wanted to be sat up and leaned forward to ease her aching back. Suze forgot about the soap.

11:35 P.M.

THE WOMAN WITH the shopping cart hesitated at the corner
of Eleventh and Wabash. From there she could see into the
dark area under the El. The El ran behind police headquarters,
down Holden Court. Underneath Holden Court was an alley
that cops used as a shortcut to the CPD parking lot. Although
it had once been paved, the tar had broken up in the freeze-
and-thaw cycle of many winters since then, and nobody had
fixed it. Huge potholes pitted the five-block stretch, making
even low speeds treacherous. Most of it was now such a mess
that to avoid potholes as well as trash, cars took a curving path
through it. The sides were wino country. Some larger piles of
muck near the uprights of the El were used by the homeless
for beds.

The old woman knew the alley was where you could get
the best bottles and cans. It wasn't just the winos that threw
them around; it was the cops, too. Or cops mostly, to be honest
about it. She'd seen more than a few cops toss cans out of their
cars before turning into the lot. Didn't want to be caught with
open alcohol, she figured.

She peered into the alley. The trouble was the El cut off
most of the light from streetlamps and the whole alley was a
tunnel into a dark jungle.

Still, with another few cans she could get enough deposit money at the All-Day-All-Nite to buy a bottle of cheap wine. She stirred the cans and bottles in her basket, counting them, but lost count at thirty-one when the ones she'd pushed to one side fell back into the uncounted pile on the other side. Never mind. She'd been doing this a long time and she knew from experience that she needed several more.

She steered the cart into the alley. There were potholes every few feet and she protected the cart from the bounces by easing the front wheels up as she let the back wheels down into hole after hole. Faintly, this stirred memories of pushing Danny in his stroller, leaning the stroller back to go down over a curb. Danny would be—what?—twenty-eight now? No, maybe thirty? She wondered where he was living. Was he married? Did she have grandchildren? Maybe a little girl? She sure would like to see a granddaughter if she existed.

Sometimes it puzzled her that so much of her life had vanished from her memory. She remembered being a child, remembered that clearly. There were bright fragments that rose into her mind unbidden. New snow. And staying home from school when there was a blizzard and her mother making lamb stew. But of the last fifteen or twenty years or so—?

Then the El clattered by overhead and the loud gnashing of metal wheels on metal tracks blew everything else out of her head. Soot sifted down.

It was like being inside a metal dinosaur here, under the tracks, inside its huge splayed metal ribs.

And near one of the uprights was a little drift of five or six Bud Light cans. Wonderful. She laughed happily.

She scooped them up in her arms and dropped them in her cart, saying "Whee!" In a pothole a few feet farther along, a band of light glinted on two amber bottles. She hoped they wouldn't turn out to be broken. Stores were supposed to take them back, even if they were, but just try to tell the clerks that.

They didn't have any respect. And people threw empty bottles anywhere they wanted, just as if they were cans. Nobody had any manners anymore.

The bottles were both broken. She put her hands to her face and cried for a little while, then wiped at the tears, smearing dirt across her cheekbones and nose.

When she took her hand away from her eyes, she saw a figure standing near her, backlit against the distant street glow.

"A lady shouldn't cry," a voice said.

"I'm not crying."

"Yes, you were. But I can make you feel better. Look what I have."

Even against the light, she could see the bottle in his hand. Light shone warmly through the amber liquid. The bottle had that expensive, tailored look. He tilted it, making the liquor lap back and forth enticingly.

"We can have a party," he said. "You'll feel much better afterward."

WEDNESDAY

CHAPTER ELEVEN

From: "Boul Mich Beat"
by Mike Rocco
Chicago Today, Wednesday, June 1

The City Council, in its wisdom, has decided to take up the problem of homelessness. But Councilman Ed Voladivic announced at the start of debate: "Why are we worrying about this? It's summer. The homeless bums out there aren't cold."

And his colleague in insensitivity, Cordell Wasserstrom, said, "I pay thousands for my kid to go on Outward Bound trips and sleep in the woods. What's the problem?"

Well, I'll tell ya, Ed and Cordy. Maybe we don't all want to sleep in the woods. And maybe sleeping on Lower Wacker is more like sleeping in a jungle.

I mean, who really enjoys a cement pillow? And if the great Chicago outdoors is so wonderful, why don't the Embassy Suites and the Holiday Inn and the Omni and the Palmer House go out of business?

Hell, why don't we rent six-foot stretches of Michigan Avenue sidewalk to tourists at big bucks? And six-foot stretches of LaSalle at cut rates. Send your kid to Grant Park for the night. Discounts for the under-twelve set.

Here's a fine new way for the city to make money. No?

BENNIS RECEIVED THE call at 3:21 A.M., and was not pleased. He got moving immediately, though. After he arrived on the scene, he agreed to call Figueroa himself. "Under the El, near Eighth," he said to her. "Can't miss it. You'll see the lights."

"All right."

Suze dressed fast in her uniform, belt, and all the accoutrements, and went down the stairs to the second floor. Since she had her own phone line, the call had not awakened Robert. She knocked on Robert's open door.

"What the hell is it?"

"I'm on call. I have to go out."

"Why do you have to wake me up?"

"You probably'll have to get the kids ready for school."

"Oh, shit!"

"Robert, just give them cereal. It doesn't have to be a hot breakfast."

"Yeah, yeah."

"And don't bother to pack lunches. Give them lunch money. If I'm not home by seven A.M., you'll have to drive them to school."

"Mmmph."

"You'll have to call school, too, and tell them the kids will be late, because Miss Sturdley won't be here until eight. You know they take roll at pre-class, too, so the school needs to be told."

"Damn it!"

"Sorry."

He knows all this himself. He just wants to complain. Why should I apologize?

Suze went on down the stairs. Robert probably would not bother to reset his alarm and so he wouldn't get up before his usual hour. He never got the kids up if he could avoid it. But JJ would wake him or would get Kath to wake him. The kids knew Suze could be called out sometimes. They all had alarm clocks.

She tiptoed down the last flight of stairs, even though the kids generally slept as if on an IV anesthetic. Except of course when you wanted them to sleep, which was when they woke up, which was why she was so careful now.

As she hit the first-floor hall, she heard a scurrying sound. Sheryl? Sheryl was often restless. She kicked and writhed as she lay there in bed. She was sleepless a lot, in fact, which wasn't surprising since she was basically bedridden.

Still Suze thought the sound had come from the other direction, maybe the kitchen. She passed through the kitchen on her way to the back door, but saw nothing.

She hoped it had been a mouse and not a rat. One of their neighbors had rats and claimed all these old houses harbored them. Suze didn't think so. The idea of rats made her shiver. Rats in the walls. Creeping along on the other side of the plaster, just inches from your head, for all you knew. Ick! Rats with their dirty yellow fangs and naked ugly tails, living with you without you knowing it, slinking slyly through the house while she slept. Horrible.

By the time she hit the street, her annoyance with Robert and her thoughts of rats had faded, overtaken by curiosity about the murder Bennis had sketchily described, and by the time she parked in the CPD lot on State Street, eagerness made the blood sing in her ears.

She didn't want anybody to be dead. Really, she didn't. But if somebody was dead, she wanted to be the cop to solve the crime.

———

Harry Pressfield was one of the first-watch uniforms, who worked eleven to seven. He ordinarily left the district just as Bennis and Figueroa came on at seven, and they knew him slightly from chatting in the locker room. Pressfield had found the crumpled body near an El support at three A.M., on his way from coffee break back to the CPD building.

It was easy enough for Figueroa to locate the crime scene. The usual group of cops and equipment had assembled around it. When Figueroa strode up, it was nearly four A.M. Bennis was peering down at the small, rigid corpse.

Mossbacher was here, too. He looked rumply and out of sorts, his eyes red and his nose pink. Was he a drinker, Figueroa wondered, or did he just stay up too late? Unable to sleep after his tour, like a lot of cops? Too jazzed? Too stressed?

The dead person was a woman. This was not immediately obvious, as the hair was bunched under the head and the clothes, wrapped around her like a cocoon, could have been worn by a lot of male homeless. The clothes looked more suitable for a woman, but the homeless wore what they could get. Figueroa was surprised, although she shouldn't have been, that it was a woman. Occasionally hookers were killed in this area. Hadn't been any for a couple of months, though.

And this was an old woman. She wore a dozen layers of clothing, despite the warm weather—a cloth coat that might have been real cashmere, probably discarded when the elbows wore through. Its hem was badly stained. Under it were a flower-patterned blouse with blue morning glories and green vines, chartreuse stirrup stretch pants, and peeking out at the waist some sort of purple tunic or leotard, shreds of purple hanging out. When Figueroa was in high school she had done a report on the Middle Ages and she had explained that the poor people in those days just put a new garment atop other older garments, letting the older clothes underneath wear out, rot, and shred, and eventually fall off like dead leaves. The other students had been horrified, of course, accustomed as they were to washing machines, clean clothes, and new clothes whenever anything wore out. But here was a present-day example.

The woman's hair was gray and thin and caked with dirt. Her arms were like sticks. Her hands were dusty. The eyes were sunken and half-closed. The ankles were grimy.

And the face was clean.

Mossbacher said "Figueroa," as if it were a greeting, and then walked over to the second uniform, a first-watch female officer who looked familiar to Figueroa, although no name came to her mind. Mossbacher gestured to the woman, showing her where he wanted her to put the yellow barrier tape. The woman tied one end of it to a telephone pole, walked the spool across the alley, and ran the tape twice around the leg of an El support. Then she moved fifteen feet farther along a sagging stretch of chain-link fencing. With the holes in the fence too small to push the tape spool through, she puzzled for a few seconds, then pulled out a three-foot length from the spool and broke off the end, pushed the end through a hole in the fence, and pulled it out another hole. Then she tied the spool end to the torn end and continued back across the alley. When she reached the place where she had started, she tied the whole thing off and took out two AUTHORIZED PERSONNEL ONLY signs. These she duct-taped carefully, one north of the body on the telephone pole and one south onto the brick side of a building. Pleased, she stood with her hands behind her back and waited for further orders.

Mossbacher took out his cell phone and dialed.

Meanwhile, Figueroa and Bennis studied the body. The woman lay on her back, legs slightly bent, one arm over her chest, the other out to the side. A shopping cart filled with bottles and cans was a few feet away.

An evidence tech circled the dead woman, taking photographs. He was a man of about forty, with hair cut to within a half inch of his scalp. He wore Levi's and a khaki windbreaker. When he figured he had enough pictures, he put the camera in a blue cloth bag and opened a black case.

"Could you photograph the shopping cart closer up?" Bennis asked.

"Who are you?" the tech asked, annoyed.

"Officer Bennis."

"I don't do what uniforms tell me."

"Officer Figueroa and I are acting detectives. You know about the detectives being—"

"I heard about it. Well, you'd better take direction from me, then. I've been doing this a long time. You don't need pictures of the cart."

"I want pictures of the cart—" Bennis said.

"And I want the cans in the cart printed," Figueroa said.

"Why?"

"Suppose the killer got close to her by handing her a few cans?"

"There's probably fifty cans there!"

"Plus I want the area around the body Dustbusted." Figueroa meant that the tech should vacuum the ground around and under the body, but she was also implying that the trace evidence picked up that way should be studied. "And watch for a Handi Wipes or Wet Ones."

The tech said, "That's crazy. There's wall-to-wall trash and dirt there."

"What the hell's the matter with you?" Bennis shouted. "Your *job* is collecting evidence."

"Shit, it's just a bag lady. She's a wino, man."

"I don't believe this," Figueroa said. "We've got a murder here. Just do as we tell you."

"You're not detectives!"

"*What's going on?*" Mossbacher yelled. He flipped his cell

phone closed and strode over, hard shoes hitting the ground like hammers.

"These uniforms are trying to order me around."

"Berkley, they're Actings! During the current crisis, you do as they say, understand?" Berkley made a gruff sound, but he pulled out his camera.

"And I want a plat drawn," Figueroa said.

The tech didn't answer, but Figueroa was confident that at this point he'd do as he was told.

Bennis, apparently agreeing with her, said to Mossbacher, "We also need to search through all this crud"—he kicked at a discarded rag on the ground—"to see if there's a Handi Wipes or a Wet Ones. Some kind of pre-moistened towelette." The tech looked daggers at him. He added, "And Figueroa and I are gonna help with that."

Mossbacher jerked his head sideways to Bennis and Figueroa, pulling them over to the squad car. "Got a hint for you."

"Yes, boss," Bennis said.

"For the present, call yourselves 'Acting Detective Bennis and Acting Detective Figueroa' and like that when you meet a tech. Or anybody. They won't know whether you're a fill-in from patrol or a fill-in who's been a dick and is now, say, vice or whatever."

"Yes, boss."

"And what in the world made you wear a uniform?"

"Well, boss, nobody said—"

"*Don't* wear a uniform."

"Yes, boss."

"And another tip. Go easy on the enthusiasm, my little friends. I know you're new and eager. But be cool. We can't fingerprint the whole world. Follow the manual."

"Manual says we canvass next," Bennis said.

"Right."

Bennis gestured at the surroundings. You canvassed for witnesses, hoping to find a shut-in or a gossip who knew the dead person, hoping somebody sick and sitting up all night had been looking out of his window. But what window? Bennis cocked a thumb at the El overhead, the parking lot, the chain-link fence, and the blank brick wall beyond.

"See what you mean," Mossbacher said.

The brick wall was the back side of an apartment building, a five-up, the limit beyond which the owners had to install elevators. Most of the wall that faced the El was windowless, presumably because nobody would want to look at the El anyhow, or hear the noise. One small window on the south corner of the west wall had been allowed in each apartment.

"Not so good."

Bennis said, "Passengers on the El wouldn't see anything going on under the tracks."

Mossbacher said, "Nope."

"How about we look for other homeless people?" Figueroa said hopefully.

Mossbacher smiled pityingly. "You can try," he said.

Figueroa said, "We're gonna have to get a memo to all the roll calls and ask if anybody parking or unparking a car saw the woman. Or whoever attacked her."

"Yup."

"And we also have to circularize everybody in the CPD building, like secretaries and janitors and so on. Ask them the same thing."

"Circularize is not a word," Bennis said.

"Yes it is."

"Plus, secretaries wouldn't be here in the middle of the night. However, janitors might be. And you're absolutely right. We do that right away." He stepped back from the body and all the way over to the side of the alley. From here, the El didn't block the view. On the other hand, it wasn't the site of the murder. "We also go to those two apartments."

"You aren't supposed to go to homes in the middle of the night unless it's urgent." But she was looking where he pointed. From here, the whole west wall of the apartment building was visible. On the third floor of the brick building, the corner window showed lights. On the fifth floor another corner apartment was brightly lighted. "Can if they're clearly awake," Bennis said. "Plus, you can canvass at any hour when you've got a violent crime, and we got a murder. We'll do the lighted places first, though."

Two adults stood in the doorway, a heavily varnished brown door half open and held in place defensively by a man of about thirty-five. A bright red angry baby screamed in the woman's arms. The man was unshaven and his light brown hair stood on end. It was obvious why they were awake at this hour.

"May we ask you a couple of questions?" Figueroa said.

Neither answered.

"You're not in any trouble," she said. The response she got sounded like "vt" and "verstandig" with many other glottal syllables in between, and "politieagent," which sounded odd, but Figueroa understood the basic meaning. Figueroa and Bennis wore uniforms. These people were frightened.

Figueroa paused. With no translator, and in fact no idea of what language this was, she was stumped.

"See out window?" she said, pointing. The small living room was just beyond, and she could see the two windows at right angles to each other. One faced south and one faced west toward the El and the area around the crime scene.

The two adults turned to look at the window. The infant turned deep purple, sucked in a breath, and emitted a blood-curdling shriek. It was furious. Its world was horrible. All was in ruins.

"Colic?" Figueroa asked, almost as a reflex.

"Ooo, colic, ja, ellendig!" the woman said. "Kinderarts!"

Figueroa nodded her head, thinking of the universal language of parents.

Suddenly the father shouted, "Marika!"

Whatever did that mean? Figueroa thought. After a few seconds, he shouted, "Marika!" again.

The baby shrieked. The mother leaned from left to right, left to right, with a little bounce included. The baby screamed louder.

Then there appeared in the room beyond a tiny girl, maybe six or seven years old, rubbing her eyes and trailing a long pink nightgown with a pattern of improbably blue roses.

"Mmmmf," she said.

Her father pointed at Figueroa and Bennis and said, "See?"

The little girl regarded Figueroa and Bennis with no fear, indeed something like quiet, thoughtful study. Figueroa was very aware of the nightgown on the child, new but bought longer than she needed so that she could wear it for several years and save money. She'd had many items of clothing exactly like that herself as a child.

The little girl quickly decided they were okay, and spoke up like a miniature adult. "What seems to be the problem?"

Figueroa explained, over occasional screams of outrage from the baby. Crime in the alley. After eleven P.M. Before three A.M. Searching for witnesses. See from here. Help the police. She was extremely careful to treat the child like a human being and not talk down to her.

When she finished, the little girl said, "You may look," and led them to the window. She was obviously more than a translator; she was an adult before her time. While Figueroa and Bennis looked, the child explained the situation to her parents in their language.

The view of the murder scene, Figueroa saw, was as bad as

she had feared. You looked right out at the El, which passed next to the west wall directly outside. It occupied about half of the entire vista. Beyond it, you could see State Street, but not a whole lot of the CPD parking lot and none of the alley. To the north, you got a diagonal view of the CPD building itself, for whatever that was worth. If you stood right up against the glass and looked down, you could see some of the access strip along the alley under the El.

The little girl spoke up.

"My mother saw nothing. She is very worried about Adrian. Adrian is perfectly all right. Babies *do* cry, you know."

"I know," Figueroa said.

"All the same I think it is very responsible of Mama to be so worried, don't you?"

"Yes, indeed. You have to take babies seriously. Did your father see anything?"

"He says he was walking Adrian at one-thirty. He says there was a man crossing the parking lot. But we see people crossing the parking lot all the time."

"At one-thirty in the morning?"

"Yes. It is a police station."

"True. What did the man look like? Tall? Short? Fat? Thin? Old? Young? Oh, and wait. Which way was he going?"

There was consultation, during which the baby screamed again, turned bright red, went stiff, then subsided into gulps. The mother decided to walk him into the back hall and let them talk.

"He looked like anybody, Papa says." Figueroa sighed. "But he was not old. Not fat. And he was carrying a brown bag. And he walked slowly toward the alley."

"Slowly?" Figueroa had never seen a cop actually stroll the alley or into it. The littered, unwholesome alley was considered something you got over with as fast as reasonably possible.

More consultation.

"Yes, slowly. And then he disappeared under the El."

"When did he last see him?"

After more talk the child said, "He's not sure. He did not see him long. One-thirty is the best he thinks. He was leaning on the window, carrying Adrian, you know. Very weary. That's what he says. Very weary."

"I wonder," Figueroa said, "if you would tell me what language you're speaking?"

"Dutch. We have come from the Netherlands."

Figueroa reached out and shook the little girl's hand. "Thank you, Marika. I really appreciate your helping us."

"Oh, I believe that most people would probably do the same."

Ordinarily a proper canvass is supposed to consist of two teams of two detectives each, supervised by a sergeant, who were to canvass all possible witnesses immediately and go back later if some were not home. In this case there were just two officers doing all the canvassing. Which in fact was not that unusual. In fact, a detective had once told Bennis that he had never in eight years been on a "perfect" canvass.

The only other apartment with a light had been on the fifth floor. Bennis and Figueroa were glad to see light still visible under the door when they got to the fifth-floor hallway.

Their knock brought someone to the door, but whoever it was didn't open it. He said, "Go away."

"Sir, since you're up," Bennis said, "we'd like to talk with you. Chicago Police Department." They had long since developed a certain kind of teamwork in which Bennis used his male-authority voice when that was appropriate, while Figueroa used an unthreatening female voice with families, women, and children.

"Go away. I don't know you."

Bennis said, "Sir, if I hold my ID up to the peephole, you will see I'm a Chicago police officer."

"Can't get up to the peephole."

Figueroa whispered to Bennis, "Disabled, maybe?"

"Look, sir, I—" Bennis weighed the problem of losing his ID and then said, "Suppose I pass my police identification under the door. Would that be okay?"

"Oh, never mind." Bolts screeched. A chain rattled. Finally the door creaked open a few inches. "I guess if you're willing to do that, you're okay."

A gust of stale air emerged, flavored with frozen-dinner smells. Macaroni and cheese. Ravioli. Chicken and broccoli and potatoes. The man sat in a wheelchair, one of the heavy kind with battery power. A gray plain blanket lay over his legs.

"May we talk with you, sir? We noticed your light was on."

"Talk? Why? It's the middle of the night." He backed up and Bennis and Figueroa entered.

Bennis explained. A murder. In the alley. After eleven P.M. and before three A.M. View from here.

"Nope," said the man.

"You didn't see anything? That window overlooks the area." Bennis walked through piles of boxes and magazines to the west corner window. It looked down on the alley from a higher angle than the Dutch family with the baby. It had a better angle on the CPD parking lot and State Street, but it seemed to Bennis as if the height made the murder scene area on this side of the El harder to see.

"Nope," the man said.

"You didn't go to the window?"

"Nope. Writing letters."

The apartment did not have a dining room, but there was a corner of the kitchen most people would have used as a dinette area. It was filled with magazines and books, an old typewriter and stacks of blank paper. It faced south, not west.

"Writing letters?" Bennis repeated. In training they taught you that one nonthreatening way to urge a witness to go on was simply to repeat his last phrase.

The man gestured at the very old Smith-Corona manual typewriter. Besides the newspapers and magazines, several law texts lay there, with markers stuck in their pages or turned over open to a saved place. "Yes! Writing letters. To the *Trib* for one."

"To the *Tribune*?"

"Yes, young man. For God's sake, pay attention. Letters to the *Tribune*. The *Sun-Times*. About the City Council. It's not constitutional, you know. We are entitled to a town meeting form of government. All citizens should be welcome. It's a constitutionally mandated foundation of our governmental system. They still have them in New England. Participatory democracy. It's unconstitutional that they close us out here. One man, one vote. The Chicago town meeting would solve all our problems. Let everybody vent. Get it all out. Clear the air. Say your piece. Then make strides forward into the future, with everybody fully informed."

"Uh, Bennis?" Figueroa said as they left. She looked back to make sure the door was firmly closed.

"You wish a word?"

"Yes, dammit. How can a handicapped person live on a fifth floor with no elevator? Does the city allow that? How does he get in or out?"

"Probably he doesn't go out. I saw a much larger jacket on a clothes hook in the kitchen. Larger than he'd ever wear. Somebody lives with him. Probably he never goes out."

"But what if he's there alone when the other person goes to work? What if there's a fire? What if—"

"Figueroa. Put in a word with Human Services. I agree with you. But I'm betting he won't be grateful."

They knocked on all the other apartment doors. People were home, which, Figueroa thought, was hardly surprising. All said they had been sleeping. All said they had seen nothing because they had been sleeping. Most of them were extremely angry that they'd been awakened, and willing to express their anger loudly.

Figueroa hoped somebody might have been sitting in the dark, looking down at the El, however spooky the image was. But even if somebody had been, residents around here would be so used to police cars and police officers coming and going that they might not have paid any attention to people roaming around. Figueroa had hoped, nevertheless. She got nothing.

It took Bennis and Figueroa nearly three hours to finish the canvass, put the paperwork to bed on the dead woman, and see her off to the morgue. They spent nearly an hour searching the crime scene for a pre-moistened towelette that wasn't there. All of which gave Figueroa and Bennis just time for eggs and biscuits, red-eye gravy, and a lot of coffee at the Snuggery before roll call at seven-thirty. In the forty minutes available to them, there was no point in Figueroa trying to get home and back, but she called in. Sheryl, Kath said, had had a restless night. Robert was irritated, J J was giggly, Maria was languid, and Kath herself sounded sweet.

It was nice to have something predictable, something regular to count on, Figueroa thought.

When they got to the district for roll call, there was a message. Yesterday's elderly dead man had been readily identified by AFIS. He was a Michael Kilkenny O'Dowd, and he had once been a Chicago cop.

CHAPTER TWELVE

SUZE WAS GRUMBLING. "I don't see why we have to spend time on *pickpockets*."

"We're too important, huh?" Bennis said mildly.

She hated it when he sounded wise and calm.

"It's not that *we're* too important, it's that the murders are too important," she muttered as he parked on Chestnut Street, making a neat one and a half pass parallel parking job in a minuscule space between two cars. "Dammit, Bennis! Three people have been murdered."

"Yes, and if this were *NYPD Blue* or *Homicide: Life on the Streets*, we'd have just one case to work on, wouldn't we?" Bennis said with perfect serenity. "Matter of fact, we're quite lucky Touhy didn't give us the vandalism on the backhoe at the lakefront. Or that one about the Porta Potti missing from the construction site."

"Yeah, fine. Why don't we get a list of overdue library books, too, while we're at it?"

"Figueroa, my man, have you ever lost your wallet?"

"Twice," she said grimly.

"You have much money in it?"

"Once, years ago. I had the rent money. And both times I was devastated. My credit cards, driver's license, Firearm Owner's ID, library card, picture of J J as a two-month-old. Look, I know what you're trying to tell me. Pickpockets can make people miserable. But *they don't make them dead*."

North Michigan Avenue was retailing's *crème de la crème*. In three blocks you had Bergdorf Goodman, Godiva, Lord & Tay-lor, Marshall Field, Armani, Brooks Brothers, Cadbury and Ma-son, Neiman Marcus, Saks Fifth Avenue, Tiffany, and a whole lot more. And those weren't even the most exclusive. There were couturiers so special they never advertised, and you had to know somebody just to be allowed in the door. However, the small exclusive shops were not where Bennis and Figueroa were headed. Pickpockets didn't go into small places with closed doors.

"So," Figueroa said, "these schmucks target the biggest stores?"

"Large stores when a demonstration is going on. Makeup demos especially. Seems you ladies can't take your eyes off a good makeover."

"Give it a rest, Bennis."

They sauntered into Cadbury and Mason, where a woman in a white coat was mixing many colors of Versace powder to match exactly the complexion of an extremely attractive model. The model wore a white smock. The demo person wore a lilac smock. She was working from several pots of powder—beige, sand, mauve, petal pink, rose, and pale amber. Twenty or thirty shoppers, all women, stood raptly watching.

"How are you gonna blend in here, Bennis?"

"Simple. I'll go talk with the chief of security. You blend in."

Following Mossbacher's orders, they had worn plainclothes, so Figueroa blended in pretty well. The crowd ranged from seventy-year-old women in beautiful wool suits and much jew-elry, their lavender hair perfectly permed, to young women in business power suits, and harried women in Levi's with children in strollers or backpacks. In addition to the thirty or so people in the crowd, others milled around on the fringe, wandering in and wandering away.

It was an ideal setup for a pickpocket, Suze thought, as she edged closer into the group of spectators, her elbow right up against the purse of a tall blond woman. On her other side was a younger woman in a black spandex jogging suit, her wallet presumably in the belly bag at her waist. That would be harder to get into, Suze thought, but maybe not impossible for an expert. In front of her was a woman with a child in a stroller. The woman wore feather earrings, Figueroa noted, and Levi's, and her wallet was in her back pocket. Figueroa stared at it.

It would take a lot of guts to be a pickpocket, Suze realized. She tried to imagine herself lifting that wallet from that tight back pocket, and simply couldn't imagine how. Wouldn't the woman feel the first touch? Suze shifted position to nudge the wallet pocket slightly. The woman didn't appear to notice. But the wallet was still wedged into the pocket.

All right, she thought. *Assuming I'm good at extracting the wallet from the pocket, the setting is ripe for it. But then what? How soon would the victim discover it was missing? Would I take the wallet and move back out of the crowd and walk to the door, right away? Of course. My first thought would be to get away.*

I wouldn't run. Too noticeable. Walk fast? Hide? Have a confederate who would distract the crowd? Maybe. Pass the wallet to the confederate and stand innocently right where I was?

If you left, even quietly, somebody in the crowd would remember what you looked like, wouldn't they?

The targeted stores were invariably the busiest stores. No surprise there. Bennis and Figueroa hit them all. By noon the two had seen demonstrations of perfumes, lipstick, eye shadow, and nail polish, and just missed one on how to tie a scarf attractively.

They met four chiefs of security and two assistant chiefs. In one case the big cheese was out sick and in the other case he was in Detroit. Their talk with Brandon Ely, the last of the six, was pretty much typical. Of the six security honchos, five were men, one a woman; three were former cops, two Army,

and one a graduate of a professional security and alarm program. All were between thirty-five and fifty-five, the assistants
being on the young end.

They sat in Ely's office while a lesser mortal brought in
Starbucks coffee (at one store it was Seattle's Best, at one it was
Water Tower mezzanine's, and the three others their own house
blend). Ely's office was cheaply paneled, which seemed to be de
rigueur for these guys. He had tan low-pile carpeting, also
pretty common. Ely was maybe fifty years old, portly and gray-
ing, and was one of the former cops.

He said roughly the same thing as the other security chiefs.
"We don't get many pickpockets. What we get is shoplifting."

"And employee theft?"

Grudgingly, Ely said, "Well, yeah. Some."

"Okay," Bennis said. "This most recent theft. What exactly
happened?"

"Sans Souci was demonstrating a new perfume. They had
a little 'educational' spiel all worked out. A lecture on the different sorts of scents. Basic categories of scents. Spicy, fruity,
floral, something like that. They passed around little pieces of
cloth with their logo on them and each was scented with a
different type of fragrance. Then a short lecture and then they
gave out free samples. Free samples draw the crowds. Most of
these women could buy a gallon of Chanel Number Five and
not blink, but they love free samples. So I'm standing near the
Michigan Avenue doors. We had some shoplifting last week, so
I'm not sitting here in my office, I'm on the floor keeping an
eye out. But very unobtrusively. I'm not standing in *front* of the
doors or anything like that. I'm off to one side looking at
leather gloves. Trying some on. I didn't look like a store employee."

"This was shoplifting? I thought we were talking pickpockets."

"We are. I'm coming to that. So the crowd starts breaking

up and one woman suddenly screams, 'My wallet's gone!' Her
handbag is hanging open and her wallet's missing."

"You were watching the crowd when she said it?"

"You bet. And before. Now, the way things are in a store,
with a lot happening all the time, other shoppers wandering
around, several aisles, browsers blocking the traffic pattern, you
lose sight of people real fast. In fact, you know stores are intentionally laid out so that you can't walk in a straight line right
through. They want to slow you down, have you go past a
variety of displays of merchandise. Anyway—there are only two
doors out of the ground floor. They're big double revolving
doors, with side doors next to them for strollers and the disabled and so on, but there's only two sets of them, one on Michigan and one on Pearson. I'm at one and our notions buyer was
at the other, studying a display of costume jewelry. You wouldn't
make her for a store employee, either, she says, any more than
you would have me. She says none of the people who left the
perfume demonstration went out the Pearson door. And I'm
watching two or three people from the demonstration leave by
the Michigan door, and I can tell you they weren't standing
anywhere near the woman who got her purse rifled."

"You get a good look at the people near her?"

"So-so. In a crowd like that, maybe four or five people were
behind and beside her. The people in front of her, I don't see
how they coulda done it."

"Me either. Can you give us descriptions of the people behind her?"

"Yeah, I guess so. Fair to middling, maybe. But frankly they
looked like a cross-section of all our customers. And that's not
what bothers me. What bothers me is, say you're gonna lift a
wallet. Wouldn't it be the first thing you do is get out of the
building?"

Figueroa said, "Sure."

"But I'm here to tell you, whoever she was, she didn't rush out the doors."

Bennis said, "Maybe she hadn't picked enough pockets."

"I guess."

Bennis and Figueroa got up. "You'll write out those descriptions?" Bennis asked. Ely nodded. "Fax me at this number. And what I'll do, I'm going to recommend that some of the patrol officers pass through the store from time to time. You understand we don't have enough people to just stand here and watch all day, though."

"I'm not sure we'd even want that. Cops looming over the customers."

"Right," Figueroa said. "It takes some of the fun out of having your nails painted chinchilla if a cop is looking."

Ely raised his eyebrows. Bennis said, "She's joking, sir, but there's some truth to that. We usually try to keep a low profile in stores. What you could do to help, Mr. Ely, is let us know ahead of time when the store is planning these demonstrations."

"Okay. I'll do that. I'll make up our schedule and fax you that, too." Ely was loosening up. In fact, he seemed to find Figueroa amusing. "After all, we can't blow a whistle at the end of a demonstration and yell, 'Everybody check your purse.' "

"I guess not," Bennis said.

"And much as you'd like to, you certainly can't frisk 'em all for contraband."

"Okay, we've wasted two hours. Can we go now?" Figueroa demanded in the elevator.

"Yeah. Over to the CPD. See about the other currency exchange robber."

"Wait. I have to call. We've got O'Dowd's next of kin's name and phone."

Death notification was one of the responsibilities of the

investigating officer, usually the detective. She and Bennis rarely had to do it and she was glad of that.

Barbara Jean O'Dowd sounded much younger than her dead husband, the retired cop, had looked. Figueroa fought down a surge of anger at a woman who could let her husband wander the streets in an old overcoat with just a bottle of wine, eighty-eight cents, and a foam cup in his pocket. Mrs. O'Dowd's address was in Elgin, far northwest of Chicago. Did she ever get into town to see her husband? Did she care? Of course, you never knew what went on inside a marriage, but still—

Procedure said the first people to talk with after eyewitnesses were the family. And Figueroa was going to talk with the family, even if she had to bite her tongue about her feelings. She was aware she was being unfair, prejudging the situation, but couldn't even one family member watch over this man?

"I'm afraid I have bad news, Mrs. O'Dowd."

There was a silence, which Figueroa broke into right away. Even though there was no record of O'Dowd having children, records weren't always right, and she didn't want this woman to think a child of hers was dead.

"We have a Michael Kilkenny O'Dowd who is, uh, he's dead, ma'am."

"Oh, poor Dowdy," the voice said. And that nickname and the sorrow in the tone took away all of Figueroa's anger. "What happened to him? I always thought the end of it would be—"

"Would be what, Mrs. O'Dowd?"

"Drink related. He'd walk into the street in front of a car. Or he'd drink and pass out and freeze to death. But it's warm now, of course. And why am I going on like this? Tell me what happened."

Figueroa told her as much as they knew.

When she had finished speaking, Mrs. O'Dowd said, "What do you need to know from me?"

"Have you seen him recently?"

"I haven't seen him in several years. Eight or ten years at least. And he didn't call. He thought it was better for me if he left me alone."

"Was it better?"

"I don't know."

"Do you—did he—did you have children?"

"No."

"Did he have friends in town here?"

"Not that I know of. I'm sorry. That sounds so sad. He kind of lost them all in the last years. Dowdy just wasn't going to be happy. And he had the grace not to share his unhappiness with anybody. Even though we might have wished he would. He was a man with a lot of grace. I'm sure there were friends he could have called on. But that wasn't him."

Figueroa said, "I'm sorry."

"I'll claim the body when you let me know," Mrs. O'Dowd said.

"All right."

"Officer Figueroa. There were very few women officers in Dowdy's early years. But he never held the view that they were out of place in the department."

"That's very good."

"Do you have family? No, don't tell me. I know that cops don't like to talk about who they have at home. Hostages to fortune. What I wanted to say is, have family. Have friends and things you do and hobbies outside the department. Have friends who are not cops. Because one day, it's all over. Dowdy was just fine as long as he was a working cop, but after that he fell apart. Have friends and keep them and make time for them. Right now. When you think it doesn't matter. Because later on it will matter a lot."

———

In only thirty-six hours, the man in the attic had become quite
an expert on the family's habits. He amused himself by sitting
on the step that was just above the halfway-down turn in the
narrow attic stairs. He wished he could sweep the stairs. Nobody around here seemed to care that they were dusty. But
someone would surely notice if he cleaned.

This position put him out of sight to the boy and the
woman cop who lived on the third floor. He listened to their
chatter as they got ready for bed at night and as they got up in
the morning. It was better than TV. The stairs acted like a kind
of speaking tube, bringing up sounds from the floors below,
even as far away as the kitchen.

This morning the cop must have left early. She was no
doubt the person who came hurrying through the kitchen in
the middle of the night, nearly catching him with the ice cream
carton. The crabbiness of Mr. Daddy this morning was the result of being left in charge. Sheesh! What a creep! Didn't he
know that the father set the tone for the whole household, for
good or for bad? It was his responsibility to be firm and com-
manding.

When the family left for school and work in the morning
and only the spaz and the nurse were left, the man crept down
the back stairs to the spot just above the turn in the flight
between the first and second floors and listened from there.
However, it wasn't very interesting. The spaz couldn't talk, and
in his opinion the nurse couldn't think.

He went back up to his attic to change shirts. In the night,
he had taken a T-shirt and a sleeveless undershirt from the
dryer in the basement. They were a little large on him, but
he smiled and whispered, "Beggars can't be choosers." And he
hated to be dirty. His own undershirt was so similar that
he thought he could probably leave it in the big plastic basket
of dirty clothes and somebody would wash it. But that would
be just too risky.

He had also found a big roll of silver duct tape and a screwdriver and scissors. He carried that nice package up to the attic as well.

Every day the nurse, Alma Sturdley, took her allotted lunch hour off. She didn't leave the house; that was part of the agreement. Someone had to be there at all times in case of fire. But she was able to sit down with a cup of coffee or tea and a sandwich and read a book, knit, or watch television as long as she kept the sound low enough so she could hear Sheryl's bell. Being a responsible woman, she did exactly as she had promised. The fire alarm she could have heard with the TV at full blast. They had tested it twice, and it was loud enough to wake the dead.

She had got into the habit of relaxing at lunch in the sun parlor. This was a room off the living room on the south side of the house. Kath was growing a variety of houseplants there. Robert had installed three chaise longues in the room and JJ had insisted that Suze also put in a small television. That way, if Kath and Maria were watching a program he didn't like on the larger TV in the living room, he could go to the sun parlor and see his own shows.

Alma Sturdley liked to watch the Channel 9 noon news or *Hollywood Squares*.

By his second day in the house, the man realized this was a regular pattern and occurred always on the stroke of twelve.

At eleven Wednesday morning he came slowly but firmly down the back stairs from his attic to the third floor. He was very familiar now with which treads creaked so that you had to step near the wall.

He had explored the third floor briefly yesterday, but not boldly. Now that he knew no one came home during the day, he could pretty much do as he pleased.

The little boy's room wasn't interesting to him. But the cop's was.

The blue carpet absorbed any sounds his feet made. The room had blue and white plaid curtains and a blue and white bedspread. There were three paintings of western scenes on the walls, and each had some blue sky or blue water in it. A color-coordinated cop. What next?

A western-look pine dresser stood between the two gable windows. The man made a note of the position of this room and where it lay under the attic he called home. He must be careful not to walk around on the attic floor that lay directly over the ceiling of this room. The goddamned cop seemed alert. He wasn't going to take any chances.

He pulled open the top dresser drawer. Sweaters and sweatshirts. He felt around under them, but there was nothing special hidden there. Shutting that drawer carefully, he pulled open the second. Underwear. Bras, some black, some flesh color. Panties, most of serviceable cotton, but some black silk as well, and some white lace. He picked up a handful, crushing them into a bouquet, and held them to his face. There was only the smell of a light perfume, no woman smell. He was disappointed but not surprised. She seemed like a clean one, always washing the kitchen countertops, making sure all the dishes went into the dishwasher at night, even if she had to help the kids do them. He heard her chattering with them as they rinsed and loaded. That was admirable, as far as it goes, he thought.

He put the underwear back in the drawer and resisted the urge to fold them more neatly than she had. Her arrangement hadn't been bad. He'd give her a B− for it.

Drawer three held socks, scarves, and some jewelry. He held a scarf up to his nose and smelled the woman's shampoo scent on it. So she didn't wash these after every wearing. He felt underneath them, but except for some outdated ID and odds and ends, stationery and pens and pencils, nothing. The bottom drawer held more miscellany. Annoyed, he pushed it in sharply, and then froze. He'd carelessly made a noise. He shouldn't have done that. Better get control of himself.

The closet, then.

In the closet were dresses, shirts, and pants on hangers. A lot of cop stuff. Blue uniform shirts. White dress shirts. Some blue ties. A cop kind of black raincoat with yellow stripes. All of it in order, cop stuff on the far right. Shoes were lined up on the floor, the cop shoes under the cop clothes.

He felt around the shelf above the clothes.

Aha! He knew it! Her extra. It had to be someplace. No cop ever had just one gun, did they?

He lifted down a stainless-steel Colt revolver. Excellent! It had been hell for him, going around without a gun, but if the cops caught you and you had one on you, you'd never get loose.

And then, he realized that the Colt had a trigger lock in place, an ugly thing like a pair of rubber earmuffs locked together. Making it safe for the little darling children. Instantly, he was furiously angry. He could feel his face get red and hot.

Stop. Get control.

Yes. He unclenched his hands. That was better. Maybe he could find the key?

Back to the dresser. He tried the two drawers that had the jumbled stuff in the bottom. And there were several keys, but even a glance told him they were not the size of the small keyhole in the trigger lock.

Where, then?

She might keep it on her key chain and carry it with her. That would be too bad. Wait. She would carry the key to her daily gun with her, of course, but the extra one? Probably not. Why risk losing it?

Okay. If it was here it was not likely to be in the closet. Too close to the gun. She was too careful for that. And he hadn't found it in the dresser. Still, it had to be near at hand to be any use to her at all.

The pictures.

The back of Yosemite Falls was just plain brown paper. So was the back of a creosote bush against the western sky. But behind Mono Lake at sunrise—a key.

The key.

He stared at it for half a minute, very pleased with himself. He held the gun near it so as to be absolutely certain it was the right one, but he did not touch it, and he certainly did not try to pull off the tape that held it in place.

Then he replaced the paintings and checked them carefully to see that they were straight. He made sure all the drawers were properly arranged. He put the gun back on the shelf.

He had never had any intention of taking it. He just wanted to know how to get to it when he needed to.

In Sheryl's room, Alma Sturdley checked her watch. Eleven-fifteen. They had done the morning set of exercises, and she could see Sheryl was tired. Her face paled because she tried so hard. Sometimes Alma had to call it quits, even though Sheryl wanted to go on. Sheryl would hold on to the chair arms and do it again and again, and once in a while Alma actually had to get firm with her, saying, "The doctor could have me fired if I let you do this, dear. Now don't make me worry."

Today they had been working on getting up from a chair without leaning sideways. Up and down, up and down. "You really are getting better, dear," Alma said. She was still not balanced, even though the movement was better. Sheryl's right arm was very strong but her left was still weak and visibly thinner.

Forty-five minutes were left before Alma's lunch break. She decided to go to the kitchen and make tea so that it could cool off, and she could have iced tea with lunch.

She rose from the rocker near Sheryl's bed and said, "I'm going to make tea, dear. Would you like some while it's still hot?"

"Am-bin," Sheryl said.

Alma Sturdley had never been able to understand much of what Sheryl said, even though she'd been here three months now. But she often got an idea of whether Sheryl was enthusiastic about a thing or not. She didn't seem to be enthusiastic about tea, so Alma said, "Well, all right, dear. Maybe later when it's iced."

In the kitchen, she filled the kettle, then emptied some of the water back out. It was silly to boil a whole kettle if you were just making a cup or two and besides a smaller amount of water would boil faster.

Alma Sturdley stood watching the pot, reflecting that it was a watched pot that never boils. Finally, she got tired of watching and turned to look out the kitchen window at the backyard. She heard a bump behind her. Whirling, she stared down the hall, but no one was there. Then the kettle on the burner made a ticking noise. The kettle danced a little hop. The water on the underside of the kettle was vaporizing on the burner, making the kettle jump a little. That must have been the sound she heard.

Alma put her wrapped sandwich on a plate to eat with the tea. She had brought Diet 7UP in her lunch bag today. It was chilling in the refrigerator, but somehow, tea had sounded nicer. She would not begin lunch until noon. She was extremely responsible.

On the second floor, the man waited a full minute next to Kath's room, without shifting so much as a single inch. He cursed the door that had swung itself into the wall.

Either the nurse down in the kitchen would come and see

what had made the noise or she wouldn't. If he heard her coming up the back stairs, he would head for the front stairs, go to the third floor, and boogie up to the attic from there.

A couple of minutes passed, but she didn't leave the kitchen and finally the kettle began to screech.

He turned back to the little girl's room. This time he was careful to hold the doorknob until the door was fully open, making sure it didn't swing into the wall.

Old houses were like that. Nothing was exactly level, and doors swung open on their own.

Had to remember that.

There were stuffed animals on the girl's bed. The bed itself had been hastily made—just pulled together, really. Didn't parents teach their children the proper care of their possessions these days? But then he reflected that the little girl's mother was unavailable right now, busy being a spaz. So why didn't the cop give these children clear orders? Or their father? Somebody really ought to teach them a lesson.

The animals were more carefully placed than the bed-clothes. There was a little white stuffed dog, a yellow Pokémon doll, a very old Raggedy Ann, a small brown bear with much of its fur worn off, a large brown bear wearing a Notre Dame shirt, and a green dinosaur with a red tongue and yellow claws. They were lined up in a neat row against the headboard on top of the pillow.

The man lay down on the bed, nuzzling his face into the pillow, between the two bears. He forced his face farther down, squeezing air out of the pillow.

He could smell the little girl.

He took deep breaths, savoring the scent.

After she came out of the coma, the world was so confused that most of the time Sheryl couldn't make any sense of what the doctors and nurses were trying to tell her. Sometimes she tried to hide inside her confusion, refusing to deal with the real world.

The broken bones made it painful for her to move. But as soon as the staff could get her moving, they became relentless. Her memories of the parallel bars would stay with her for the rest of her life. Hold on, walk, walk straight, hold on, hold on, keep going! And the therapist was always on her left, the weak side, forcing her forward.

"There are five somewhat different approaches to rehabilitation after a head injury," the therapist told her, when she was first able to concentrate a little. Or maybe he had told her the same thing many times before and she just didn't remember. The days blurred a lot. Events overlapped.

"The approaches are Root, Bobath, Brunnstrom, proprioceptive neuromuscular facilitation, and Carr and Shepard. They're all helpful. However, most of us believe that Bobath is the most successful for hemiplegia caused by brain injury."

He spoke quite slowly and distinctly, but without talking down to her, which she remembered appreciating and wishing she could speak well enough to tell him that she was grateful.

"Bobath goes on the assumption that the sensation of movement is what's learned, not movement itself. Sort of like what you feel is what you get."

He smiled. She thought maybe she smiled. She certainly tried to.

"A cerebral injury causes abnormal patterns of movement. What we're going to do is elicit normal patterns of posture and movement and so on. Think of this as motion providing normal feedback to the brain. Moving normally will produce normal stimuli to the injured parts of your brain. And of course it will inhibit abnormal patterns."

In one of those completely unpredictable events, like the sun coming out from a tiny gap in the clouds on a rainy day, she said, "Easy."

He was delighted. "Wonderful! Wonderful! Except of course it won't be easy. It will be very difficult. Sometimes it will be painful. I will be merciless. The right side of your brain was injured, and therefore the physical deficit is on your left. I won't let you get away with leaning over to the left. When you do, I'll make you do every motion again and again."

Which they did.

Before Sheryl was allowed to go home, the therapist schedule was put in place. In addition, Alma Sturdley took two days of training in Sheryl's specific daily exercises. The therapist told Alma that even though Sheryl had to do these exercises and do them correctly, she wasn't supposed to do them to the point of exhaustion. If anything, Sheryl was too desperately eager.

"Tire her," he had said, "but just a little bit."

On the stroke of twelve noon, Alma Sturdley picked up her cooled tea, poured it over ice cubes, and walked down the hall to Sheryl's door.

"I'm taking my lunch now, dear," she said. "If there's a problem, you just ring that bell."

The bell was actually a button that sounded a loud buzzer mounted on the wall. Sheryl didn't ring it much, partly because it was a strain for her to reach unless she was lying on her back with her right hand next to it. And also, Alma believed, because poor Sheryl hated to be trouble to anybody.

Alma sighed. Alma thought Sheryl felt she was a terrible burden. And indeed why shouldn't she? She *was* a burden, or at least a responsibility, and for sure her accident made everybody else in the house do the work that a mother would normally do.

But it wasn't her fault. Alma just hoped that Sheryl realized that. You couldn't quite come out and say something like that, though, even with the intent of being kind. Alma also hoped Sheryl believed she was getting better. Alma had seen for herself in the months she had been here that Sheryl's walking had improved. Why, she could stand up all by herself now for a half minute or so, and when Alma had first arrived she could hardly stand at all, even with two people holding on to her to steady her. Her speech had not improved so much. It must be terribly frustrating, all those thoughts locked inside. Alma, who loved to talk, sighed deeply in sympathy.

Sheryl had a small television set in her room. Alma wished Sheryl would watch some of the comedy shows. Surely they would cheer her up. One or two were just so hilarious. But she never seemed to watch, even if Alma turned them on. She rolled on her other side and didn't look. How strange.

Alma sighed again as she settled in front of the television in the sun room. Poor thing. It must be hard.

Alma reminded herself not to show any pity. She had found over the years of caregiving that usually they hated that most of all.

Sheryl lay quiet. Frequently, she tried to lie just as still as she possibly could, and listen to her body. This wasn't always possible. Sometimes her left arm trembled for no reason. Sometimes her left foot would point and straighten, point and straighten, until she thought it would make her crazy. And nothing she could do, no mental exercise, no relaxation technique, no force of will, not even making some kind of counter move to "distract" it, ever stopped it until it just decided to stop on its own.

And sometimes she was just too achy with all the lying in bed to hold still. She would change position as if compelled to do so when the ache in her back or shoulders or neck became unbearable. She'd wiggle, and arch her back, cringe in on herself like a shrimp, then stretch out as long as she could make herself, then do it all over again.

But now she seemed able to lie still for a few minutes.

Grateful, she felt the sheets under her body, and studied carefully the coolness, touched the fabric with her fingertips, sensing, being aware of the temperature, the texture, the light weight of the cloth. Then she drew in a breath and felt the air with her nose and mouth and down into her throat. It was cool, too, and moved smoothly. The air on her skin was her next focus. There was very little motion in the room, very little passage of air. Instead, it seemed to hang rather heavily over her. Air was called a fluid, and she felt very much as if she were under a pool of fluid. The sensation wasn't unpleasant, but the thought was disturbing. Humans were frighteningly dependent on this body of air, but unaware of it. Probably it was a good thing they were unaware of it. Had there been sunlight in the room, she thought she would feel the weight of that, too, not just the warmth.

Stretching, then settling back to motionlessness, she assessed the muscles and joints that she had become so very painfully aware of in the last four months. Nowadays it amazed her that she had casually spent the first thirty-five years of her life hardly thinking about the parts of her body. Just using them as if they were always going to be there, always going to do what she wanted them to do, as if she were the puppet master, pulling the strings to her arms and legs. Maybe infants, she thought, went through a process of discovering the parts of their bodies and trying to get them to do what their minds wanted.

She could almost feel the electricity buzzing in her nerves. Down the spinal cord, her senses running out to the fingers and the soles of her feet, the toes—

But generating the messages was the problem. During the weeks she had spent in the hospital, when she had been so angry at the feet that didn't do what she asked them to, the eye that looked someplace else, the mouth that wouldn't talk, one of the neurologists had told her that her anger was a good thing.

"Brain injuries are bizarre," he had said. "And especially

brains coming out of comas. People who can't move their legs at all will tell you they're just the same as they ever were before the accident. People who can hardly speak will say there is absolutely nothing wrong. It's very, very strange, and I'm here to tell you that nobody really understands why. It's one of the mysteries of coma. We think it's more common in right-side injuries, like yours. There's a theory that the right side of the brain looks for trouble and the left side of the brain looks for okay-ness. So when the trouble monitor is turned off, so is awareness of it."

She had replied in nonsense syllables but he understood her intent.

"No, it's not because they're trying to look on the bright side of things. They honestly seem to believe that they're doing all the things they always used to do. The people who don't react that way get better sooner."

"Ah, ah, ah!" she had said. Or something like that.

"I know you're frustrated. And impatient and angry. But you need to understand that feeling that way is a good sign."

When she was first coming out of coma, Sheryl had heard sounds, and that was all. She couldn't see or speak, and she didn't really feel herself move, but she heard rushing water. Later the doctors told her that the first of the lost senses to return after coma is hearing.

She was at Niagara Falls. She knew it for certain. And someplace around was Maria, who was only two years old. They were playing near the falls.

A week or so later, farther into her recovery, she realized that it must have been the sound of the respirator she thought was the falls, but she had been so sure. And after Niagara Falls she slipped into utter terror. The sound was not falling water, but flames. She had died and gone to hell and she would be here forever.

And devils were stabbing her with their pitchforks. Over

and over, for days, they stabbed her. They were breaking her back. Some of them poked at her eyes. Or shot flame into her eyes.

Now Sheryl put the past out of her mind. Its only use today, she told herself, was so that she could reflect on how far she'd come. She could stand up. She could see quite well now, even though the world sometimes looked to her as if the left eye focused a little higher than her right eye, making her feel spacey and out of sync.

She would walk again. She knew this, without question. The primary problem now was mental. There were times when she wasn't really sure where she was. She would be eating dinner with the family and suddenly be convinced that she was at work. Or much worse, back at the hospital, waiting for some painful test while machines made noises. Because she was aware of her confusion, it was both less and more scary. She could rationalize it. But the idea that her brain could run away with her was deeply upsetting.

Most frustrating on a moment-to-moment basis was language. It was frustrating because she was so sure she ought to be able to master it. She would think the word "cat," picture a cat clearly, and get her mouth all ready for "cat" and out would come the word "evil." Or "fork." She tried very hard not to burst into tears when she couldn't talk, because she knew it bothered the children when she cried.

What she'd been doing lately in reaction to this was cowardly and she knew it, but she couldn't help it. She'd been talking less and less so she wouldn't get upset. Dr. Gregorich would have something to say about *that*.

She could practice now, of course, when there was nobody to hear her. She would say "It's a warm day."

"Bast," she said. "Corner-gah." She started to cry.

———

With the nurse in some distant room eating her lunch and playing the television, the man was free to come down the last flight of stairs. At the door to the kitchen he paused and studied the downstairs hall.

He had come this far at night. Several times in fact. But it was important to him to see the rooms by daylight, so as to know exactly what was where.

First, on his left as he started down the hall, was a broom closet. Then, on the right, a bathroom. Now he silently examined the bathroom for three or four minutes to fix it in his mind, noticing where the window was, just in case, and how it opened, a sash window with a simple turn latch.

Time to go look in the spaz woman's room. It was just beyond the bathroom, also on the right. The archway to the living room was beyond it on the left. A glance into the living room told him the nurse wasn't there. Sound came from the sunroom television. He crept softly to the bedroom door. The woman might see him the instant his head appeared around the doorjamb, of course, but more likely not. She couldn't possibly spend the whole day staring at the doorway. And even if she did, she couldn't tell anybody what she had seen.

If she saw him, he would be back up the stairs before the nurse could get here.

No time like the present, he said to himself.

He leaned boldly around the doorjamb.

The woman was much smaller than he had anticipated. She lay on her right side, her legs drawn up a bit, facing away from him. There was a red and blue floral quilt over her, pulled up to her waist.

He noted her window, which was just like the bathroom sash window but larger. It was open a couple of inches at the bottom.

He noted the bottles of medications, an insulated carafe, a plate of cookies, a jar of dried fruit, cards made by the children, all on the nightstand. He noted the hospital bed with rails, the rails raised so that she wouldn't fall out. He noted a kind of swinging bar over the bed, which she probably used to exercise.

There were two chairs, one straight and one soft stuffed one. A rack held several dresses and robes on hangers. All of the clothes that he could see buttoned or zipped in front.

And especially he noted the call button on a wire looped over the bed rail, in easy reach near the spaz's right hand if she was lying on her back.

That call button was important.

As he padded carefully back up the stairs to the attic, he ran over in his mind everything he had seen, but the location of the call button was the big detail, first and foremost.

CHAPTER THIRTEEN

AT TWENTY-SIXTH AND California, the Cook County Criminal Courts Building, Figueroa and Bennis caught up with ASA Malley. Malley said, "He's flipped on his buddy."

"No honor among thieves," Bennis said. "And come to think of it, how sweet that is."

"What changed his mind?" Suze asked. "Did you convince him, Mr. Malley?"

"In a manner of speaking. I asked him how it happened he got to go into the currency exchange and take all the risk and his pal got to stay in the car where he couldn't be ID'd. Pointed out that the way it went down, anything goes wrong, Herzog gets caught and the other guy gets away."

"And?"

Malley frowned. He preferred people to listen to his stories and not prompt him. But he liked the sound of his voice more than he liked silence, so he went on. "Says he's gonna do a deal. Gives us the name of his pal. He seems to be one Stanley Sisdel. Lives on West Addison. Herzog picked him up there once."

"That's in the Nineteenth. They get him?"

"Nope. They went there. Turns out to be a rented single room in a real dump. I mean, this guy must have figured on the currency exchange cash to upgrade his lifestyle. You messed him up a whole lot, guys."

"Good for us," Bennis said.

"So where do we look now?" Figueroa asked.

"Who knows? I'm no cop, thank God. Know what else?"

"What else?"

"The asshole in the car? Sisdel? Herzog says he wasn't even carrying."

"No gun? Why not?"

"Case they were caught. I mean, even Herzog realizes that now. Herzog is not real bright. In fact, he's got the brains of a block of tofu. Your guy, Sisdel, is real bright. But Herzog, he's finally worked it out—maybe with a little help from yours truly—he's finally worked it out that if they were busted on the spot, Sisdel was gonna claim he had no idea what Herzog went into the currency exchange *for*. Cute, huh?"

"Very cute," Figueroa said.

"Not a nice guy," said Manny Jiminez, more cheerfully than he should have, given the info he was getting off his machine. Manny looked exactly like the kid reporter, Jimmy Olson, from the old Superman comics. All he needed was a bow tie, Bennis thought. Maybe one of those straw hats with the red band. Manny had a ham and Swiss cheese sandwich on an onion roll on his desk. Figueroa and Bennis hadn't had time for lunch. It was now past two, and the sandwich smelled like heaven. They averted their minds. As much as possible anyhow.

Manny was the Area Four computer whiz. He had just searched NCIC, Cook County, and Illinois for wants and warrants on the missing currency exchange bandit. "Aha," he said, "I have our known but flown."

The name Herzog had given up was Stan Sisdel, but it turned out Stan Sisdel was an aka and Stan was really Harold Valentine, an improbable name for an extremely unappetizing man.

Manny said, "Seems our Harold likes little girls."

"Likes little girls *and* robs currency exchanges!" Bennis said. "A double threat man."

"Triple threat. Felony stuff relating to scams, too, and other stuff."

Figueroa said, "All right, all right. Give us something we can use. Known associates?"

"No known associates. Maybe he's not a buddy-buddy type. I can only give you what I got. DOB 10-04-65. Social—here—place of birth—mm, yes—I'll print all this out for you. Haydn High School, graduated in 1982. Two years of junior college. Became—well, lookee there. A commodities trader. Lasted four months. He seems to have tried some sort of Ponzi scheme. Mostly by mail looks like. Maybe he's not a real slick talker in person. Just a guess. Arrested the first time right after the CBOE booted him. Lemme get that from another source."

"Be my guest."

"And now—ta-da! National Sex Offenders Registry. Nice that we have it. The registry I mean. No reason whatsoever we couldn't have had one twenty years ago. But don't get me started. Course now we got the Registered Sex Offenders Act, too, so they have to register where they live. Who says life doesn't get better? Yes. Here you go. Our Harold was picked up hanging around a junior high school playground. But since he didn't have any record back then, he basically got away with saying there's no law against sitting on a park bench *outside* a playground. Which there isn't. Of course, it wasn't much later that—oh, my, my Harold!"

Figueroa said, "Tell me."

"Harold's a sucker."

"Any crook is a sucker," Bennis said.

"No. A sucker is a sadistic form of a biter."

"A biter is already sadistic."

"A sucker is more sadistic. A sucker is a very, very angry person. True, they bite the victim. In Harold's case he mostly bites little girls around ten, twelve years old. The sucker takes a bite and holds on and sucks. Makes a quite distinctive mark.

A central area of ecchymoses with a starburst pattern around it. One of the vice guys could show you pictures. Very distinctive. Know it in a second, once you've seen one."

"Oh, swell. So if he's so busy biting, what's he doing knocking over currency exchanges?"

"My guess is he needed the money."

"Valentine got nabbed for abducting the kid, not the biting," Calvin Waters said. Any of several special units could be involved in sex offense cases—Violent Crimes, the Youth Division, the SIU. Calvin was from Vice, and was definitely not cheerful. He had deep grooves from his nose to the sides of his mouth and down to his chin. He looked like a sad puppet.

He went on. "There were three or four other cases he was tied to, but they couldn't tag him for sure."

"I thought tooth marks were distinctive," Figueroa said.

"They are in a lot of instances. Especially on stuff like, say, cheese or fudge. But flesh is quite movable. It's what we call plastic. If you get a nice clear mark on firm skin, you can probably match it. But you get the best marks on cadavers. These particular cases—well, you know how live kids wiggle."

"Especially if they're being bitten," Bennis muttered. "I'd wiggle too." He didn't like this whole discussion, Figueroa saw. Bennis had told her he had never wanted to deal with crimes against children, and he'd never agreed to work Youth. He knew he'd be too angry at the parents.

"How come he's out so soon?" she asked.

"Doesn't say. He served thirty-nine months. Supposed to stay a hundred yards away from any playground or school."

"So what do we do, look for him a hundred and one yards from schools?"

"I surely wish you would," Waters said.

"Why so urgent?"

"This sucker type isn't your ordinary fondler. Suckers have a lot of anger. Generally speaking they escalate."

"To murder?"

"Child rape. Sometimes murder. Yeah."

CHAPTER FOURTEEN

FIGUEROA AND BENNIS had specifically asked if Dr. Percolin could do the dead woman's post. Apparently he was free and willing, and he was waiting for them when they arrived.

"Got O'Dowd's blood alcohol level," he said. "It was point three five."

"That's high," Bennis said. "Arrested a driver once who blew point three. He thought he was flying a plane into Newark."

"High enough to be comatose. We call point two to point three grossly impaired. For drivers point one is considered impaired."

The dead woman's old clothes lay on a table, and her wallet and driver's license were with them. The license had expired eight years earlier, but told them her name was Abigail Ward.

Old, naked, gray, and small. Figueroa saw the woman as a crumpled throwaway. Percolin, in his dignified manner, had draped a paper sheet over the body, but the old woman was fundamentally naked nevertheless. Even her reddened eyelids and pallid face looked emphatically naked. When Percolin and the diener turned her over, her bones squeaked on the stainless steel of the table. The left elbow made a sound on the metal like a crying cat. Her buttocks were flat and colorless. The knobs of her spine stood out.

Percolin went through the usual introductory remarks about the external condition of the body, but Figueroa hardly heard. She was very much afraid she was going to cry, and by the time she realized it would embarrass her a lot to cry, she felt tears that had already run all the way down her cheeks.

"Suze, my man—" Bennis said, startled.

"I'm not crying!" she said.

Percolin said, "Officer Bennis, Officer Figueroa is not crying, is that clear?"

"Yes, boss," Bennis said. "I hear you."

Percolin stepped on the voice activator pedal. Today he was wearing penny loafers and his socks were yellow. "There are no serious abrasions or contusions on the dorsal or ventral surfaces. A few small red marks on the ventral skin of the abdomen may represent an attack of insects or members of the tick family. The face has been recently washed."

Figueroa stared at the deflated breasts, like balloons that had lost air, their nipples hard brown knots like dried figs. She got hold of her sadness, not eliminating it, but putting it in some back compartment so that her analytical brain could function.

Percolin took up his scalpel and made the Y incision. He peeled the soft tissues back from the chest. He reflected the flaps he had made.

Then Percolin reached for the bone saw. This was much like a circular saw for wood paneling or drywall, but with smaller teeth and a smaller diameter blade.

Figueroa watched the saw cut through the ribs. Percolin wore a Plexiglas mask, similar to welder's gear. There was a smell of hot, burned bone fragments and a fine mist in the air of blood, bone, and tissue.

He removed the chest plate.

"Heart's not at all bad," Percolin said encouragingly, as if he were telling Figueroa that her child might make All-State. "She does have a few little lung problems."

"Such as what?" Bennis asked.

"Must've had TB a while back. Don't get worried. Old case.

It looks like it's all encased in calcium. I'd bet this was before the new drug resistant strains."

"Make my day," Bennis said.

"Also recent pneumonia. Still a little juicy right here in the left lower lobe." He poked the lung with his index finger, producing a *squish-squish* sound like pressing a wet sponge. "Sleeping out. No medical care. Hardly surprising."

Time went by while Percolin worked and Figueroa worried. How did you find a killer who swooped in on people like this who were rootless? People who had nobody? People nobody was waiting at home for? Nobody missed them. She was startled by Percolin saying, "Figueroa?"

"Yes, Doctor."

"You said 'poor old lady' at one point. Well, how old do you think she is, mmm?"

"Seventy?"

"My guess is she's not more than fifty-five. And if we were doing an office pool and closest guess wins, I would say forty-nine."

"Really?"

"Give the driver's license a look. And she's had a baby. Maybe two but I don't think more than that. Probably thirty years ago."

Figueroa went to the effects table. Percolin was close. Abigail Ward was fifty-one.

Once again, Percolin took a good look at the stomach lining. It showed, he said, the changes typical of prolonged alcoholism. He asked Figueroa to smell the contents. She said, "Booze. But I'm no good at telling what. I'm a beer person."

"Officer Bennis?"

He sniffed. "Bourbon. Good bourbon, in fact."

"My opinion exactly," Percolin said.

Figueroa said, "Is there any way to tell exactly what brand,

Dr. Percolin? If it's not generally available, we might be able to narrow down where she got it."

"Yeah," Bennis said. "Suppose the killer took her to a fancy bar."

"In that outfit she was wearing?" Percolin asked. "I doubt it."

"Or brought it along and fed it to her," Bennis said. "We might be able to find out where it's sold."

Figueroa said, "O'Dowd had good scotch in his stomach, remember."

"Problem with identifying it," Percolin said, "is that so much of the alcohol is absorbed so fast. Fifteen minutes, in most cases. And the stomach acids also would be mixed with it. No, wait a minute. What am I saying? It's right here. We can smell it. This last amount was administered after several earlier drinks; the killer must've fed her a whole lot of alcohol. She absorbed the first five, six, seven shots. They weren't mixed with water as far as I can tell, or at least what's left wasn't. It just basically went into her bloodstream and then he fed her more and more until the stomach was nearly paralyzed. So the stuff that's left here might be pretty pure."

"You *could* identify it?"

"You can identify almost anything if you're willing to pay enough for the analysis. Here's one parameter. If this contains urethane, it's probably bourbon."

"We already know it's bourbon from the smell," Bennis said.

"If this gets to court, you want to be going in and testifying that your nose knows?"

"No. I guess not."

"Urethane is a by-product of the production of bourbon and an unfortunate one because it's carcinogenic. But two or three of the top-priced bourbons are quite low in urethane. That might narrow it down without doing some expensive chemical profile. Suppose this bourbon is low in urethane. So let's say it's a high-priced bourbon. How does that help you?"

"Well, there's maybe a hundred bars in the Loop area I know she didn't go to, if so," Bennis said. "And a hell of a lot of liquor stores I know our murderer didn't buy it from."

"Whatever. If that helps you, so much the better. I'll send this off and we'll see."

Percolin used a ladle, identical to a soup ladle but smaller, to scoop a portion of liquid from the stomach. Figueroa sighed sadly.

It was an hour later that Percolin wrapped up. He snapped off his gloves, slapped them into a bin marked DANGER MEDICAL WASTE, and, crooking a finger at them, led them to a small library off the hallway, densely packed with books and journals. "Canadian limit on urethane is a hundred and fifty parts per billion."

"A hundred and fifty parts per billion doesn't sound like much."

"It is when it's urethane. See here, there are some plum brandies that have two thousand parts per billion. But that's not our problem. Look."

His thick index finger ran down a column of figures next to an alphabetized list of the name of various bourbons. "See, most of them run between seventy and a hundred and fifty parts per billion. Some as high as three hundred. These pricey ones, though, are in the fifty parts per billion range. And one of the Makers Mark lines is zero."

"I see that."

"The other thing is, how fast is urethane absorbed? I'm not a chemist, but I'd guess pretty damn fast. We'd hope at the same rate as alcohol so the ratio remains the same. Anyhow, we can give this a try. There may be other ways a chemist can tell bourbons apart. Each one probably has a characteristic chemical profile. For all I know, the FBI may have a library of chemical profiles of all sorts of booze. I'll save some of the stomach contents here, just in case we need to order more tests later."

Most posts took under an hour, as Bennis and Figueroa well knew, and the fact that Percolin had taken closer to two hours all told, plus Percolin's seriousness, plus the fact that he had left cause of death open, impressed them.

Bennis said, "Tell us what's going on. What exactly did she die from?"

"I wish I knew. My best guess is she was suffocated."

"Like the old man yesterday, then?"

"No. Not strangled like the old man yesterday was. I'm going to need some of these tissue samples looked at by an expert." He'd taken a lot of samples, some that he'd stuck on glass slides and blown fixative at, some that he'd dropped into small phials with tops color-coded to identify the kind of preservative inside. The diener had attached case number labels to all of them. But Percolin gestured at three he'd taken from the lungs.

Figueroa said, "What do you expect to find?"

"My wild guess is they'll show she was sprayed with a fire extinguisher—now, hold it and let me explain. There are a number of fire extinguishers made especially for fires in and around computer equipment where you don't want to use water or foam or anything that leaves a residue."

"I'm aware of that."

"They're also used in restaurant kitchens because you can put out a fire without getting any crap in the food. Halon was one of the early ones, but there are maybe a dozen different types now. They all have the same action. They use a gas that keeps oxygen away from the fire. Argon or some such. I think the killer got her drunk, which wouldn't be difficult. When she was lying passed out on the ground, he kept spraying her with the fire extinguisher until she died."

"Outdoors? I can imagine doing that in a closed room, but

outdoors seems like 'using with adequate ventilation.' "

"She was already in run-down health. She was immobile from the bourbon. She wouldn't fight being smothered. And I think the gas they use in the extinguishers is heavier than air. Anyway, at least you should check to see whether there was any wind last night. If there was, maybe I'm wrong, mmm? That's your job, Officer Figueroa. And in a couple of days we'll see what the lung sections tell us."

"Manualo was smothered, O'Dowd strangled, this woman Ward maybe snuffed with a fire extinguisher. Three dead people and three different methods of murder. That isn't very typical of a serial killer is it? Don't they get into rigid habits?"

"Ask a profiler. You have at least one in the department. But if you're asking me as an amateur in the profiling business, I'd say it told you something about the killer's psyche. These murders all cut off the oxygen supply. Within that overarching requirement, I'd say the variations mean the killer is teasing us. And having a lot of fun doing it."

They left Dr. Percolin looking for similars over the past eighteen months. "Love this computer stuff," he said. "Suddenly I can do searches without breathing paper mites and library glue and paper dust."

Back at the district, Figueroa did some net searching while Bennis made phone calls. She reported back to him. "I got last night's weather report. Virtually no wind. Temperature never got below sixty-eight."

"I thought so. It was a sultry night."

"Was that Yolanda or Miranda?"

"Sultry? Neither. You're obsessed with my lady friends. And it's Amanda not Miranda."

"I don't want to hear about it."

"Yah. Haf a Mr. Valentine," the building super said. "Not a bad guy. May be trying to run out on his rent, though. Paid through the end of May. Haven't seen him. Hasn't brought in a check."

The building had deteriorated and had never been beautiful. Yes, Figueroa thought, Valentine needed the cash from the currency exchange robbery.

"You have him make out a form when he rented the room?" Bennis asked.

"Yah. Sure, we always do that."

"I'd like to see it, sir."

After a brief rummaging in a drawer, the form was produced. It had a "previous address" box, which Bennis would bet was false but nevertheless copied in his notebook, a line agreeing to the rent, with Valentine's signature appended, and not a great deal else.

"You get next of kin or anything like that?"

"No. Don't need it. Last month's rent and damage deposit. That's what we need."

"You said he was not a bad guy. Not a bad guy in what way?" Bennis asked.

"I dunno."

"You hang with him at all? Go out for a beer?"

"Nah."

"Well, help me out here. In what way was he not a bad guy."

"Quiet."

"You ever talk with him? Discuss anything? The Bears? Bulls? The Cubbies? Prothonotary warblers?"

"Nah. Talk in the hall."

"About what?"

"Like 'heat's off' or 'hi.' Like that."

"So he was a good tenant. Why?"

" 'Cause you didn't hardly ever see or hear him."

———

"Valentine? Who's Valentine?" the man with three stiff hairs in a wart on his nose said to Bennis.

"Your neighbor. Lived in the apartment right under yours."

"Under mine? You expect me to know who lives downstairs?" The man slammed the door in Bennis's and Figueroa's faces.

"Lovely," Bennis said.

"Look on the bright side. You didn't want to spend time with that guy anyway."

"Valentine. Right next door?" Bennis said. "Right there?" He pointed to the right, at Valentine's door. There was no name on it, but it was marked 4D in cheap black plastic numerals. The hall smelled of onions.

"Huh? That's 4D," the woman said.

"I know. The man who lived there was named Valentine. Or maybe Sisdel?"

"No kidding? Funny damn name, either of 'em," she said in a slow, dull tone. "Sistel, huh? My ma had a sistel rug on the porch when we were growing up."

"I think that's sisal," Figueroa said.

"Right. What I said."

"Ever see him? Mr. Valentine?"

"Maybe. Come in with groceries maybe."

"Say anything?"

"Nope. Turned his head away, what I remember."

"Valentine. Right next door," Figueroa said to the woman, pointing to the left, toward the door. By now they'd decided to let Figueroa talk with the women, although the stratagem didn't seem to work miracles.

"Uh, yes."

"Did you know him at all?"

"No!" the woman said.

"But you saw him go in and out?"

"Sometimes. No. Not really."

"Ma'am, could we come in and talk with you?"

No response. Suze Figueroa looked past her into a room containing a turquoise sofa entombed in a thick plastic cover.

"Ma'am? Could we come in and talk?"

From somewhere out of sight came a voice. "Mommy? Can I have some potato chips?"

The woman said, "Um—"

A girl appeared at her side. She was about ten and wore a red skirt, white tights, and a white sweater.

"Ma'am," Figueroa said, "if you could just tell me about Mr. Valentine—?"

"Mommy!" said the girl.

"We don't know anything," the woman said.

"Mommy, is that the bad man?"

"No," said the woman.

"I don't mean the lady!"

Figueroa said, "Ma'am, does your daughter mean that Mr. Valentine is a bad man?"

"We don't know anything!" the woman said. She slammed the door.

"Well, hell," Bennis said. "We sure are striking out."

"Or look at it the other way. We know that Valentine lived here. We're pretty sure he hasn't been here in a while. And we're bloody damn sure he was a loner."

"Oh, that's a big help."

"Give me a card." He gave her his callback card.

Figueroa tapped on the door. There was no response, but she called loudly, "Ma'am, if Mr. Valentine comes back, please call this number. Don't approach him. Don't ask him anything. Just call. Please?"

There was still no answer. Figueroa slipped the card under

the door, with just a tiny white corner left sticking out like the sail of a ship. She waited thirty seconds. It disappeared.

The building super had simply given them the key to Valentine's apartment. Sometimes it took you days to get a warrant and they still acted like you were there to steal the spoons. Sometimes they practically urged you in.

"Probably he doesn't like Valentine," Bennis said.

Figueroa turned the key in the lock and the door swung open. "You know we could be accused of trespassing."

"Only if somebody finds out."

"You know if we find any evidence against Valentine, it can't be used in court if we don't have a warrant."

"Then we go away and ask the district to send somebody and discover it all over again."

"Then the super will tell them we've already been here."

"Probably only if they ask him."

"Oh, all right."

They stood still and gaped at the apartment. The furniture was cheap and worn. The curtains looked like original equipment, as if they were JC Penney circa 1930. The walls were a hideous aqua. But the place was spotlessly clean.

There was a plastic or melamine coffee table. On it were three magazines, squared up perfectly with the edge. Two pens and one pencil were lined up parallel to the edge of the magazine and precisely parallel with each other. Bennis and Figueroa headed to the bedroom.

The bed was made, corners army-square. They opened the closet. "Good Lord," Figueroa said. "Who spaces hangers exactly two inches apart?"

"Valentine, obviously."

In the bathroom, the bath towel, hand towel, and washcloth had been folded precisely in half and hung in size order, precisely spaced. Figueroa pulled open the medicine cabinet.

"I figure the guy for an order nut. But what kind of order is this?" The medicines were carefully lined up, all half an inch from the front of the shelf, but were not categorized, the stick-on bandages next to the aspirin, which was next to the Bromo-Seltzer, but the big square Telfa bandages were on a shelf below.

"Believe it or not, alphabetized by brand name," Bennis said. "Look. Band-Aids, Bayer, Bromo-Seltzer."

"After this, when my kid says a little mess is healthy, I'm gonna agree."

The kitchen was even stranger, because there were more canned goods than there had been medications. Campbell's soups were alphabetized in the "C"s, while the Heinz soup came right next to Hershey's syrup. And there was only enough food to line up with the front of the cupboard shelves, no cans in back, no piles.

The sink was dry; the sink sponge was lined up with the edge of the counter and was bone dry.

"Well, he certainly hasn't been here in a while," Bennis said.

"This is not a well man."

They took the key back to the super. The super said, "Sure. I'll call. If he ever turns up."

"Great. We know where he isn't," Figueroa said as they got into the car.

"Exactly. The big question is where is Valentine now?"

CHAPTER FIFTEEN

WACKER DRIVE SNAKES through the center of the city of Chicago by edging along the south branch of the Chicago River, then hanging an eastward right-angle bend and following the Chicago River to Lake Michigan. Thus, there is South Wacker Drive, North Wacker Drive, West Wacker Drive, and East Wacker Drive, to the despair of out-of-towners.

For Chicagoans in the know, however, there is also Lower Wacker. This underground semisecret road is a specialty of taxi drivers, because they can avoid the traffic that clogs the street up above where the daylight shines—and there are no pedestrians to slow you down. Lower Wacker gives access to basement delivery ports of major hotels and civic buildings. Part of Lower Wacker is lighted by green bulbs, a strange but atmospheric notion thought up by some Department of Transportation honcho.

Lower Wacker is also home to the homeless. Warmer than ground level in the glacial Chicago winters, and cooler than the sunny streets in the stifling summers, many homeless live in Lower Wacker the year round.

Tunnels branch off from Lower Wacker in all directions, running for miles under the city. Some are unlighted. Some lead to underground iron-groined chambers and low-ceilinged tunnels that have not been traveled or even mapped since the late 1800s when they were used to deliver coal to Loop office buildings.

Last year one of the hotels was replacing cracked cement

steps next to their Lower Wacker delivery ramp. A day or so later, delivery people heard desperate knocking noises coming from the steps. A homeless man, sleeping in a narrow tunnel behind the steps, had been cemented in. They chopped up the steps, dug him out, and later poured another set of steps.

Bennis and Figueroa parked their squad car next to an iron support.

"First we're in Neiman Marcus and Bloomie's, now Lower Wacker," Figueroa said.

"Yeah, these are the enchanting discontinuities endemic to the life of an urban police officer," Bennis said.

"Actually, I can't stand working this way," Figueroa said. "What I want is to spend all my time on one case, the murder, solve it, put it to bed, and start the next case."

"Then you're in the wrong line of work, aren't you?" Bennis muttered.

"There's a man over there. Unless it's a pile of rags."

They approached the sleeping man. He had found himself a large shipping carton and several pieces of fabric. He had filled the carton with a layer of foam packing "peanuts" and laid a blanket over them, creating for himself an insulated mattress that protected him from the dampness of the sub-sidewalk.

"You got the bag?" Figueroa said.

Bennis said, "Whattaya think this is?"

"I guess I only said that hoping it would wake him up." The man didn't stir. Figueroa, well aware that some cops rousted the homeless brutally, said, "Good afternoon, sir."

The man sat up sharply and looked scared. He was unshaven and very thin.

"I wonder if we could speak with you, sir," Bennis said.

"What do you want?"

"We'd like to show you a couple of pictures of some people you might know. We thought that while you looked at them you might enjoy a snack."

The man said nothing but studied both of them, staring them up and down from his sitting position. Finally, he said, "Cops?"

"Yes, sir."

"Don't like cops."

"Can't entirely blame you," Bennis said. "Coffee? Cream? Sugar?"

"We also have these Quarter Pounders with cheese," Figueroa said. "And pie."

Figueroa, who had missed lunch, had to admit that the cheeseburgers smelled irresistible, and fortunately they were to the man as well. "You can call me Nate," he said.

"I'm Norm."

"And I'm Suze."

Bennis showed him photos of the dead woman and two dead men found near the CPD. "I'm sorry the way these look, Nate," he said. "I'm sure you realize—"

"Look dead. I can recognize dead, mister. I'm not an idiot."

"Have you seen any one of them?"

"Don't think so." He took his time and studied the pictures seriously.

"Nope."

Bennis and Figueroa sipped their own coffee, while Nate sipped his. "Anybody else around here we could ask?" Bennis said.

"Hmm."

"We're harmless," Figueroa said, hoping that they were. "And there's more lunch in the car."

While Nate's home was close to the roadway, it was nevertheless out of sight of the traffic, behind a cement barrier-type divider, and the whole area was dim. Figueroa, whose eyes had become used to the dimness, looked up and down the hidden walkway and saw no more people, homeless or otherwise. Cars and trucks kept up a steady hum ten feet away.

"Suppose I got the food from the car," she said. "Would you take us to somebody else around here?"

"Ain't around here. Ain't nobody else much likes the front porch."

"Someplace else, then?"

"Could be."

Figueroa went and picked up two more large bags of burgers, apple pies, and hot coffee. She winced inwardly, realizing a cheeseburger or two was not anywhere close to what this man needed. He needed a home, running water, and regular meals. But she couldn't think what else to do right now, and she had her own goal to keep in mind. By the time she got back, Nate was standing up and Bennis and he were chatting, of all things, about the 1954 Buick Century.

But from there it was into the rabbit hole.

While on the main roadway most of the lightbulbs were working, and some were even enclosed in wire cages, Nate led them into a side tunnel that was oddly broad but with a very low ceiling, and absolutely without lights. There was a yellow glow at the end of it, though, where it vanished into a T-junction. They had their flashlights, of course, but the light, though dim, was adequate for moving along. Both Figueroa and Bennis, without consulting about it, believed that taking out their large Kelites would make them look like cops or, equally bad, sanitation inspectors.

Passages led right and left from the dead end of the first tunnel. The yellow light came from a dim but working bulb that Figueroa took to be just fifteen watts. Nate led them into the left-hand tunnel. This one, as well as its mate that went right, was tiled, oddly enough, in pure white glazed ceramic.

She whispered to Bennis, "You think this used to be a subway station?"

"You don't have to whisper," Nate said. "Yeah, this was gonna be a subway stop. Subway here never got built."

The floor was cement, and the farther in they went the cleaner it got.

"Nate, is this clean because people clean it, or because—"

"It's clean because it's so far from the cars and the riffraff."

"Oh."

"Although somebody drops stuff, we pick it up. Can't just let the place go to rack and ruin."

Figueroa raised her eyebrows at Bennis, who shrugged.

Nate's cronies were four men, no women. Two of the men were black, two were white, and all were grayish. They lived in an alcove far from the roadway. They had two working fifty-watt bulbs, the sudden glare making Figueroa blink. She estimated they were three hundred yards or more from the car, and they had made five turns getting here. She was afraid that if Nate didn't take them back they would never find their way. And she didn't think their radios would work down here.

One of the black guys muttered all the time. One of the white guys had heavy scar tissue like a mushroom where his left eye should be.

Nate passed around the burgers and pies himself. He allowed Bennis to pass the coffee. Then Nate told the group, "I don't say these cops are okay, you know. But they treated me polite, and I think we could look at their pictures. This here's Norm and that's Suze."

The four said nothing. Figueroa, after a few seconds of disappointment, realized that this meant a conditional yes. Nate took the photos and passed them around.

The four made a circle around the pictures, ducking their heads, not letting Bennis and Figueroa watch them react. There was some whispering. Then the muttering man said,

"Back of the yard

"Bool and a card

"Baby it's hard.

"Mami is low

"Mami does know,

"Abby the gal."

It wasn't rap and it wasn't word salad. Schizophrenic word salad, she thought, would have more internal rhymes, like abby-cabby-yellow-cabby-tabby. Figueroa decided it was just this man Mami's personal response to a difficult life. Bennis and Figueroa looked at Nate for help deciphering it. "Mami here says the woman's name is Abby."

Suze said, "Actually, we knew that. Was she a friend of his? Does—did she have friends? Somebody we could talk to?" It was the first rule: find friends and relatives of the victim.

Mami shook his head. Nate said, "No. No friends."

"Does she—did she hang around with anybody we could talk to? It's important."

Mami shook his head.

"Relatives?"

Nate conferred with the man and said, "Never mentioned any."

"Were there any people you saw around her? Asking about her? Or anybody following her?"

"Hey, you. You trying to pin her death on one of us? On a homeless guy?" He was angry.

"No, we're not."

"I mean, that's real easy. Always pin everything on the bums, you know."

Figueroa said, "Listen, you know as well as I do that not every homeless person is a saint. Be real, here. I wouldn't try to tell you that every cop in Chicago is a saint."

This elicited a huge gust of laughter, even from the silent ones. The little guy laughed so hard he lost his breath and had to sit down on the ground. Suze winced. Well, not every cop was a saint, okay?

"If there's somebody going around killing you," she said, "don't you want to know it? Don't you want him stopped, whoever it is? Suppose the killer is somebody dressed up to look like he's homeless? Help us out here."

"You got a point." Nate looked intently at the other four, especially Mami. They shook their heads. "But I don't guess they saw anybody like that."

"Did Abby usually hang around South State Street? Eleventh and State? Like under the El over there?"

More conferring. Finally Nate said, "Yeah. More fool her."

"Why's that?"

"We never go there. That place is dangerous."

Figueroa hesitated. "You mean—recently? You've stopped going there recently?"

"What's recently?"

"Well, the last month or so, I guess."

"Nah. More like the last year or so."

"God, those cheeseburgers smelled so great! I really should have saved one in the car," Figueroa said as they drove back toward the CPD parking lot.

"Well we didn't know we'd have to feed five people."

"And I guess it was sort of worth it."

"Time is it?"

"Five. We missed the wind-down at the Furlough."

"And we oughta take a look at the murder scene at night."

"I can't. I have to go home and make dinner."

"Suppose I drive you home and pick you up about seven?"

Figueroa called home on her cell phone, got J J, promised to provide dinner, then called ahead to the ultra-fast, ultra-thick toppings take-out pizza place the kids liked best and put in an order.

———

Holding three pizza boxes balanced in a leaning tower, Suze struggled out of Bennis's car.

"Sure you don't want to come in and eat some of these?"

"No, I want to catch up with a guy who can tell me how to find a pickpocket. I'll be back to get you around seven."

"Yeah, that and you don't like Robert much, either, right?"

"If you can read my mind, why do we talk?"

When she got inside, she found Maria had set the table. Kath pushed Sheryl's wheelchair to the open space on the side. There was no time for niceties. Suze dealt out the three pizzas right down the middle of the table and went to get lemonade and milk. She was so tired her body buzzed.

"I have to go back out for a while," she said as they sat.

Robert said, "Speaking of going out, I have to take my managers to dinner Friday night. The new manager for Ravenswood needs to meet the managers of the five existing stores."

"Sure. When do we expect you back?"

"Well, the stores don't close until nine. So, say we start eating at nine-thirty, finish by eleven-thirty. I should be home by midnight."

"No problem."

"What's this?" Robert asked, opening one of the boxes.

Suze said, "Pineapple and Canadian bacon." Before Robert could say he didn't like it, she added, "JJ likes his pizza that way. He'll probably outgrow it. The pepperoni and green olives is there, in that one, and the other one is your favorite. Onions and ground beef."

"Mom, how come you have to go out?" JJ said.

"Norm and I have some special cases because we're temporary detectives."

"Why are you temporary detectives?"

"Because a whole lot of the real detectives got sick."

"Why did they get sick?"

"They all went to a dinner and ate some food that was bad."

"Why did they eat it?"

"Because—"

"J J!" Robert shouted. "Stop it!"

"Well, all right," J J said, "but just tell me what the special cases are."

"There have been a couple of homeless people killed," Suze said cautiously. She didn't like bringing her work home, and she really didn't like talking about assignments involving death.

"Why are people homeless?" J J asked.

Robert said, "Because they don't want to work."

"Well, that's not really always true," Suze said. "Some of them can't work. Like, they've had an injury."

"Almost anybody can work if they have motivation."

"Or they've been let go because the factory downsized."

"In which case they should look for a job someplace else," Robert said. "After all, a hundred years ago lots of men worked as blacksmiths. Then people stopped using horses for transportation. The industrious men went into automobile repair. You can't wait for the world to find something for you to do."

"Some people have disabilities and they don't have health insurance. And a few years ago most of the mental hospitals closed, so mentally ill people are out on the streets."

"There's always a job somewhere, if you look," Robert said.

"If you lose a job, like the plant you worked in suddenly closes, you can discover you don't have enough money for rent. So you get behind and finally you are put out on the street."

"People shouldn't get bigger houses than they can afford. If you plan ahead and save your money, you won't get caught short. You'll have something to fall back on."

"If you're homeless, then it's harder to get a job because you can't get your clothes cleaned and pressed and you don't look carefully shaven."

"A lot of them are just drunks and druggies," Robert said.

"Well, those are addictions. Good people can have problems. Well-meaning people can have addiction problems. Or sometimes like I said, they have a mental problem but nowhere to go for help," Suze said.

Kath said, "Somebody should make good housing for them. I read that most shelters aren't safe."

"And here we are," Suze said, "in a nice house, with good food and a roof over our heads. We should be grateful. And sympathetic."

Robert said, "They're nuts or they're drunk or they're on drugs or they're lazy. Why make homes for people like that? Susanna, I don't think it's good to give children the idea they don't have to work. I work all day, and nobody ought to pay me if I didn't."

Suze said, "Oy," under her breath. Then she realized there hadn't been a sound from Sheryl since dinner started. She looked at her sister. Sheryl was trembling, her head bobbing on her thin neck and her right arm twitching, the left held like a claw up against her chest. Suze jumped up.

"Honey? What's wrong?"

Kath and Maria got up too.

Suze checked her eyes and her pulse. "I think she's just having an anxiety attack," Suze said. "Robert, can you help me get her to bed?"

"Sure."

"Kids, you eat," Suze said. "I want to get you started on the dishes before I have to leave."

But what Suze really believed was wrong with Sheryl was terror. She should never have allowed the argument—call it a discussion—about homelessness to go on so long. She would bet a lot that Sheryl was picturing what her life would be like now, if she were disabled, as she was, but had no family.

While Suze ate pizza, Norm Bennis was in Skokie, a large suburb immediately northwest of Chicago. He had a contact there, and had notified the man to meet him in one of the village parks.

"My gypsy friend," Bennis said when Harold Pigeon strolled past the swing set and over to the bleachers near the small baseball diamond and sat near Norm.

"Haven't I told you, you shouldn't say gypsy? It's considered pejorative."

"Yeah, you told me. I'm not a politician, Harold. I don't have to be p.c. I'm a cop. Everybody knows how insensitive we are."

"You know, what this world needs is a 'Proud To Be a Gypsy' T-shirt."

"Maybe you could make 'em and sell 'em. White on dark green is very nice. I also like blue on cream." Harold had been Bennis's source in a few busts of scams on the elderly. The relationship developed when Bennis had traced three women in their thirties who buddied up to men in their seventies and in one case eighty, took them traveling on the men's money, partied with them, and got them to sign over their bank accounts. Harold had been involved, having introduced the women to their victims. In fact he had been the connection that tied the cases together for Bennis. But he was harder to convict than the women, since he had not been directly involved in touching the money, and there was no paper trail involving him. Nothing had been signed over to him. He got kickbacks in cash from the women. Anyway, he was ultimately more useful to Bennis as an informant.

"Harold, I need somebody to tell me about picking pockets."

"What makes you think I'd know anybody like that?"

"Don't play with me. Elaine would probably love to get her sentence reduced, now that she's had time to think it over. Betty

I'm not so sure of, but Elaine is not a stand-up female. She'd rat."

"Well, there is one guy."

Suze and Norm got out of Norm's car in the CPD parking lot, under the peach-colored lighting. "This is the most horrible color anybody could have picked," Figueroa said. "Green would be better." In the light, Bennis's brown skin looked orange, which was not so bad, but she knew she looked sickly yellow. "Whoever invented this should be sentenced to four years in a detox ward."

"Don't be crabby."

They walked together from the parking lot to the El tracks. The El ran along Holden Court, behind the CPD building at the second-floor level, like railroad tracks in the air. Its great iron legs splayed out and down, elbows at train level, the feet set in concrete pillars on the street level. A giant anchored.

State Street, that great street, paralleled the El tracks, one block west, running in front of the CPD central offices building. Because it was also the headquarters of the First District and many courts, the area was busy by day—and never had anywhere near enough parking. The CPD lot was permitted to officers and CPD employees only, and the many other lots that had been randomly placed here and there along State Street north and south of the CPD had gradually been lost to gentrification. New apartment buildings were required to provide plans for under-building parking for tenants before they received construction permits but that didn't help visitors to the area. And most of the street remained patchily run-down.

It was not quite dark even now. Darkness came late to Chicago in June. It would be full night by ten, but at nine the sun had just set. Still the shadows of the buildings and the tracks gave the place an urban gloom.

"Bennis, did you know that during Prohibition you could

smell the illegal alky brewing on Maxwell Street all the way over here?"

"Never heard that."

"If you brewed for Johnny Torrio, you could make ten times what you earned digging ditches. He'd advance you some corn, some sugar and yeast, and one of the old people in the house who'd be home anyway would sit there and watch the corn likker brew. One house could make a couple of hundred gallons a week. Torrio's trucks would come around and collect the booze in tanks. Thousands and thousands and thousands of gallons. The whole district reeked of fermenting mash."

"And your point is you can't keep people away from booze?"

"No, my point is maybe that's a better use for old people than letting them wander around homeless."

"That's not a bad point."

Figueroa gazed up and down the El track and the darkening street. "You know what, Bennis? It seems smaller here at night. The El looks like a fence, an overhead fence. It clamps down on you, doesn't it?"

She glanced at him as if thinking he'd mock her, but he said, "Yeah. Like a tunnel."

"And State Street with those orange lights on all that asphalt is kind of toxic. It looks like the Deadly Dessert that kept people from getting out of Oz."

"What's the matter with you? People didn't want to get out of Oz."

"They did if their Auntie Em lived in Kansas. Anyway, suppose there was a deadly Oz you did want to get out of?"

"Now you're weirding out. Let's not get nuts. Let's look at it up close and personal."

Figueroa put her hands on her hips. "Okay. You're absolutely right. And let's be systematic while we're at it. The first known murder by our killer was Manualo. Ten days ago now.

Close to the El but not right under it. Let's go look."

Jimmy Manualo had been killed about a block north of the CPD building, past what was known as the Annex. The Annex was an undistinguished blocky structure contiguous to the CPD. It had been cobbled onto the bigger building about thirty years ago when the department found it needed more room. Unfortunately, the Annex had never been intended to be part of the CPD, and its floors were not on the same level. This meant that inside, when you walked from the CPD part on any given floor into the Annex, you walked down a sloping ramp of ugly vinyl tile.

The entrance to the First District Police Station was in the main CPD building, next to the Annex. The east side of the Annex and the east side of the CPD building faced the El. There were upper-floor windows on the Annex's east side, but they looked directly out at the El tracks, just like its sister building did, and there were no lower-floor windows.

Bennis and Figueroa stood in the deep purple gloom between two legs of the El and looked at the Annex with dismay.

Bennis said, "It's no better, is it?"

"Why didn't they just put some damn big windows on the first or second floor?"

"Because there's no view. Nobody wants to look at the El and hear all the noise, Suze."

They walked to the exact spot where Manualo had been found. It was a good block north of the Annex, and not near anything, really. A parking lot between the El and State Street was being torn up, probably for a high-rise. A crane was parked on the cracked asphalt. Nobody would have been sitting in the crane all night, watching for murderers.

And next to the track, even though they knew they were in the right spot from the plat drawing they'd brought along, there was no sign of anything unusual. It was as if Jimmy Manualo had never existed and his dead body had never lain in that alley.

Trash was everywhere. Apparently no one had ordered a complete collection of potential evidence on the ground after Manualo's death, so some of this must have been here when he died ten days before. Bennis and Figueroa kicked through it. There were gum wrappers, candy wrappers, McDonald's, Wendy's, and Burger King bags. There were long red wrappers from microwave burritos, a few dried french fries, and a dozen or so cold drink cups. There were several foam hot drink cups, a muddy squashed mitten, a few condoms, part of a car muffler, a few pennies, and an entire car door, painted light blue. There was a child-size T-shirt, and one smashed Reebok. And there were bottles and cans, mostly beer, and some bottles that had contained cheap wine. Most of the glass bottles were broken. Suze and Norm looked for discarded Handi Wipes or Wet Ones, but didn't see any. There was a lot of Kleenex and other tissues, ranging from fairly new to so deteriorated they were slurry, but you could tell they were paper, not pre-moistened towelettes, when you scuffed them.

Bennis said, "Civilization, huh?"

"Pretty smart to kill under an El track," Figueroa said. "Nobody can see you. And if you pick your moment right, when there's an El going over, people could be standing three feet away and not hear a thing. Even a scream or a struggle."

"Yeah, clever."

"Why do homeless people want to sleep here, of all places? It's noisy."

"They sleep all over town. They get moved out of the bus station and the El stops. And out of O'Hare. Plus none of those places have benches you can sleep on anymore. They've put in armrests every couple of feet so nobody can lie down on them."

"Maybe the homeless feel safer here, near the CPD," Figueroa said sadly.

They walked south.

The site of O'Dowd's death, or to be more accurate, Bennis

pointed out, the place where O'Dowd was found, was a side alley, but just off the El tracks and one block south of the CPD. There was as much trash here as directly under the El, and the area was just as secluded. It looked as if the techs had collected very little trash for examination, just like the Manualo murder.

By now the sky was dark. Only the sickly peach lights made it possible to see. The eye couldn't pick up any details. "I'm glad we came here, Bennis," Figueroa said.

"Yes. It's different at night."

"Seeing it the way they saw it, you begin to realize how long the killer could toy with them. They could have had a two-hour picnic sitting right here with a bottle of scotch or bourbon and watched the trains go by overhead."

"But you can see people driving by on State. Which means they might see you."

"Right. And cars going down the alley to park in the CPD lot. And some pedestrians on State Street."

"Would anybody notice? A couple of homeless people sitting around?"

"You never know." She thought a moment. "I doubt it. But if I were the killer, I'd still be cautious."

"Which tells me that the murders happened after the eleven-to-sevens reported for duty at eleven and the three-to-eleven guys had left."

"Which would be late enough so there wouldn't be any pedestrians at all."

Bennis said, "And which would be consistent with the ME's time of death estimate."

"One murder May twenty-first, then ten days of no attacks, then two in two days, May thirty-first and June first. Depending on how you count—whether they happened before or after midnight. I wonder what that sequence means."

"I hope it doesn't mean he's found out he really enjoys it," Bennis said.

Having got the feel of the area in its own dim light, they took out their multi-cell Kelites and did another search. Holding the flashlights low to the ground, they scanned the broken asphalt and gravel for anything new. The raking light gave them a better view of the contours of the ground and highlighted some small litter that they would not otherwise have seen. But there was nothing that looked like evidence.

They clicked the lights off and walked to the spot a block farther south where Abigail Ward's body had lain. This was still blocked off by yellow CRIME SCENE DO NOT CROSS barrier tape and the AUTHORIZED PERSONNEL ONLY signs.

Figueroa said, "I guess nobody took this down."

"Why should they? Nobody needs this place. You can get into the CPD lot by coming down the alley from the north, and you can get in from State Street."

"Yeah." Peach light discolored the parking lot and the side of the CPD building. It turned the red brick of the apartment building a dreary tomato soup color. But it didn't give much illumination, and in contrast to its odd hue, the shadows became greenish. Figueroa said, "Bennis, did you see that?"

"What?"

"Over there. Somebody's watching us."

Both froze, looking for a sign.

They stood unmoving for several minutes, Figueroa's knees beginning to ache.

There was a hint of movement near one of the legs of the El. Bennis sprinted to top speed from a standing start. Figueroa ran too, but at an angle to Bennis, a little farther under the El, hoping to head off whoever it was. She clicked her flashlight back on, and the light bounced ineffectively off the ground and buildings.

They pounded down the alley toward the rear of the CPD. "Stop! Hold it, sir! Police!"

The figure vanished.

"Stop! Stop!"

"Police!"

But they knew they were yelling only in the hope of getting the man to show himself. They had no idea where he had gone, and after three minutes of running had taken them past the torn-up parking lot with no sign of anybody, they gave up.

"Where'd he go?" Figueroa said, gasping.

"No doors back here. He coulda slipped under a fence. It's too dark to see between buildings."

"Did you see what he looked like?"

"Not much. Wearing a cap. Young, maybe from the way he ran."

"Jeez. I'm creeped out."

"Let's go get a beer."

"Yeah. I can make some phone calls from there."

Far in the distance they heard the El train coming.

The Furlough Bar was two blocks south of the CPD building and just the other side of State Street. They fled there, each more grateful for the other's company than they wanted to say.

Mary Lynne Lee was twenty-three. She had been a popular girl at New Trier High School, a beautiful girl, had lots of dates, and had played a very good game of soccer.

From her first years in school, everybody liked her. In grade school, teachers had called her "sweet," or "a very peaceful child," or "obedient."

Mary Lynne's grandfather on her father's side was Korean. A nuclear physicist, he had taught for many years in the Tech Institute at Northwestern University. His wife was French and had been an early founder of Montessori schools in the rich suburbs north of Chicago—Wilmette, Winnetka, and Glencoe. She had published numerous articles on early childhood education. Mary Lynne's maternal grandparents were both professionals also, her grandmother an architect and her grandfather an architectural engineer. Mary Lynne's mother was an obstetrician practicing at Evanston Hospital, and her father was an electrical engineer who had got in on the ground floor of computer hardware manufacturing and made lots of money, selling parts to Motorola in Schaumburg, among others. This was not a particularly unusual family history for the north shore area.

Mary Lynne's brother was in school at MIT. Her younger sister, Pamela, had won every academic prize in mathematics the New Trier school system had to offer.

Mary Lynne was beautiful and sweet, but not very bright. Always a C student at best, she tried and tried and tried and did her homework, and listened to the teachers, and tried and failed. After she failed ninth-grade algebra, she was put in remedial math for two years. The school advised her not even to attempt the sciences.

New Trier divided students according to levels, which was a politically correct way of saying they had a tracking system. Level four was the hardest class in its category. A level four English class was for the brightest English students, and within that level they were graded A, B, C, or F. A level three course was average, but not bad. Level two was for those who weren't doing very well. Same for math. Same for history. And so on.

Mary Lynne was of low-average intelligence. She did not qualify for special help. She was not placed in level one. All of her classes were level twos, but even there, competing only against the poorer students, she got Cs.

Which might have been all right, if she had not been Mary Lynne Lee. Her teachers liked her. She did her work; and after all, not everybody in the world had to be academically inclined. If they weren't Mary Lynne Lee.

Mary Lynne spent her life in a family entirely made up of high achievers, and she knew she didn't measure up. Every day, every night at dinner, the family talk was about her brother's scholarships or another article her mother was writing on obstetrics. Her grandfather, now in his late seventies, won several major physics awards, for one of which he had to fly to Paris and for another to the Hague. He took Pamela, Mary Lynne's younger sister, with him, since, as her parents told Mary Lynne, "Pamela can appreciate the award." Pamela had been in level five math, which was only for those especially talented.

Meanwhile, Mary Lynne was playing pretty good soccer.

When she graduated from high school, Mary Lynne took a summer job in a Montessori preschool. In the fall, at the advice of her grandmother who knew schools in the area well, she started at a local small private college that gave lots of personal attention. Mary Lynne wanted to study early childhood education, maybe out of a desire to please her grandmother. But the school discouraged that and suggested phys. ed.

But even that was academically too hard for her.

Frustrated by classwork, Mary Lynne started drifting into Chicago for the weekends, hanging out at singles bars, trying to blot out the humiliations of the school week. The weekends began to stretch into noon on Monday and start earlier, right after class Friday, then Thursday night. For a while she told herself that everybody cut Friday classes in college, but it wasn't true.

She drank more, went to the dorm less, and spent nights downtown with a variety of men she met in bars.

She thought she'd take a little room downtown in a cheap SRO hotel, hoping her family might not realize she wasn't in the dorm most nights. But she needed a source of income other than her parents' allowance to make it work.

Mary Lynne became a weekend prostitute.

For months she continued to turn up at classes on Tuesday and Wednesday. But just before Christmas she was called in to the office of her adviser.

Her choice was to get to every class for the rest of the term or withdraw.

Mary Lynne promised to attend class. But the thought was so depressing that she decided she would go party that night and start being really good the next morning.

She never went back to school.

After Mary Lynne Lee started staying in downtown Chicago on a permanent basis, her parents sent a detective to find her. Four times in the first year, she was discovered and brought back to their house in Winnetka. Four times she slipped away again.

Mary Lynne was not particularly expert at covering her tracks. She had never been sly or dishonest, only sad. But the fourth time her parents brought her home, she overheard them talking with the family internist about "protective residential housing." While not certain what that meant, there had been enough hints that her parents thought they couldn't control her, and the school couldn't control her, and therefore they needed a specialist to control her.

They loved her; she knew that. But her whole family, she believed, was not right for her.

The fifth time she disappeared, she didn't go back to her small hotel room. She stayed with a man she hardly knew, because she reasoned that if she hardly knew him, her parents and their detective would have no idea of his existence at all. Nobody could find her and make her feel bad.

That nobody could find her, she was absolutely right. As to whether anybody else could make her feel bad she was dead wrong. The man she stayed with hit her when he was drinking and ignored her when he wasn't. She decided to leave him and sleep on the streets, at least until the weather got cold.

Mary Lynne tried cocaine for a little while, but she didn't like it much. Later on she tried crack at the urging of another prostitute. But she didn't like it, either. Neither one appealed to her as much as alcohol.

When she was tricking for money, Mary Lynne wore a

short, short skirt with cutouts on the side in the shapes of hearts. When she wasn't tricking, she wore sweatshirts and Levi's. But she soon found that if she put her hair up under a baseball cap when she went out in the sweatshirt and Levi's, the world was a nicer place. People thought she was a boy and they didn't hassle her or call her ugly names.

She was minding her own business just wandering Wednesday night near the CPD building on State Street when the two cops almost walked up on her. Automatically, she ran away. What were they doing out there anyway, poking around under the El with nothing criminal going on? She finally lost them simply by burrowing under some trash bags. After they were gone, feeling slimy and gritty from the trash, she got up and wandered north on State Street, back toward the Loop. Maybe later she could come back and sleep here someplace. It seemed kind of safe to be near the police department.

The address on Abigail Ward's long-expired driver's license was in District Thirteen. During the day, one of the officers from Thirteen went to the address, which turned out to be a bed and breakfast. Nobody there had heard of Abigail Ward, but they had records going back years.

"Just ledgers, really," said a motherly woman of about sixty, "but you're welcome to look at them."

The cop did, and found Abigail Ward's check-in information. She claimed to have arrived from Albany, New York. And she had given her address there.

"So I called the Albany, New York, PD," Figueroa said to Bennis as they sat in the Furlough.

"And?"

"They put me on to the local precinct, and maybe it wasn't a busy day, but one of the cops actually went over to the address where the Wards had lived, which wasn't far from the station. That part's the good news."

"The bad news is there's nobody there named Ward anymore."

"Right. However, the next-door neighbor gave the cop the phone number of a Daniel Frank Ward who still lives in the Albany area."

"He say how old?"

"Thirty-eight."

"That's about right. So call."

Suze called.

"Yes, this is Dan Ward."

"Mr. Ward, I'm Susanna Figueroa, from the Chicago Police Department. I need to be sure I'm talking to the right person. Is your mother's name Abigail?"

"What's happened?"

"You're the correct Daniel Ward?"

"If she—yes."

"I'm very sorry to have to tell you, we have an Abigail Ward who is deceased."

"Well, thank you for calling. Good-bye."

"Don't hang up, please. I need to know when you last saw your mother."

"Why?"

"We're trying to trace her movements. Your mother was killed yesterday."

"By a car?"

"We think she was murdered."

"Thank you for calling. Good-bye."

"Please! Do you want to come to Chicago and claim the body?"

"I don't want my mother and I don't want her body. She wasn't there for me. Why should I care? She—we asked her, we all begged her to stop drinking, and she didn't give a rip, Miss Figgero. I haven't seen her in a decade. Don't even try to lay a guilt trip on me. She was an adult when I was an infant. It was not my doing. I don't have a mother now and I never had one when I needed one, either. Don't bother me anymore."

Sinking onto a bar stool, Figueroa blew air up at her eyebrows. "Jeez. Don't ask. Forget Abby Ward's family."

Bennis said, "Okay."

"We've got three murders. They should tell us something. What do we actually *know*?"

"The victim. Did you get background on Manualo?"

"Finally. The investigation those detectives did is only—at best—well, Mossbacher aside, I'd have to call it perfunctory."

"Go ahead. Call it perfunctory."

"You're a saint. Manualo was a jockey, of all things. Raced at Arlington, Maywood, lots of other places. In the seventies and early eighties he won a hell of a lot. He was major. He was actually famous."

"Got it."

"Then—well, this is kind of sad. A lot sad, actually. Then at the age of forty or so, he started to gain weight. He was a little guy, naturally. Five feet one, ninety pounds tops."

"Kind of like you."

"Smaller than me if you can believe such a thing. He started to gain weight. Went to his doctor, apparently. No hormonal problem, no diabetes, no congestive heart failure, no nothing. He was eating the same as ever. His metabolism had changed as he got older."

"I keep telling my mother that. Don't send care packages of food anymore."

"Naturally, as he got heavier, he slipped down the rank of jockeys. Eventually he became unemployable. Lots of people said he should just eat less. He told one jockey friend he'd spent his whole life calling a lettuce leaf and one boiled clam lunch, and he just couldn't go lower than that."

"So he's unemployed."

"And starts to drink. He'd always allowed himself one ounce of red wine to unwind at the end of the day. *One ounce!* That's one third of a normal glass."

"And it got away from him."

"Yup. And he wound up on State Street in May. High blood alcohol level. Smothered with a coat and a sort of pillowlike thing he was carrying. And his face was washed. He had no close relatives in Chicago. Honestly, I don't see following up his possible enemies or heirs. He was in the wrong place at the wrong time."

"So," Bennis said, "what do we got? Well, victims: we got a white guy, a Hispanic guy, and a white woman. So race and gender is no object to our perp."

"Fine, but what do they have in common?" She picked up her beer. "Just one of these. I'm driving."

"I can drive you home."

"Aw, Bennis, you already drove me once today. Thanks, but I can do it."

"You've had a hard day. You deserve two beers if you want them."

"Bennis, you *sweetheart!*" She threw an arm around his shoulder and kissed his cheek.

"Figueroa! Are you insane?" He jumped back and looked around the bar, which was fortunately deserted. "They'll think we're having a cliché squad car romance."

"Okay, okay. Calm down. So—what we know is this. First, all three murders probably took place after midnight."

"All three were homeless people."

"*Visibly* homeless. Unkempt. Unhealthy-looking."

"All three were alcoholic. And all three didn't do dope."

"True. But in the over-forty age group that isn't so unusual. Maybe the asshole is intentionally killing older people. The dusters and crankers and your random dopers tend to be the younger gang."

"And of course all three had their faces washed."

"Exactly."

"Okay. And all three were within two—mmm, call it three blocks of the Chicago Police Department."

Bennis put down his beer and frowned. "There's something about that fact I don't particularly like."

CHAPTER SIXTEEN

FIGUEROA DROVE HOME after just one beer, as she was determined to do. It was past midnight when she got to her part of town. The nearest parking place was four blocks away.

Oh, gee. Extremely bad luck. No, come on! That's absurd. In fact, she thought, it was stupid. The reason there were fewer parking places was the late hour. She usually got home around four-thirty or five, and most nine-to-five workers got home later. No wonder she often had the pick of parking places.

She let herself in the back door with her key, quietly, so as not to wake anybody.

The first thing she always did after locking her gun was to look in on Sheryl. After her sister's distress earlier tonight, Suze was worried about her. Tomorrow she ought to call the doctor and engage in some serious in-depth questioning about how Sheryl was really doing. If she could report that the doctor saw progress, it would be a good idea to make that extremely clear to Sheryl.

And if the doc *didn't* see progress? What then?

Cross that bridge later.

Early in Sheryl's rehabilitation, Suze visited the surgeon who had reset the fragments of her fractured skull. "I seem to be more frustrated every day that she can't talk," Suze said. "And if *I'm* frustrated, think how frustrated she is."

"Be glad she's come this far," the doctor said.

"But she's so—it's like she's locked up in there."

"No she isn't. There actually is a condition called 'locked-in syndrome.' "

"I already don't like the sound of that."

"In that condition, the patient is actually fully awake and thinking, but the body is completely paralyzed. Some of them can communicate by blinking. Some can't. Some can't do anything whatsoever to communicate with the world outside their bodies. As a doctor, you see these patients and you feel absolutely useless."

"That's like—like 'The Premature Burial,' isn't it?"

"Just about. So when you see Sheryl struggling to get words out, and she will have to struggle for months, you know, you need to be aware of how much worse it could be. Even when she gets most of the way well, there'll be setbacks. It's not just Sheryl who will be frustrated. You and her husband and children are all going to be resentful and angry over and over again."

"It makes me so angry for her."

Dr. Sager nodded, not unhappy to hear this. He was a great advocate of involving the family, and a family member empathizing with the patient was no bad thing in his view.

"You're probably more aware of it than she is right now. She's disoriented, and dealing with muscle injuries, and fractured ribs and arm bones that hurt. Her aphasia is only one small thing to her in a sea of things right now."

"Well, even so—"

"Even so, she soon will be aware of it. Let me show you what the problem is."

Sager pulled over a model of the human brain that he kept on his desk. It opened on a hinge, showing the inside.

"Your sister has had several areas of her brain damaged. The paralysis on her left side was caused by an injury to the right side of the brain. Aphasia—the inability to speak—is caused by injury to the cortex of the left hemisphere in the posterior frontal and anterior temporal lobes. Right about here." He pointed to an area that would be roughly in front of Sheryl's ear.

"What she has is called nonfluent aphasia. Sometimes it's called Broca's aphasia because the site of injury is called Broca's area. It's in the frontal lobe close to the area of the motor cortex, and controls the movement of the lips, jaw, tongue, soft palate, and vocal cords. This is very much like the way other motor areas control arms and legs. Damage to Broca's area causes a difficulty in expressing thoughts verbally and in writing. The ability to understand remains intact."

"In other words, she can think of what she wants to say, but she can't produce the sounds."

"Exactly. Broca's contains the memory for motor patterns of speech. There are other kinds of aphasia, fluent aphasia for instance, where the patient can talk up a storm but none of it makes any sense."

"I was hoping she might be able to use her computer instead. You know she worked as a computer engineer before the accident happened."

"Yes, I knew that."

"I thought she could use a word processor to tell us what she was thinking."

"I don't think that's going to happen. I'm sorry. But patients with Broca's can't write, and mostly they can't type, either."

"What *is* going to happen?"

"She'll improve. It'll be slow but it'll come."

"By 'improve' do you mean just a little bit, or will she be entirely well again?"

"I can't tell you that. All I can say is that the biggest improvement will happen in the first three to six months."

Sheryl was asleep. The faint green light of the night-light showed the peaceful rise and fall of her chest.

Breathing a sigh herself in sheer relief, Suze hurried to the back stairs. She had to be up by six, and the sooner she got to bed the sooner she'd get to sleep. And she was just utterly, totally exhausted.

Stepping onto the first stair, she halted. The oddest feeling crept over her.

Now and then, with another cop, she would do an Officer Friendly talk at a grade school or high school. Their goal, besides trying to make children more comfortable with the police, was to steer children away from potentially dangerous situations. One of the difficulties was that bad people often looked perfectly nice, and you had to explain to the child that he or she should listen to his instincts, even if nothing really looked wrong.

Suze felt as if there was something wrong.

Well, take your own prescription, she thought. She removed her foot from the step and walked back down the hall. Sheryl was still asleep and *definitely* breathing. Suze listened carefully through six full breaths to be sure that she was not only breathing but breathing normally. Feeling like a fool, she also crouched down and looked under Sheryl's hospital bed, but there were no monsters there.

Having decided to do a patrol, Suze checked the first-floor bathroom without turning on the light, so as not to wake Sheryl. Her sister found it hard enough to sleep; waking her for no reason would be cruel. Suze could see quite well in the dim night-light by now. There wasn't any monster behind the shower curtain.

She paced into the living room, across to the sun parlor, then turned back and walked slowly through the dining room, finding nobody lurking anyplace, and finally back into the kitchen. Except that the kids had left a few dishes out of the dishwasher, there was nothing wrong.

She leaned to look down the cellar stairs and flicked on the light, knowing it was far away enough not to disturb Sheryl. She walked down to the landing, and from there she could see most of the basement.

She hesitated a few seconds, then decided she was being stupid. She walked down the cellar stairs. The lightbulb Robert had installed was so dim the light looked brown. Suze walked over to the clothes washer and pulled the cord of the bulb overhead.

Bright blue-white light flooded the cement room. Suze stepped slowly past the washer and dryer. Beyond them was a cement room scarred by old dark streaks. She thought it once had been a coal storage space. It was damp and low-ceilinged.

Retreating, she backed up to the stairs. No monsters in the basement either, except for feelings of threat.

By now she was starting to feel distinctly foolish. The house was full of people. Of course there weren't any monsters. This was all happening just because she was overtired. Too long a day and too much stress. She turned and went up the back stairs, pausing for a full minute on the second-floor landing to listen. Robert slept with his door open so as to hear Sheryl's bell or the fire alarm, although both were loud enough to hear through closed doors. Kath and Maria slept with their doors shut. Everything was just as usual.

As she turned to go on upstairs, Suze noticed a patch of lighter color in the corner where the second-floor hall met the main stairs. Trying not to make noise, she crept over and looked down. It was a pink cloth. When she picked it up, she realized it was a pair of Maria's underpants. Maria was going through a stage of wanting "older" underwear, not little-girl cotton anymore. Suze had insisted that whatever she bought had to be either machine washable or Maria had to hand-wash them herself. This was the result—silky pink undies made of nylon that could be machine washed and even machine dried.

It was strange that Maria dropped them here on the landing

of the main stairs. If she'd been carrying laundry up from the basement, she'd drop something near the back stairs, wouldn't she? But really, that was being too analytical. Maybe she'd stopped here to talk with Kath or somebody and not noticed she dropped them.

Suze hung the underwear on Maria's doorknob, where she'd probably be horrified to find them in the morning, and went on upstairs.

On the third floor, she stepped into JJ's room. He was making little-boy snuffling sleeping noises. Just as usual.

Good.

She studied the stairs to the attic. Really, she should go on up if she were going to do a thorough job. But there was nothing of value in the attic and no reason anybody would go there. It would just be hot and empty. And besides she was just so tired.

And feeling even more foolish.

In her own room, Suze stripped off clothes that she had worn now for twenty hours. She thought she could take a shower without waking JJ. JJ was not like Sheryl. He could sleep through everything except the smell of bacon.

But under the shower, water sluicing down her naked body, she still didn't feel comfortable. She was in her own bathroom, in her own home. Why did she feel so exposed? The water was warm. Why did she feel chilly?

THURSDAY

CHAPTER SEVENTEEN

Thursday, 7:00 A.M.

From Your Morning, *the drive-to-work chat show on AM 98:*

This is Steve Mumford sending you a happy good morning. The weather over the Chicagoland area is mild and lovely, with a projected high in the mid-seventies. Traffic with Brand Goddart in four minutes.

At ten past the hour I will be interviewing Sandra Cascolinelli, the new appointee to the post of press rep for the Chicago Police Department. We'll talk about the CAPS program and the recent shooting inside a Seventh District lockup.

The City Council has decided to table any discussion of safe shelters for the homeless until early fall. The underlying thinking seems to be that it's warm out. Well, that's true. It's warm right now. I find it's often warm at the beginning of the summer, don't you?

But do you parents out there remember the story of the monkey's house that we all read our children? The monkey troop was caught in a terrible hurricane. It blew away the bananas they'd collected and drenched the monkeys and kept them wet and miserable for three days. "This is horrible. We've got to put up a shelter," the lead monkey said. "We need a roof and walls. We need a house. We'll build one tomorrow."

Tomorrow came. The storm blew itself out. The sun rose and the land dried off. All was wonderful. One little monkey said, "Shall we build our house now?"

But the boss monkey said, "We don't need one. Look. The sun is shining and the land is warm and dry." So they played and foraged for food and had a wonderful time.

But after a while another hurricane came. And it blew away their food and left them cold and wet and miserable. "We have to build a house," they all said. "We'll start tomorrow."

And then the storm went away and the sun came out. And what do you suppose the boss monkey said?

You guessed it.

In Chicago we know that winter comes every year. We're smart enough to have picked up on that. I've certainly noticed it, haven't you?

We need reliable, clean, permanent shelters for the homeless. Not scraped-together, temporary, unsafe, overnight cots in vermin-filled rooms. And we need to build them while the sun shines.

IT WAS MORNING in the Figueroa-Birch household and everybody was running late. Suze hadn't had enough sleep and was fighting the mental fuzzies. She'd dropped the frying pan, trying to make scrambled eggs. The frustration of having to clean up slippery raw eggs from the floor and then serve bowls of cold cereal, which she didn't particularly like, almost made her cry. When she looked at the paper towels, printed with a repeating pattern that said, "Home is where the heart is," she was extremely annoyed. Then, when J J and Kath, who loved scrambled eggs and also didn't especially like cereal, were kind and helpful and said, "Never mind, it's okay," she actually did shed a tear. She skillfully concealed it by pouring herself another cup of coffee.

Maria, of course, didn't eat eggs. Or sausage or bacon or sweet rolls. A glass of orange juice and half a bowl of instant oatmeal was all she wanted. She was dieting.

Just as Suze started out the door with J J, Kath, and Maria, she realized she'd left her handcuffs upstairs. "Hold it!" she said. "I'll be right back."

She ran fast up the rear stairs. Most of the time Figueroa used the rear stairs, and she was sorry to admit to herself, one of the reasons was so that she could avoid Robert.

Robert is a good person, really, she constantly told herself. *He goes out every day and works hard to make money for his family. He brings home his earnings and he supplies food, clothing, and shelter.*

Robert's string of five or so dry-cleaning stores made steady money, but it was no way to get rich. There were staff problems, building problems, zoning problems, pilferage problems, and so on. The opening of the sixth store in Ravenswood was taking a lot of his time. And his patience.

Robert's problem was that he was crabby, nit-picking, complaining, impatient, and sarcastic. So Suze avoided him when she could. Especially first thing in the morning.

She ran up the back stairs, trying not to clump too hard in her heavyish work shoes.

She stepped lightest at the second floor, so as not to get

Robert fussed. As she passed the second-floor landing, she smelled male sweat. You couldn't miss it.

How odd. Robert never used the back stairs. And where would he have been going, anyway? He hadn't come down to the kitchen. In fact, ordinarily it would be half an hour before he even got up. Would he have gone up to the third floor? Only J J and Suze lived up there, and he certainly hadn't sought them out this morning to ask them anything.

When she got there, he wasn't on the third floor. Suze found her handcuffs on her nightstand, and there was for sure no Robert around.

Well, what difference did it make if he was roaming around? It was his house. And anyhow, these old houses were weird. There were creaks and groans you could swear were human, but it was just the house breathing. On the third floor, once in a great while, you could actually hear the furnace turn on in the basement. Most of the time you wouldn't. The sound of the water heater turning on might carry up through the pipes. Or not. Sometimes you could smell what was cooking in the kitchen. Other times you could fry enough onions for the whole First District and not get a whiff of it up here.

Must be a combination of wind direction outdoors, and who had which doors and windows open, she thought. And whether the heating system was on or off.

Anyway, as she came back down the stairs there was no sweat smell remaining in the air.

Sergeant Touhy said, "Bennis and Figueroa. Get to Mossbacher at the area ASAP. No, not ASAP, forthwith!"

"Yes, boss," Bennis said.

Mossbacher was angry.

"You can't just run up hours of tech time."

"Look, Sarge, if there's gonna be evidence anyplace it'll be in transfer evidence on the ground."

"There's a limit, kids. I'll allow somebody to fingerprint the crap directly under the body, and even within one foot of it. Also bottles and cans nearby. But let's not get crazy here. And I'm not talking just about the ton of shit from the ground around the body that you wanted examined. I'm also talking about Dr. Percolin ordering some complicated testing of the stomach contents and some weird analysis of face swabbings."

"How'd you know about this so fast?" Bennis asked.

"Are you kidding?" He gestured at his keyboard and monitor. "You think I can let you two inexperienced hotshots blunder around without any supervision? We got a crisis, but thank God for Bill Gates, I can cyber-supervise."

"Boss, we need this info. We may have a serial killer on our hands."

"Serial killer! Don't say that." Mossbacher looked annoyed and a little worried. "On the basis of three dead bums? You're out of your gourd, Bennis. Drop it."

"There's all these similarities—"

"They washed their faces? Spare me. You're suffering from beginner's enthusiasm. The wonders of techno-sleuthing. You've been reading too much crime fiction."

"But, seriously, sir, if we knew what booze they'd been drinking, we might be able to figure out where these people had been just before—"

"The idea that tracing a brand of booze or a face wash, even if there is one, is just too remote. People can pick up good bourbon or bad bourbon anyplace. Listen, Bennis. Let's say you wanted to do a tox screen. Routine. Let's say the standard tox panel costs a thousand dollars."

"That much?"

"Probably more. This is a for-instance. But say it doesn't turn up anything. So you've got a hunch. *Got* to be something there, right? You want to do fifty more rare poisons. Mercury, chokecherry, radium, theophylline, peyote, whatever. Maybe that's ten thousand dollars. With me so far?"

"Yeah, sure, boss. But—"

"Still no result, so you think of another fifty poisons even rarer. Maybe a hundred thousand dollars. There are three to four thousand tests for things people have around the house every day. There are respiratory drug panels and cardiac drug panels. Where do you stop? What about the trace evidence? You could pick up every morsel of dust and crud and flecks of human skin and bits of human hair and wings of flies in the alley and study them, do DNA on the hair and skin fragments, but do you have any idea how much lab time the city'd be paying for? WE DO NOT DO THIS IN CHICAGO! Can't. The city budget is not infinite. You want your potholes patched? You want fire engines?"

Bennis said, "We're not stupid, boss. We know there's a limit. We'd draw the line someplace."

"You're not hearing me, Bennis. You've already drawn the line *too far out!*"

Figueroa said, "If the dead guy was the mayor, you'd order every scrap of evidence eyeballed. Minutely."

Mossbacher surged to his feet. His face was red and congested and his eyes were half buried between lowering brows and bunched cheek muscles.

"Figueroa, if the dead guy was the mayor, *you would not be on the case! Now get out!*"

They hurried out of the door, but not fast enough. Suddenly Mossbacher appeared behind them. "And *don't* talk to the goddamned press!"

His door slammed hard.

"Say, I could be wrong, Bennis, but I kind of get the idea we're on our own."

"Yes, Suze, my man. We're on our own, and I'm not even sure they want us to get anyplace."

"These homeless people are throwaways."

"Murder victims, but negligible human beings."

"Makes my blood boil."

"You bet, Tiger. We'll forge on."

"Three musketeers, Bennis?"

"Two anyhow. One for both and both for one."

"My buddy."

"My pal."

CHAPTER EIGHTEEN

"LET ME GET this straight. You want me to tell you if you have a serial killer?"

"Right," Bennis said. He put the three file folders down on Jody Huffington's desk. It was nine-thirty Thursday morning and coffee was brewing in a pot on the file cabinet. Jody was a middle-aged man starting to show flecks of white at his temples.

"These days everybody thinks they've got a serial killer."

"I suppose. But we just might."

"Actually, to be honest, they're not as rare as you might think. Right now we have three serial killers of prostitutes operating just in the Englewood area."

"So why do people keep telling us not to jump to conclusions?"

"Because you shouldn't jump to conclusions. These days everybody thinks they know all about serial killers," Jody said. "They throw around 'profiling' and 'organized serial killer' and 'disorganized serial killer.' It's the result of an overdose of TV. In the real world, it's not as easy as that."

"Well, we've got three cases with a lot of similarities."

Bennis and Figueroa sat in Huffington's office in the basement of the CPD Annex building. Metal shelving sagged under books and slabs of paper. Figueroa had never seen so many books in any cop's office.

"You need to understand what I do here," Huffington said. "And what I don't do. The FBI runs training courses for officers from police departments around the country training in profiling. This is a help. We can pick up on cases early. There are three of us in the CPD who took the course. But if it really looks to me like there's a serial killer here, I send all the specs to Quantico to get the series analyzed."

"Fine. Whatever you say."

"When the Behavioral Science Unit of the FBI developed the notion of profiling," Huffington went on, "it was considered pretty abstruse stuff. Almost like magic. And there was a lot of doubt about whether it would work."

Bennis said, "I know. I remember hearing cops talk about it. Black magic nonsense."

"Frankly," Huffington said, "they thought it was stupid. But then the predictions started coming out pretty good."

"I saw one of the first questionnaires they ever developed."

"They developed them and then refined them over several years. With questions like the place where the bodies were found—in a house, in a public building, in a store, in a school, outdoors in woods, outdoors on a street, all that kind of thing. You filled it out and sent it along with the crime scene photos and any tech results in to the FBI and they'd score it and send you back what to look for."

"So help us out here. What do we look for?"

"We're not at that stage yet. Leave me the files. Go get coffee or something and come back in half an hour. I'll skim them and see what I can tell you. Then if you want me to do a more thorough analysis, I'll copy them and keep them a day or two."

"I have to say I'm not sure. You've got three different murder methods—"

"But they all stop the breath. Strangulation, smothering, that fire extinguisher stuff."

"And the victims differ about as much as they possibly could. Except for the alcoholic homeless aspect."

"We're aware of that. But the locations are close together and the time of the murder is about the same in every case."

"You don't know the time of death in the first one. He was half-hidden and the ME wouldn't pin it down because several hours had passed."

"Well, it had to have been night at least. Killing somebody there in daylight is too risky."

"Look. I'll give it the benefit of the doubt. Say it is the same killer for all of them. I'm gonna show you something. Two kinds of serial killers, from the 1985 FBI Law Enforcement Bulletin."

"Organized and disorganized?"

"Right. Look." He shoved two sheets of paper at Bennis and Figueroa. The letters were slightly fuzzy, as if they were photocopies made from photocopies of photocopies.

Crime Scene Differences

Organized

Planned offense
Victim a targeted stranger
Personalizes victim
Controlled conversation
Crime scene reflects overall control
Demands submissive victim
Restraints used
Aggressive acts prior to death
Body hidden
Weapon and evidence absent
Transports victim or body

Disorganized

Spontaneous offense
Victim known
Depersonalizes victim
Minimal conversation
Crime scene sloppy
Sudden violence to victim
Minimal use of restraints
Sexual acts after death
Body left in view
Evidence or weapon often present
Body left at death scene

"So see how well you think each fits your crime scenes. Now, let's say for purposes of discussion that the same person actually did commit all three of your killings. The bodies were left in view at the probable death scene. That's disorganized. But the main features—planning, targeting a certain kind of victim, plus weapon and evidence missing. That's organized. Anyway, here are the two profile possibilities."

Profile Characteristics

Organized

Average to above-average intelligence
Socially competent
Skilled work preferred
Sexually competent
High birth order status
Father's work stable
Inconsistent childhood discipline
Controlled mood during crime
Use of alcohol with crime

Precipitating situational stress
Living with partner
Mobility, car in good condition
Follows crime in news media
May change jobs or leave town

Disorganized

Below average intelligence
Socially inadequate
Unskilled work
Sexually incompetent
Low birth order status
Father's work unstable
Harsh discipline as child
Anxious mood during crime
Minimal use of alcohol
Minimal situational stress
Living alone
Lives or works near the crime scene
Minimal interest in news media
Significant behavior changes

"As between the two, to my eye he's organized."

"But, excuse me, Lieutenant Huffington," Figueroa said. "This doesn't point us anyplace. We can't very well go around looking for smart guys with clean cars who read the papers and watch the news. Not in Chicago. Hundreds of thousands of people fit that description. This doesn't give us anyplace to *start*."

"Usually it doesn't at first. What it gives you is a way of narrowing things down when you get suspects."

"We don't have even one so far."

Bennis said, "Huffington, paint me a word picture of these guys."

"All right. A disorganized offender is a loser, living with his mother, maybe, or by himself in a place that's basically a dump. A real mess inside. Most likely it isn't far from the crime scene. The guy is dumb and socially inept. He's probably between eighteen and thirty-five. He doesn't own a car, or if he does, it's crappy and dirty. He's impulsive and kills in a blitz attack. No subtlety. His victims are often people he's seen around his neighborhood. He often mutilates his victims. He's the easier one to catch, of course."

"And an organized offender?"

"All this is hypothetical, you know. But on the average, he's different. Methodical. Smart. Very verbal. Plans carefully. He owns a car or a van and it's in very good repair. He murders fairly far away from home. And probably not near his work. His victims are strangers. But they're a 'type' that he wants to kill. In your case homeless people. He finds some way to control them before killing them. In your case, he's controlling them by getting them drunk, which given their addiction, works remarkably well. He doesn't leave evidence most of the time, and he loves to make fools of the police."

"Man, oh, man, our guy has certainly done that."

"Another thing you need to remember, besides that there's no pure case of organized or disorganized, is that they can change. The disorganized offender doesn't become organized. He doesn't have the self-control. Or the smarts, either. But the organized offender can morph into a disorganized killer as he spins out of control. Or like Ted Bundy, who was very organized, deteriorated into a spree killer near the end. A spree killer kills again and again in fast succession without a cooling-off period."

"If we have one of those, we're in real trouble."

"What I'll do, I'll send this stuff to the FBI and see what

VI-CAP says. See if they think this is a legit serial killer. I'm also gonna advise you to go to a friend of mine. Dr. Ho. He can paint you a better picture of this guy." He paused.

"Assuming there is a guy."

CHAPTER NINETEEN

"YOU THE CHARACTERS that wanna learn about magic?"

"What?" Bennis said.

"Are you the law enforcement *individuals* who would like *instruction* in the *art* of *prestidigitation*?" The man giggled at his own wit and bopped from foot to foot, dancing up and down the cement esplanade near the lake.

"No, what we're looking for—" Bennis began, but Figueroa kicked him sharply in the shin.

"Yup. That's us," she said.

Eddie Charles was jumpy. He looked like a puppet on strings, thin to the point of scrawniness, long-limbed, with big knees, big elbows, big joints in his fingers. Thin as a one-sided board, Figueroa thought. For a few seconds she wondered if he was nervous about meeting with them, but she soon decided he was just naturally hyper.

It was just past ten-thirty A.M., and both they and Eddie had been on time at the meeting Bennis had set up the night before.

They had met on the lakefront, just north of Navy Pier. And Eddie was walking back and forth while talking. Out in the lake, the Victor Schleger fireboat was doing some sort of practicing, squirting water high up into the air in an arc that caught the sunlight. Rainbows flickered in its mist.

"I ain't a pickpocket, y'know. I'm a magician. I do magic shows."

"Where you played lately?" Bennis asked. Figueroa elbowed him in the ribs, seizing a moment when Eddie looked out at the water.

"And plus I teach magic. I'm only doing this because Harold asked me to help you, y'know."

"We appreciate it," Figueroa said.

Eddie bounced up and down on the balls of his feet. *Coked up?* Figueroa mused, but she didn't think so. He didn't have the signs. *That's just our Eddie*, she thought.

She said, "So tell us, how can a person pick a pocket without being noticed?"

"It comes down to three things. Distraction, distraction, and distraction." He laughed, pretended to punch a punching bag. "Ba-ba-boom!"

"Well, can you be a little more specific, Mr. Charles? I was standing in a crowd behind a woman who had a wallet in a tight back pocket. Suppose I want to take that wallet out. She's looking at a perfume demonstration. Shall I just ease it out slowly?"

"Absolutely wrong, wrong, wrong! Worst thing you can do. Totally wrong technique. Plus that perfume thing prob'ly isn't enough distraction. You bump her, pat her, collapse, whatever you need to do, and at the very same instant as you grab her arm, like this, you whip the wallet out of the pocket."

"Okay—"

"Like this," he said, giggling, and holding out Figueroa's wallet.

"I see we came to the right place," she said grimly, taking her wallet back. Some joggers on the lakefront glanced at the three of them, wondering if there was a crime going on. But Bennis smiled blandly at them and they jogged on.

"The basic thing you need to know is that the human mind can only focus on one thing at once."

"But you just said that it wasn't enough for the woman to be looking at the perfume demonstration."

"It ain't *enough*. Now if she sees a car careening at her kid, *that's* distraction enough. But see, it's the *type* of distraction, too. You want somebody not to feel a physical touch, you gotta give them some bigger physical distraction. Now, when I got a mark—that is, in my magic shows, a member of the audience—and I'm gonna pick his pocket, I say, like 'Now, I need you to stand over here,' and I take his arm real firmly. Squeeze it. I put more pressure on the arm than I'm gonna make removing the wallet. Ya get me?"

"Yes, I think I do."

"Like this. Watch. Now you can keep your hands on your wallets, or whatever," he said, grabbing Figueroa's left wrist and Bennis's right wrist and dragging them toward the very edge of the cement walkway, which was eight feet above the water. Figueroa and Bennis, in fact, both placed their hands on their wallets and paid close attention to their sidearms, which they were really determined not to lose, no matter what.

"So I got your attention by pulling you over here. Right?" He pulled them almost, not quite, to the point where all three of them might fall into the water.

"You bet."

"So where's your watches?"

"What?" Bennis whipped his wrist forward. No watch. Figueroa turned her arm to look at her own wrist. "All right, Eddie, you made your point," she said, not knowing whether to marvel at him or be annoyed.

"Sure. I sure did. Here." He produced both watches. Bennis's was on a clasp band, Figueroa's on an expandable band. Hers was cheap, but she knew Bennis's had cost a fair amount.

"Now tell me something," Eddie said. "Before I told you they were missing, didn't you really *feel* your watches as if they were still in place?"

"Yeah, kind of," Figueroa said, thinking back. Bennis nodded curtly.

"That's because I squeezed your wrist. Your body retains the memory of it, y'know?"

"Okay, but how'd you get them off?"

"Put 'em back on and I'll show you." He put his hand over Figueroa's wrist, slipping his fingers under the expandable band on four sides and moving it forward over her hand. For Bennis's watch, he flicked the tongue of the latch with one finger as he squeezed the wrist. Having released the latch, he let the watchband open up, then just lifted it away.

Bennis growled.

"Course," Eddie said, "I distracted you by walking you a little too close to the edge of the water, too."

"I see," Figueroa said.

"Now that squeeze. Or the grab to the arm before you take the wallet—among us magicians, we call this the distracting force."

"No doubt."

"Distraction, distraction, distraction." Eddie bopped over to the edge of the water, then back. He snapped his fingers half a dozen times, both hands. Figueroa admired this; she could only snap her fingers right-handed.

"Other good things to know," he said, snapping his fingers once more. "Don't look at what your hand is doing. Look away. I looked at you and then the water. Keep a straight face. You're interested in something else, see, not the person you're working on. Lotta times, now this is onstage, y'know, lotta times you can use a false arm. People see both your hands, they ain't gonna think you're picking their pocket, right?"

"Right. But—"

"Course, say that's no good for your perfume demonstration. But then again it might be possible, y'know. Mmm. Might be."

"Like how?"

"Say you put a coat over your arm. Say you put a rod in

the coat or in one of the sleeves so it stays rigid, like your arm is under it? Your other hand just goes and does its work. See?"

"I do see. Except this is warm weather for a coat."

"Shopping bags? Garment bags?"

"Could be."

"Well, hey. Is that all you need?"

"I guess," Figueroa said. "We certainly do appreciate you coming and helping us out this way."

"No prob."

"And before you go, let me and my partner here just make sure we have our wallets and watches and so on."

Eddie laughed raucously. "I like you. You make a good joke."

"I wanted to arrest that little bastard," Bennis said.

"Yeah. You weren't exactly friendly."

"I wasn't feeling friendly."

They got to the lockup by eleven. "So, Herzog, my man," Bennis said to the prisoner. "What we need here is for you to show your good faith."

"My lawyer takin' care of that."

"No, see, we have your lawyer's permission. We wouldn't be talking with you otherwise. You're making yourself one very fine deal, my man."

"Yeah, you're a smart guy, Herzog," Figueroa said, glancing up for lightning bolts.

Herzog did a little side dance with his head.

"So tell us here," Bennis said, "how'd you meet up with Valentine?"

"That his name? Thought it was Sisdel."

"It's his real name. Harold Valentine. Trust me on this."

Herzog thought for a few seconds, but didn't seem to get

much out of the exercise. "Whatever. I was in this bar, see? And this guy comes up to me."

"Okay. Back up just a touch. Was he there first, or did he maybe follow you?"

"No, no. He was there first. I would be onto that, otherwise."

Onto what? Figueroa wondered, but as long as the idiot was talking, what the heck.

"So he'd been drinking a while? Talking with people?"

"Dunno. Drinking, maybe. But he wasn't with anybody. And he didn't talk much. He, like, sat and listened."

"For a long time?"

"Yeah. Like an hour or so. I'm talking with a coupla buddies. You know. And finally he comes over, says he's got a proposition. Picked me out of a crowd, he said."

"Slick talker, huh?"

"Uh. No. Not exactly. Kind of talked in short bursts, you know?"

"Curt? Abrupt?"

"Yeah. Abrupt. But he needed a guy for this job where he knew we could get a lot of cash, see? He'd set it all up, but he needed a guy with brains and guts he said."

"And you were it."

"Well, don't make fun. He was right, you know. There was a lot of cash in that place."

"You willing to identify him?"

"You got him, I'll identify him."

"Well, so far we don't got him."

Noon. The man in the attic, Harold Valentine, knew that the nurse would just be starting her lunch in the sun parlor. For a while he toyed with the idea of paying the spaz a visit. Still, it would be much nicer at night when there would be more time.

Instead, he went over to the place where the roof made a

point, creating a wedge-shaped space in the attic. It was so low that he had to walk in on his knees. At some time in the past, there had been a water leak here—at the place where the wedge met the upswing of the central roof. On the outside, this would be what roofers called a "valley." And that made sense, because that would be right where water might leak in. Inside, several floorboards had warped from water damage. Two of them had bowed upward like rocking-horse runners. That left a hollow space above the ceiling of the third floor. This was where he hid the remaining cash. It wasn't much money. Far less than it should have been, he thought with a surge of anger.

And wasn't it silly of him to check it every few hours? Ridiculous! After all, nobody came up here, ever. Therefore nobody could have taken it. But he couldn't help checking every so often, just in case.

He'd been anxious, ever since the first money flew away. He couldn't have escaped from the cop if he hadn't thrown the money into the air, but he'd been so sure the cash from this robbery would give him a new start. He wanted to have all of it.

When he got away from the cop after the car chase, he had hailed a cab, and there went more money. He'd had the cab follow the two cops and that idiot Herzog back to the cop-shop and drop him there. He'd wait as long as he had to, and get even.

He sat on a fence near the CPD parking lot.

He saw them come out of the cop-shop at three-thirty, and when he got a good look at the Suze bitch, he realized he hated her more than the man. And then, to add insult to injury, they spent an hour in a goddamn bar across the street.

But the Suze bitch came out of the bar first. That was a break. And headed to her car. And while she did, he got another cab.

And after all that bad luck, here he was in a house with a sweet little girl. Who ever said things don't balance out?

CHAPTER TWENTY

SUZE FIGUEROA AND Norm Bennis were just talking about lunch when his beeper went off. He called the district.

Sergeant Touhy said, "We have two new pickpocket reports. What are you two doing out there? Painting your toenails?"

"Which stores, Sarge?"

"I want this resolved, Bennis."

"Sarge, we got three murders going on."

"That's Area Four. Not my department. I've got ritzy stores exceedingly upset."

"Okay. Tell me which ones. We're on our way."

While Bennis drove toward the Miracle Mile, Figueroa cellphoned the two stores that had just suffered another pickpocketing. As before, the wallets had been lifted while the women watched product demonstrations. Then she called the other four stores to confirm from the lists they had faxed of the times today the stores were having demonstrations.

There was time to visit the targeted stores first, then the other four.

As Bennis eased the car around a Chicago flexible bus, the kind in two segments with a rubber middle, Figueroa screamed, "Bennis!"

"What?" Bennis hit the brakes.

"No! Don't stop. I've got it!"

"Figueroa, you nearly made me hit the bus. Do you have

to be so mercurial? Why can't you be measured and calm and rational, like me?"

"Babies, Bennis! Babies!"

He cast his eyes at the sky, then immediately back at the road.

"Distraction, just like Eddie said. What's more distracting than a baby? What's more natural in those crowds of women than a couple of babies? What makes it easier to lean forward, lose your balance, and grab somebody's arm than a screaming kid?"

Bennis waved his hand. "Say! What makes it more reasonable to have stuff hung over your arm? Diaper bags, extra clothes. Suze, my man. I think you've got it!"

Cassius Mullen was the head of security at the first Michigan Avenue store they visited. The uniforms had already taken particulars of the pickpocketing.

"Two wallets in the same crowd," Mullen said with disgust. "And I can't imagine how you'll ever find out who did it."

"Were there women with children in the crowd?" Figueroa asked.

"Sure. Almost always are."

"Do you have any other demonstrations lined up? My chart says you plan a lipstick demo at twelve-thirty."

"That's right. Do you think we should call it off?"

"No. Let us observe."

"Mr. Mullen, your demos and the other stores' demos are concentrated around the noon hour, from eleven or so to one-thirty. I would think that's a crowded enough time already. Why do you do that?"

"It's not like the old days. We used to have demos in mid-morning or midafternoon. But women work these days. A lot of them only get lunch hour off."

"What about the idle rich?"

"Even the idle rich don't want to be idle any longer."

"Mr. Mullen, I'm going to hang out in the crowd. I have a radio. You and Officer Bennis wait out of sight. And here's how we're gonna do this—"

Nothing out of the ordinary happened at the lipstick demo, except that Figueroa learned she ought to call it "lip gloss."

Fortunately, the stores were clustered in the space of four blocks. There were demos scheduled at two other stores, at one and one-thirty, and because they were so close together Figueroa and Bennis could get to them easily.

At Batchelder Shops at one-thirty, they watched as a sultry woman gave a mascara lesson. And finally, Figueroa hit pay dirt. Two women in the crowd had infants in strollers. Figueroa edged her way into the crowd and stood about equidistant between the two. She didn't notice any suspicious moves, but after a few minutes, one of the children began to cry impatiently, then a few seconds of silence, then cry angrily again. The mother reached forward, giving the baby a bottle, dropped the bottle, fell a stagger-step toward the woman near her, caught her balance, and said, "I'm sorry."

"No problem," the other woman said.

Figueroa's radio was inside her jacket. She mumbled a description into her neckline.

Czielski, the security boss at Batchelder's, had been adamant that he and his staff and only they would stop any suspect and talk with her. Not the cops. So Figueroa just kept watching. The demo came to an end fairly soon. The supposed pickpocket had waited until it was breaking up so as to escape under cover of a lot of people walking off in different directions. Figueroa saw the suspect and baby stroller head off toward a spot where she knew the security man could easily intercept her. Figueroa herself kept an eye on the other woman with a baby in a stroller, so that nobody would confuse her with the suspect. At the same time, she approached the probable victim and showed her police ID.

"Ma'am, Officer Figueroa, Chicago Police Department. I wish you would check your purse. We think there are pickpockets operating in this area."

The woman looked at her purse. It hung open. She gasped.

When the crowd had finally dispersed, and the second stroller had passed out of the doors, Figueroa took the victim with her and caught up with Bennis and security. Czielski stood near a woman with a baby in a stroller. He was saying, "I'm terribly sorry, ma'am, but I certainly appreciate your letting us look."

"I don't mind. It's a good thing that you're trying to protect people." The baby screamed. The woman handed the child a graham cracker.

The woman and the baby and the stroller moved off. Figueroa left Czielski to explain to the victim why they didn't pounce the moment they had a suspicion—not an easy thing to do. Very awkward. "We couldn't tell whether someone touched your purse or not, ma'am—"

Figueroa drew Bennis aside and whispered, "What happened?"

"No stolen wallet. She let us search her own purse, plus the stroller, and the diaper bag, and the baby, and even feel the baby's diaper. And the mother wasn't wearing the kind of clothes that conceal anything."

"Dammit, Bennis!"

"Yeah, yeah, I know."

"We pretty much have to find stolen stuff on the suspect, or we can't arrest 'em."

"Well, we musta got the wrong woman. Did she look like your suspect?"

"I'm not sure. I only saw her from behind in a crowd. They both had fairly long dark hair. But mine had a dark blue shirt,

I think. This one was wearing a black shirt. Shoes—well, I couldn't see mine's feet because of the crowd."

"We got the wrong woman! Hell!"

"It really looked like the same stroller, though. One of those light, foldable ones. Hell. I guess there are a lot of them around."

"And the same baby?"

"Yeah. But then one stroller looks a lot like another. And for that matter, one baby looks a helluva lot like another, too."

"Even more so."

CHAPTER TWENTY-ONE

MARY LYNNE LEE woke up a little past noon. Unrested and unhappy, she had tried to fall asleep again. She had been awake until four in the morning, turning tricks in cars that picked her up on Rush Street. The last guy had been a real sweetie and had taken her to a hotel, a cheap hotel, but one with sheets and hot water. When he left at six A.M., he told her he had paid for the room for the whole night and that checkout time was one P.M. He said he wished her well.

They weren't all like that. In fact, they usually weren't like that at all.

She knew the hotel manager would be around on the stroke of one to roust out anybody left. Her one chance to get a real shower was right now.

But she just felt so sad. She wished she had her own place. She wished she had a nice apartment, because then she could have a dog. A medium-size dog, not one of those tiny ones you were always afraid of stepping on. A tan cocker spaniel, maybe. Or an Afghan. She wanted a dog with long, beautiful hair that she could brush and comb.

Mary Lynne started to cry. Somehow time got away from her once she started crying, and it seemed like only five minutes later that she heard knocking at the door.

"All right! All right!" she called. "I'm leaving."

Now she didn't have time for a shower. But at least she had money. She dragged on her horrible-looking clothes, thinking for just a moment that she could buy a new shirt. But before long she was thinking instead about what she would buy when she got to the liquor store. She could afford vodka today. But then, for the same amount of money she could get two big bottles of cheap wine. Better get the wine. It would last longer. And anyway, weren't there some vitamins in wine?

When the hotel housekeeper let herself into the room, Mary Lynne was dressed and ready to walk out.

Figueroa said, "Bennis, today we are going to eat lunch or else."

"I promise."

"Let's go get enchiladas."

"Soon. Right after we see Dr. Ho."

"What your profiler Jody thinks of as disorganized serial killers and organized serial killers I think of a little differently," Dr. Ho said. His office at Northwestern University Medical School was distinctive. Figueroa wondered whether she liked it or hated it. Dr. Ho collected seashells. One entire wall contained nothing but display cases, floor to ceiling. The shells were grouped in categories, hundreds of shells, all labeled with beautifully handwritten calligraphic labels—black conch, cone shell, pectin, lace murex, measeled cowrie, olive shell, juonia, sunrise tellin. The other three walls were filled with bookshelves, and one small window peeked through the books, giving a view out toward Lake Michigan.

"I think of them as psychotics and psychopaths. Disorganized killers are primarily psychotic and organized serial killers are almost always psychopaths. But you need to realize the psychopath who kills is a rarity among the large group of psychopaths out there, just like far and away most psychotics don't kill. Most of what we call crazy people are much more dangerous to themselves than to anybody else."

"Wait," Figueroa said, "aren't psychotics and psychopaths the same thing?"

"No. Small wonder you make that mistake. It's just too bad the words 'psychotic' and 'psychopath' are so similar. Almost everybody confuses the two. For a while I hoped we might use the word 'sociopath' for psychopathic people, but it didn't stick." Ho gave a small but attractive smile. "And I wrote so many extremely convincing articles on the subject, too."

"So what is a psychopath?"

"They're people without a normal sense of empathy. They don't understand why they're supposed to care about other people. They're often described as being without conscience."

"But they don't all kill?"

"Of course not. Why should they? Most of them aren't angry, for one thing. Let me describe a pure psychopath for you. He or she is irresponsible. He doesn't see why he has to fulfill commitments he makes. He loses jobs. He's the kid who says he'll be home for dinner and just doesn't show. He comes in when he darn well pleases. Most of them aren't even very self-protective about it, even though they're smart. A psychopath doesn't really learn from punishment. He steals from his mother's purse and even if you spank him he'll just do it again. A psychopath is very charming. People who don't have to depend on him think he's wonderful. Remember how charming everybody said Ted Bundy was? Well, of *course* psychopaths are charming. They don't have to believe the things they say, like the rest of us do, so they say whatever will please you."

Bennis said, "I just bet a lot of them become politicians."

"Sure. Some mild psychopaths are politicians. Some are doctors. Some are lawyers. They seem 'nice.' They're neatniks, usually, unlike psychotics, who if they're really disorganized, may live in absolute squalor. Psychopaths behave very attractively, like Ted Bundy. If you'd seen his defense table, you'd have thought he was one of the lawyers. So they come in under your radar. And that's the problem. When they're bad, they're very, very bad. The killers among them are the people we really have to warn our kids about—they are people who look nice and act nice, but are deadly dangerous."

"So unless you see them in action for a while, you can't tell who's a psychopath?"

"Pretty much. But not entirely. Psychopaths make mistakes in their charm. They study normal people, and imitate them, but they just don't get the *reasons* why normal people say certain things. So sometimes they'll say something they think is charming and the people they say it to don't think so at all. My mother-in-law is mildly psychopathic, I think."

Bennis laughed, but Ho said, "No, I'm serious. She doesn't kill anybody. But she has very shallow emotions. And considerable charm. People who don't have to depend on her think she's an absolute darling. But she gets her charm just a little bit wrong at times. For example, my wife's brother is very much overweight, and he's sensitive about it. *Every single time* he comes to a family gathering, the minute he walks in the door, Myra says, 'Why, Todd, you've lost weight.' Which, of course, immediately calls attention to the fact that he's fat. I took her aside at one point and said, 'Maybe he doesn't like having you call attention to his weight like that.' And she said, 'But I was complimenting him. I said he'd lost weight.' I said, 'Myra, suppose you're Mikhail Gorbachev and you have a great big birthmark on your face and you're sensitive about it. Would you like it if every time you walked into a room somebody said, 'Gee, Gorby, your birthmark is smaller'?"

"What did she say?"

"She just stared at me. She could *not* understand what I was talking about. She has other psychopathic behaviors too. Starts jobs and quits. Says she'll be home at six and comes in at eight. Nothing major. Indulges in little lies that she calls fibs. Like she'll say she's late getting home because she stopped to pick up a stray dog. But she carries in half a dozen shopping bags from Marshall Field's. Hardly bothering to cover up, see? She just doesn't *get* it."

"She must have been a real treat for your wife to grow up with."

"Psychopaths befuddle and infuriate their families. My wife spent the first thirty years of her life trying to figure out whether her mother just didn't understand her or hated her. In fact, my wife kept thinking she was a deficient daughter in some way. Not a good enough little girl. After we married, I showed her some literature on psychopaths. She kind of jumped up and yelled, 'That's Mom!' "

"But your mother-in-law doesn't kill people."

"She's not angry. And like I said, she's a *mild* psychopath."

"Our guy—"

"I believe you do have a serial killer. And your guy is nasty. He's belittling those homeless people when he washes their faces. We had one man a couple of years ago who was killing prostitutes, and for some reason, after he killed them, he painted their noses green. When we caught him, of course we asked why. The psychoanalytical types were trying to think of reasons—like the term 'blue nose' means prude and 'brown nose' means a suck-up. But green nose doesn't mean anything especially that we could figure out. We were avid to find out what it was. He told us he thought the green color contrasted well with their pink skin tones. And he meant it. He couldn't understand why we looked at him like he was a monster."

"Bad upbringing?"

"No, not necessarily. The current thinking on psychopaths is that there's either a developmental problem or a birth injury. Something in their brains just doesn't develop. Which given the complexity of the human brain isn't that surprising. Remember, thirty years ago psychiatry thought autism was caused by bad mothering. The 'refrigerator mother.' There were families devastated by that, and mothers who killed themselves in remorse. But it now seems clearly to be organic. Some brain-injured people recover from the injuries but come out with totally different personalities."

At this, Figueroa felt a chill. Suppose when Sheryl began to speak, what she showed was a different personality? But she wouldn't, would she? She seemed to be the same person. Figueroa realized that Bennis, aware of her fear, was carefully not looking at her. Dr. Ho sensed something amiss.

"Did I say the wrong thing?"

"No, Doctor," Bennis said. "We were just thinking about a mutual friend. Go ahead, please."

"Well, whatever the cause, some researchers think maybe two to five percent of the population may be psychopathic."

"That's very scary."

"Most of them never kill people. They're con men. Ne'er-do-wells. They're irresponsible mothers or fathers. Petty thieves. They may be quite good surgeons. Or lawyers. Or salesmen. They're the charming young men who prey on older women. And they're the charming young women who prey on older men. Every hospital has a doctor or two who are known to do procedures unnecessarily painfully. The psychopaths you have to be scared of, though, are the ones who happened to be born into a cruel childhood. Without a conscience, they become human monsters."

"But they're not crazy?"

"Not in the usual sense. Perfectly normal children can be made into psychotic killers, usually into what Jody calls 'disorganized serial killers' by a cruel childhood. They kill out of rage. Their killings are often committed impulsively, in a sudden fury. Psychopaths can be made into organized serial killers. They kill because it's fun."

"Jeez!"

"My belief is there are four categories of crooks. The first is the cultural criminal. A child grows up in a family of thieves and turns into a thief."

"Seen a lot of that," Bennis said.

"Anyhow, a cultural criminal is usually not a killer. They just steal stuff."

"Okay."

"Then there's what I call the ruined soul. Someone so abused as a child that he or she just can't develop normally. Some of them have so much anger that they kill. And when they kill over a period of time, they're called disorganized serial killers. But some of them are the sexual predators. They have been damaged at some sexual level, and they play out their lives compulsively on that level."

"Okay."

"Then there are the true psychotics. People with a real mental illness. Sometimes it has a genetic component. Schizophrenia runs in families. So does depression. Sometimes the psychosis is caused by chemical exposure or disease. The man who shot all those people at a McDonald's in California several years ago had been exposed to heavy metals. Cadmium, I think."

Bennis said, "And then there's the psychopath."

"Right. My own belief is that a psychopath is a psychopath from birth. But the psychopathic *killer* probably has also been abused as a child. I often say about killers—some we make, and some we make worse."

CHAPTER TWENTY-TWO

DR. HO HAD brewed a fragrant batch of coffee that Bennis, always attuned to food, found superb. He said so. Dr. Ho said, "Thank you. And to go with it—tah-dah!"

"Oreos?" Bennis said, taking two. "Thanks." Ho passed them to Figueroa, who took one and then Ho took two himself.

"Sure," Ho said, watching Bennis rotate the top and bottom of the cookie apart, exposing the white inside. "I find that how a person eats an Oreo says a great deal about his character."

Figueroa froze, a bite taken out of hers still in her mouth. She had not unscrewed the cookie. She watched as Ho dunked his in his coffee.

Bennis sat still too, his open Oreo held in front of his mouth.

"And you believed that?" Ho said, laughing uproariously. "Eat it any way you want. I can't tell a bloody thing about you from it." He smiled more calmly. "People are just so uneasy with psychiatrists. They think every move gives them away somehow."

"Yeah," Bennis said. "But I'm taking the safe way out." He dunked his Oreo in his coffee. "Say, that's not bad."

Figueroa said, "Describe a psychopath, Dr. Ho. Charm, a history of changing jobs, what else?"

"Petty thievery sometimes. A history of petty crimes. Sometimes silly, unnecessary, obvious crimes. People say, 'He's too smart to have done this.'"

"But even so," Figueroa said, "how do we find somebody like that?"

"It's not easy. Despite what the FBI leads the media to believe, you very rarely *find* an organized serial killer in a large metropolitan area on the basis of the profile. In small towns with a limited suspect group, you might. Organized serial killers usually hide in plain sight. Or to put it another way, unlike the disorganized killers, who usually go to ground, they don't really hide at all. Usually they're caught because they do something foolish and an alert cop spots it. But there are two possibilities that might help you. First the zone of comfort."

"Explain, please."

"You already must know that people go to customary places, where they feel comfortable. For instance, if you have a park you sometimes go to, you'll probably always sit on the same bench. Same in restaurants. If you're allowed to choose your own table, it's probably always the same table."

"But isn't that because I like that table? Maybe it's against a far wall and I can see the door?"

"A cop table? To watch the door? Sure, maybe it is. And maybe your bench in the park is far from the street so you don't smell the car exhaust. But what difference does that make? It's your choice and you'll go back to it. Plus, if there are two benches equally far from the car exhaust or five tables against the back wall, you'll still go to the same one if you can."

"All right. That's a normal human behavior."

"But don't you see? Killers have mostly normal human behaviors. And a screw loose."

"That's a technical description, Dr. Ho?"

He smiled. "Ought to be. On the whole, organized serial killers try to pick a place to kill or to dispose of their victims that won't be directly connected to them. That's your challenge, I guess. But usually in fact it's a place they know. And a whole lot of them choose places close to them. We had a bunch of bodies that were discovered in Wisconsin when a cow barn, a milking barn, actually, was bulldozed to make a foundation for a new house. The bodies had been buried there over a period of years, from about 1969 to three weeks before we arrived. Naturally, we tore the life histories of everybody who had worked there into little tiny threads. Nothing. All the owners, absolutely every little scrap of their entire lives. Nothing. After literally months, we worked our way back to a man who had been a custodian, cleaning up the barn in the 1958–1961 period. People who remembered him said he abused the cows. Hit them when they wouldn't stand still for milking. He was let go. Apparently you can't do that. A happy cow gives more milk."

"He killed the victims?"

"No, he was dead. Been dead fifteen years, which was why he hadn't appeared on our lists. But his wife and son had lived there at the time, and his son accompanied his dad to work. We think he was abusive to both of them. So to make a long story short, that was the place the son remembered and felt comfortable in. Comfort zones. Sometimes they're far in the past, but sometimes they're close. Remember Ed Gein, the Wisconsin grave robber and cannibal who, if memory serves me, hung the home-tanned skins of his victims in his own barn? Or John Wayne Gacy, whom I am sure you remember—"

"Who could forget?"

"Right. Buried his victims in the crawl space under his *own house*! Imagine the risk! But that's not at all unknown in these cases. Or Jeffrey Dahmer. He kept his victims in his *apartment*, for God's sake. Some of their heads on a shelf."

"So we look for somebody who lives in the area?"

"Lives or works in the area. And I'm sorry to add this—or who *used to* live or work there."

"Well, okay, I can buy that," Bennis said. "We could get records on everybody who has lived in that brick apartment building over the years."

Figueroa said, "Plus DOT workers, El employees, garbage pickup men, electric workers, maybe?"

"Maybe," Bennis said. "But otherwise—if that doesn't work, there can't be much sentimental connection to the El track."

Dr. Ho said, "You never know."

"I mean, what killer could really be comfortable virtually in the shadow of the police department?"

"I thought you'd never ask."

Figueroa and Bennis were silent. Ho poured more coffee. It was obvious what he meant, and they didn't like it. Finally, Figueroa said, "All right. Maybe he works in the CPD building. Maybe he worked there twenty years ago." She didn't want to say, maybe he's a cop.

"Inadequate personalities gravitate to jobs that give them authority and status. Jobs like security guard, rent-a-cop, cop, paramedic, firefighter. And when a stressor happens in their lives, like loss of a job, or divorce, or whatever, they snap."

"C'mon. Now that you've freaked us out, give us some good news."

"I can do that to a certain extent, as a matter of fact. The second of the two possibilities I mentioned. Psychopaths do have one Achilles' heel. They take risks, sometimes risks that seem insane, given the fact that they're smart and they clean up clues around their killing zone. I don't know whether it's because they think they're so much smarter than the police that they take the risks just to prove it, or whether they love the adrenaline rush of it, or whether they actually want to get caught. If I had to guess, I'd say they don't think they can be caught, or in some weird way they don't think it matters. Ted Bundy carried the heads of his victims around with him. Now, is that self-protective behavior?"

"I wouldn't think so."

"They tend to escalate, kill more often, take more risks, and finally get caught. There was a serial killer in New York named Joel Rifkin. He had committed at least eighteen murders, and he goes out driving in a truck with no rear license plate, without headlights, and the rotting body of a victim in the back of the truck. He gets stopped by some New York State Troopers for a totally unnecessary traffic violation. Gave *them* a surprise."

"What do you think of profiling, Mort?" Bennis asked, back at the Furlough.

"I hate art."

"No, I mean like criminal profiling. Like when the FBI does a profile of a serial killer based on the evidence at the crime scene."

"Ah, that shit ain't worth a bootful of piss."

"Go ahead," Figueroa said. "Don't hold back. Tell us what you really think."

"That psych stuff is crap."

Bennis and Figueroa had picked up a bag of White Castle hamburgers and taken them to the Furlough at three-thirty, hoping to see the gang. This detective job, Figueroa had found, tended to isolate you from your old friends.

Mort started to uncap a beer for the Flying None. She said, "Wait!"

"Wait, what, dammit?"

"I'd like something different for a change. How about a pink lady?"

Mort's mouth dropped open. "Arrr—" he said.

"I'll do it," Corky said. He pulled a bar recipe book from the shelf. "Oops. Can't. Egg white, grenadine, cream, and gin. We only got the gin."

Mileski said, "Drat."

"How about a peach blossom?" Sandi said.

Corky checked. "Needs a peach."

"Sloe gin flip?" she asked.

"No sloe gin."

Mort said, "I'll flip you."

"My dad used to drink Pall Mall cocktails," Kim Duk said.

Mileski said, "A cigarette cocktail?"

"Don't be silly," Bennis said. "It's named after a famous street in London. So are the cigarettes."

Mileski started to say, "How come you know so much?" when Corky cut in.

"But I can make you an orange blossom," he said. "*That* we got."

"Well, get it over with," said Mort, walking out from behind the bar and letting the flap in the counter slam down.

Corky said to Figueroa, "Don't let Mort bother you. There's a lot to that profiling stuff."

"Thanks, Corky."

"Did I ever tell you I spent two years in the Green Berets?"

"No. That's amazing."

"Well, I was young and foolish. But anyhow, we used a lot of the results of early profiling. You know, if you're going into a situation, like, say, you want to rescue a downed airman and he's being held by a rebel group."

"Yes?"

"You need some psych background on the group. What is it they value? Physical strength? Strategy? The ability to negotiate? Might be that more than anything they don't want to lose face. Or are they impulsive, like your disorganized offender? If so, you better get in and out fast and strong. You don't use subtlety with those guys."

"I never heard you had that kind of background."

"Oh, you know me. I like variety. It was fun for a while. Beirut. Eastern Europe. Parts of North Africa."

"I would think it was more dangerous than fun."

"Yeah. That too."

Stanley Mileski said, "I was in the army, but jeez, I wouldn't volunteer for anything like that."

"Aw, c'mon Lead Balls," Bennis said, "you'd give 'em hell."

"You been out all day?" Mileski asked Bennis.

"Us?" Figueroa said. "Yeah. We went to roll call. Been out since then."

"Then you haven't heard. Another one of the detectives died."

"Oh, shit. Of E. coli?"

"Yup. And they say there are eight on dialysis."

Bennis said, "What a goddamn shame."

Figueroa was paged and saw the phone number was Dr. Percolin's. She called back and talked with him. Finished, she went back to Bennis.

"Percolin found one case. It was a homeless man, a black guy, sixty-one, alcoholic. Killed closer to Congress Street, but that's not more than six blocks. The man's face was washed, although that wasn't in the autopsy protocol."

"How come he didn't tell us about it before this?"

"He didn't know about it. It wasn't his case. One of the other pathologists did the post. And Percolin almost missed it in his search. He was just using homeless and alcoholic and this general part of town as parameters."

"So how does he know the guy's face was washed?"

"He was going to pass this one, but he noticed the man was smothered. He had a blanket pushed over his face. So he asked the other doc."

"And he remembered?"

"When he was prompted. Percolin says you couldn't take it to court."

"When was this?"

"A year and a half ago. Percolin's still doing searches."

"Jody Huffington said killers sometimes step up the pace as they deteriorate."

"I know. I know."

By four o'clock Bennis and Figueroa were out of the Furlough and walking to the CPD headquarters. Since the murders had occurred late in the evening, and all of them pretty certainly after eleven P.M., they wanted to question everybody they could find who was on the three-to-eleven shift. They might have seen something out of the windows of the building. Or they might have seen something when they went to the parking lot to get their cars. Or—possibly one of them was the killer, and hung out after work to do his murdering.

They'd have to repeat with the eleven P.M. to seven A.M. people. Fortunately, since this was primarily an office building, there were fewer of them.

Figueroa and Bennis decided to start from the top floor and work down. It was a default decision, one they made without much discussion, since they were both distressed and unhappy with the idea of asking CPD people where they were at the time of the killings. Suze and Norm hoped the cops, secretaries, janitors, and so on would have no idea they were under suspicion. Still, they were edgy. Bennis said, "I couldn't feel any more uncomfortable if there were sea urchins in my underwear." Suze and Norm were genuinely interested in finding out whether any of these people had seen anything, and asking that would help cover the other reason, but underneath they knew one of these people could be the killer.

All shifts had received their memos by now, asking anybody who had noticed anything suspicious on the late night to early morning of May 21, May 31, or June 1 to beep Bennis or Figueroa. So far, nobody had.

The thirteenth floor was the "penthouse," housing the women's lockup. The senior guard, an administrator named Forbes who would have been called "matron" in an earlier era, was a tiny woman who looked like she could be Katie Couric's grandmother.

"Of course you can come in," she said when they explained why they were here.

As in any lockup, they had to deposit their sidearms in a box outside the jail facility itself. That way there was no possibility of prisoners getting their hands on guns.

"I don't know exactly what you can see from here," Forbes said. "But you're welcome to check. Our prisoners couldn't have seen anything at all. They're all housed in inside cells."

Thinking about the Manualo murder, Figueroa said, "Can I get a view to the north from this floor?"

"Sure."

The Annex, which was attached to the main building, was only seven floors. When Figueroa and Bennis looked out of the north windows here, they saw the roof of the Annex and nothing of the ground level just north of it. Nobody could have seen the Manualo murder from this floor.

"Thanks," Figueroa said. Forbes led them back to the lockup. The cells, in two double rows down the center of a huge room, with the cell backs against each other, were tiny and very public. The bars in the front were the full width of the cell and included a door made of bars. The woman yelled, "Man coming through!" as they walked. Some of the women prisoners in underwear made no move to cover up. The ones who were screaming mostly went on screaming. Each cell had a toilet, a sink, a slablike bed, and one—just one—blanket. Therefore the whole facility was kept very warm.

Figueroa noticed the shoes on the floors outside the cells. Tradition said the shoes should always be placed outside so that the prisoners wouldn't hang themselves with their shoelaces, but most of the shoes had no laces and they were outside anyway. Sometime she thought she would ask why. Hanging was also the reason why they weren't given sheets.

"Over here," said Forbes.

The wall that faced the El, the east wall, was almost entirely windowless. Apparently even in a jail nobody wanted to look at El trains. There was a single east window on the corner adjacent to the south wall. The CPD parking lot was to the south.

Against the south wall was a bank of four microwaves above a counter on which stood two coffeemakers. Next to the counter was a refrigerator. There were several chairs and a low table, scuffed around its edges. Figueroa assumed that the scuff marks were from guards sitting on the chairs and resting their feet on the table edge, although none of them were doing that now, with the administrator looking at them. Two stood at the microwaves, warming sandwiches on paper plates.

"Bologna sandwiches," Forbes said. "You know this is a temporary holding facility, not a residence facility, so we don't do real meals."

"You serve—"

"Bologna sandwiches for breakfast, lunch, and dinner. But we do offer them either cold or warm, depending on which way our guests like it best."

"Oh. Gourmet dining."

"So what do you want to see?"

"This." Figueroa and Bennis stared out the single east window. There was a good view of the El, but they couldn't see the alley underneath it. The south windows that overlooked the parking lot gave a diagonal view of the place where Abigail Ward had been killed, but it was a long way away.

"If you could call all the guards together, I'd like to tell them some dates and ask them what they saw."

While the woman was gathering everybody, Figueroa remarked softly to Bennis, "All we can do, I guess, is watch body language and try to get each one of them to talk so we can get an idea of what they're like."

"Looking for Dr. Ho's characteristics?"

"What else can we do? We have to start someplace."

"I don't believe the killer is a woman."

"I doubt it myself. Think positive. Maybe one of the guards actually saw something down there."

One had.

Five female guards shook their heads and shrugged. But one said, "Yeah. May thirty-first."

"What did you see?"

"It wasn't from here. I got out of here late because my relief didn't show. Idiot woman. She's been fired. Good riddance. Anyhow, they got in a replacement twenty after twelve. So I'm in the parking lot and see, I'm short."

"Yes. About my height."

"Right. And I'm standing near my car, trying to figure out why my keys aren't in my key pocket where I always put them. Turned out to be in my hand. And I see this guy crossing the lot. He doesn't see me because the car is taller than I am."

"What did he look like?"

"Well, you gotta realize I'm seeing him through two car windows and they aren't that clean. I just basically noticed him because he passed in front of the light at the far end. Which meant, see, that the light was behind him."

"But what *did* you see?"

"Medium tall. Wore a hat. Baseball cap, I think. Short jacket. Walked like a youngish guy."

"You sure it was a man?"

"Pretty damn sure. Walked like it."

"Heading which way?"

"Well, see, that's why I noticed. He came from the street onto the parking lot, so you figure he's going to a car, right? But he walked right on through and out the other side."

"Toward?"

"Under the El."

"How come you remember the date?"

"My kid's birthday. I hadda work that night, so we were celebrating the next day. Kid was freaked. Who knew that ten-year-olds could be so formal about ceremonies?"

Bennis and Figueroa repeated the process with the men's lockup on twelve. Here they didn't even bother to check from the north windows. The view would only be worse than from thirteen.

None of the guards remembered anything at all out of the ordinary on the nights of the murders. "Nothing unusual outside," one of them said. "In here every day there's weird shit happens."

Eleven, ten, and nine produced next to nothing. On eleven, the suits had several years earlier declared a cafeteria. Almost nobody ever ate there, largely because the food was putrid. A hot table with real, live, and hideously bored cooks ran along the east wall, the wall that backed onto the El. There were no windows whatsoever in it and if there had been they'd have been as steamed up as the plastic covers over the hot table. The only hot foods left in the stainless-steel bins at this hour were creamed chipped beef and some grayish sort of meat, with an orange barbecue sauce half stirred into it, giving a marbleized effect. The cooks stared morosely at thick white plates of wilted iceberg lettuce.

There was a long row of coin-op machines along the south wall. They had been set down in a row regardless of the fact that there were windows behind them. As a result, nobody could possibly have seen down into the parking lot or over toward the El, without standing on top of a coffee machine, which nobody was likely to do casually. If the killer had been looking out to see whether there was a homeless person walking by, he didn't do it from here.

The cooks had seen nothing, knew nothing, and didn't give a good demonstration of caring much, either.

On eight, the Personnel offices still hummed, but showed signs of closing up for the day. A secretary with big hair the color of overripe mangoes showed Bennis and Figueroa her south-facing window, which looked like it hadn't been washed since it was installed. There was another window next to it that was actually rather clean, about as transparent as lightly used dishwater. But the several potted plants growing there would have made it hard for a person to look out without being conspicuous about it.

Except if nobody else was in the office.

"When do you leave for the day?" Figueroa asked.

"Five. Normal time."

"Ever stay late?"

"Hardly ever. Not in the last three-four weeks."

"Can we talk to the commander?"

And they did. Commander Cole, a tall, slender black man with a reputation of being highly professional, was outraged that somebody would do murder near the CPD. However, he couldn't help much. He often worked late, but in the last weeks had been out of there by eight, going to community meetings. He also admitted, after a little chat, that he had not asked to be Commander of Personnel. "Borr-rrring!" he said. He wanted to be back in Detectives or Patrol.

Seven and six were administrative offices. Nobody knew anything and everybody said they left by five, which Bennis and Figueroa thought actually meant four-thirty at the latest.

Five and four were Dispatch.

The Dispatch Center was something else again. Absolutely state of the art when it was built in 1961, it had been visited by police departments from all over the world and copied a thousand or more times. Six months from now, it would all be gone.

Arranged around an open center were stations consisting of desk space, microphones, zone maps, and special maps. A dispatcher staffed each work station, which covered a specific zone of the city. The special maps were of parks, lakes, and such, where giving street addresses didn't work and where fleeing felons could easily get themselves lost. The cops could get lost, too, if no one had a clear map of the area.

911 calls come into Dispatch, but are first categorized by a real live human being. If the concerned citizen has a cat up in a tree, 911 may try to get Fire or Animal Rescue to deal with it. Chicago has been famous—or famously foolish—for decades for trying to run on every 911 call, but no more. In a time of overload, there's prioritization.

However, once vetted, a call goes to the dispatcher appropriate to the district involved. He or she puts it out on the air. The dispatcher is in charge of choosing the most appropriate car, usually the closest, but if he or she knows a car is about to go to lunch, and if the call seems like it will lead to a long interaction, a missing child for example, another car just up from lunch will be chosen. Lunch is the meal in the middle of the tour, regardless of the time of day.

All of this will be completely computerized in the new building, and will include "live" radios in the squad cars, which will read out on the screen exactly where the car is. All will be computerized, that is, except for the dispatcher, who will still be in charge of making the big decisions.

Dispatch is always busy.

When Figueroa and Bennis strode in, lights were flickering on and off along the fronts of consoles, phones were ringing with muted buzzes, like a field full of crickets at night. The air was filled with quiet, flat-voiced talk, dispatchers speaking into mikes, ordinary stuff mostly, issuing assignments, returning wants and warrants. But as they walked past, Figueroa heard one say, "Stay off the air, Thirty-three has an emergency. I have a ten-one at Sixty-third and State—"

She imagined the Third District squad cars all suddenly spinning around wherever they were, running to help a buddy in trouble. It would be only one or two minutes at most before the dispatcher was telling them, "Everybody stay where you are. I have enough units on the scene."

"Well, lookee there," Bennis said, pointing at the wall.

"We knew this, didn't we?"

The windows of Dispatch were covered with sheetrock to keep light off the consoles.

"I guess so," Bennis said. "Damn. Well, maybe it narrows things down."

"It doesn't really. It just makes it hard to talk to people here. Can't exactly say we want to find out if they saw anything."

"Sure we can. They get off at eleven. We can ask what they saw in the lot."

But it came to nothing. They got no information on the third, second, or first floors either, and had to spend ten useless minutes with a press secretary who was a glad-handing idiot. He'd had a dozen different jobs, exuded charm, and had emotions about an inch deep. "Sorry to hear about a murder in our area here. Very sorry."

As they turned away from him, Bennis said, "I'll bet he drives a new car in good condition, too."

"So he's a psychopath. I think he's a happy psychopath."

They did the north side of the Annex and found out nothing of any use. They walked slowly to the parking lot. Bennis said, "Talk with Dr. Ho a few minutes and you start to see psychopaths everywhere."

"Maybe they *are* everywhere. Oh, jeez! I have to get home. It's nearly five, and I want to catch the neurologist!"

"We ought to talk to the first watch in the building."

"Meet you in the Furlough at eleven tonight when they come on?"

"Done."

Of all the doctors and nurses and therapists that had treated Sheryl since the accident—and Suze thought they would number more than a hundred by now—the one she liked best was the neurologist, Dr. Hannah Pettibaker.

The one she liked least was a condescending and sappily cheerful physical therapist who had come just for a couple of weeks after Sheryl got home. He was named Jonathan Roon. His job, he said, was to return Sheryl to a "realistic" level of competence. Whatever that meant. He taught her what he called "activities of daily living," which he shortened to ADLs. He had the habit of bounding into Sheryl's room and asking brightly, "And how are our ADLs today?"

Dr. Pettibaker was straightforward, no nonsense, and not saccharine.

The first time Suze and Robert met with her, about a week after the accident, she said, "I'm going to give you the general background picture, and then we'll apply it specifically to Mrs. Birch. And by the way, I don't approve of doctors calling themselves Dr. Pettibaker and calling the patient by the first name, like Sheryl. But we could be Hannah and Sheryl and Robert and Susannah, okay?"

"Okay, as long as I'm Suze."

"Done. Now that we know Sheryl is not going to die, we move into the next phase. We assess the extent of the injury. You'll hear us use a lot of terms, not necessarily the way laymen use them. We're not trying to impress you with them, and they're not secret. So let me explain them."

When they talked about impairment, she said, they meant damage at the organ level. It was the actual damage done to the tissues of Sheryl's body. "When we use the term 'disability' we're talking at the person level. It's what the person can't do. And when we talk about 'handicap' it's at the societal level. The ways in which the disability interacts with other people."

Robert said, "Is she going to be handicapped?"

"We're not sure yet. Right now we're going to deal with short-term goals, given her acute disability."

"Does that mean she's disabled?"

"She is now. But acute disability is a specific term that refers to early, reversible damage. When we talk about chronic disability, that's permanent. Our short-term goals are to get her sitting, and then maybe walking again."

Suze said, "Maybe?"

"Well, yes. Then we get into the difference between optimal goals and realistic goals. It's realistic to think she'll be able to stand, and probably to walk after a fashion. Optimally, we'd like to get her walking normally."

Suze sighed, pressing her hands together. She was utterly terrified.

"Your sister," Dr. Pettibaker said, having noticed Suze's reaction, "is now into stage two. Stage one, immediately after the accident, was the time when she was in a coma. In stage two the patient shows a lot of spasticity. This is normal. It lasts up to four or five weeks. You'll see her making exaggerated responses to normal stimuli, jumping at ordinary noises, twitching when they draw blood. Her head might jerk back and forth. It will seem strange but it's entirely expected and you shouldn't let it frighten you. There's been a tremendous insult to her brain. After stage two, she will go into stage three. What she will be doing then is called synergy. When she tries to bend her elbow, for example, she will also move her whole shoulder and hand."

"And then?"

"If all goes well she will go into stage four. At that point the patient is nearly normal, or as normal as she is likely to get.

Normal motion comes back proximally first, which just means that she'll regain normal use of the parts near the center of the body, arms and legs, before the more distal parts, like feet and hands."

Robert said, "How long will all this take?"

"Most of what function she's ever going to recover she'll recover in the next six months."

"Dr. Pettibaker, it's great to see you! I mean Hannah," Suze said, coming into the living room. It was always good to see Pettibaker. The world felt better after she'd been there. Suze thought that very few doctors would make house calls. Pettibaker was very much aware of how nervous Sheryl got when she was driven to an appointment outside the house.

"Hi, Suze. Your girl here is doing well."

Sheryl actually smiled. Pettibaker always told Sheryl exactly what she thought.

"Be specific for us," Suze asked.

"Sure. I've just started explaining to Sheryl, but once more is good. You're doing a lot less listing to one side, Sheryl. The leg is stronger. I don't think you realize it, but because I see you once a week, the improvement is more noticeable to me than it is to you."

Sheryl said, "Bastard."

"She often says that when she means 'better,'" Figueroa said.

Pettibaker grinned. "I'm your neurologist, not your physical therapist, but I think you're pushing the exercise kind of hard. Your right side is like iron. Your left side is good and getting better, but my guess is you're overcompensating. Be good to your left side. Help it out."

Sheryl said, "Gah."

"I know it's frustrating and you're frustrated about your

speech. It will get better. It really will. Aphasia can be quite stubborn, but your last MRI was encouraging."

"Ahhhh."

"I think that was an intentional 'ah.' "

Sheryl smiled again, lopsidedly, but genuinely.

You didn't "walk Pettibaker to her car." You wouldn't get any more information anyhow, and she wouldn't get herself into situations where the patient could even think the doctor was telling the family stuff the patient didn't know. Suze admired that.

After Dr. Pettibaker left, and Robert had come home, Suze said, "We're going to celebrate. I'm gonna call for Thai food."

After dinner, Suze, J J, and Maria did the dishes.

"Aunt Suze," Maria said, "Emily's having a sleepover to-morrow night. Can I go?"

"Well, I don't see why not. Your dad has to go out, but I'll be here."

"I'll be here, too," J J said.

Suze said, smiling, "That's right. With me and J J and Kath, your mom should be fully protected. Speaking of which, I have to go back out tonight."

J J said, "Aw, Mom, do you really?"

"Yes. I'm sorry but they pay me for this. I should be back by one A.M."

Valentine was sitting in his favorite spot for the family dinner, halfway down from the second floor. When he heard Suze say, "I should be back by one A.M.," he was quite pleased.

He whispered to himself, "That will work out nicely."

CHAPTER TWENTY-THREE

SUZE GOT TO the Furlough at ten forty-five and found Norm already there. "Miranda stand you up?" she asked.

"Amanda, and no."

"Been working?"

"If you absolutely *must* be nosy, I spent the time since I left you at the laundromat doing my laundry."

"Ohhh. Testy, testy."

"What do you think, Figueroa. Is the Furlough our zone of comfort?"

"Must be."

Corky came down to their end of the bar and said, "It's warm out there tonight. Get you a beer, Figueroa?"

"Not while I'm working. Thanks, though. Afterward, maybe." She looked pointedly at Bennis's beer.

"One beer is like food," Bennis said.

"Can't do it after," Corky said. "We close at twelve."

Bennis chuckled. "Just long enough to mellow up the third shift?"

Mort said, "Jeez, Bennis. Even us bartender types gotta sleep sometime."

"Although some would say," Corky said, laughing happily, "that we spend our days asleep at the switch."

The first-watch guys started to straggle in. Figueroa knew they were not supposed to drink before going on duty, but what was she, their mother? She poked Bennis. "Let's hang out in the lot."

Third watch was leaving, and first watch was arriving. Bennis and Figueroa hung halfway between the parking lot and the CPD building. It was a chance to ask the ones arriving and parking if they'd seen anything on the target dates. And also a chance to catch the ones leaving, of course. Since they arrived over a period of maybe half an hour, you could spend a little one-on-one time. Both shifts had heard the memo read at roll call, but there was always a lot going on at roll call, plus a group doesn't respond like an individual. Besides, Bennis and Figueroa thought that catching these guys outdoors and gesturing at the El and the alley might jog somebody's memory.

For ten minutes Bennis and Figueroa split up, trying to talk with cops one at a time. They spent more time with departing third watch, since they could also run down the arriving first-watch cops again in a few minutes at roll call.

However, when Suze and Norm walked toward each other in front of the CPD, each knew in a glance that the other had found out nothing much.

"Zip," Figueroa said.

"Zero."

"Goose egg."

"Nada, damn it!"

"Well, up and at 'em," Figueroa said. "Into the building."

The women's lockup was much the same as it had been at four o'clock. Mrs. Forbes was gone but her assistant, a burly woman named Ms. Lotogath, was energetically in charge. When the guards were rounded up and asked by Bennis and Figueroa whether they'd seen anything suspicious, Lotogath practically ordered them to come up with something. Figueroa, fearing that one of the cowed women employees might invent a suspect just to please the boss, had to intervene.

"We don't want to put any pressure on you. Don't force it. If you don't remember, you don't remember, that's all."

"We know our guy is trying *not* to be seen," Bennis added. After they left he said, "Sheesh! I'd hate to run into Lotogath in a dark alley!"

"You don't suppose—"

"No, I don't."

By twelve-thirty they'd cruised the whole building. There was nobody in Personnel or the head honchos' offices. The cafeteria was even more depressing than earlier, if possible. One of the veggie choices for dinner must have been brussels sprouts, and the room still smelled sulphurously of them.

The Dispatch floors were exactly the same as they had been hours earlier. Only the faces had changed. Virtually nothing was going on in the north side of the Annex.

"Another great day for law enforcement," Bennis said.

They walked north on the sidewalk in front of the CPD building. Just north of the Annex, they cut to the right, through the construction area, past the backhoe and bulldozer, and over to the alley under the El.

The night was warm and very still. An El train had passed as they stepped out of the CPD doors, and a few flakes of rust were still sifting down. The trains ran less frequently after midnight. Very few cars were passing on State Street.

"Spooky here," Bennis said.

"Now don't creep me out, Bennis."

"Which means you feel it too."

"Yeah."

They stood without moving for several minutes. Figueroa tried not even to breathe loudly, and after a few seconds she realized Bennis was doing the same. Then, as if they had consulted with each other, both began to stalk quietly south.

They passed silently behind the CPD building, careful not to brush against discarded paper and other trash. Slowly they worked their way south to the fence that backed up against the CPD parking lot. They stopped there and still didn't speak.

They heard a rustling.

Bennis grabbed Figueroa's arm to quiet any idea she might have had of chasing the sound. It was too far away and they'd been fooled before.

It was somewhere in the open area under the tracks, not in the parking lot. But from the faintness of the whispery noise, it had to be more than half a block away, farther south.

Bennis put his head down, right against Figueroa's ear.

"Either you or I gotta walk back around to the front of the building. Come in from that side."

She took his head with her hands and turned it, leaning her mouth to his ear.

"I'll stay here. You go walk around front, and unless I yell, get into your car. Go out of the lot by the front, and if I still don't yell, go around the block and park and come in the alley from the south end."

"Good. Except you go. I'll stay here."

"Bennis, do *not* patronize me. We've been together too long."

He sighed very, very softly, then faded down the alley northward, without a sound.

Figueroa stood unmoving in the shadow of a telephone pole. Very little of the peach light from the streetlamps reached back here, but why take a chance? Really, the only two things that would attract attention were sound and motion. If she had not already been spotted, standing still should take care of it. And if whoever was out there believed someone had been here, the motion of Bennis walking away down the alley might satisfy him.

A minute and a half went by. Figueroa felt a shiver of fear

run up her back. She would never admit it to a soul. Well, she'd admit it to Bennis, but nobody else. A partner was unique.

Finally—finally!—she saw Bennis walking south on the sidewalk in front of the CPD. He turned into the parking lot and without a glance in her direction headed toward his car. He got in and started the engine with a sound that seemed louder than it had ever been before. He flicked on his lights, backed out of his space, and drove slowly down the row of cars toward the exit to State Street. As he turned, his headlights had passed across the east side of the lot and shined into the alley under the El.

Figueroa had expected this. They hadn't talked about it, but they'd worked together a long time and she knew he'd swing his lights into the alley for her. It was also part of the reason she had placed herself behind the telephone pole. As the lights swept the darkened alley area, she thought she saw a round shape move.

Somebody's head?

It was hard to be sure, since the motion of the headlights made everything seem to move, but this moved differently, against the direction of the other shadows. She focused on exactly where it was, and spotted objects nearby so as to be able to find the place, then looked slightly to one side of where it was. The tail of the eye picked up motion better than the center of focus, she knew. That old mammalian need to see things sneaking up to eat you.

Bennis would now be parking somewhere around the block. He would come into the alley from the south, while she held her position here, behind the north corner of the CPD building.

She heard a scrape. A rat? A cat? A human being?

Nothing moved.

Figueroa tensed and released the muscles of her legs without making any external movement. She wanted to be ready to jump into action if she had to. And she probably would have to get going fast, once the hidden man realized Bennis was coming down the alley. This was no box canyon. There were openings to Wabash Street between the buildings on the east. The brick apartment building had narrow walkways on both sides of it. The CPD was not fenced, and even though the parking lot was fenced on three sides, there were driveway openings on both west and east.

After two or three minutes, Bennis appeared at the far end of the alley, half a block away. He had changed his jacket, so he didn't show the same silhouette against the streetlights. He came shuffling into the alley with the exaggeratedly careful walk of a drunk, as if he were trying hard to balance his head on his neck.

Figueroa stayed where she was, unmoving.

He came closer, slowly, looking about as unthreatening as anybody could.

Closer still, past the far end of the CPD parking lot, along the fence, closer to where Figueroa had glimpsed a person. He neared the gate into the lot. In another ten feet, she thought, he should be near the spot.

Suddenly, a runner broke out of the shadows, racing down the alley and into the walkway next to the brick building. Figueroa went to a run from a standing start. Bennis changed in a split second from a drunk to a sprinter.

The fleeing person ran like a young boy, but with a floppy gait. His cap flew off. Figueroa put on a burst of speed. She jumped the cap, Bennis right after her. They came out on Wabash, amid garbage Dumpsters and parked cars. The runner was ducking and weaving. Now there were a few street people on the sidewalk, a group standing around an all-night diner entrance.

The runner ducked around the group, between cars, and into an area-way littered with cans. There were several ways out, Figueroa saw. She couldn't see the runner, but picked one of the possible routes, knowing Bennis would pick another.

Hers was a dead end, and no other person was in it.

She ran back to the Wabash entrance.

She heard Bennis running down a sidewalk into an enclosed courtyard and heard him say "Damn!"

She ran past, catching sight of him coming back.

"Where'd he go?"

"Could be anyplace," he said. "Damn it!"

They stood quiet and listened for running feet or toppling cans. Nothing.

"Hell," Figueroa said.

On the way back to the CPD lot, they picked up the cap. Figueroa put it in one of the paper evidence bags she carried in her car.

"Why do that?" Bennis said.

"Who knows? Maybe Trace can find something on it. Hair anyhow."

"No, I mean why bag it? Let's take it up now."

"They don't work at night."

"So? They can get started first thing in the morning."

They went into the building and up to the tech floor. Suze filled out the forms. She took the cap out of her paper bag. The evidence bag to put it in was also paper. Plastic kept out air and some biological material would degrade in it, so you weren't supposed to put evidence, especially blood or anything they might get DNA from, like hair follicles, in plastic. "Look at this," she said to Bennis.

There were several hairs caught in the clasp at the back where you could snap a band to make the cap larger or smaller.

"Long, aren't they?" he said.

The hairs were black and straight and very long.

Figueroa said, "Well, this isn't so bad. We know something

already. It's straight. So our guy is probably not African-American."

"Yup, you're right."

"Also, it's coarse hair, a thick shaft, don't you think?"

"I guess."

"So probably not one of the very northern of the northern Europeans."

"Like you're a hair and fibers expert."

"Help me here, Bennis. We lost him. We've had no luck so far. Send me home happy."

"Well, the lab will tell you. But—don't hit me—I think in general you're right. An analysis of this oughta give a pretty decent description of the perp. Maybe even age. This doesn't say old guy to me."

Figueroa stared at the hairs. "I thought it was a boy when he was running. Do you think it was a girl?"

"With all the guys out there wearing long ponytails? I wouldn't want to guess."

"What do you think this is—fifteen, sixteen inches?"

"My spread hand is eight inches. Yeah," he said, measuring from the end of his little finger to the end of his thumb without touching the hair. "Sixteen it is."

"Of course, this guy could be anybody. Doesn't have to be the killer."

Bennis said, "Why'd he run?"

"Didn't want to be questioned by the cops."

"Well, maybe."

Figueroa said, "Maybe he had drugs on him."

"Look, he didn't run quite the way a homeless person runs. Most of them are pretty deteriorated. This isn't a big area for drug sales. It's too near the CPD. Drug use, maybe. Small amounts don't get you in big trouble. He could be anybody, but I think the odds are decent that he's our killer."

"As I said before, send me home happy."

Lying flat in the shadows underneath a Dumpster just off Wabash, Mary Lynne Lee cowered and shivered, peeking out at a thin slice of pavement. Their feet had disappeared several minutes ago, and she thought she was safe.

They'd almost got her. And if they did, they'd throw her in a squad car and drag her home. She started to cry soundlessly. The whole world just wouldn't leave her alone, and it was so wrong. Why couldn't she just live her own life? She wasn't hurting anybody. When in her entire life had she ever hurt anybody?

Well, actually she had. Her mother and father. They were terribly, terribly disappointed in her. And her grandmothers, both of them, and her grandfathers, both of them. They expected more. Especially her grandfather Lee who had said, "I expected more of you, Mary Lynne," and almost tore her heart out saying it. She loved her grandfather Lee.

They were terribly disappointed, and probably very worried, too. The best thing would be if they never heard of her again. That way, they would never know how bad it was. If they never saw her again, they wouldn't ever know for sure how she'd been living.

When those cops chased her, the running had consumed the little bit of energy she had gotten from a short bottle of red wine. Wine had made her sleepy when she first started drinking; that was one of the things she liked about it. But a half bottle hardly affected her now. Briefly, it had made her invincible once she started to run flat-out. Now it was all gone. All the energy and all the—what?—protection. And all her stash of wine was gone, too.

She didn't dare stay here. Peering out from beneath the Dumpster, she saw a large homeless guy with flowing hair, a familiar figure she thought of as BAD, strolling up the alley.

Over her months in the streets, she had got used to categorizing people as good or bad on the instant.

There was a bad guy lying on the sidewalk where the alley met Wabash, too. She was way past the naive stage where she thought anybody without a shave and who smelled sweaty was a bad guy. But she'd seen this man push a smaller person into the path of a car a couple of days before, and she didn't want to get near him.

What she had to do was slip really sneakily around back to the police department building. She could sleep there.

But before that, she needed a drink.

Figueroa drove Bennis to his car. He gave her a good-night gesture, shooting his index finger at her. Figueroa shot back. She said, "Well, tomorrow is another day."

Bennis said, "Fiddle-de-dee."

CHAPTER TWENTY-FOUR

SUZE SANK GRATEFULLY into bed. Her knees hurt, her eyes hurt; her feet hurt; her head hurt. Finally she took an inventory of what didn't hurt, and since there were more of those—her eyebrows didn't hurt, or her nose, elbows, neck, ears, and a few more—she told herself to quit bellyaching, be grateful, and get some sleep. It was nearly two A.M. and she had to be up at six.

She couldn't stand too many more days like this. If there had been more progress, or if she and Norm had achieved some major success, she knew she would feel less exhausted.

There were only two windows in the attic. Neither one was much use. They were very small, one at the far north under the peak at the top of the roof, and one at the southwest, under the lower peak of a dormer. Both were in the positions where you ought to have attic vents if you had any sense, Valentine thought. In fact, he believed that they had once been the positions of attic louvered vents and the vents had been removed and replaced with windows in the early seventies during the fuel crisis. They were framed in a certain kind of matte aluminum that he knew was seventies-period.

But trying to save on heat in the winter meant that moist air would accumulate up here and eventually the wood would rot.

People were so shortsighted. They just didn't *know* anything.

Neither window opened, so he got all the stale air from the

house. Wouldn't you think almost anybody, however stupid and penny-pinching and inconsiderate, would provide decent air for a guest? A minimum gesture, wasn't it?

Of course, he was an uninvited guest, he reflected, giggling softly.

Outside one of the windows was the top of a huge sycamore tree that obscured his view from the north, toward the street. The other window looked down on the backyard, which wasn't particularly interesting. And both were terribly dirty. Shiftless, these people.

He picked up the screwdriver he had taken from the basement. The aluminum window was held in place by eight screws, two on each side near the corners. He had previously removed them all, then replaced and screwed in only the two in the top bar. The other six he simply pushed back in as far as they'd go, which was not all the way. In an emergency, he might possibly be able to jump out of the window into the tree and escape.

But it was even more useful than that. He pulled the window out and set it down on the floor. Then he urinated out into the tree.

This got around a lot of the danger of being heard flushing toilets. And truth to tell, it also gave him a good laugh.

Now he put the window back in place and pushed the screws in. As far as he could determine from looking out both windows, this and the one at the other side, all the lights were off downstairs. There were no patches of light in the yard or on the tree. His watch, which was still running, told him it was two-thirty A.M.

He crept down to the third floor. Stopping at one of his favorite spots, just inside the third-floor hall, he listened. There was no sound from the door at the end, which he now knew to be the lady cop's room. He stuck his head into the little boy's room, knowing the kid didn't wake easily. Yes, there he was, dead to the world.

Now down to the second floor. There was a light halfway along the hall, but it was dim and green. The night-light in the bathroom.

And on down to the first floor. Valentine entered the kitchen. On the counter was half a loaf of whole wheat bread. He took out two slices, buttered them heavily with the butter he found on the counter. Okay, where do you keep jam? He opened one cupboard, found it in the second place he looked. A good omen for a fun night.

He spread jam thickly on the other slice of bread and then put them together, giving the two slices of bread a little extra push, because he didn't like sandwiches that fell apart, then sat down at the small kitchen table, and ate, with great satisfaction. He popped a can of Coke. He put his feet up on the other chair. Excellent.

Finally he wiped crumbs from his hands, wiped and re-placed the knife, and—he was ready.

Sheryl lay on her back in the faint glow of a blue night-light. The call buzzer hung over the bed rail almost touching the knuckles of her right hand. He stepped quickly to the bed and lifted the buzzer over the rail, letting it fall quietly the length of its cord, to a point an inch above the floor. Out of her reach. It would take her a long time to get it into her hand, even left to herself.

Then he tickled her foot.

Sheryl woke slowly, which surprised him because he assumed that lying around all day would make her sleep lightly. Valentine watched consciousness come gradually to her eyes, and watched her focus on him. He leaned right over her, up to within a foot of her face. Awareness came more slowly than consciousness. As her eyes widened, first going to the place on the bed rail where the buzzer should be, he recognized the very instant when she was going to scream or call for help, or whatever she was able to do in her condition. When she drew in a breath, he moved fast, picking up the extra pillow near her head and bringing it down over her face.

Sheryl's body arched and she thrashed from side to side, trying to free herself. Her right hand grabbed at the pillow, and her left hand tried to, but repeatedly scrabbled ineffectively down the length of the cloth, as if the fabric were slippery. Her right hand was strong, stronger than he had expected, but he held it down on top of the pillow.

Valentine giggled a little, careful to make hardly any noise.

When Sheryl's struggles had all but stopped, he pulled the pillow away. With wide eyes, Sheryl stared up at him, sucking in air. She was pale, but not quite blue. She took in three whooping breaths, which he judged too faint for anybody in the house to hear. With great interest, he watched the pink come back into her cheeks. "Whit-ne-" she said, meaning nothing he could decipher, but he knew it meant "why?" or "who are you?"

"A nightmare," he said, and put the pillow back over her face.

CHAPTER TWENTY-FIVE

SUZE JUMPED STRAIGHT out of bed and started to run in place before she realized where she was. What was going on? She was sure that she was in the Academy and the trainer had just blown the whistle that meant run the track.

Buzzer, not a whistle. Oh, God.

Sheryl!

Suze ran for the door, never mind she was wearing just a nightshirt. Hyperventilating, she kept saying, "She rang the bell, she must be okay, rang the bell, must be okay, rang the bell, must be okay—"

Taking the back stairs two or three at a time, she practically crashed into Kath on the last flight. Robert was pounding down the front stairs.

They piled into Sheryl's room together.

"Oh, God, you're okay!" Suze said, seeing Sheryl sitting half up, half tangled in the bell cord that she had apparently pulled toward herself through the bed-rail bars, even though it should be looped over the top rail.

She wasn't okay, though. She was alive. But Suze immediately took in Sheryl's gasping breaths. Her face was blotchy, both red and pale, tear-streaked, her hair pushed upward. She was trying to talk and saying, "Aah, gah, gah, ahh, ack."

Robert said, "What's the matter, Sheryl?"

"What happened, Mom?" Kath asked.

Maria came into the room. "Mom! What's going on?"

"Gah-gah-gah-evil."

"She's had a nightmare," Robert said.

"GUH-det!" Sheryl said. "Hose."

Robert said, "She must have knocked the buzzer off the rail."

Suze almost said, "Don't talk about her as if she isn't here." But she had trained herself not to interfere between Sheryl and Robert. In the long run, she could only make trouble if she did.

But how could she have knocked the buzzer off? The cord was always wound around the rail.

"Sheryl, honey." Suze took her hand. "What happened? Are you sick?"

"Uh-uh-uh." If Sheryl was upset she spoke more poorly than usual.

"Take a breath, honey. There. Again. Did you have a dream?"

Sheryl twisted around, almost as if indignant at the thought. But Suze saw what she considered a touch of doubt in her eyes.

"You're not sure?"

"Gastrop."

Kath took Sheryl's other hand. "Mommy, can I sit here with you a little while?"

Sheryl settled back, not quite as panicky. Suze went for the sedative the doctor had prescribed for times that Sheryl was agitated. They tried to use it very sparingly, but this seemed like the sort of thing it was intended for. "Sheryl?" she said, holding up the bottle of tablets. "How about it?"

But Sheryl thrashed around, nearly as desperate as when they had first arrived.

"I guess not."

Robert said, "What happened? Tell us."

Tears came to Sheryl's eyes.

"Honey," Suze said. "It's three A.M. How about we get the kids back to bed and then either Robert or I sit here and sleep in the chair with you."

Sheryl smiled.

Robert and Suze sent the children back to bed in order to get two minutes in the kitchen to talk softly.

"All right," Suze said, "what do you think happened?"

"Like I said, a dream."

"She hasn't had any this bad."

"She hasn't had any this bad in the last month."

"Okay. True."

"Look, what else could it be? Do you think she's having some sort of seizure?"

"Didn't look like it."

"No," Robert said. "I don't think so either."

"She got quieter as soon as she realized it was us. It was almost like some monster got in and scared her."

"A monster in a dream," Robert said.

"I don't think it was a seizure. You know Dr. Pettibaker was here today and she said she 'likes' how Sheryl's doing."

"Good."

"Do you think Pettibaker's the reason? She put her through a lot of tests today."

"Pettibaker's very professional, and very soft-spoken."

"I know that, Robert. But Sheryl still knows she's being assessed, no matter how subtly it's done. Maybe Pettibaker thinks Sheryl's doing well, but the tests made her think she's not. You know she's never as good as she wants to be."

"Maybe. We'll probably never know."

"We will when she's well. She's going to tell us about all this stuff. Robert, you don't think—I know this may be dumb, but what if we had a real burglar and she saw him?"

"Don't be silly. The rest of us didn't see anybody."

Just then Kath came around the door.

"Honey," Suze said, "you should be in bed."

"Well, I was just wondering—"

"Wondering what, sweetie?"

"I wondered if Mommy saw the ghost."

"The ghost?" Figueroa felt chilly. "What ghost?"

"Last night. A ghost looked into my room."

"What did it look like?"

"It looked just like a regular man, except it was pale."

"Did it do anything?"

"No, it just stared at me real hard."

Annoyed, Robert said, "Kath, that's enough. We have real problems to deal with. We don't have time for foolish stuff."

"But it was real."

"A real ghost?" Robert said scornfully.

"Well—I really saw it."

"You were dreaming. Go back to bed."

Kath caught her lower lip in her teeth. Suze said, "Honey, whatever it was, we're here to protect you. Don't worry."

"Okay." Reluctantly, Kath went upstairs.

Robert said, "Suze, you have to back me up when one of the children is acting stupid."

"Look, I don't know what she saw, but Kath is a very reliable child. I can't just automatically 'back you up' until I know the facts."

"Well, you'd better."

"What? Why?"

"We're putting you and J J up here, you know."

"Putting us up? I pay rent."

"You pay rent for accommodation in this big house, with use of a big kitchen, clothes washer and dryer, two TVs, a whole floor to yourselves, basement, and a big backyard with play equipment. If you rented an apartment for the same money, you'd get a tiny bathroom, a kitchenette, and two tiny bedrooms if you were lucky."

"Robert, I do *all* the grocery shopping, *all* the cooking. What would you do if I weren't here? Send out for pizza seven nights a week? Which would cost more, too, by the way. Plus, I do *all* the laundry except a small amount that Maria does. And probably half of the Sheryl care. It would cost you a fortune to replace me."

"Maria could do the cooking."

"Not only can she *not* do the cooking, in the sense that she doesn't know how to cook more than one or two things, but she shouldn't. Maria needs to concentrate on her schoolwork."

"She's not doing that now. She spends all her time thinking about boys and clothes and makeup."

"Exactly. I have to keep after her just to get her to finish her homework. This is not the time to take up her energies working as 'little mother' to a family."

"Oh, I guess you know everything. If you're so overworked, why do you stay?"

"Sheryl." She said it simply and quietly.

He said, "Sheryl. Right." And there was something in his tone that told Suze a lot. Oh, no. God, no. *No, no, no.* Robert has a girlfriend. Hell, hell, hell, damn!

Holding her annoyance in, Suze said, "Whatever Kath thinks she saw, we'd better check the house."

"You're catering to her."

"There is nothing wrong with reassuring a child, let alone the fact that she won't even know we're doing it. She's gone to bed. Tell you what, Robert. You go in and sleep in the chair, and I'll check that the windows and doors are locked."

"Can't. I have a busy day tomorrow. I need my sleep. You go sit with her, and I'll check the windows and doors."

"Well, listen. I had a hell of a day today—oh, never mind. Go ahead. I'll stay with her."

FRIDAY

CHAPTER TWENTY-SIX

Friday, June 3

From "City Beat" by Charles Horgue

Sandra Jordan gets up each morning and gives her daughter Casey, eleven, a breakfast of peanut butter and jelly on whole wheat bread, Casey's favorite. Then Sandra walks Casey to school. During the morning, Sandra goes to the laundromat and washes her clothes and Casey's, leaving some in the dryers while she waits table at lunch at a local diner.

Casey plays basketball after school. Her mother picks her up there at four-thirty and they walk home together.

Casey would like to invite friends home after school to play, but she doesn't, and she very rarely goes to her friends' houses because she can't reciprocate. In fact, she's not supposed to tell anybody, including the school, where they live. Since Casey's father left, they get their mail at the home of a friend of Sandra's.

Casey and Sandra live in Sandra's car.

SERGEANT TOUHY WAS on a rampage. "I'm getting pretty damn sick of half of you getting pulled off to play detective. Most of you are only half alive anyhow!"

"Where's Bohannon?" Bennis asked, trying to deflect her. "And Moose Weatherspoon?"

Touhy ground her teeth. "You wouldn't believe," she said.

"Aw, c'mon. Tell us."

Touhy had started roll call a little early, which she often did when she was mad. It made everybody have a minute of worry that they were late. She thought starting their day with a little dose of fear was a good thing. Kept the troops in line.

Finally, she said, "They're being interviewed by the commander."

"Sarge, why would that be?" Bennis said.

"Might as well tell you, Norman," she said. "You'll only find out sooner or later."

"Sooner," Figueroa muttered under her breath. She didn't think Touhy heard. Touhy gave Figueroa a nasty look because she deduced approximately what Figueroa had said.

"Officers Bohannon and Weatherspoon were sitting on an apartment while the detectives swept up witnesses after a homicide last week. Unfortunately"—Sergeant Touhy paused for effect—"they decided to while away a weary hour watching porno on the guy's TV."

"Is that so bad?" the Flying None asked.

"It was pay per view. The lawyer for the family closed everything down last night—gas, electric, phone, charge cards, like that—to make sure there were no extra expenses. Everything buttoned up, up to the minute. My goodness, he says, the ME told us Mr. Sharpe had been dead for three days when he was found. How could he possibly have been watching TV on Thursday? *And run up all these charges?*"

Bennis said, "Oh, dear."

Touhy said, "Indeed. Then those two shit-for-brains said they just turned it on to check out whether the TV was working. Why they imagined they had to do that we don't know.

And, wonder of wonders, they just happened to hit the porno pay per view in passing."

"That's possible," Bennis said.

"For six and a half hours?"

"Oops."

"I want this to be a lesson to all of you. You don't drink the victim's Coca-Cola, or his Macallan, you don't eat his Frango mints, you don't nuke his leftover pizza, you don't watch his TV. You're really, really parsimonious about breathing his air."

Bennis started to say, "Parsimonious—" But he thought Touhy was in no mood for jokes about using big words. While he considered asking whether parsimonious were those vegetables you used in soup, Touhy's cell phone rang. She answered.

Then Figueroa could say, no, that's parsnips and he could say aren't parsnips like ministers, and she could say that's parsons and he could say aren't parsons like missing parsons—but then again maybe this was better kept for the Furlough—

"BENNIS!"

"Oh, yes, boss."

"I've been talking to you."

"Sorry, ma'am."

"You and Figueroa, up and out."

"Where to, sir, ma'am?"

"Don't wind me up, Bennis. Get out back. Under the El."

Bennis looked at Figueroa. Figueroa looked at Bennis. They both mouthed, "Oh, shit!"

It was all happening again. Mossbacher was standing near a squad car. There was a different evidence tech. Today's evidence tech was a middle-aged black woman who was circling the body, photographing absolutely everything, as far as Figueroa could tell. The body was half hidden between two Dumpsters, but appeared to be a young man dressed in the dirty clothing of the homeless. It was located a little bit farther south than Abigail Ward's body had been, leading Figueroa to wonder if the killer was moving farther from the CPD to be safer.

Figueroa didn't get close enough to be sure. Mossbacher grabbed them as they came down the alley. "Do what you need to, wrap this up, and come and see me."

"I'd like to give Dr. Percolin a heads-up," Bennis said. "Have him ready to do the autopsy."

"I have no problem with that. If he can do it right away, fine. But come see me right after. And *don't talk to the press.*"

"Yes, boss."

Mossbacher strode away. A first-watch uniform started to string barrier tape. An elderly man from the ME's office arrived to pronounce death. Figueroa pulled out her cell phone. "Bennis, want me to call Percolin?"

"Yeah. Sure."

While she spoke into the phone, Bennis located the first uniform on the scene.

Figueroa said, "Percolin will be there waiting. He's just finishing one up. By the way, he says Abigail Ward's blood alcohol was 'paralytic.' "

"That's consistent. I guess she wouldn't have fought being sprayed with the fire extinguisher. Figueroa, this is Officer Meeks. Meeks is gonna tell us who found the dead guy."

"Great."

"Secretary coming in to work saw the body."

Obviously, Meeks was not a chatty type. "Coming to work at the CPD?" Figueroa asked.

"Yup."

"What is her name?"

"His. Bill Marcantonio."

"Meeks, help us out here," Figueroa said. "Try to be a little more narrative about this. Start with who he's a secretary for."

"Chief of Patrol Archibald Davis."

Figueroa thought, *Oh-oh*. Meeks went on. "He sees the shoe, parks, goes back to look, sees the body, comes inna the building, and tells us."

"What made him see the body? It's pretty well hidden."

"Dunno. He said he thought it was funny a shoe bein' there and sticking up. Toe-up, like. I guess he figured a shoe oughta fall down."

"He's right, too. Then what?"

"Well, I was goin' off. I was practically out the door. I mean, I had one foot in the locker room, but Sarge says go see. Came out. Saw the body. Stabilized the crime scene. Didn't let nobody touch nothin'. Called the honchos. If I'd'a been just a little faster gettin' to the locker room, I'd'a been home by now."

"I feel your pain."

The tech, whose name was Barbara Carter, came over to Bennis and Figueroa. "What specific extra stuff do you want me to do?"

Hot damn! Figueroa thought. Somebody is finally treating us as if we know what we're doing.

Bennis said, "We need the trash around the body collected."

"Then the pavement underneath Dustbusted," Figueroa said.

"Sure thing. Anything else?"

Figueroa said, "Keep an eye open for Handi Wipes kinds of things." Bennis glanced at her face. She knew he could tell she didn't want to see the body, or any dead person in this place. She felt like a failure. What should they have done? Stayed here all night? If they had, would they have prevented a murder?

Bennis said, "Let's go take a look."

The evidence tech had not disturbed the body, and the doc had seen at once that there was no chance of resuscitation, so he had not moved it very much, either. Figueroa and Bennis approached the shoe. It was indeed vertical, and attached to a leg wearing very ratty blue denim.

The other leg was bent up and leaned against one of the Dumpsters. "It's a kid," Bennis said. "A teenage boy."

The doc said, "No, it's a girl."

"We got all the pictures we need?"

Figueroa thought Bennis, too, hesitated to take that last step. She said, "I think so."

"Well, let's do it."

The tech was already wearing gloves. She laid a body bag on the ground while Figueroa and Bennis pulled on gloves. Then they and the doc pushed their way between the Dumpsters.

Rigor mortis had begun in the jaw, neck, and most of the upper body, but the legs had some flexibility. They carried her like a log out onto the body bag. The young woman wore a flannel plaid shirt over a white T-shirt, but both were soiled and torn. A plastic carryall bag lay on the ground where her body had been.

Figueroa glanced at the bag, which was flattened. A glittery gold material stuck out of it a little way. Well, they'd see to that in a minute. But experience told her the bag contained the young woman's trick clothes.

Gently, they lowered the woman onto the open body bag, where her hair made a dark spill around her face. Figueroa at last looked directly at her.

"Oh, God," she said.

Bennis said, "What?"

"How long would you say her hair is?"

"Oh, man, oh, man. About sixteen inches."

CHAPTER TWENTY-SEVEN

"IF WE'D CAUGHT her last night, Bennis, we might have saved her life."

"I know. Don't beat it into the ground."

"I'm not forgiving myself."

"Listen, Figueroa, she ran away from us. It isn't as if we made her go hang out in the alley."

Not consoled, not even really listening to him, Suze said, "And there we were, running after her, probably scaring her, and all the time we were so convinced that we were chasing the killer!"

"If we'd scared her away from there, she would have been all right."

The body had arrived at the morgue separately from Bennis and Figueroa. The two cops caught Dr. Percolin as he entered the autopsy suite. Percolin saw them and lifted his arms out to the side, as if he felt helpless. Then with a sideways lean of his head, gestured them in to the autopsy suite.

"Did you know," he said, "that they're not authorizing an analysis of the face swabbings?"

"What!" Bennis said.

"They who?" Figueroa barked.

"The Chief ME." Percolin held up his hand as Figueroa drew breath. "Don't yell at me. This is a governmental agency with a budget—just like yours, and the President, and Streets and Sanitation. They review what gets requested, and they decide whether the chances of results are worth the costs. They say in this case the potential results don't justify the cost. And frankly, it *would* be expensive. What I wanted was an analysis of all the stuff on the faces of O'Dowd, Ward, and this one, so we could tell what kind of wipes the killer used."

Figueroa said, "Suppose we get a suspect and he has wipes in his pocket or car. What are we supposed to do?"

"Bag 'em I suppose. Meanwhile I'll keep the swabbings."

"I'm sorry, Dr. Percolin."

"Not your fault. Dammit! This is stupid! This is short-sighted!"

"Yes."

"It is also"—here his voice rose higher—"not what they hire us for! Damn! We're supposed to be highly trained and highly qualified investigators? Give me a break! Let us investigate! Hey! Is that too much to ask?"

Figueroa was stunned. It was a shock to see Santa Claus well and truly pissed. Bennis, however, agreed and was furious himself.

"Shit, shit, shit!" Bennis said.

Figueroa said, "He doesn't usually swear much."

Percolin said, "God! I feel exactly like he does. All I know at this point is that the faces have propylene glycol on them." Technical stuff seemed to quiet him. "And that's not too much help, because three-fourths of all the individually packaged Wet Wipes kinds of towelettes have propylene glycol in the liquid formula."

They turned toward the tables. There were several other autopsies going on, but Figueroa and Bennis saw their corpse at once.

She lay on the cold steel, covered to the chin with a sheet. The sheet was tented over her knee, where the leg remained bent as it had been on the pavement under the El. Her black hair spread out around her head and a wave of it fell over the table edge. She had been a beautiful young woman, even though she was much too thin, and her color was unhealthy.

"A poorly nourished female, possibly of part Asian ancestry," Percolin said into the mike. He gestured at her.

"Her face is clean," he said. "Like the others. Although, for that matter, her hands are pretty clean." He leaned over and smelled her face. "You too," he said to Bennis.

Bennis smelled the face. "Lemons." He smelled her hands. "Soap."

Percolin drew fluid from the eyeball for a check of ethanol and other drugs. Figueroa knew it was necessary. That didn't make her hate any less seeing the thick needle go into the eye.

The diener and Percolin turned the body over. Rigor was well established now, and the young woman turned like a log of wood, even the bent leg holding its position.

"Scratches," Percolin said, pointing to lateral red marks on the rib cage.

"He scratched her?" Bennis said. "That's different."

"Doubt it. She's been working as a hooker, I think. Probably got scratched a day or so ago. Look. They're dry," he said, rubbing one of the marks. It made a rough sound.

The diener and Bennis rolled the body onto its back again, while Percolin dictated into the recorder.

Now the woman lay facing up at the light, unblinking. A few strands of the long black hair had pasted themselves to her forehead and another swatch lay across her neck like a cut. Figueroa stared.

She said, "Why is there so much mucus in her nose and mouth?"

Dr. Percolin hesitated. "It's not mucus," he said finally.

"What is it, then?"

He picked up a hemostat and touched the material in her nose. It resisted, firm but rubbery. "Translucent, slightly whitish, rubbery," he said to the recorder. "I think it's silicone caulk."

Figueroa ran from the room.

After ten minutes she came back, sheepish. Bennis said nothing. Percolin only said, "Figueroa, look at this."

He had eased the plug of caulk out of the young woman's throat. Two smaller plugs, the ones from the nostrils, lay in a shallow stainless-steel tray.

"I do believe we've got something."

"What?" She came closer, fighting back her nausea.

"I think our man has made his first mistake."

Dr. Percolin pointed at what appeared to be a short brownish thread embedded in the silicone caulk. "It's a hair," he said. He already had a magnifying loupe focused at it.

"How do we know it's not from the victim?"

"It's a little lighter color than her hair, and it curves just a bit. See?"

Bennis had grabbed up a magnifier from the instrument counter along the wall. "I see."

"Fate has smiled on us at last. It's not a cut piece of hair, like might be left in your collar after a haircut. See the taper at the end? I'll bet our man shot the caulk into her nose first. And I'll bet the tip of the caulk tube was sticky after that, and it brushed his arm and pulled out one of his hairs. And that means—"

"I know what it means," Bennis said. "The root is still on the hair."

"And that means that when you catch the guy, we can match his DNA and pin it on him. You can get DNA from cut pieces of hair without the root, but this is *very* much better."

Figueroa said, "And *that* means all we have to do is catch him."

"Okay, Figueroa," Bennis said in the car. "Let's go feed you. You missed lunch the last two days. We'll have midmorning breakfast. Brunch. Whatever. It'll be good."

"I can't. I feel sick."

"You've been up late too many nights. You're worn out. I always say, if you can't sleep, at least eat."

"You're ashamed of me."

"I am *not*! You're one of the strongest people I know."

"But I couldn't stand it. I ran out on the autopsy."

"You came back. Anyway, Suze, if I'm gonna think less of you because you had a runaway attack of sympathy for the dead, what kind of person am I?"

CHAPTER TWENTY-EIGHT

SHERYL BIRCH LAY in bed, exhausted from her morning set of exercises. She found her mind wandering as Alma Sturdley talked about the problem her sister was having with varicose veins.

"And her husband said, if you can believe it, that her legs looked just like a road map! Can you *believe* the insensitivity of the man? I said, you should have told him you would have been just as pleased if *he'd* been the one to carry four children to term."

Sheryl did not really hear her. She was tormenting herself about the ghost, or the nightmare, or the devil she had fought with the night before. Was it really possible that she had imagined that evil face? She did sometimes experience things that weren't real. She accepted that. Dr. Pettibaker had told her to expect it for some time to come.

There couldn't be a real intruder in the house. The house was full of people.

"The brain is coping with a lot of changes. You have to expect that the wires get crossed occasionally."

Wires crossed indeed. It was more like the world turned inside out.

No! She needed to tell somebody. Last night *couldn't* have been a dream or hallucination. She could still feel the pillow over her face. She had been sure she was going to die. If she could only speak a whole, clear sentence, she would have asked Suze to check the pillow. Surely she had bitten it or slobbered on it or maybe she had torn it when she struggled with the man.

Or—that would be true even if she had had a dream or hallucination, wouldn't it? Oh, God.

And anyway, she couldn't speak a whole clear sentence or even a whole clear three words.

Bennis was eager to put some space between the autopsy and Suze. The autopsy itself had confirmed what they knew already. The woman, Mary Lynne Lee, was twenty-three. She had grown up in Winnetka, which was unusual for homeless, but not entirely unknown for high-priced call girls. Which she wasn't. Clearly something bad had happened to Mary Lynne at home or as a young person. But what it was would take some finding out.

She showed signs of having used IV drugs, but not recently. Like the other three dead homeless, she liked alcohol. She lived on the street most of the time, to judge by her clothes. Even her trick bag clothing was cheap and worn. She had some health problems related to homelessness, like skin parasites, and some VD related to prostitution, but Bennis did not think any of these were going to lead to her killer.

Dr. Percolin didn't think so either.

Her stomach had been full of scotch.

"Enough to put her so far under that somebody could squirt silicone caulk in her mouth and nose?" Bennis had asked him.

"Absolutely. Enough to make her absolutely paralytic. Yes," Percolin told him. "But she wasn't forced to drink it. There's no sign at all of a physical attack, in the sense of anybody pouring stuff down her throat. Maybe—poor thing—she was just thrilled to get the very best stuff for a change. This guy has access to good scotch and good bourbon."

Bennis said, "Suze, I have today's schedule of store demos."

"Okay. As a matter of fact, I've got this extremely excellent idea about that," Figueroa said.

"Oh, that'll be a first."

"Bennis, you know all my ideas are good."

"Look, I don't want to be the Grinch. Let me say that you have occasionally had an idea that worked out very well. What's this one, anyhow?"

"Let me try it out and we'll see."

"That's hardly the scientific approach. You should tell me first, for purposes of external verification."

Figueroa and Bennis began at eleven-thirty to make the rounds of the large stores. Four were presenting demos, the first at eleven-thirty. Having informed the security chiefs on the way there about what they would be looking for, the setups, including radio communication, were very much better than they had been on Thursday. Figueroa had brought along a change of clothes and a pair of glasses on the theory that the pickpocket yesterday might have seen her. On the way over, she tugged her hair back into a fairly neat chignon and applied more makeup than she usually used. She began to have misgivings, though, the closer they got, and thought she needed an even better disguise.

She asked the security chief at their first stop, "Mr. Lermontov, can you give me a scarf or a cheap wig?"

"We don't sell cheap wigs," he said somewhat huffily. Then he relented and entered into the spirit of the thing. "Let's see what we can do."

He took Figueroa to the "better jewelry" counter, and consulted with the head buyer. "Something just a touch too flashy," he said.

After a moment's thought, the buyer gave Figueroa a pair of amethyst earrings. She studied herself in the mirror as she put them on. They weren't anything she'd ever wear, but she thought they looked very nice. Not too flashy at all. But then, what did she know?

Lermontov next escorted her to scarves. He himself pointed to the one he wanted—a head scarf, lavender to match the earrings, the fabric shot with fine fibers of silver. Suze fumbled around with it until the saleswoman tied it for her.

Bennis said, "I guess we shouldn't've missed that scarf-tying demonstration."

Today's demo was mascara. The representative of a cosmetics company, a thin, birdlike woman, stood on a little dais that raised her twelve inches above the sales floor. With her were two absolutely gorgeous women, wrapped in powder-blue smocks, seated on high silver stools. One woman was a pale blonde, with fair skin, ash-blond hair, and light eyes, which Figueroa had to agree would look brighter with a little makeup. The other was an equally beautiful black woman, with sleek cocoa skin, hair that was black but with reddish highlights, and dark eyes that were highlighted by long dark lashes. Figueroa couldn't imagine how mascara would improve woman number two.

"Now, we're going to take a Polaroid photo of my two lovely assistants before we begin, so that you can compare later," the thin woman said. "This is Margo, and this is Elaine. I'm going to start with Elaine."

Elaine was the blonde.

Figueroa watched the demo with what she hoped was fascinated attention to eye shadow and liner. The blonde grew brighter eyed—or as the thin woman put it, the eyes began to "pop." Figueroa considered this an unfortunate choice of words. She scanned the crowd from her position to the rear of the group. There was only one baby present. This one was sound asleep in a white and blue padded stroller that did not look like the foldable ones from the day before. Of course, you couldn't go by that. The pickpockets could have any number of strollers and costumes.

These demos were always short. Unfortunately, by the time Margo's eyes were done—and Figueroa admitted that they, too, looked more defined, even though the difference was less noticeable than in Elaine's case—nobody had shouted out that their wallet was missing. And Figueroa herself had noticed no suspicious moves by the woman with the baby or anybody else. The Polaroids had been passed around, amid exclamations of delight, and the crowd dispersed. Many of the women bought products, which was the point, of course.

Sighing, she met Lermontov at the elevators. "We'd better get over to Cadbury and Mason. They're doing perfume at noon."

Lermontov said, "Would you like to keep the earrings and scarf for the day?"

"You trust me with them?"

"Hey, you're the police."

When they got to Cadbury and Mason, Brandon Ely told them, "I don't really believe the pickpocket will come back. After all, she's been here twice that we know of. It's taking too much risk. She'd have to be terribly overconfident."

"And your point is?" Figueroa muttered.

Bennis said, "Yeah, she's right, Mr. Ely. That's why they get caught. They keep doing it."

Ely, who had shown signs of liking Figueroa before, chuckled understandingly.

Figueroa said, "She's gotten away with it every single time. You have to assume this whole sequence of events is making her overconfident."

Neither Figueroa nor Bennis thought the pickpocket had seen them yesterday. "But the woman and baby might have seen you, Bennis, when they were stopped and searched."

"I know that. I'm staying well in the background. I'm back in Swiss chocolates."

Cadbury and Mason's perfume counter was a thing of beauty. Backed with forty feet of mirrored panels six feet high laid out in a gentle curve, and fronted with thirty feet of beveled glass display counters, it sparkled in much the same way as a high-priced bar. In front of the mirrors were ranged hundreds of beautiful bottles on glass and gold shelves. Cut-glass bottles, blue glass bottles the intense shade of Noxema containers, ruby-red bottles, clear bottles shot with gold or silver filaments, tiny silver flasks, big balloon-shaped spray bottles for cologne, and all the brand names known in the world of fashion—Chanel, Armani, Estée Lauder, Clinique.

The demo woman was glossy too, wearing a gold lamé wraparound sarong.

"Today," the woman said, "we are going to consider only the herbal fragrances. These have become tremendously popular of late. As I'm sure you know, florals were terribly popular in the 1920s and 1930s. One can almost picture Theda Bara floating along on the scent of camellias. We all wore simple scents during the World War II years when women worked in defense plants. Then the fruitier scents came in. But of late the more natural herbals have made a big advance, especially among young people, who don't care for artifice—"

There were perhaps thirty people in the audience, Figueroa thought. Several of the women looked vaguely like some of yesterday's crowd. Three of them had children in strollers, one cuddled a tiny baby in a papoose carrier.

Without appearing to study the audience, she pushed in a little way and was able to keep in view the three women with strollers. This position made it impossible for her to see the fringes or back of the crowd without turning her head, and she just had to hope that her guess about babies was right.

She had a view of the left shoulder of one woman and the

back of her stroller, the back of another but not much of her stroller, and the right arm and most of the baby in the case of the third.

By using the edge of her vision, she could be aware of movement of these parts of these three women without moving her head or even cutting her eyes back and forth very much.

The baby on her left started to cry. The mother leaned forward and plucked a bottle out of a diaper bag. She handed it to the baby, slightly jostling the arm of a woman next to her. The woman to Figueroa's right jumped when her child threw his pacifier into the air. In so doing, she grabbed the sleeve of a woman ahead of her and said, "Oh, I'm sorry."

"No problem," the other woman said.

The woman directly in front of Figueroa plucked her baby out of its stroller. This meant Figueroa got her first look at the child, a little boy eight months old or so in a plaid baby suit, just at the moment that the baby kicked the woman in front of her. Figueroa had never before realized how much physical activity occurred in a group watching a demo.

Also at that moment, one of the older women in the front of the bunch decided that she didn't want to stay for the rest of the demonstration. She turned and pushed her way out, right past Figueroa. The older woman was wearing pointy-toed high-heeled shoes—the kind Figueroa believed had been developed by orthopedic surgeons to create more business—and as she neared Figueroa she turned her ankle, falling heavily against two people, the woman with the baby on Figueroa's left and a young girl standing nearby.

The older woman said, "Oh!"

The teenager said, "Are you all right?"

"Yes, I think so, dear," the older woman said. Her face had flushed with embarrassment. She patted the teenager and smiled as if she were fine, but as she moved away she limped heavily.

Figueroa had now seen so many "contacts" she didn't know who to watch. Two of the four babies present started crying. The demo came to an end. The group broke up like an expanding bubble, people moving off in all directions. Figueroa was utterly at a loss about whom to suspect. When a chubby little woman started to yell, "Where's my wallet?" Figueroa had nothing useful to say into her microphone.

She walked fast, but she hoped unobtrusively over to Bennis and Ely, who stood next to the elevators.

"Who was it?" Bennis asked.

"I have to go take care of that woman," Ely said, looking at Figueroa as if she weren't as much fun as he'd thought.

"Bennis, stay right here. Don't get any nearer; we don't want the pickpocket to see you. But watch me; watch where I go."

Suze strolled to the women's rest room and pushed her way inside. There was a young woman washing her hands at the sink. She had long brown hair, dangling earrings, and wore a red silky shirt. A large black purse was next to her feet. Figueroa could not specifically remember whether she had been at the demo. There was no one else in the place. Figueroa went to a sink, looked into her left eye, pulling the lids apart, blinked a few times, rinsed her face with water, and after drying her hands left the rest room.

She went immediately to a long rack of pastel summer jackets and hid behind them, watching the rest-room door. She was aware that Ely would be looking for her soon, but this was more urgent.

Several minutes went by. An older woman went into the rest room and came out two minutes later. Still the young woman remained inside. Then Figueroa saw the rest-room door open and somebody peer out.

She waited.

A teenage boy emerged, carrying a gym bag with a baseball

mitt hung over the strap. He wore a ponytail, a Cubs T-shirt, and Levi's.

Figueroa pounced on him and said, "Gotcha!"

"The bag turned inside out," Brandon Ely said. "The earrings came off, of course. The hair became a boy's ponytail. The makeup came off in the bathroom sink. And Levi's are unisex, of course. But the 'boy' was really a young woman."

"You carry a baseball mitt," Bennis said, "you look like a boy."

"Who would not have been watching a perfume demo," Figueroa said.

"She handed the stroller and the baby to a confederate. She kept the stolen wallet because the person with the stroller might be searched, and she went to the bathroom, figuring that if anybody got followed it would be the woman with the baby."

"Who was dressed similarly," Bennis said. "What I'm sorry about is that the confederate got away."

"Well, we can follow up on this one's associates. Now that we know where she lives, we can find her relatives. Somebody will talk."

"What I don't get," Ely said, "is how you knew she'd be in the *women's* rest room."

"She had to watch the demos as a female, or she'd really look out of place. So at some point she had to change to a boy. She had to do it right after the demo ended; she couldn't control that. So for all she knew, she'd be going into a rest room that had other people in it. So it couldn't be the men's. They'd freak. Once she changed clothes, she could wait around inside the women's rest room until it was empty. If somebody came in she could duck into a stall. She could peek out and make sure nobody was especially watching. By the time she got outside, a few feet away from the door, nobody would notice that a boy had come out of the ladies' room."

When Figueroa went back to the other store to return the scarf and earrings, she found she had lost one of the earrings in the brief scuffle.

Lermontov said, "Forget about it. It's a small price to pay. Congratulations."

CHAPTER TWENTY-NINE

"I AM SO psyched," Figueroa said.

"Well, it was good work," Bennis said. "Just the same, I think it's unseemly to crow about it quite so much."

"When you gotta crow you gotta crow."

Even Sergeant Touhy had been pleased when they walked in with their pickpocket. Touhy showed this by not snarling. However, she said, "I have a couple of new jobs to give you."

Bennis said, "We have to canvass on the murder, Sarge."

"All right. I'm giving you the benefit of the doubt. For now."

As they started to turn away, she added, closing one eye and looking sideways at them, "Oh, gee. I guess I must've just forgotten. Go see Mossbacher."

"Figueroa. Bennis. Sit down."

Mossbacher was more subdued than usual. He can't possibly doubt that we have a serial killer now, Figueroa thought. And then she had a sudden throb of apprehension. If he thought it was an important case, he'd put somebody else on it.

He said, "I want to know what you've got so far."

Figueroa looked to Bennis. He flicked a glance back at her, but courageously started to explain.

"A series, boss. The cause of death in all four cases has been a variation of smothering—choking, smothering with a bunch of fabric, cutting off the woman's oxygen with a gas fire extinguisher, and now stopping the mouth and nose with silicone caulk. There's a pattern there."

"Not much of one."

"And there's a pattern in the selection of the victims. All homeless. All poorly or raggedly dressed. All alcoholics."

"And all different ages and genders and races," Mossbacher said.

"And all with their faces washed," Bennis said.

"All of them?"

"Including the last one. Mary Lynne Lee."

Mossbacher steepled his fingers in a gesture Figueroa thought was rehearsed rather than genuine. Nevertheless he looked genuinely annoyed. "And so?"

"A serial killer isn't going to stop. We need to get pro-active. We need to put out decoys. We need to let the community know he's out there. We particularly have to get word out to the homeless to stay away. They should be warned."

"No. The press would get wind of it."

"Use the press. The press can warn them. That's one way the press is actually useful. And warn anybody else in the area. Maybe the press doesn't care so much about the homeless, but we can't be sure that he won't turn to drunken party-goers next."

"No can do, Bennis. Won't make Chicago look like fun city. We're right at the beginning of the tourist season. We got the Air and Water Show coming up, then the Taste of Chicago. The Fourth of July celebration. One thing right after another. They may be homeless, but murder still isn't good advertising. We're gonna handle this quietly."

"But he's hitting fast now—"

"And what's more, you don't know who Mary Lynne Lee is."

"We've got an address. We want to talk with her relatives next."

"I've already sent somebody to do that."

Bennis said, "What?"

Figueroa was shocked. Why wouldn't he let them do the investigating? Meanwhile Bennis, who had only paused half a second, was asking, "Who is she, then?"

"Well, matter of fact, as herself she isn't anybody. But her parents and grandparents are. They're doctors and engineers and corporation CEOs, and the whole lot of them live in Winnetka."

"Oh."

"Oh is right. They're hopping mad already. We do *not* need them to know that she wandered into a serial killer situation. One that we haven't been able to solve."

Figueroa couldn't stand it any longer. "Boss, if we got some support, we *might* solve it now. Dr. Percolin can't do the tests he wants. The stomach contents. The face swabbings. The trace evidence around the bodies wasn't—that is, you didn't let us—I mean, we only got about a tenth of it analyzed."

"It will be now, Figueroa."

"Thank you, sir. That'll help."

"Well, it may help, Figueroa, but it won't help *you*."

"Sir?"

"By tomorrow, barring any E. coli relapses, I should be able to get a couple of detectives on the case. Real detectives, I mean."

Bennis said, "Sir, we should have started earlier. A tox screen is going to take another two weeks."

Figueroa said, "Boss, we've put in a lot of time on the case. We've got leads."

"Then I suggest you follow them up. You've got twenty-four hours. Surprise me."

As they went out the door, he called after them, "And make sure you've written up all your notes so your replacements can get right up to speed."

When they were far enough away not to be heard, Figueroa

said, "Is that his technique? Waits until you're practically out the door and hits you with another punch?"

"Still think you want to be a detective?"

At three-thirty, carrying brown bags filled with pastrami and mustard on onion rolls, Figueroa and Bennis arrived at the Furlough Bar.

"Man!" Figueroa said. "I'm dead on my feet."

"Don't fold yet," Bennis said.

Mort, never chatty, said, "Beer?"

"One. We gotta go back out soon."

Mort pulled the beers and then leaned back against the dishwasher door and stared at the ceiling. Corky gave them a big smile, though. "How's the murder investigation going, guys?"

Bennis said, "Slow."

Kim Duk O'Hara came in, with Mileski and the Flying None right behind him.

"Man!" Kim Duk said, "Am I ever tired of prostitutes!"

Everybody laughed. "Well, I mean, I've interviewed twenty working ladies today, and all they do is make fun of me."

Everybody said, "Aw!"

Mileski said, "Wish they'd make fun with me."

"You can laugh, but you'd think when one of their own gets killed they'd try to help."

Mileski said, "Yeah. I really would have thought so."

"Hadn't seen anything, hadn't heard anything."

"Did you say please?" Sandi the Flying None asked.

Mileski said, "I solved both of my cases."

Sandi said, "Both of *our* cases. One of 'em, we get sent to a call of a woman screaming and find her husband on the floor dead, and she's standing over him with a knife. We say, 'Who stabbed him?' She says, 'I did.' This detective stuff isn't so hard. Corky, can you make a maiden's blush cocktail?"

"Do *not* make any jokes," Figueroa said.

Mileski said to Figueroa, "I hear you're working with ASA Malley."

Figueroa said, "And?"

"He used to be in private practice. Had a guy once come to him to defend him against a sexual harassment thing. Making lewd remarks about a woman in his office. So they go to court. Daley Center, civil case, see? On the way in, they're following this really great looking babe and Malley says, 'Was she like that? Just look at the ass on that woman!' The woman turns the corner, he says, 'And great hooters.' He says, 'Harassment or no harassment, you just gotta burst out with comments sometimes.' "

"And?"

"And the woman turned out to be the judge."

Figueroa said, "You know, that sounds like Malley."

Corky said, "Bennis and Figueroa were just going to tell us how their case is going."

"Oh, man," Bennis said. "We got four homeless people dead. And nobody sees anything. Most recent one last night."

Figueroa said, "We canvassed the area on the first three cases—"

"You need to canvass all over again," Mileski said firmly. "I mean, the fact that hardly anybody saw anything the first three times doesn't mean they didn't see anybody this time."

"I know. Easy for you to say, though."

"And you know what else you have to do? Interview the people who found the bodies. In a lot of cases, the person who reports a murder is the killer."

"They were all different people."

"Right," Bennis said. "And they were all cops. Like, Harry Pressfield, who's a uniform, found Abby Ward's body, for instance."

Figueroa said, "Except the secretary who found Mary Lynne Lee."

"Oh, all right."

Mileski said, "Listen, I take it back. I sure don't think a cop is going around killing people."

Challenging that, Bennis said, "Dr. Ho, our friendly serial killer expert, says killers often kill where they're comfortable. Cops are comfortable near the CPD. Serial killers are control freaks. Cops are often control freaks. Well, don't look at me that way! You never met a cop who was a control freak?"

"Oh, all right! Maybe."

"This kind of killer is a control freak for sure. Immobilizes the victims and kills them. The ultimate control. People become cops to clean up the city. Well, this guy is cleaning out the bums."

And cleaning their faces, Figueroa thought, but she didn't mention it aloud. Best keep something in reserve. Another thing about cops—cops were the world's worst gossips.

"I hate the idea of a killer cop," Mileski said.

"Well, you were right the first time," Bennis said. "The first thing we have to do is find out where the cops who found the bodies were at the times of the murders."

"*And* canvass the neighborhood," Figueroa said, getting off the bar stool. "Again."

"I'm coming." Bennis followed her over to the door. "All right. Let's get efficient here, Suze. Let's split up. I'll take one and you take one. Which do you want?"

"I'd a hell of a lot rather run around to all those apartments and all the CPD offices than ask some cops where they were at the time of the murder."

"Fine. Meet you back at the district at—when?"

"Five? Maria is making dinner tonight, so I don't have to be home until sixish."

CHAPTER THIRTY

HENRY LUMPKIN SMILED almost all the time. A black man of fifty-nine, he had the face for smiling, a round face like a moon, with jolly plump cheeks. He had smiled pretty much all the way from St. Louis, up Interstate 55, through Springfield, the capital of Illinois, through Bloomington-Normal. Up what used to be famous old Route 66. And they were now closing in on Chicago.

The guy in the big rig who had picked him up thought Henry was the greatest hitchhiker he'd ever had. Hitchhikers all helped pass the time, but some were dangerous, which was why Jon Smigla kept a sawed-off baseball bat on the floor to the left of the driver's seat.

Most of the hitchhikers had their problems. And he had figured out what Henry's was when he wanted to stop for beer or wine in Springfield. Smigla didn't care if Lumpkin drank, but he had to do it while they were stopped. There were a zillion Illinois State Police around, plus truck weighing stations, and he wasn't going to have open alcohol in the cab.

So while Smigla fueled up and got himself a burger and fries in Springfield, Lumpkin knocked back a couple of beers. Later, when Smigla stopped for coffee, Lumpkin got another couple of beers.

Lumpkin was running out of money, though. He knew that by the time they got to Chicago, he was going to have to start panhandling, and he hated that.

"Why are you going to Chicago?" Smigla asked.

"My hometown, Chicago. Lost my job downstate. I useta drive a street-sweeper. I loved that job. You're out at night when the streets are practically empty. I useta pull circles up and down the streets. Like waltzing on a highway."

He lost the job drinking, and his wife had died a few years back. He'd lived twenty-five years in St. Louis, because it was Adelaide's hometown, but somehow now he just wanted to go back to Chicago.

Lumpkin was just as pleased with Smigla as a fellow traveler as Smigla was with him. Smigla had that kind of wiry curly hair that looked like he'd stuck his finger in a light socket. And the fact that it was red made it look even more so.

When they came up into the greater Chicago area, and Interstate 55 became the Stevenson Expressway, Smigla said, "I hate to see you go, Henry."

"Me too."

Smigla was well aware that Lumpkin had done nothing but drink all day. "You gonna be all right?"

"Absolutely."

"Well. Where can I drop you?"

"Don't want to put you out."

"I'm going right downtown. Going to Congress Street."

"That's good for me. Can you let me off at Congress and State?"

At five o'clock Figueroa walked into the First District canteen and found Bennis drinking coffee. "Get anything?" she said.

"Most of them can prove where they were most of the time but not the whole time from eleven P.M. to three A.M. all four nights. Small wonder. I mean, even when you're working, there's usually a half hour here or there when nobody sees you."

"I suppose if a guy is alibied for one of the killings, he's clear."

"If so, we got two in the clear and two not. You get anything?"

"One of the women's lockup guards saw somebody ducking around when she got off work at midnight. Couldn't describe him. Otherwise nothing. Except this. Ta-da."

She poured a bag full of small boxes onto the table.

"Walgreen's Antibacterial Moist Wipes?"

"Wet Ones Lunchkins Antibacterial Wipes."

"Baby Wipes."

"Wet Ones Moist Towelettes with Aloe."

"Yum."

Figueroa took out a second bag and piled another four brands of wipes on the table in the middle of the canteen. Then she opened her laptop to make notes.

"Benzalkonium chloride."

"How come you can pronounce that, Bennis?"

"I thought you always said I knew everything."

"Of course. Go on."

"Water, SD alcohol, PEG 75, lanolin, fragrance, propyl-paraben."

"Sounds delicious. Next?"

"This one is water, SD alcohol, propylene glycol, aloe vera gel, sodium nonoxynol, fragrance, lanolin, citric acid."

"Next."

"Water, propylene glycol, aloe gel, PEG 75 lanolin, poly-sorbate 20, methylparaben, fragrance, citric acid."

"Next."

"Water, propylene glycol, lanolin, aloe gel—"

"That's the same one. You just did that."

"No. Different order."

"Well, how are the analysts supposed to tell them apart?"

"Some of these have more lanolin, and some have more antibacterial stuff—"

"Sure. But on the skin of a dead person who's been lying outdoors all night, aren't they all going to evaporate?"

"Look, I don't know. What am I? A chemist? Let's do what we planned. Let's smell them."

"The Lunchkins won't work. They're not lemon. They're berry."

"Don't prejudge. You close your eyes. I'll hand you the wipes." Bennis closed his eyes and Figueroa opened the first mini-pack.

"Fruit of some kind," Bennis said. "But not lemon."

"Right. Lunchkins watermelon scent."

Two of the wipes smelled like a hospital, quite antiseptic. One hardly smelled like anything. The CVP Baby Wipes smelled like baby powder. Figueroa held it to her nose for a few seconds, letting it take her back to J J's infancy in the way only scents could do.

Osco Baby Wipes also smelled like baby powder.

"Funny," Bennis said. "I thought more of them would smell like lemon."

"Me too. I wonder why I thought so, now."

"Beats me."

They had gone through seven of the eight packs when Bennis said, "Lemon!"

Figueroa read from the box. "Best-Wipes."

"Where'd you get them?"

"Drugstore on State Street. They're sold in pocket-size carry-packs and large 'economy-size' boxes."

"Okay. They smell like lemon. But are they the *only* ones that smell like lemon?"

"Who knows? They're the only ones of these that do. We do what we can, right?"

"Also, does the lemon scent evaporate?"

"Here, Bennis. You rub one on your arm or face and I'll rub one on me. We'll see in the morning."

"It'll come off when I shower."

"Bennis, I don't want to shock you, but this one day, forget about your shower."

CHAPTER THIRTY-ONE

ROBERT, OF COURSE, was not at home. He was working at
the new store, and when it closed at nine would take the manager of the new store to dinner with the more experienced ones
from the older stores.

J J met Suze at the back door, very excited because his best
friend Doug—who used to be called Dougie until this year—
wanted him to sleep over. Suze nevertheless called Doug's
mother, made sure it was all right, and then said yes. She felt
guilty that Maria was not going to be able to go out too.

Maria had cooked. She made steak, baked potatoes, and
green salad, and was very, very proud of herself.

Figueroa said, "This is such a great dinner, I feel guilty
about what I have to tell you."

"What is it?"

"I know you had a sleepover planned. But I've absolutely
got to go back out. And we need you to stay home and take
care of things."

Maria was silent. Figueroa quailed inwardly. She knew the
thoughts going through Maria's mind. Guilt that she wanted to
go out while her mother was half paralyzed. Resentment that
her life was so changed. Unwillingness to hurt her mother's
feelings by saying how upset she was.

Kath and even little J J knew how disappointed Maria was.
You could tell because they kept dead silent. So did Sheryl,
which made Suze sadder still. Sheryl was perfectly aware that

if she had been well *she* could take care of Kath, and Maria could go out.

Finally, Maria said, "Do you *have* to go? I mean, they have a whole police department. I mean, thousands of cops, right?"

"Yes, but just Bennis and I have this case. And I told you about the detectives getting sick."

"I know. I know."

"I don't want to claim it's life or death exactly, but we really are trying to prevent another murder."

She heard Sheryl gasp. Sheryl had never been quite at ease with Suze's job.

"Your dad won't be home before eleven at the earliest. And I might have to be out a lot later than that." She didn't say, didn't have to say, that Kath was just too young to leave alone with a paralyzed woman. Too much could go wrong—fire, break-ins, who knew?

"I'll make it up to you, Maria. In fact, my first day off, which now that I think of it is day after tomorrow, I'll take you to the mall and get you—let's see—I promise two sweaters." To Sheryl, she said, "Some people call this bribery. I prefer to go along with the psych students and call it positive reinforcement."

Maria said, "Thanks, Aunt Suze."

"So I'd better get going. J J, get your overnight stuff and I'll drop you at Doug's. Maria and Kath, take charge. And Sheryl, keep on trucking."

Sheryl smiled with the right side of her face.

The man on the stairs smiled with his entire face.

On the way in, Figueroa caught the news on her car radio. Mary Lynne Lee's mother said to a reporter, "The police knew there was a killer loose. They knew it and they didn't do anything about it."

An interviewer said, "Do you feel they neglected these cases because they involved the homeless?" Figueroa cringed. The guy was hoping the mother would say something nastier than he himself would be allowed to.

"My daughter wasn't homeless! She was just going through a difficult, but very human, period of transition."

Cutting off the sound bite of Mary Lynne's mother, the radio voice said, "The Chicago Police Department, reacting to the recent illness of many officers in the Detective Division, appears to have assigned two inexperienced patrol officers to investigate this series of killings of the homeless. Ironically, all these murders occurred a stone's throw from the central office building of the police department itself. Whether experienced detectives could have brought this series of murders to a close earlier will never be known. Whether the murders were not given priority because of the nature of the victims is a question the City Council plans to take up in days to come. This is Dave Hodges reporting from the Chicago Police Department at Eleventh and State. Back to you, Art."

Figueroa ground her teeth and kept driving.

CHAPTER THIRTY-TWO

THE HOUSE WAS like those boxes of chocolates with all the different centers. There was a woman or girl in every room, practically, and all different. He might just sample that one and sample this one. Like nougat, and caramel and raspberry cream. Mmm, his favorites—soft centers.

Valentine giggled. What it came right down to, they were all soft centers, weren't they?

Henry Lumpkin was having a wonderful time. He would have smiled continuously, except that he knew if you walked around panhandling and smiling broadly, sooner or later somebody would think you were a psycho and call the cops. So he held out his hat and only smiled broadly when a person dropped coins into it. Other people, seeing this, would drop in coins too. Henry was not really aware that it was the sweetness of his smile to the earlier donor that made the next several people give him coins.

There were occasionally crabby people, as there were any-place, but in general he thought Chicago was wonderful.

The main reason he wanted to smile, though, was that he recognized so much of it. It was Chicago, like he remembered it all these years. He stood on the steps to the Art Institute for a while, getting several dollars in coins and just remembering, remembering those music school buildings across the street, whatever they were called, and good times with his family at festivals in Grant Park.

True, there were huge new office buildings and glitzy architecture that was unfamiliar, but that only made him proud. He walked west on Congress as evening came on, figuring the tourists near the Art Institute would taper off.

Since Smigla dropped him on State Street, he had made a full circle north along Michigan Avenue and south on LaSalle and now he was back on State, with night coming on, looking for a liquor store or a bar. He had a whole *lot* of coins now, and he was running through his head what he could buy.

On Wabash in a lower rent area, he sighted a package store and went in. He expected to be treated with some rudeness, because he was poorly dressed, but in fact the clerk, who looked Greek to Henry's experienced eye, was very nice. He let Henry put his pocketful of coins out on the counter, and they discovered Henry could afford to buy two bottles of cheap red wine. "Thank you," the clerk said when Henry paid.

"And thank *you*," Henry said.

"How about a package of cheese crackers? On the house."

"Sure. Thanks." The guy was trying to make him eat, which made Henry feel he might not look so healthy, but nice was nice.

Henry was not naive. He realized that a store like this made their money from people like him. But some such places were courteous and some weren't. Some would make their money from you and all but kick you out the door afterward.

Henry wandered on to State Street to sit somewhere, drink, and watch the El trains go by.

Bennis and Figueroa met in the CPD parking lot and stared at the alley. The sun was setting somewhere over The Land Beyond O'Hare, and the sky was purple.

"You know, I really thought I'd see some patrols out here," Bennis said.

"There's one." A squad car drove slowly down the alley

under the El, carefully avoiding potholes. When it got to the south end, beyond the parking lot, it turned east and headed toward Michigan Avenue.

"Oh, great," Bennis said. "That's *it*? They need plainclothes guys hiding in the alley, dressed like the homeless. Any killer with two neurons between his ears can hide while a squad car goes by."

"I was afraid of this."

"And even if they scare the guy away for a few nights, how does that help?"

Suze said, "Well, let's go see if they have some decoys in the alley."

But even though they walked the alley from Roosevelt Road all the way north to Balbo, they didn't see any cops. There was one old black guy who might have been a disguised cop, trying to look like a homeless man. But the instant he saw them he got up and moved away.

"Hey, don't stay here, sir!" Figueroa yelled. "It's not safe for transient people here."

"He's gonna think you just wanted to move him along because cops always move homeless people along."

"Right now I don't care what he thinks about the reason. I don't want another murder."

"Problem is, he'll probably just come back."

It was only eight-fifteen P.M., too early for the killer to show, so they went back to the Furlough to think.

The Furlough Bar was deserted. Corky watched Figueroa and Bennis come in, looking troubled.

He said, "Hey, Bennis, Figueroa. Did you hear three of the sick detectives, three of the ones that were on dialysis, are planning to retire?"

"Why?"

"Well, it's not because they're scared of cop banquets."

This was not so funny and neither Figueroa nor Bennis laughed. Corky went on. "They've got permanent kidney damage. They go to dialysis three times a week."

"That's awful!" Figueroa said. "Last week they were healthy, active people and now they're permanently handicapped?"

"Well, at least it's a job-related disability. Full pension."

When Corky wiped and swabbed his way down to the end of the bar, Figueroa said, "Okay. Focus, Bennis. Our killer is somebody who lives or works in this area."

"Or used to live or work here."

"Or played around here as a child?"

"Like that case of Dr. Ho's? I doubt if kids have played around here in decades. There hasn't been any real residential housing here in years, except maybe that building behind the CPD. And those kids don't play out on these streets. It's too dangerous. And if it was somebody who played here forty years ago, they'd be in the wrong age group for the profile."

"Right. So—somebody who lives or works here, or used to, probably not too long ago."

Corky said, "I'm gonna go out and have a smoke."

Mort said, "Don't take too long."

"Oh, right. Somebody's gotta handle all the rush orders."

Mort growled.

Figueroa said to Corky, "I never knew you smoked."

"Well, how would you? With the lifestyle police out telling everybody they're gonna die from secondhand smoke. I mean, can I run my life or not, baby, right?"

"Right. It's a problem."

They watched him leave. Bennis thought about it a couple of minutes.

"Hey, Mort. Is there a law about not smoking in bars?"

"Don't think so. One more regulation and I'm going postal."

Figueroa said, "Bennis, you ever heard about Corky smoking?"

"Nope. But who knows? Everybody's got stresses. That's when those bad old habits return."

Corky crossed the street and angled toward the CPD. One didn't want to be too casual, take too many risks, but sometimes the excitement just started to build. He decided to make a turn through the parking lot, holding the lighted cigarette that he didn't really need or want.

The cars all sat there like dead cows, or as he thought about it, like dead hippos. The whole world was like that, mostly dead. Dead to the world, how funny.

It was only eight-thirty, so he was just scoping out the situation. See which members of the lame civilian community were in the area. What members of the even lamer cop community were trying to play detective.

He stood around, pretending to smoke his cigarette, which validated his presence to anybody. For a few seconds, he reflected on how the cigarette police had made all kinds of hanging around on street corners and in alcoves and so on perfectly explainable. Nonsmokers saw your discomfort with glee. You never needed an excuse for standing in some otherwise weird place smoking a cigarette.

You were a cigarette pariah! A nicotine outlaw. A fume felon. A toxic toker. You could go anywhere outdoors and no questions asked.

Cigarette in hand, he strolled through the parking lot and into the alley under the El. He headed north, behind the CPD building itself. Just past the Annex, he took another puff and leaned one shoulder on the wall. About a hundred yards away, down in the construction area, an old black bum was sitting on the ground, his back resting comfortably against the big rubber tire of a dump truck.

Corky watched as the old guy unstoppered a wine bottle, put it to his lips, and turned it bottom up. Corky could almost see the man's throat work as he drank. He frowned at the ugly sight.

CHAPTER THIRTY-THREE

AT EIGHT-THIRTY KATH and Maria decided they would give their mother a new hairstyle. It was necessary, of course, to get her agreement, and they marched into her room together. Alma Sturdley had given Sheryl a shampoo today, along with her bath, so they were being quite honest when Maria said, "Gee Mom, your hair is so nice and shiny."

"And fluffy," Kath said.

"And so out-of-date," said Maria.

"Yeah, I mean, it's so *twentieth century!*"

They watched for her reaction. They could not always tell whether Sheryl was trying to convey yes or no, or whether she was pleased or not pleased by something. Life would be much easier if they could. But now she smiled, just on the right side of her face, but nevertheless it was a wide, definite smile.

"So we thought it was time for a change," Kath said, holding up the scissors. Part of Sheryl's hair had been shaved off at the hospital after the accident and the brain injury. The rest had been cut short. It was now uneven lengths.

Maria had brought a big sheet. They transferred Sheryl to the upright chair, a movement that she could mostly do on her own as long as they watched so she wouldn't fall. Then they spread the sheet to catch hair clippings and Maria went to work, with directions and giggles from Kath.

Wasn't that cute, Valentine thought, from his position on the stairs. It would keep them busy a little while, too, which was good. He went up to the attic floor and assembled his kit, which included duct tape, a change of shirt, a pillowcase, scissors, a screwdriver, and some other odds and ends.

Then he went down to the third floor and let himself into the cop's room. On the whole, he was glad the little boy they called J J was not going to be home tonight. He didn't like little boys—nasty, loud, dirty creatures. He didn't want to have to deal with one.

He took the picture of Mono Lake at sunrise down from the wall and pulled the key off the backing. Then, just to be on the safe side, he replaced the picture on the wall and made sure it was straight.

The handgun was on the closet shelf in its special place. The key fitted, as he had known it would. He unlocked the trigger guard, put the earmuff-shaped pieces in the drawer, made sure the gun was loaded, opened the window, and just for amusement, threw the key out into the yard. Ultimately, maybe somebody would blame the cop bitch for having an unsecured handgun in the house.

CHAPTER THIRTY-FOUR

CORKY PITCHED HIS cigarette stub in the gutter and returned to the Furlough. Mort stood at the bar with his arms folded, studiously ignoring a gaggle of unwashed beer glasses on the drainboard.

"Oh, come on!" Corky said. He opened the dishwasher and loaded them into it. As he slammed the dishwasher closed, the door of the Furlough opened. An elderly black man entered. Figueroa thought he looked like the man she and Bennis had tried to move along.

"Can I buy a bottle of wine here?" he asked. He wasn't drunk exactly, but walking very, very carefully.

Mort said, "No!"

Corky said, "Sorry, but we don't have a package store license."

Henry Lumpkin stood trying not to sway. He said, "Uh— do you know where the nearest—?"

Mort said, "Get outta here."

"Wait, wait." Figueroa got to her feet and approached the man. She drew him toward the door. He was such a sweet-looking man, with such a lovely smile; she could not bear the thought of seeing him on a steel table in the autopsy suite tomorrow morning. Could she arrest him to save his life? There was nothing to arrest him for. "Look, let me take you outside." She walked him out to the curb. "If you head up that way"— she pointed north—"there's a package store up at Congress. But please, sir, don't come back here."

"Why's that, officer?"

"There's a killer around here at night. Really. I'm serious. Please. Don't come back."

He smiled at her.

She saw him mosey north, calling, "Thank you, officer," but she also saw him shrug a little when he thought she was no longer watching. He didn't believe her.

Sitting at the bar, Bennis dropped his head in his hands. He'd drunk just one beer, so Figueroa knew he wasn't overcome by hops and alcohol. In fact, he looked like she felt. It was just as well there weren't any other customers in the place.

"We gotta do something," she said.

"No kidding. What?"

"Well, sitting here is just wasting time. We could go back and look around the alley. We could hide in the alley for that matter."

"I think we should. But it's nine o'clock. We've got over two hours before there's any point."

"That's true. Where'll we hide?"

Bennis said, "What about me pretending to be a homeless guy? I got some truly beat-up clothes in the car."

"And if I fill you up with beer it won't even be an act."

"Pour it over me instead. I need my wits about me."

Corky sauntered over, polishing a glass. "You gonna get up a disguise?"

"Lordy, I don't know," Bennis said, wondering why the guy was so interested. Bored, most likely. "Maybe. Maybe it's the best I can think of."

Mort opened the flap in the bar and went out, letting it fall with a slam as he did. The falling flap made a terrific crash, but nobody jumped. They were used to it.

"What's his problem?" Figueroa asked.

Mort went on his way to the men's rest room.

Corky said, "Nothing, probably. He's always like that."

Figueroa and Bennis sat without speaking for a minute or so and Corky stepped over to the rack of glasses to put some away.

"At this rate," Figueroa said, "I might just as well be home."

"No. Can't do that," Bennis said. "We're going to be replaced tomorrow. We'll slip out there and slide out of sight and wait and we'll catch him."

"Darn right."

"You know, when we were canvassing the CPD, we also should have questioned Mileski and the Flying None and Kim Duk and all the guys."

Figueroa said, "Why?"

" 'Cause they're right here after work every day. They might have seen something."

"No, they leave before five, most of them. Latest by six. Hey, you're not suggesting that one of them is the—our—no, you're not. Right?"

"I'm not. Right."

Mort came back, slamming the flap again. "You guys gonna nurse one beer all night?"

Bennis said, "Yup."

Figueroa said, "Yup."

Corky said, "That's perfectly all right."

"Be right back," Figueroa said. She went to the women's rest room, way down the hall from the men's. It was less convenient, and although she had never been in the men's room, she heard their room was bigger.

She figured a bathroom break right now would be a good idea because she and Norm were going to go back out and spend several hours hiding in the alley. It would also be a good idea to call home. She had told them she'd be back by midnight, which was stupid of her. She should have realized it could take longer.

Yeah, take longer and maybe achieve nothing, she thought.

Still, with Maria in charge and Kath as backup, and Robert getting home by twelve, there shouldn't be a problem.

She'd call anyhow.

She washed her hands, dried them on one of the brown paper towels from the dispenser, and grabbed one of the pre-packaged towelettes that had appeared in a dispenser in the washroom a year or so ago.

She gave her face a good, brisk wiping off. Nice lemon fragrance.

Lemon fragrance? Oh, my God!

Figueroa came up behind Bennis at the bar. "Mort, we both could use one more beer, but I'm going to take it to a table. Okay, Norm?"

"You all right?" Bennis said. "You don't look well."

"Yeah, everything all right?" Corky said.

"So-so. That bar stool is getting to my back."

Bennis took both beers and followed Figueroa to a table, one of only four in the place, where she sat stiffly down, her back to the bar. This pretty much forced him to face the bar.

"Sheesh! What's the trouble? You need a doctor?" he said. He knew she never made a fuss unless there was a real problem.

"Look right at me and no place else. Right into my eyes."

"Suze, you're all funny. It's all white around your lips and you're trembling."

"Forget about how I look, Bennis!" she hissed. "Just listen. We're looking for somebody used to being around here. Comfortable with cops. Somebody glib. Somebody who's frequently changed jobs. Somebody superficial. Somebody who is free after midnight."

"Suze, shit. You're giving me chills. All right, I hear you. But Mort doesn't fit the profile. He's a slob and he's charmless."

"Not Mort. Corky!"

"What—"

"Don't look up! *Look at me, not him!*"

Bennis sat thinking, staring down at the table. That was one of the things Figueroa liked best about him; he didn't make light of anything that mattered, and he took her seriously. "And who," he said, agreeing, "has access to all the best booze in the world without having to buy it?"

When Bennis looked about finished with processing the idea, she reached into a pocket and took out a Best-Wipes towelette, which she placed on the table. It smelled of lemons.

Bennis said, "From?"

"The women's rest room."

"Oh, shit."

"So what do we do now?"

"Corky," Bennis said, "I'd like you to accompany us to the First District."

"Why?" Corky stood next to Mort, behind the bar. He looked, Figueroa thought, as innocent as the day was long.

"Step out from behind the bar, please," Bennis said.

"What is this?"

Corky opened the flap and left it open, coming out in front of the bar.

"We'd like to ask you some questions about the homeless people killed here recently."

"Me? I don't know anything."

"Look, just come along with us to the District. If you can explain everything, we'll forget about it."

"I don't *have* to explain anything. What's to explain?"

He looked so good, so innocent, so handsome, really, so charming, that Figueroa lost her cool. "Well, actually, there's some DNA evidence, and we thought you might like to supply a blood sample to clear yourself."

Corky shouted at her, a loud wordless yell, but it was a

diversion. At the same instant, he was grabbing Bennis's gun, swiping the snap tab up, and pulling the gun out of the holster. Bennis turned with a roar, clutching at the weapon, pushing it up to point at the ceiling. Corky dragged it down from Bennis's grip, toward Bennis's chest, just as Figueroa drew her own side-arm.

Bennis was between her and Corky, but she dove at both of them, jamming her gun up under Bennis's armpit, trying to push the muzzle past his flesh, where she could fire at Corky.

She saw Corky bring the gun closer to Bennis's skull. She knew if she fired now, she might crease Bennis's side. She didn't know what damage the blowback and muzzle flash would do to him. It would burn him, for sure. Would it blow a gas hole in his chest?

The three of them rolled against the bar, slamming each other into the wood edge, but their relative positions didn't change. Corky held a death grip on Bennis's gun. One more inch and it would be in Bennis's ear, and she would have to take the chance and shoot. She'd do it, too. Five, four, three, two—

Then there was a crack and Corky's eyes went unfocused. He fell like a sack of rocks, the gun spinning off uselessly onto the floor.

Mort stood over Corky, holding a large bottle of Aquavit by its neck.

He said, "I always knew he wasn't worth a bucket of warm spit."

CHAPTER THIRTY-FIVE

AT NINE O'CLOCK, Valentine decided that the house was just right. Kath was in her room playing some music CDs. Her door was closed. Maria was talking on the telephone. Apparently her parents allowed her to have her own phone, he thought, and he was angry with them for being so indulgent. You could spoil a child so easily. And they're spoiled forever. But then he realized it was probably a portable phone that belonged to the whole family.

He tiptoed down the hall and stood outside Maria's door. She sat on the edge of her bed.

"Well, I *wish*!" Maria said. Pause. "Oh, that's fun! It would go with your coloring. Not mine. I have some peach pink—what do they call it?—oh, here it is. 'Rose Tapestry.' It has little sparkles in it."

Pause.

"Next week. And she's going to buy me something. A sweater, I guess. Oh, I know, I know. She really *tries*! Okay. You go ahead. But I'll call you back in an hour. Okay?"

The instant she hung up, he pounced on her from behind. She made a little "Ooof!" sound, but he had his hand over her mouth instantly and pushed her face into the pillow. He whispered in her ear, "Hold still or I'll kill you," and he had the point of the screwdriver in her back as he said it. Would feel just like a knife. She stopped struggling but trembled from head to foot. A bottle of nail polish rolled onto the floor and spilled enamel into the rug.

He slapped a short piece of duct tape over her mouth. Then he ran tape around the back of her head, pulled the head up by the hair and covered her mouth more securely. She started to fight him again, but now that he didn't have to worry about her screaming, he flipped her over on the bed, knelt on her stomach, and grabbed her hands. He ran the tape around one wrist. She pulled the other away, but he had lassoed the first hand with the tape and he held the second hand next to it, pulling it so that both were together. Then he wrapped the tape around both of her wrists, three or four times.

He did the same with her ankles.

He picked her up like a package and straightened her out. The bound feet he moved near to the rail of the bed's footboard. Wrapping the sticky tape back and forth around her ankles and the rail, he attached her firmly to the bed.

Just to be on the extra safe side, he wrapped one long piece around her elbow and from there to the post of the headboard.

"If you stay right here and keep quiet, you won't get hurt. Understand me?"

After the arrest, and the caution, which Figueroa read to Corky in the presence of two third-watch cops she didn't even know but was using for extra witnesses, there was a raft of paperwork. The arrest slip, the call to the detectives, the felony minute sheet, the call to the state's attorney, the booking and charge, everything had to be done and Figueroa wanted it done to perfection.

Fingerprinting was simple these days. You rolled the fingertips on a glass screen and the machine did the rest. It would automatically go into the AFIS computer. Corky's fingerprints would be on record from his time as a cop. Maybe they'd find that those fingers had committed a crime someplace else in the country. If they were in the system, AFIS would probably pop them out. There were still some fingerprint systems around the country that didn't talk to AFIS, but not many.

By nine-thirty, Mossbacher had arrived. So had the ASA, fortunately not Malley. The felony review unit responded twenty-four hours a day, but they didn't send the senior people late at night. It was a young guy named Fritz Haber, whose blond hair stuck up straight, despite his nervous habit of running his hands over it constantly. His job was to determine whether they had enough for a charge.

Figueroa spent half an hour on the arrest paperwork, the general offense case report, while Bennis shepherded the other procedures. She eavesdropped on what he and Mossbacher were saying.

ASA Haber told Bennis and Mossbacher, "This is quite tenuous. You can only hold him twenty-four hours."

Figueroa said, "What about assaulting an officer?"

"Yeah, I suppose you could use that as a hammer."

"Why not?" Bennis said. "Otherwise, we could be here all night. He's not talking."

Mossbacher added, "Plus he's lawyering up."

"Well, he'd better," Figueroa said. "I bet we'll find a caulking gun in the supplies room at the Furlough. The ME has a hair with the root on it. They'll be looking at a DNA match."

"Found?" Haber asked.

"Inside the mouth of the most recent victim. Stuck there with the weapon."

"Which is?"

"Silicone caulk. The clear kind." Since he was still staring at her as if she was making it all up, she lost her cool and said, "You know. The kind that looks like snot. He has a sense of humor, our Corky."

Outside Kath's door Valentine had to stop and breathe methodically for a minute—in-out, in-out. This was so exciting he could hardly stand it. Much as he might hate Suze, he loved Kath. Kath was the one he really wanted.

He estimated that Suze the Cop Bitch wouldn't be back before midnight. And Robert had said he'd be back by midnight, but Valentine would bet that meant closer to one A.M. People always said midnight when they just meant really late, and the guy was a selfish bastard anyhow.

Plenty of time. Take a deep breath. Pull another short piece of tape from the roll. Eight inches is good. Cut it with the scissors. Turn the knob slowly.

He burst into Kath's room even faster than he had Maria's. She was sitting at a pine desk, making pictures with markers, the music playing loudly in the background. With her back to the door and the music playing, she never heard him at all until he seized her and slapped the tape over her mouth. Her little soft mouth, half open in a soft little "O" before he covered it.

Such big, beautiful brown eyes, with soft eyelashes, looking over the top of the tape.

She tried to kick and fight, but he just picked her up from behind and held her in the air. She couldn't get any leverage that way, and when he held her tightly up against his side, she couldn't even kick him, although she tried to. With both of his arms around her arms, squeezing her, she couldn't raise a hand against him.

She was wearing a little, little light blue fuzzy robe that zipped up the front.

So fast that she didn't expect it, he dropped her onto the bed on her back and whipped a length of duct tape around her wrists. He was very careful to make the tape just tight enough so that she couldn't pull the wrists apart or twist them around, but not so tight as to cut off her circulation.

She kicked her feet while he did this, but it didn't matter. He took one or two blows on his forearm and then grabbed both ankles and taped them. He also wound her knees to immobilize her legs completely.

The little girl lay on a twin bed, and now he had a really good, new idea. He ran tape over her waist, over the mattress, and down the side to the floor. There he unwound more tape and gave the roll a little shove, until it was far enough under that he could reach it from the other side of the bed and pull it out. From there it was up, over her waist again, and down the other side, plastered down to stick to itself.

Two more turns and she was nicely anchored to the bed. Much more elegant than what he had done to Maria.

Learning by doing. How nice!

Then he sat down on the bed.

He stroked the sweet little leg. It was soft and smooth. That was what he loved so much about little girls. They were smooth. There was no ugly hair on them, on their legs, or crotch, or armpits, just creamy softness.

He brushed the ankle, then the knee. Only in little girls was the knee this beautiful. By the time they were women, the knee had grown bony and coarse and ugly.

Smooth. So smooth and soft.

He bent over the thigh. Closer, he put his lips down on the soft flesh. It smelled fresh and clean. Then like a kiss, he took a bite.

Kath thrashed back and forth but she could hardly move because of the tape, and it was no trouble to hold her leg still. No trouble at all.

He bit until the flesh was firmly in his mouth and then he began to suck. The soft, smooth flesh and skin came up into his mouth.

As Mossbacher and the detective brought a smirking Corky Corcoran out of the interrogation room, Suze impulsively said, "Hi, Corky! We got you!"

Corky, who was handcuffed, nevertheless halted and stood as unafraid and calm as if he were the Pope. He stared several seconds at Figueroa.

"You really think that?" he said.

"You're going to jail and I'm going home," she said.

"Nobody catches Corky, you know. Corky is too smart. You didn't find me. I gave up. Corky arranged it this way."

Somebody, it may have been Mossbacher, said, "Mr. Corcoran. You know you've been cautioned. Anything you say—"

But Corky went on, overriding the words. "Corky could have been more elusive. More deceptive. You know that. Corky could have cleaned out a bum here and a bum there. On Lake Shore, on Michigan Avenue, down on Sixty-third Street, up at Belmont. Way west. Corky could have cleaned out a new one every night. And you would never have known. Or cared, would you?"

"I would have cared if I'd known."

"No. People just say that. Who moves the bums out of O'Hare? Huh, Figueroa? Bad guys?"

"No. Cops."

"Damn right, the cops. Nobody wants bums. Bad for tourism. Bad for everybody. They're ugly, dirty, smelly, and cause crime. Corky has been helping, making the city cleaner. The city will realize this. And it won't be long from now. Really, in their hearts everybody feels just the same as Corky does. Everybody. Everybody hates drunken bums. All the clean, nice people like you and me and the sergeant here and all the people who aren't sloppy drunks lying in the street."

CHAPTER THIRTY-SIX

"I REALLY HAVE to get home," Suze said. They had finished the paperwork and Bennis thought they should celebrate.

He said, "I thought Maria was in charge."

"She is, and that's fine as far as it goes. She's very responsible. But still, I feel better being there when Robert is out. Plus, I'm totally tired." She caught the skeptical look on Bennis's face. "Well, okay. So I'm pretty damn energized by the arrest. But I still need sleep."

Bennis said, "We did good."

"We did great!"

"Damn right."

"This has gotta go in our personnel jackets, don't you think?" Suze said. "I mean, we're the heroes of the hour."

"It can't hurt. You really want to put in for detective?"

"Yeah. Don't you? Let's both do it. We're good at this, aren't we?"

Bennis said, "We missed Corky for quite a while, though."

"It's funny how something can be right there in front of you and you don't see it."

"It's like when I go to get a piece of cold pizza in the refrigerator. I know it's there, 'cause I put it there the night before. But I look all through the fridge, move things around in back, push stuff aside, and I can't find it. Why can't I find it? Because it's right in front, that's why. I looked right past it. And that's the thing. It's what's right in front of you that you don't see."

Now that he had Maria and Kath immobilized, he had time to get ready. He went to the master bathroom on the second floor and turned the water on in the shower. While it warmed up, he padded into the master bedroom—or Robert's bedroom actually, since Mrs. Robert was downstairs being a spaz.

The closet in Robert's room held a lot of nice clothes. Valentine picked out a soft cotton shirt in a nice powder-blue. *Matching Kath's little robe.* He thought a pair of navy deck pants would go nicely with it. And of course these good quality cotton briefs. Clean socks. Navy to match the pants.

He carried the clothes into the bathroom, placing them carefully on the top of the hamper, out of the way of any spray. Likewise the gun, screwdriver, scissors, and roll of tape.

Robert's clothes. They all called him Robert. Self-important sounding guy. You just knew he never let them call him Bob, or even Rob. *Maybe I'll call him Robbie-boy when he comes home tonight. I ought to have some real fun with him.*

The shower water was glorious, that was what he whispered to himself, glorious, after all those days in the attic. Those days of purgatory were the cop's fault. Suze. Bitch Suze. But in the shower, he felt as if it all washed off him. There was beautiful, wonderful, hot, hot, *hot* water sluicing down all over him. And on the wall shelf was Ivory soap, minty soap, coconut soap, or oatmeal soap, and three kinds of body wash. Three kinds!

He smelled each bottle of body wash with great care and chose the cinnamon one. Hey! You only live once.

Then he washed all over his whole body, going very quickly, as usual, over the nasty parts. When he was done, he stood under the hot water, and slowly turned the hot tap down until it became warm, then lukewarm. He didn't go to cold, even though he knew that everybody should. He giggled a bit, thinking that he could do exactly what he wanted.

When he stepped out of the shower, he realized he had not brought in a towel. He didn't want to use any on the racks, because they had probably been used to wipe somebody else's body. Robert's, probably. And that idea was very unpleasant. But he opened a door under the sink and found a whole pile of towels. He took two, both dark blue.

He rubbed them briskly over his skin. It felt so good to be clean.

CHAPTER THIRTY-SEVEN

"**ALL RIGHT**," **MOSSBACHER** said. "It's up to the suits now."

Figueroa said, "I can go home. Yay."

Mossbacher said, "Figueroa, Bennis, you did a good job. I have to admit it. A really good job."

"Thanks, boss."

"I'm proud of you."

They walked out to the parking lot. Bennis jiggled his keys. Hesitating, he said, "Well, we've earned a rest."

"Right. Good night, Norm."

"Suze—what's wrong?"

"Wrong? Nothing. I'm tired."

"You're not yourself. And you haven't been all week. Something at home?"

"Not that I know of. I mean, all the usual. Sheryl's recovery is *so* slow. And uncertain. We don't know how far she'll get, either. And Robert—well, you know Robert."

"Yeah, but that's always going on. It feels to me like something else. Kids okay?"

"Yes, they're fine. Don't worry about me. There's nothing wrong. I'm heading home and it's high time for a full night's sleep."

She revved up the car and headed north on State Street. It was ten-thirty. Home was twenty minutes away.

Valentine had everything planned. While he believed that Suze and Robert wouldn't get home until midnight at the earliest, he still needed to be warned if they came in unexpectedly early. He got the bags of trash out of the two garbage cans, the one in the kitchen and the one at the head of the basement stairs. He piled one near the back door, just overlapping the frame so that the door would brush it when it opened. Then he opened the second bag at the top, partway, and piled it on top of the first. Rummaging inside, he found two empty cans and an empty glass bottle and balanced them precariously at the very top. When the bottom bag was jiggled, even a little bit, the cans and the bottle would fall over on the floor and make a lot of noise. And the beauty of it was, it wouldn't alert whoever came in that it was a booby trap. It would just look like one of the kids had started to take the trash out and forgot. Or was too lazy. Whichever.

If it was Robert, he'd probably yell angrily for the kids, which would alert Valentine even further. And Valentine could just shoot him or maybe wound him, if everything went really well, and then play with him awhile. Robert was a bully and they always whimpered like babies when you hurt them.

He went to the front door and bolted it from the inside. As far as he could tell almost everybody came in the back door, but it didn't hurt to be extra cautious. If Suze or Robert tried the front door first, it would seem normal. It certainly made sense for the girls to lock the door when they were going to be home alone.

Home alone. Wasn't that a grand joke? The family hadn't been home alone since Monday.

Suze was the one he had to get even with. As far as Maria and the spaz were concerned, he thought he'd just play with them a little bit and then kill them. His interest in them was superficial. Robert he might shoot slowly, piece by piece, just because he was an asshole. But Robert wasn't by any means the dessert in this banquet.

That was Kath.

If he sequenced the events properly, around about two A.M., after everybody else was dead, he would be left alone with Kath. And then he'd have all night. Maybe well into the next morning. Surely that kid J J would play at his friend's house for quite a while on Saturday before wanting to come home.

Kath and he might have many, many wonderful, exciting hours.

Excellent. Couldn't be more perfect.

Valentine walked firmly along the hall to Sheryl's room. Whoever said he didn't have a sense of humor? he thought as he strolled smartly in.

He said, "I'm baaa-aack!"

CHAPTER THIRTY-EIGHT

SUZE FELT GOOD. After all, she and Norm had made a very, very seriously major arrest. At the same time, she was slightly unsettled. What Bennis had said as she was leaving stuck in her mind.

Was there something wrong with one of the children, something just below the level of consciousness? There was a time, when she was in high school, that she had a strange sense of something wrong in the house. A couple of days later, her mother was rushed to the hospital with appendicitis. Thinking about it later, she realized her mother had winced now and then in the days leading up to the crisis. But she hadn't said anything about pains and nobody, including Suze, had really paid attention.

JJ seemed fine. So did Kath and Maria. And Robert— maybe Robert was the problem.

Well, she'd call home. Let them know she was on the way. It was kind of late to call, or would be if it was a school night. But one thing was certain. Maria would be up. Teenagers had a union rule—no going to bed on Fridays or Saturdays until after midnight.

Suze dialed her car phone with one hand and listened while it rang.

It rang eight times, no answer. Ten times.

I must have misdialed. They're there. They really can't go anyplace else.

That's what you got for dialing one-handed. She dialed again, more carefully, and it rang again.

And rang and rang.

Valentine pulled the buzzer button out of Sheryl's hand and dropped it down to the floor. "Even if you used that thing it wouldn't help you."

Sheryl made gulping noises, but Valentine responded as if she'd asked him a question.

"That's because the girls are all tied up."

At that, Sheryl went very still. There was no sound in the room, not even the sound of Sheryl breathing, until Valentine laughed.

"Now, you," he said, "you couldn't identify me. I mean, I could certainly let you live." He looked in her eyes for any sign of relief there, but didn't see it. "But then again, I'm sure you wouldn't want to go on living with your beloved husband and daughter gone. You notice I said daughter. By that I mean older daughter. I haven't quite decided about the little one yet. I might just take her with me."

Sheryl's eyes were huge, but she didn't make any effort to speak.

"I could stay here a day or so I suppose," he said. "I can't believe anybody would seriously look for you all on Sunday. Oh, what am I thinking? J J will be coming home. Why yes, we really do have to get this all done tonight. Then I can take Kath and the car—Robert's car. Suze's car is too old and unpleasant."

He reached out and lifted the bed safety rail nearest him, clicking it sideways and letting it down. This gave him better access to Sheryl.

"I've never been the kind of person to pick on the handicapped," he said. "Plus, this part isn't my favorite. This part I just plan to get over with."

He lifted one of the three pillows lying on the bed and brought it down on her face.

CHAPTER THIRTY-NINE

FOR ABOUT THREE minutes, Figueroa told herself that Maria and Kath must be playing their music too loudly. They simply didn't hear the phone ringing. It was kept on a recharger stand in the hall. And Sheryl, of course, would hear it but couldn't do anything about it.

Suze was ten blocks from home when she realized she didn't believe this. Not only did she think it was improbable, but she felt an increasing general uneasiness. Bennis was absolutely right. There was something wrong, or something odd, going on at home, and it wasn't as simple as stupid Robert having a stupid affair.

Maria? Could *Maria* be having a sexual relationship with some boy? Could she be pregnant? Could she have gone out with the boy and left Kath alone to take care of Sheryl?

Or could the boy be there in Maria's room and that was why she wasn't answering the phone? Kath didn't have a phone, and she did play loud music.

Or could Maria have gone out to the sleepover? Disobeyed?

But Maria was too responsible for that, surely. And too kind. She was a teenager, and they could be nuts, but Maria was not that nuts.

Suze hoped. A minute or two to home.

As she came down the street to their house she found she was trembling. When she saw that the house was still standing and not on fire, she let out a huge breath of relief.

————

The only parking place she could find was three blocks away. Bad luck. *Oh, don't be silly. The house looks fine.*

She ran all the way from the car to the house, though.

She came up the alley into the backyard and put her key in the door. Turned it. Pushed open the back door.

There was a crash of breaking glass, a rattle like falling cans. Frightened, she pushed the door open fast.

It was just a bag of trash. Two bags in fact, that the kids had forgotten to take out.

Sheryl felt the pillow come down over her face for the third time. Why had he even bothered to tell her he didn't torture the handicapped? Just to torture her further, she realized. Just like he had done before. It was fun for him.

She fought for air. She felt herself smothering, actually felt herself dying. Then over the roaring in her ears, she heard a crash.

The pillow lifted up.

She saw the man turn and listen. He was on her far side, away from the door, and now he ducked down behind her. From somewhere in the kitchen came Suze's voice saying, "Hi, guys! I'm home early."

The man took a gun out of his waistband. Suze's footsteps were coming down the hall. Sheryl yelled, "Awka! Daddnot!"

The man hissed, "Shut up!" Sheryl knew Suze could not hear him.

Suze walked into Sheryl's room, saying, "Hi, kiddo. How is everything? I called, but—"

Valentine stood up. He fired a shot at Suze, narrowly missing her. Suze drew her sidearm fast. Valentine pushed Sheryl up to a sitting position between them, holding her up with his left arm, firing again, knowing that Suze couldn't return fire without risking hitting Sheryl.

Sheryl grabbed his wrist with her strong right arm, but she couldn't quite get hold of the gun. He fired again, and missed again as Suze jumped sideways. Suze still couldn't shoot because he had Sheryl pulled against him.

Sheryl swiveled her head up into the man's neck and sank her teeth into the strap of muscle there. She bit down and held on. She felt blood leak out, running over her mouth and flowing down her chin, and she was energized! She bit harder. Clamped her teeth in a death grip. She hated him! Hated him!

The man screamed, pulled the trigger, firing into the floor. And Suze came up fast and cracked him on the head with her gun. Sheryl let go. He fell over the bed rail, half on top of Sheryl, then slid bleeding to the floor.

There was blood everywhere. Sheryl trembled.

"Are you okay?" Suze yelled at her. Suze said, "He's down," and pulled the man over to the radiator near the window and handcuffed his wrists around a pipe.

Sheryl twitched and shook. She wanted to talk and couldn't speak. She realized that the girls hadn't appeared, despite all the shouting and shooting. But she couldn't get the words out to tell Suze.

"Oh! Oh, God!" Suze said suddenly. "The girls!"

Sheryl thought, *Oh, God! They're dead. And I'm helpless. My own children and I couldn't save them.*

Suze ran from the room.

Suze was back in three minutes. "It's okay! It's okay!" she yelled.

Sheryl sank back exhausted.

"They're okay. They're taped up but alive. I have to go get some scissors and cut the tape off."

She looked at the man handcuffed to the radiator. Blood was leaking from his neck, forming a pool on the floor. Wondering how long it would take him to bleed to death, Suze said,

"Jugular vein. Shall I call 911? Naw, I'll get the girls first. Let him ooze."

Sheryl said, "Bastard."

They both laughed and then both burst into tears.

CHAPTER FORTY

ON SATURDAY MORNING, after the police investigation of Valentine had quieted down, long after Valentine was removed to Cook County Hospital and then jail, and all the evidence collected, Robert took Suze to the kitchen to talk. He said, "You brought this on us."

She'd been feeling the same way, herself. "I didn't have any idea, Robert. But I wish it had never happened."

"He followed you here."

"I know."

However, Suze thought Robert had a guilt problem of his own. Last night, three hours went by after Valentine's attack before Robert got home. The girls needed him; Sheryl needed him. But nobody knew where he was. At a restaurant? There were a thousand restaurants. He had said he'd be home by midnight and got home at two A.M., after all the danger was over and the house was full of cops. Suze suspected that he'd spent a couple of hours that night with a woman, probably one of his managers. This was not her business, although it worried and saddened her; ultimately it was up to Robert and Sheryl.

Robert said accusingly, "Well, that's what comes of trying to be a cop."

"Trying?"

"Yes, trying. It's bad for all of us."

Suze didn't lose her temper. She thought seriously for a moment and then said, "Well, Robert, maybe it would be better if J J and I moved out. I know you think we're a drain on you."

Then she watched the wheels go around in his head. She could almost see them turn. He'd have to stop and get groceries on his way home from work. He'd have to pay for an extra nurse or sitter for Sheryl when the kids were in school and Ms. Sturdley wasn't on duty. Somebody would have to be home all day Saturday and Sunday. Somebody would have to cook. And what about the housecleaning and clothes washing?

Suze had an immense feeling of satisfaction when he said, "Don't jump to conclusions, Susanna. You know we value your contributions."

It was a good thing Suze didn't have to go to work Saturday. She spent the whole day watching the girls. Maria had trembled and cried most of the night, and kept her light on, of course, which seemed normal to Suze. Suze slept in Maria's room the whole night and Kath left her door open. When Robert finally got home, Kath slept in his bed.

Maria was no better during the day Saturday. She cringed at sounds and refused to talk about the experience. By lunch-time, Suze told Robert they'd better look for a counselor for her.

"She'll get over it."

"No she won't. I'll call Pettibaker and ask if she can give me a recommendation."

Robert opened his mouth to object, but Sheryl stared at him with such a look that he quit.

Kath, however, bounced back like rubber.

"What a gross, grotty freak!" she said.

Maria said, "Don't talk about it."

"Can if I want. What a crustified idiot. A true jabroni." And she raised her eyebrow and turned her head in a manner that Suze recognized as pre-teen-today.

Suze caught Kath later in the kitchen. "You want me to

find you somebody to talk to? I'm getting somebody for Maria. This was a horrible experience—"

"Truly the worst. Let me tell you about the face he made when he was unrolling that tape. It was *sooooo* scrub."

So, Suze thought, maybe Kath didn't need counseling.

Sheryl was visibly improved. Suze and Kath called her the Vampire. At this, Sheryl actually laughed. Her mood lightened, and to look at her, Suze thought she felt less achy. Her face was less drawn. When she did her afternoon exercises under Suze's supervision, her step was lighter and stronger.

By Saturday night, Suze was calling Sheryl The Vamp. JJ was home now, utterly disgusted that he had not been there to "destructo" the intruder. "I'd've smeared him! I'd protect everybody!" he said. Maria burst into tears and ran to her room when he said this, but Kath giggled and Suze said, "Maria's still upset. But I know you'd have done great, kid."

The kids, of course, had no idea what a vamp was, or how sinister and important they were in early movies. But they loved the name and Sheryl, who did know the earlier connotations, appeared to think it was excellent.

Sheryl The Vamp bloomed.

MONDAY

CHAPTER FORTY-ONE

INSIDE CHICAGO

Monday, June 6

In a surprise move, a Chicago City Council subcommittee has moved on the proposal to establish permanent homeless shelters. The proposal was reported out of committee early today, possibly in response to Alderman Paul DeSario's comments to this paper on Sunday, after the arrest of a man who allegedly has murdered five or more homeless in the south Loop area. DeSario, reached for comment this noon, said, "Even if the proposed shelters were built tomorrow, they would house less than a third of the homeless wandering our streets. But it's a start."

[see HOMELESS, p. 21]

MONDAY, IT WAS all back to reasonably normal at the Furlough Bar. Bennis and Figueroa had spent a quiet tour, their first since their four detective days, driving around in a squad car wearing uniforms again, and some of the sick detectives were back on the job. The old gang at the Furlough was trying not to say anything about Mort's part owner who was now in jail. At the first court call on Monday, the judge had refused to grant bail to Corky. But even though everybody else was avoiding the topic, Bennis said, "Hey, Mort, you said you knew Corky was no good. How'd you know that?"

" 'Cause he's an asshole on legs."

"No, seriously. Why?"

"You're a cop bartender and you mix pink squirrelly drinks, you're tryin' to be something you ain't."

Bennis said, "You won't get any sense out of him."

"Maybe he makes more sense than the rest of us," Figueroa said.

The Flying None said, "Say, Mort. My aunt has some money she wants to invest in a business. If you don't have Corky anymore, how about my aunt and me buying in?"

Mort said, "Over my dead body!"

"I could learn to make all the drinks. I just learned a whiskey swizzle. I made some for my mother."

Mort walked out from behind the bar and slammed the flap loudly. They watched his hunched back disappear as he headed to the rest room.

"He needs somebody to help out," the Flying None said.

Bennis and Figueroa left the Furlough at four-thirty as usual. In the parking lot, Figueroa grabbed Bennis's arm. "Look."

"That's the old guy who came into the Furlough."

"Right."

They walked over to where Henry Lumpkin sat, drinking a beer under the El. Bennis said, "Hi, my man."

Lumpkin said, "I remember you. You were movin' me on."

"For good reason. There was a guy killing people out here."

"I read about it."

Figueroa said, "You had a pretty near escape."

"Say, that calls for a celebration. You wanta buy me a drink?"

Bennis and Figueroa laughed. For a minute Figueroa

MONDAY

thought—gee, the man drank way too much already, but then she said, "Sure. Let's go."

Inside the Furlough, Bennis ordered three beers. They both expected Mort to snarl, but Henry smiled at him. Mort didn't go so far as to smile back, but he pulled the beers without complaining.

"You ever need a bartender?" Henry said suddenly.

"Don't need a bartender that drinks up the profits."

"I wouldn't do that."

"How do I know?"

"Try me."

A week later, Bennis and Figueroa came into the Furlough after work, and for the first time were not surprised to see Henry behind the bar. They were actually getting used to it. They ordered their beer.

"Drink fast," Mort said. "We gotta close at five."

"Just for an hour," Henry said smiling. "You can come back."

Figueroa said, "Not once I get home, thanks. Where you guys going?"

"Don't tell 'em," Mort said.

"AA meeting," Henry said.

Figueroa, astonished, realized that in all the time she spent in the Furlough, she had never seen Mort take a drink. After a few seconds, Mileski said, "I heard Corky didn't quit the department like he told us; he got fired. Too often late, too many no-shows."

The first homeless murder had happened a week after Corky had been fired, Figueroa now knew. But she didn't mention it.

Kim Duk said, "I heard his parents were both alcoholics and that's why he hated drinkers."

"And worked in a bar?" the Flying None said.

"Happens that way a lot," Mort said.

Figueroa and Bennis had heard all of that too. They'd heard that Corky's mother had left the family when Corky was a young boy and that Corky had come home one day from high school and found his father dead, choked on his own vomit. Everybody thought that offered some sort of explanation. Figueroa and Bennis had talked about it.

"There's fuel for any point of view," Figueroa said. "Corky seems to have stayed home to take care of his father after his mother left. The social workers say they suspected that he was doing all the cooking and housekeeping, and even washing his clothes. But neither of them would admit it. The father doesn't appear to have been the tidiest person about his personal hygiene."

Bennis said, "On the other hand, both parents are said to have been basically kind. Just what my dad would have called 'weak.' So, who knows?"

"Maybe getting fired was his stressor. Plus the CPD building closing, everything here ending. The cop-shop moving and the Furlough having to move soon."

"Maybe."

Neither one of them could really believe serial murder had a simple explanation.

"Ah, well, let's chalk it up to the deep and abiding mystery of the human animal," Mileski said, and everybody groaned.

Figueroa almost quoted Dr. Ho, "Some we make and some we make worse." But then she decided just to drink her beer in silence.

AUTHOR'S NOTE
PSYCHOPATHS AMONG US

THE QUESTION "WHAT is a psychopath?"—by the name psychopath or another—has fascinated humankind for generations. Who are these people who seem to have no conscience, who have none of the normal human sympathy?

One of the classic and still popular works about psychopathy is *The Mask of Sanity* by Hervey Cleckley.

Among many fictional stories about psychopaths is one by Mary Astor, the actor who among other roles starred in *The Maltese Falcon* with Humphrey Bogart. Astor became a writer in later life and wrote a fascinating novel of a psychopath, *The Incredible Charlie Carewe*.

Oceans of ink have been devoted to the question of whether psychopaths are born or made. An interesting discussion of the human mind comes from Dr. Antonio R. Damasio, University of Iowa College of Medicine. His book *Descartes' Error: Emotion, Reason, and the Human Brain* is filled with fascinating cases.

For a thorough discussion specifically of psychopaths, you might read *Without Conscience: The Disturbing World of the Psychopaths Among Us*, by Robert D. Hare, Ph.D. Hare estimates that there are two to three million psychopaths in North America. He also theorizes that even if every serial killer were a psychopath—which clearly isn't the case—there would be twenty to thirty thousand psychopaths who were not serial killers to every one who is.

PET scans (positron emission tomography) of human brains have shown that psychopaths show a different pattern of cerebral blood flow during the processing of emotional words.

In any case, whether born or made, it is clear that there are such people. Psychopaths move among us and may make up as much as 5 percent of the population—certainly not all homicidal. The rare ones who are killers are likely to look clean; they sound good; they are very pleasant. They are very dangerous.

And after all, every serial killer lives next door to somebody.